# Modern Techniques of
## Track and Field

# Modern Techniques of Track and Field

CLARENCE F. ROBISON

CLAYNE R. JENSEN

SHERALD W. JAMES

WILLARD M. HIRSCHI

*Brigham Young University*
*Provo, Utah*

Lea & Febiger  *Philadelphia · 1974*

HEALTH EDUCATION,
PHYSICAL EDUCATION, and
RECREATION SERIES

Ruth Abernathy, Ph.D., Editorial Adviser
Professor Emeritus, School of Physical and Health Education,
University of Washington, Seattle, Washington 98105

*GV 42*
*1060.5*
*.M6*

**Library of Congress Cataloging in Publication Data**

Main entry under title:

Modern techniques of track and field.

(Health education, physical education, and recreation series)
    Bibliography: p.
    1. Track-athletics.  I. Robison, Clarence F.
GV1060.5.M6        796.4'2        74–850
ISBN 0–8121–0424–2

Published in Great Britain by Henry Kimpton Publishers, London

PRINTED IN THE UNITED STATES OF AMERICA

# Preface

Almost three thousand years have passed since the Greeks first met at Olympia to determine who among them would win. Since then, and also prior to that time, men have consistently striven to run faster, jump higher and throw farther. They have put themselves in contest with each other, and in their efforts to win, they have worked ingeniously to improve training and performance techniques. Through the ages, old techniques, fascinating and rich in tradition but scientifically unsound, have been discarded, and new techniques have evolved, based on insight and understanding. As a result of this constant evolution, man is today running faster, jumping higher and throwing farther than ever before.

For centuries, progress toward better performances was very slow, but in recent years dramatic improvements have taken place in every track and field event. Improved techniques, combined with better facilities and equipment and perhaps a stronger will to excel, has resulted in some astounding performances.

Numerous articles containing current and sound information on track and field are written each year. Unfortunately, the information is scattered and often not accessible to those who need it. Several good books on track and field have been written, but most of them are outdated due to much new found knowledge and the rapid changes that have occurred. In view of these facts, this book will serve a worthy purpose. It includes the most current and useful information on track and field, and the material is well-illustrated, scientifically sound, and described in a simplified and readable manner. Coaches, athletes, and athletic fans all should find the book interesting and useful.

The authors acknowledge the significant contributions of their students and several of their colleagues. Special credit is given to Keith A. Mac-farlane for preparing the illustrations and to L. Jay Silvester for his contribution to the chapters on the throwing events.

CLARENCE F. ROBISON
CLAYNE R. JENSEN
SHERALD W. JAMES
WILLARD M. HIRSCHI

*Provo, Utah*

# Contents

PART I. *Preparation for Performance*

                     *Introduction* . . . . . . . . . . 3

CHAPTER 1    *Basic Performance Traits* . . . . . . . 5

CHAPTER 2    *Factors Related to Conditioning and Performance* 25

PART II   *Running Events*

CHAPTER 3    *Short Sprints* . . . . . . . . . . . 43

CHAPTER 4    *Quarter Mile Sprint* . . . . . . . . . 63

CHAPTER 5    *Distance Races* . . . . . . . . . . 72

CHAPTER 6    *High Hurdles* . . . . . . . . . . . 106

CHAPTER 7    *Intermediate Hurdles* . . . . . . . . 119

CHAPTER 8    *Relay Races* . . . . . . . . . . . 136

PART III   *Jumping Events*

CHAPTER 9    *High Jump* . . . . . . . . . . . 147

CHAPTER 10   *Long Jump* . . . . . . . . . . . 163

CHAPTER 11   *Triple Jump* . . . . . . . . . . . 177

CHAPTER 12   *Pole Vault* . . . . . . . . . . . 188

PART IV *Throwing Events*

 CHAPTER 13 *Shot Put* . . . . . . . . . . 207

 CHAPTER 14 *Discus Throw* . . . . . . . . . . 222

 CHAPTER 15 *Javelin Throw* . . . . . . . . . 236

 CHAPTER 16 *Hammer Throw* . . . . . . . . . 250

PART V *Administration of Track and Field*

 CHAPTER 17 *Promoting Track and Field* . . . . . . 271

 CHAPTER 18 *Organization and Conduct of Meets* . . . . 278

 CHAPTER 19 *Track and Field Construction* . . . . . . 290

PART VI *Appendices*

  A *Conditioning Exercises* . . . . . . . . 303

  B *Track and Field Records* . . . . . . . 321

  C *Distance Conversion Tables* . . . . . . . 323

  D *Decathlon Scoring Values of Commonly Made Marks* 325

  E *Books, Journals and Articles* . . . . . . 327

  F *Glossary* . . . . . . . . . . . 336

INDEX . . . . . . . . . . . . . . . . 341

# Part I
# Preparation for Performance

# Introduction

In the year 776 B.C. and at the time of the full moon of the month of Appollonius, there was a great foot race in a meadow alongside the river Alpheus at Olympia, and young Coroebas was the winner. He was crowned with a wreath of olive leaves taken from the tree that Hercules had brought from the land of the Hyperboreans and planted in the sacred grove near the Temple of Zeus at Olympia. The Olympic Games had been born, and were henceforth held every four years for eleven full centuries. Then in 394 A.D. by decree of Roman Emperor Theodosius I, the games were halted, not to be conducted again until more than 1500 years had passed.

On the morning of April 6, 1896, King George I of Greece, with the Duke of Sparta on his right and the members of the diplomatic corps around him, stood erect in the royal box in a new and magnificent stadium in Athens and formally opened the first of the modern Olympic Games. The ancient games had been revived in the city where they had long ago enjoyed their glory.

Other important dates stand out in the history of modern track and field. On March 5, 1864 teams representing two different universities, Oxford and Cambridge, met for the first time in a track and field match. The meeting was held on the Christ Church ground at Oxford. Two years later, on March 23, 1866, the first English championships were held at Walham Green, London. The program consisted of twelve events. Before the turn of the century, national championships were held in several European countries. The first United States championships, organized by the New York Athletic Club, were held at New York in 1876.

Since its revival in the 1800s competitive track and field has spread through the public schools of the U.S. and many other countries of the world. It has become an almost universal sport in colleges and universities, and a host of amateur track and field clubs have been successfully organized.

3

At the present time track and field is—on a worldwide basis—the most widely accepted of all sports.

Even though accurate records are not available of the performances made in the ancient Olympic Games, it seems safe to assume that they were inferior to the performances of today. Probably there are hosts of competitors who now run the race better than Coroebas did when he won at Olympia in 776 B.C. This would tend to be supported by the fact that the record books have been practically rewritten every decade since the revival of modern track and field. Because of the great number of youths and adults who now participate and because of the high standards set by competitors of recent years, the price to be paid by those athletes who really want to excel becomes steadily higher. Not only must they train harder in order to improve on past performances, but they must also be more serious students of correct techniques.

CHAPTER 1

# Basic Performance Traits

There are a number of general athletic traits which are important to performance in track and field, and it is important for coaches to understand the best methods of developing the traits so they can design effective training programs for their athletes. Among the traits that coaches often desire to improve are strength, endurance, muscular power, speed of muscle contraction, flexibility, reaction time and specific skills.

## STRENGTH

Strength is the ability of the body to apply force. Because vigorous activities depend on the application of great force, increased strength often contributes to better performance. In certain cases improved strength can be the most important single contributor to better performance.

Strength involves a combination of three components:
1. The contractile forces of the muscles causing the movement.
2. The ability to coordinate the several muscles involved.
3. The mechanical ratios of the lever (bone) arrangements.

The *first* component depends upon the maximum contractile force of each muscle contributing to the movement. This can be increased significantly through heavy resistance strength training. The *second* component depends upon the ability to coordinate the contractions of the several muscles involved, while relaxing the muscles which are antagonistic to the movements. This can be improved by practicing the particular movements many times. The *third* component depends upon the amount and type of leverage involved. Sometimes this can be advantageously altered by changing positions of body parts.

A considerable amount of the information in this chapter was taken from Jensen, Clayne R. and Fisher, A. Garth: *Scientific Basis of Athletic Conditioning,* Philadelphia: Lea & Febiger, 1972.

### Methods of Increasing Strength

In order for muscles to increase rapidly in strength, two principles must be applied: *overload* and *progressive resistance*. The muscles must be contracted regularly against heavy resistance (this is overload) and the resistance must be increased as the muscles become stronger (this is progressive resistance). Any form of exercise which applies heavier than usual resistance to muscle contractions will stimulate an increase in strength. Strength building stimuli may be provided by:

1. Hard manual labor or vigorous athletic performance.
2. Specific exercises against body weight, as in pull-ups or dips. (Additional weight may be added to body weight.)
3. Exercises against external movable resistance, such as weight training equipment, wall pulleys, etc.
4. Application of muscle tension against a fixed object or another body part.

The first three methods result in isotonic (dynamic) contractions, meaning the muscles change in length as they contract, and movements of body segments occur. The fourth method involves isometric (static) contractions, meaning the muscles apply tension but do not shorten, and movements of body segments do not occur.

*Isotonic (Dynamic) Strength Building Methods.* Prior to World War II, strength building programs were used very little in athletic conditioning. They were considered taboo because it was believed that "muscle boundness" resulted from such programs. During World War II, great success was experienced with heavy resistance exercises in the rehabilitation of hospital patients. Subsequently, much research was done to determine the effectiveness of this type of training for improving athletic performances. It was learned that increased strength was highly beneficial to certain athletic performances, and that heavy resistance exercise was the most expedient method of increasing strength. Hence, weight training gained much popularity among athletes and coaches (Figure 1–1).

Strength can be increased most rapidly by exercising against very heavy resistance for few repetitions. After much study and experimentation, DeLorme and Wilkins[4] recommended the use of three sets of 10 repetitions each. They specifically recommended the following program to be adhered to every second day:

1. One set of 10 repetitions with $\frac{1}{2}$ 10 RM.
2. One set of 10 repetitions with $\frac{3}{4}$ 10 RM.
3. One set of 10 repetitions with 10 RM.

(RM means repetition maximum. Ten RMs is the maximum weight that can be lifted successively 10 times. One-half 10 RMs is $\frac{1}{2}$ of the weight that can be lifted 10 times).

Subsequently, other investigators have learned that fewer than 10 repetitions with heavier weight is more effective. For instance, Berger[2] found

Figure 1-1. Two arm press exercise (isotonic).

that strength increases most rapidly when four to eight RMs are used with three sets. Other studies have added support to Berger's findings. Currently there is lack of agreement among experts as to the exact program that is best, but the following points are well-established and generally accepted:

1. Exercises must be selected to work the specific muscles in which strength is desired.

2. Muscles should be worked regularly (every second day) against *heavy resistance.*

3. Near maximum weight for eight or less repetitions should be used.

4. The weight must be progressively increased as strength increases, in order to continue to provide overload to the muscles. (This is progressive resistance.)

Suppose you wanted to design a strength program for a shot putter, an event which requires great strength and speed. In analyzing the putting action it is apparent that the following muscle groups are major contributors: ankle plantar flexors, knee extensors, hip extensors, trunk and hip rotators, trunk extensors, shoulder girdle elevators and protractors, shoulder flexors (horizontal position), elbow extensors, wrist flexors and finger flexors.

When the specific movements involved are known, an effective exercise program can be designed. A typical procedure would be as follows:

1. Select exercises which will work the muscles that are involved in the performance.

2. Determine the maximum amount of weight that can be lifted for one repetition with each exercise, and use 70–80% of maximum weight.

3. Perform at least three sets of each exercise doing as many reps (repetitions) as possible in each set. (If you can do more than eight reps the

weight is too light.) Some mature athletes prefer to do more sets (5–15) with fewer reps (2–3) and very heavy weight (80–90% of 1 RM).

4. Rest two to three minutes between sets.

5. Do the workout on alternate days (i.e. Monday, Wednesday and Friday).

6. Increase the resistance as much as possible each week.

Ideas on specific exercises to be used for strengthening certain muscles can be found in Appendix A and from weight training charts and books. If you are in doubt, the exercise movement which most closely resembles the skill in which you are interested will probably be the correct choice. Remember that the resistance must directly oppose the actions of the muscles you want to strengthen.

*Isometric (Static) Strength Building Methods.*  Studies which support strength building through static muscle contractions were introduced by Theodor Hettinger and E. A. Muller, of Germany in 1953. Since that time numerous studies have been published, most of which generally support the idea that strength can be increased at a rapid rate by use of isometrics.

Muller and Rohmert[14] learned that strength will increase more rapidly by use of isometrics when near maximum contractions are used, and 6–10 repetitions are employed. Also, they established the idea that strength will increase more evenly throughout the range of motion if the contractions are performed at various positions (Figure 1–2).

On the basis of available evidence the following guides are recommended for isometric programs:

1. Near maximum contractions for five to six seconds should be used and repeated at least six times with a few seconds rest between contractions.

2. The exercises should be done daily.

3. The contractions should be applied at various points through the range of motion, if maximum strength is desired throughout the full range.

Figure 1–2. Two leg press exercise (isometric).

In some cases, as in ballistic movements, strength may be needed mostly at the beginning of the motion. In such cases exercises should be designed accordingly.

*Comparison of Isometric and Isotonic Methods.* When the programs described above are used, strength gained from isometric and isotonic methods is about equal. However, each program has certain advantages and the final selection should be based on administrative feasibility and personal preference. Following are some guides:

1. For some individuals there is a psychological advantage that occurs from isotonic exercises because they see heavy work performed.

2. Slightly more muscle hypertrophy and also more muscle endurance results from isotonic exercises. Some experts claim that isotonic exercises develop strength more uniformly and have a more favorable influence on coordination because they require use of the muscles throughout the range of motion.

3. The greatest advantage of the isometric method is administrative economy. It requires less time, less effort, less space and much less equipment than the isotonic method. A reasonable amount of ingenuity can make a good isometric program possible with the equipment normally available in a gymnasium and by having athletes work in pairs to provide resistance for each other.

*Other Strength Building Methods.* In addition to pure isometric and isotonic methods, some programs combining the two methods have received attention, and several training devices for this type of training are sold commercially. Reasonable success has been experienced with the following procedure (Figure 1–3):

1. Contract the muscles isometrically against a rope or cable arrangement. After tension has been held for about 10 seconds reduce the resistance which holds the rope, allowing slow motion isotonic contractions. This combines isometric and isotonic contractions into a single exercise.

2. Repeat each exercise 5–10 times daily.

Another method is "functional overload" where the performance of the activity itself is done under resisted conditions. Weighted vests, ankle weights and weighted objects and implements are used; some track athletes practice running against resistance. Functional overload has the advantage of more closely integrating the strength gains into the activity pattern, but some experts think it reduces coordination and timing.

*Underlying Principles.* The primary objective of most athletes who engage in strength building programs is to gain the greatest amount of usable strength in the most efficient manner. To accomplish this, a few basic concepts must be applied:

1. Although the contractile force of a muscle is maximal when the muscle is fully extended, the mechanical advantage is less than optimum, and strength is less than maximum.

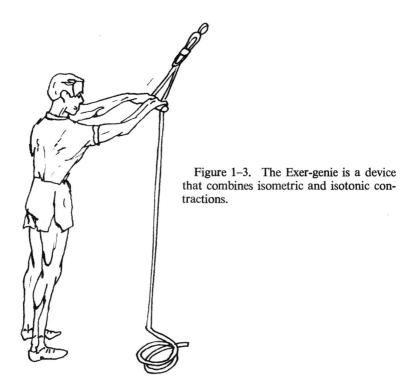

Figure 1–3. The Exer-genie is a device that combines isometric and isotonic contractions.

2. As a muscle goes through its range of contraction, the mechanical ratio changes and this results in a strength curve. To experience maximum strength gains, a variable resistance to match the strength curve would seem to be an advantage.

3. The resistance should always directly oppose the direction of the body movement (omni-directional resistance) and be carried through the full range of motion.

4. In order for a muscle group to apply maximum force it cannot depend on weaker muscles to transmit the resistance. In other words, a body part should be isolated so the resistance can be applied directly to it.

### Physiological Changes Which Accompany Changes in Strength

Several changes accompany increases in strength, of which the following are the more significant ones:

1. The muscles hypertrophy (enlarge) due to increased size of muscle fibers, increase in connective tissue and more capillaries. However up to a certain point the external measurements of the body segment might not increase because fatty tissue might decrease as muscle tissue increases.

2. A greater proportion of the muscle fibers become active, meaning

they respond to stimuli. (In a weak muscle a high proportion of the fibers are dormant.)

3. There is an increase in the amount of protein and fluid in the muscles.

### Factors Influencing Strength

Several factors relate to strength and influence the rate that it develops and how long it is retained. Following are brief discussions of these factors.

*Strength in Relation to Muscle Size.* The contractile force of a muscle is directly related to its cross-sectional measurement. As muscular strength increases, the cross sections of the individual muscle fibers increase. This results in a greater cross-sectional area of the total muscle. Theoretically, this measurement is proportional to strength; however, this is not always true because other factors are involved. For instance, 1) two muscles having equal cross sections may differ in strength due to different amounts of fatty tissue; fat lacks the ability to contract and causes friction and interference with the shortening of muscle fibers; 2) the proportion of active fibers differs in muscles and this influences strength; 3) the efficiency of contraction has an important influence on strength, but the fact remains that muscle size and strength are related.

*Not All Muscles Respond Equally.* When the same training program is used, the amount of strength gain varies with different people. Also, within each individual certain muscles respond better to strength training than other muscles. When put on a strength building program of equal intensity, some muscles may increase at five percent weekly, while others increase only one percent. This is partly explained by the fact that some muscles are in better condition at the beginning of training. Those in poor condition ordinarily increase more rapidly.

*When Training Is Discontinued Strength Decreases.* Research shows that when a strength building program is discontinued, the athlete begins to lose strength within 8–10 days. Strength developed at a slow rate lasts longer than strength developed rapidly. After training ceases, strength is lost at approximately one-third the rate it was gained, but a small amount of the increased strength remains indefinitely. If a segment of the body is completely immobilized, as when placed in a cast, strength decreases very rapidly (about 20% per week).

*Strength Relates to Age.* Strength increases at a rather steady rate from birth to about age 25 for men and age 18 for women, at which time it levels off and then begins to decline at a gradual rate. But as a result of training a person can maintain near maximum strength for several years beyond age 25. A person's strength development curve is influenced by his rate of maturation and the amount and kind of activity he does.

*Strength Differs Slightly on the Two Sides of the Body.* Even though right-handed people use the right side of the body considerably more than the left side (vice versa for left-handed people), the right side is only slightly stronger, and its musculature is only slightly larger than that of the left side. The fact that the muscles on the two sides are of about equal size is generally attributed to the cross transfer theory, which in essence means that use of one side of the body will influence the development of like muscles on the other side.

*Reserve Strength Becomes Available Under Stress or Excitement.* The reserve strength theory is supported by observations of people who have performed great feats of strength while under emotional stress or excitement, and who could not voluntarily perform the same feats after the emotional state had passed. This idea has little support from research, probably because the topic is difficult to treat experimentally. The excitement and stress cannot be provided under controlled conditions. Physiologists have explained reserve strength as a condition resulting from 1) increased secretion of adrenalin, causing the muscles to become more responsive; or 2) a stronger stimulus from the central nervous system and a reduction of inhibitions, causing more muscle fibers to respond. It is probably true that a limited amount of reserve strength becomes available under exciting competitive conditions.

### ENDURANCE

Endurance is defined as resistance to fatigue and quick recovery after fatigue. The definition may apply to the body as a whole, to particular body systems such as the respiratory and circulatory systems, or to a local area of the muscle system. We usually speak of two kinds of endurance— *cardiovascular* and *muscular.*

A person with a high level of endurance can persist in vigorous performance. When endurance gives way to fatigue as a result of muscular work, several elements diminish which are important to good performance: strength, timing, coordination, speed of movement, reaction time and general alertness. Increased endurance postpones the onset of fatigue; therefore, endurance contributes to improved performances in activities where fatigue is a limiting factor.

#### Methods of Increasing Endurance

The need to apply the overload principle for the development of strength has already been discussed. That principle must also be applied if endurance is to be increased. Overload for endurance means working the system beyond previous endurance levels.

*Muscular Endurance.* Local muscle endurance is dependent upon the quality of the muscles, the extensiveness of their capillary beds and the nerve mechanisms supplying them. It has been established that strength contributes to muscle endurance. In fact, there is a very high correlation between strength and *absolute muscle endurance.* Absolute muscle endurance is the amount of times a person can work against a certain resistance regardless of strength. When different persons work against the same resistance, the stronger ones are able to continue exercise longer than the weaker ones. Conversely, there is very little relationship between strength and *relative muscle endurance*. If the resistance is adjusted to correspond to each person's strength, then the weaker person displays as much endurance as the stronger one.

Since increasing strength is an effective method of increasing muscle endurance, the strength building methods described earlier may be used for this purpose (heavy resistance with few reps). However, if increased endurance without increased strength is desired, then the program must be altered. Research shows that 20–30 RMs with three sets (light weight with many reps) will increase muscle endurance at a fast rate and will affect strength and muscle size very little. Hence, if increased endurance without increased strength is desired, many RMs (20–30) with light weight should be employed.

Even though weight training has been used to illustrate how to increase endurance, it should be recognized that muscle endurance can be increased by any form of exercise which results in overloading the muscles (either in weight or repetitions).

*Cardiovascular Endurance.* Cardiovascular endurance is the ability of the circulatory system to keep the muscles supplied with oxygen and nutrients, and to keep the muscles free of waste products during heavy exercise. When many muscles are worked hard the circulatory (and also the respiratory) system is heavily loaded because this system directly supports muscular work. The effectiveness of the system then becomes the limiting factor in endurance. It is agreed that in vigorous activities of long duration, oxygen supply to the tissues is the main limitation. Therefore, the primary objective of cardiovascular endurance training is to improve the supply of oxygen to the working muscles.

It should be pointed out that there are two forms of work—*aerobic* (oxygen is present) and *anaerobic* (oxygen is not present). Likewise, there are two forms of cardiovascular endurance—*aerobic* and *anaerobic*. Aerobic endurance is the ability of the metabolic processes which require oxygen to resist fatigue. Anaerobic endurance is the ability of the processes which require no oxygen to resist fatigue. Anaerobic processes are not actually involved in cardiovascular endurance except as they are called into play as a result of inadequacy of the aerobic processes.

*Aerobic Training.* The ability of the body to supply the cells with oxygen (oxygen consumption) is the key to cardiovascular endurance. When oxygen is not available in the cells in large enough quantities, the energy production shifts to the anaerobic (absence of oxygen) process. The anaerobic process produces ATP (energy) very inefficiently and it increases the fatigue toxin lactic acid. When large quantities of lactic acid are produced, activity must be lowered to a level below which no additional acid will accumulate. This is fatigue.

Because of the importance of oxygen in the production of ATP (energy) for muscular work, the endurance level of an athlete can be evaluated in a laboratory by measuring the amount of oxygen he absorbs from the air per kilogram of body weight (oxygen uptake). Those with high oxygen uptake can generally work longer at a faster rate than those with low oxygen uptake. Of course the reason is that the greater oxygen supply to the cells allows the body to use the more efficient aerobic method for producing energy, and thus avoids the buildup of lactic acid, which causes fatigue. The purpose of aerobic endurance training then is to increase the ability of the oxygen transport system (cardiovascular system) which results in more oxygen uptake, and in turn a better oxygen supply to the cells.

This type of endurance (aerobic) can be developed by working *continuously for long periods* of time such as in cross country running, long distance swimming or cross country skiing. However, perhaps the best method is the one known as *interval training*. This technique consists of a series of work bouts with short rest interval between bouts. Astrand and Rodahl[1] found that a work load which could only be tolerated continuously for nine minutes could be carried on for an hour when done intermittently (interval training). This means that much more total work can be accomplished before fatigue when interval training rather than continuous training is used.

In order for an interval training program to be effective over a period of time it must be increased as endurance is gained in order that overload will continue to be applied. In other words, as an athlete becomes better conditioned he must do more work during each training session to develop additional endurance. Interval training workouts may be increased four different ways: 1) the number of work bouts can be increased; 2) the length of each bout can be increased; 3) the intensity of each bout can be increased; and 4) the rest periods between bouts can be shortened. It is recommended that the work bouts be three to five minutes in length, with light activity or short rest periods between the bouts. The number of bouts, intensity of each bout and the amount of rest between bouts should be geared to the level of the athlete's condition. The athlete need not be fatigued at the end of each work period, since there is no evidence that anaerobic processes must be used to develop aerobic endurance.

Heart rate should be used as the criterion for determining the optimal training load. It should be maintained at a rate within 10 beats of maximum heart rate during each of the three-to-five-minute work bouts. The rest periods between bouts should be equal to or less than the time of the work bouts. A training program of this type involving a sufficient number of bouts during each workout will result in optimal changes in the effectiveness of the oxygen transport system. It should be noted that if less than the optimal rate of increase in aerobic endurance is desired, the heart rate does not need to be maintained within 10 beats of maximum during each bout.

Cooper[4] suggested that the heart rate should be above 150 beats per minute for at least five minutes. In most athletes, 150 beats per minute will produce gains in aerobic endurance, but the gains will be less than optimal. Karnoven[11] recommended that the heart rate during each bout be at least resting heart rate plus 60 percent of the difference between resting and maximum. It is very questionable whether Karnoven's plan is vigorous enough to produce significant gains in trained athletes.

In summary it should be said that aerobic endurance will develop at an optimal rate as a result of doing a sufficient number of successive bouts of work, three to five minutes in length with short rest periods in between, where the work bouts are intense enough to cause the heart rate to be maintained within 10 beats of maximal rate. Further, aerobic endurance can be developed at less than optimal rate by doing bouts of work that are less intense and, therefore, do not maintain the heart rate within 10 beats of maximal rate. Also, aerobic endurance can be developed at a reasonable but less than optimal rate by doing continuous work over an extended period of time at considerably less than maximum intensity, such as cross country running.

*Anaerobic Training.* Anaerobic endurance refers to the effectiveness of the processes of the body which provide energy for muscular contraction in the absence of oxygen, or in other words, when sufficient oxygen is not available to produce enough energy aerobically. Anaerobic endurance is very important in activities requiring maximum effort for a short period, such as running a 220 or 440 yard sprint, or in activities such as basketball and football which require short bursts of vigorous exercise.

Anerobic endurance training is accomplished best by repeated *short bouts* of maximal effort, with brief rest periods between bouts. Extremely high levels of lactic acid are found in the blood following four or five work bouts of this type, indicating great use of the anaerobic mechanisms in the cells. Well-trained athletes are typically able to tolerate much higher lactate levels than untrained athletes.

It is important that the work periods for anaerobic training not be too short. Research indicates that 10–15 seconds of vigorous work *do not* increase lactic acid levels a significant amount and thus would have little, if any, effect on anaerobic endurance. Successive vigorous work bouts of about one minute in length are the most effective for this type of endurance. The number of successive one-minute bouts that should be done depends upon the condition of the athlete and the emphasis placed on anaerobic endurance. The rest period between bouts will be influenced by the athlete's condition and the number of bouts done in succession.

*Aerobic-Anaerobic Relationship.* Training programs usually involve both aerobic and anaerobic training because most activities involve both aerobic and anaerobic processes. But it is important to know that for certain performances, aerobic endurance should be emphasized, while anaerobic endurance should be emphasized for other performances.

Falls[7] presents valuable information (Table 1) which illustrates the relationship between different track events and the primary energy-yielding components involved.

From the data presented in Table 1, it becomes apparent that an athlete who is training to run the mile should devote 20 percent of the training program to speed, 25 percent to aerobic development, and 55 percent to anaerobic development. This table is also applicable to training for other activities. Notice that the time of the event has been included. Regardless of the kind of event, the time is related to the energy-yielding systems involved. Therefore, for a swimming event lasting four to five minutes, the athlete would use approximately the same training program as for the mile run, which also lasts four to five minutes. The main difference would be the kind of activity used in the training program (running or swimming). Table 1 can be used successfully in combination with Table 2, also presented by Falls.[7]

Table 2 lists various types of training programs involving speed training, aerobic training and anaerobic training. (For descriptions of the different types of training, see p. 17.) An athlete can refer to Table 1 for the type of program needed in the training for his event, then refer to Table 2 for a description of the training program to be used. For example, a two-miler would find out on Table 1 the breakdown of speed, aerobic capacity and anaerobic capacity needed for the two-mile run. He would then attempt to match these percentages to a training program listed in Table 2. Speed play or fartlek training is the kind of training most nearly matched to the training requirements of a two-miler, but repetition running could be used with good results.

### Physiological Changes Which Accompany Changes in Endurance

When endurance overload is applied regularly, the following changes are brought about:

1. The circulatory and respiratory systems become more efficient in transporting oxygen and nutrients to, and waste products from muscle cells. This results from a number of specific changes in those systems.

2. The temperature regulating system enables the body to adjust more effectively to the increased heat caused by muscular work.

3. Body movements become more efficient as wasted movements are eliminated and the coordinated actions of muscles become more refined (skill increases).

4. The carrying capacity of the blood is improved, resulting in better

transportation of oxygen and food products to the cells, and better disposal of waste products.

5. The active muscles may become stronger (depending on the type of training program used) and this will contribute to muscular endurance.

6. There is an increase in capillaries where gas exchange takes place in the lungs and at the tissues. This allows greater exchange of oxygen and carbon dioxide.

## TABLE 1
### Percentage of Training Time Spent in Developing the Energy Sources for Various Track Events*

| Event | Performance Time | Speed % | Aerobic Capacity % | Anaerobic Capacity % |
|---|---|---|---|---|
| Marathon | 135:00 to 180:00 | 5 | 90 | 5 |
| 6 mile | 30:00 to 50:00 | 5 | 80 | 15 |
| 3 mile | 15:00 to 25:00 | 10 | 70 | 20 |
| 2 mile | 10:00 to 16:00 | 20 | 40 | 40 |
| 1 mile | 4:00 to 6:00 | 20 | 25 | 55 |
| 880 yards | 2:00 to 3:00 | 30 | 5 | 65 |
| 440 yards | 1:00 to 1:30 | 80 | 3 | 15 |
| 220 yards | 0:22 to 0:35 | 95 | 3 | 2 |
| 110 yards | 0:10 to 0:15 | 95 | 2 | 3 |

## TABLE 2
### Endurance-Development Programs Specifying Type of Training*

| Types of Training | Speed % | Aerobic Endurance % | Anaerobic Endurance % |
|---|---|---|---|
| Repetitions of sprints | 90 | 4 | 6 |
| Continuous slow running | 2 | 93 | 5 |
| Continuous fast running | 2 | 90 | 8 |
| Slow interval | 10 | 60 | 30 |
| Fast Interval | 30 | 20 | 50 |
| Repetition running | 10 | 40 | 50 |
| Speed play (fartlek) | 20 | 40 | 40 |
| Interval sprinting | 20 | 70 | 10 |
| Acceleration sprinting | 90 | 5 | 5 |
| Hollow sprints | 85 | 5 | 10 |

* Both tables are taken from Falls, H. B., ed.: *Exercise Physiology*. New York: Academic Press Inc., 1968.

### Conditions Influencing Endurance

Several factors influence endurance. The following are brief discussions of the more important factors.

*Strength.* Suppose a man has a given amount of strength and with that strength he is able to move a particular resistance through the range of motion 100 times. If his strength were increased 50% he would then be able to move the same resistance with greater ease; thus he could repeat the movement considerably more than 100 times.

*Skill.* A certain amount of energy is wasted in unnecessary and uncoordinated movements. The skilled individual wastes less energy than the unskilled. It has been found that an unskilled swimmer may use more than five times as much energy as a skilled person in swimming a given distance. Similar but less dramatic differences exist between skilled and unskilled runners.

*Fatty Tissue.* Fat lacks the ability to contract, thus it is noncontributing in motor performances, and it hinders performance in three ways: 1) fat within the muscles causes friction and contributes to inefficient contractions; 2) fat within and surrounding the muscles adds dead weight, increasing resistance against the movement; and 3) fatty tissue places an overload on the circulatory system. It is estimated that one pound of fat increases the vascular system one mile.

*Efficiency of the Circulatory and Respiratory Systems.* In order for muscles to continue to function, the individual muscle cells must receive oxygen and nutrients from the circulatory system. Also the circulatory system transports waste products from the muscles. In turn, the respiratory system supplies oxygen to the circulatory system and receives carbon dioxide and other waste from it. If the circulatory and respiratory systems do not keep the muscles adequately supplied with oxygen and nutrients and free of waste products, then fatigue occurs.

*Age and Sex.* Endurance increases with age up to a certain point, after which endurance decreases as age increases. Among trained individuals, maximum endurance usually occurs slightly later than maximum strength: the early 20s among women, and the late 20s among men.

Comparing adult men and women, there is only a slight difference in endurance in moderate exercise, but the endurance of women in strenuous activities is considerably less than that of men.

After maximum endurance is reached, it holds fairly constant for three to five years, then begins to decline gradually because of several changes that occur in the circulatory and respiratory systems with increased age. Men in their 70s or 80s have lost about one-half of their capacity for transforming energy aerobically. The ability to supply blood to active tissues has decreased, and skeletal muscles are weak. Nevertheless, when working within the limits of their ability, many men well-advanced in years can carry on work with a lower heart rate and less evidence of fatigue than that exhibited by certain younger men. It should be noted that the loss of endurance at any stage in life can be reduced significantly as a result of training.

*Temperature.* Grose[9] found that endurance is adversely affected by immersion of the arm for eight minutes in water at 120° F. Conversely, the effects of cold have proven to be advantageous, until a muscle temperature of 80° F is reached. According to Clark et al.[3] 80° F appears to be the optimal muscle temperature for endurance, and muscle temperatures below this level produce adverse effects on endurance.

*Acid Waste.* The processes of muscle contraction result in acid waste products, primarily lactic acid. Muscular activity is greatly hindered by a high lactate level in the blood. Therefore, a person's endurance is influenced by his ability to keep the lactate level low, and by the ability to tolerate this by-product. The tolerance level seems to increase as a result of training.

*Pace.* In running and other locomotive activities, stopping, starting, accelerating and decelerating are very costly in terms of energy. Therefore, the most economical approach is to distribute the available energy evenly over the entire distance, meaning that theoretically a four-minute mile should consist of four 60-second quarters. However, this is not practical because the quarters are influenced by the start and finish, and by the necessity of gaining and holding position during the race.

## MUSCULAR POWER

Muscular power, often called explosive power, is a combination of force (strength) and velocity (speed). It is the ability to apply force rapidly. Power is typically demonstrated in projecting the body (as in jumping) or an object (as in throwing). The muscles must apply great force at a rapid rate in order to give the body or object the momentum necessary to carry it the desired distance.

It is possible for a person to be extremely strong and still not be very powerful. Also, he may be able to move with great speed against a very light resistance but lack the strength to move rapidly against heavier resistance—and thus he is not powerful. But if he possesses great strength combined with great speed of movement, then he is powerful.

Power is very important to vigorous performances because it determines how hard a person can hit, how far he can throw, how high he can jump and, to some extent, how fast he can run. Running is a series of body projections, therefore leg power is essential to fast running.

### How to Increase Power

Power can be increased by increasing strength (see p. 6) without sacrificing speed, or by increasing speed of movement (see p. 20) without sacrificing strength, or by increasing both speed and strength. Increasing strength affords the greatest potential for improving power because strength can usually be increased a significant amount, while speed can be improved a very limited amount.   Strength and speed can both be stressed by applying strong force through rapid (explosive) motion as is done in explosive weight training.

## SPEED OF MUSCLE CONTRACTION

The speed of contraction of different muscles varies considerably among individuals.   For example, person A may have faster leg actions while person B has faster arm actions.   In other words, speed is specific to individual body movements.

A. V. Hill[10] pointed out that speed of contraction is apparently inherent in muscle tissue, because even when muscles receive constant artificial stimuli they contract at varying rates.   DeVries[6] states that the difference in speed of contraction is apparently due to differences in biochemical and physiochemical properties of the contractile materials within the muscles and has no relationship to factors outside the muscle tissue.   The chemical environment of muscle tissue, and its chemical makeup can be altered a limited amount either by training or by nutrition, and this may result in faster body movements.

### The Essence of Speed in Performances

The speed of muscle contraction is basic to speed in moving the body or an object.   Speed (velocity) of the body and of objects is extremely important in track and field.   An increase in the rate of speed is referred to as *acceleration*.   The opposite of acceleration is *deceleration*.   Acceleration may be uniform or varying but, like velocity, acceleration is seldom constant.

In the running events, *average velocity* (distance/time) is the important factor, because this is what determines how long it takes to cover the distance of the race.   Velocity at any particular time during the race is relatively unimportant.   Conversely, in the field events (throwing and jumping) the real concern is *final velocity* of the body or object.   This is the velocity at the climax of the thrust, the moment contact is broken.   For instance, when an object is thrown, the speed at release is the primary factor influencing the distance it will travel, assuming it is projected at the correct angle.   The same is true of the human body when jumping.   The velocity over the total effort (average velocity) is of little concern.   If velocity is built to a climax at the correct instant, it is invariably the result of muscular forces producing a sequential acceleration toward that climax.   This calls for precise timing, and its achievement is often the difference between the skilled and unskilled performer.

Greater muscle force is necessary to produce the same velocity in a heavy object as is produced in a lighter one.   For instance, a 16-pound shot provides twice as much resistance as an 8-pound shot; therefore, considerably more force is required against the heavier shot to achieve the same velocity. Likewise, an increase in the body weight of a jumper can seriously reduce his final velocity, and thereby decrease the height and distance he can jump. Increased body weight has a similar effect on running speed.

### How to Increase Speed of Contraction

A muscle practically always contracts against some resistance, even if the resistance is only the weight of the body segment. Because of this, *strength* can influence the rate of contraction. As the amount of resistance against a movement becomes greater, strength has more influence on speed; where resistance is very light, strength has little if any influence on speed.

Increased *coordination* of muscles (skill) can increase the speed of specific movements. As the several mover muscles become better coordinated, they can overcome the external resistance with greater speed. When muscles are well-coordinated, one contractile force arrives at the peak velocity of the previous force. Consequently, the second force is more effective. Also as the agonistic and antagonistic muscles become better coordinated, the antagonists furnish less resistance to the contractile efforts of the agonists. If increased speed is desired in a particular performance, the skills should be practiced at rates equal to or exceeding those used in competition.

A. V. Hill[10] claims that speed of contraction can be increased by approximately 20% by raising body temperature 2° C. The magnitude of this claim lacks sufficient evidence, but it is well-established that increased body temperature does increase rate of contraction to some degree. Such increase is apparently due to a decrease in viscosity within the muscles. Raising body temperature a measurable amount requires much work. This is one of the arguments in favor of a thorough warm-up in preparation for explosive type performances.

It is believed that the efficiency of muscle contractions can be increased through training and this may result in increased speed. For example, training causes a reduction of fatty tissue within a muscle and this results in greater efficiency and faster contractions.

If the flexibility of antagonistic muscles is inadequate, then by increasing flexibility those muscles will furnish less resistance to the movement, and this may result in greater speed. Also reducing neural inhibitions as a result of training will allow the performer to voluntarily call upon greater numbers of available motor units. The more motor units involved, the greater is the strength and the more quickly the resistance can be overcome.

### Influence of Speed on Power

When the mechanical ratio (leverage) of a body movement remains constant, then the speed of movement is directly proportional to the speed of muscle contraction. If the rate of contraction were increased by 5%, the speed of movement would increase by the same percentage. In turn, the increased speed would contribute to power ($P = F \times V$). If other factors remain constant, power will increase in proportion to speed.

### Influence of Speed on Energy Cost

The energy cost of a muscle contraction varies with the cube of the speed of contraction. For example, if muscle X contracts twice as fast as muscle Y, the energy cost of muscle X is eight times as great as that of muscle Y. Whereas if muscle X contracts three times as fast as muscle Y, the energy cost of muscle X is 27 times as great ($3^3$) as that of muscle Y. This relationship has great significance, and it explains why maximum efforts cause fatigue so rapidly. Further, it explains why spurts of speed and unnecessary rapid movements are undesirable in endurance events.

## FLEXIBILITY

The range through which a joint can move is limited by three factors: 1) bone structure of the joint; 2) amount of bulk (muscle and other tissue) surrounding the joint; and 3) the extensibility of the muscles and connective tissues which cross over the joint. The third factor is of the greatest concern in trying to increase range of motion.

Hurdlers, high jumpers, triple jumpers, pole vaulters and discus throwers are among those who need more than normal flexibility in certain body regions.

### How to Develop Flexibility

Flexibility is developed by stretching the muscles and connective tissues regularly. Even though flexibility can be developed by dynamic stretching (bobbing type movements), static stretching is a better method. The recommended approach is to stretch the muscles gradually until the "stretch pain" is felt, then hold the position for about 10 seconds while consciously allowing the muscles to s-t-r-e-t-c-h. Release the tension for a few seconds and repeat the exercise five or six times. Flexibility exercises produce the best results when they are done daily. Hard jerky-type stretching causes mild injuries to the muscle tissue, so it should be avoided.

## REACTION TIME

Reaction time is the time that lapses between the onset of a stimulus and the response to the stimulus. It is very important in some athletic performances, such as basketball and tennis. However, in track and field the influence of reaction time is limited mostly to starting. Whether a sprinter wins or loses the race may be determined by his ability to react quickly to the starting signal.

Research supports the following: 1) reaction time improves up to age 20–25 after which it gradually declines; 2) reaction time is slightly faster in men than women; 3) reaction time shortens as the stimulus becomes more intense (louder in the case of an audio signal); 4) reaction time is shortened by tensing the muscles in readiness for a quick movement; 5) preliminary signals given rhythmically, such as rhythmic counting prior to the signal, shorten reaction time; 6) distracting noises lengthen reaction time; and 7) repeated practice of a particular response shortens reaction time.

### How To Improve Reaction Time

Reaction time can be improved by 1) practicing the response until it becomes conditioned (automatic) or semi-conditioned; 2) anticipating (concentrating on) the signal or stimulus; 3) increasing the person's alertness; 4) causing emotional excitement which usually accompanies competition; and 5) increasing the intensity of the stimulus.

## SPECIFIC SKILLS

Skill is the ability to perform a combination of movements smoothly and efficiently. It is the effective coordination of all the different muscles involved, whether they are agonists, antagonists, neutralizers or stabilizers. In other words, skill is the ability to use the correct muscles at the correct time, with the exact force necessary to perform the desired movements in the proper sequence.

### How to Improve Skill

Skill is primarily a characteristic of the nervous system because muscle contractions are directed by nerve impulses. To take a systematic and effective approach to improving skill, a person must analyze the specific movement patterns in the performance and attempt to improve those patterns. Movement patterns must be practiced correctly over and over until they become naturally smooth and efficient. For example, pole vaulting involves a number of specific body movements which must be put together in correct combination. The movement patterns must be practiced correctly over and over until they are perfected. When a person accomplishes this he has developed a high level of skill in vaulting.

## SELECTED REFERENCES

1. Astrand, P. O. and Rodahl, K.: *Textbook of Work Physiology.* New York: McGraw-Hill Book Co., 1970.
2. Berger, R. A.: Optimum repetitions for the development of strength. *Research Quarterly* 33:329, 1962c.
3. Clark, R. S. J., Hellon, R. F. and Lind, A. R.: The duration of sustained contractions of the human forearm at different muscle temperatures. *J. Physiol.* (London), 143:454, 1958.
4. Cooper, K. H.: *Aerobics.* New York: M. Evans & Co., Inc., 1968.
5. DeLorme, T. and Wilkins, A. L.: *Progressive Resistance Exercise.* New York: Appleton-Century-Crofts, 1951.

6. DeVries, H. A.: *Physiology of Exercise for Physical Education and Athletics.* Dubuque: William C. Brown & Co., 1966.
7. Falls, H. B., ed.: *Exercise Physiology.* New York: Academic Press Inc., 1968.
8. Gardner, J. B. and Purty, G. J.: *A Computerized Running Training Program.* Tafnews Press, P.O. Box 296, Los Altos, California, 1970.
9. Grose, J. E.: Depression of muscle fatigue curves by heat and cold. *Res. Quart. Amer. Ass. Health Phys. Educ.*, 29:19, 1958.
10. Hill, A. V.: The mechanics of voluntary muscle. *Lancet*, 261:947, 1951.
11. Karnoven, M. J.: Effects of vigorous exercise on the heart. In Rosenbaum, F. F. and Belnap, E. L., eds.: *Work and the Heart.* New York: Paul B. Hoeber, Inc., 1959.
12. Mathews, D. V. and Fox, E. L.: *The Physiological Basis of Physical Education and Athletics.* Philadelphia: W. B. Saunders Co., 1971.
13. Morehouse, L. E. and Miller, A. T.: *Physiology of Exercise.* 6th ed., St. Louis: The C. V. Mosby Co., 1971.
14. Muller, E. A. and Rohmert, W.: Die Geschwindigkeit der muskelkraft zunahme bei isometrischen training. *Int. Z. Angew. Physiol.*, 19:403, 1963.

# CHAPTER 2

# Factors Related to Conditioning and Performance

There are several factors related to training and performance that deserve attention in this text. By being well-informed about these factors, coaches and athletes can act intelligently in their approaches to conditioning and preparation for performance.

## NUTRITION

As a result of their unusual desire to find ways to improve, many athletes are easily influenced by the success of others whose training regimes may include strange diets or fad foods. Typically, when these foods are tested by scientific methods, it turns out that the athlete's success was achieved in spite of and not because of his unusual dietary modifications. There is no evidence that athletic performance can be improved by modifying a basically sound and nutritious diet. Conversely, an athlete can reduce his performance considerably if his diet is less than optimal. Thus, a nutritious diet is an important consideration in athletic conditioning.

There are so many nutritious foods that many different combinations can result in a sound diet, and individual differences exist in our sense of taste and also in our dietary needs. Therefore, it is not possible to prescribe a "best diet." It can be said, however, that an athlete's diet should be well-balanced, nutritious and composed of foods which are satisfying and not disrupting and which are sufficient to maintain a normal body weight. Such a diet does not need to be supplemented by fad foods; it is even doubt-

A considerable amount of the information in this chapter was taken from Jensen, Clayne R. and Fisher, A. Garth: *Scientific Basis of Athletic Conditioning*, Philadelphia: Lea & Febiger, 1972.

ful that food supplements such as vitamins and wheat germ are of additional value. On the other hand, if the diet is not sound, food supplements might be beneficial.

### Recommended Proportion of Different Foods

It is known that the human organism utilizes *carbohydrates* first for energy during muscular activity even though it is also capable of utilizing *fats*. Carbohydrates have a distinct advantage because in the oxidation process they yield more kilocalories of energy per liter of oxygen than do fats. Therefore carbohydrates are more efficient. In addition, several studies have shown that endurance diminishes on a high fat diet as compared with a high carbohydrate diet. In spite of this, it is not recommended that fats be excluded from the diet. Aside from the important vitamins and certain essential fatty acids in fats, there appears to be a fat-contained factor that is necessary for the normal metabolism of carbohydrates.

*Protein* is needed in the diet mainly for building new body tissue. Only under conditions of insufficient carbohydrate and fat supplies is the protein of body tissue consumed for energy. During athletic training there is an increase of muscle mass; hence an abundance of protein is required for the formation of new capillaries, connective tissue and sarcoplasm.

It is well-established that over 50% of the athlete's diet should consist of carbohydrates, while fats and protein compose less than 50%. Morehouse and Miller[5] recommend the following proportions:

1. For *long duration* events: 700 grams of carbohydrates, 150 grams of fats and 100 grams of protein.

2. For *speed and power* type performances: 350 to 400 grams of carbohydrates, 100 to 300 grams of fats and 210 grams of protein.

Best and Taylor[1] recommend the following approximate proportions for the athlete who uses 3000 kilocalories daily: 380 grams of carbohydrates, 133 grams of fats and 70 grams of protein.

### Principal Sources of Carbohydrates, Fats and Protein

*Carbohydrates:*
    Grain and cereal products—breads, cornbread, grain cereals
    Vegetables—corn, potatoes, beans, rice
    Fruits—bananas, grape juice
    Sugars—honey, candies, jams, jellies
    Pastries—pie, cakes
*Fats:*
    Certain meats—pork, mutton, goose (influenced by the fatness of the
        meat)
    Certain fish—salmon
    Nuts—pecans, almonds, peanuts
    Cooking fats—animal fats, vegetable oils

Margarine, butter, lard
Mayonnaise, salad dressing
Whole milk
*Protein:*
Lean meat—beef (pot roast, steak, tongue), lamb chops
Fish—tuna, white, sword, cod, blue, cat, trout
Fowl—chicken, turkey
Milk—skim, powdered
Cheese
Eggs
Soybeans
Dried Yeast

### Food Supplements

Often good performers claim their success is due in part to supplemental or so-called special foods. It is difficult to know whether this is true, and whether the benefits, if any, are physiological or psychological.

*Vitamins.* In the past it has been believed that the requirements for vitamins increase more rapidly than the increase in metabolism due to exercise. Recent research indicates that vitamin needs increase in approximately the same proportion as metabolism. Thus, it can be reasoned that ingestion of more food as a result of heavier work automatically provides the needed increase in vitamins. This assumes that the diet is well-balanced and sound. Based on research and reasoning, it is recommended that vitamins be obtained as much as possible from their natural sources (food), rather than from purified synthetic sources. It is commonly believed by nutrition experts that if a person is on a well-rounded and nutritious diet there is no need for vitamin supplements. Conversely, if the diet is not sound, supplementary vitamins will likely prove beneficial for both athletes and nonathletes.

*Minerals.* Like vitamin needs, mineral requirements increase in the same proportion as food requirements when there is increased exercise. Most of the experimental results indicate that an adequate supply of minerals is present in a well-balanced diet. Under the conditions of such diet it is questionable whether mineral supplements are of any value, but here again, if the diet is not sound then mineral supplements might be beneficial.

*Wheat germ.* Wheat germ is a rather complete food composed of a large number of nutrients. For this reason, some people have reasoned that regular consumption of wheat germ will assist in overcoming deficiencies in the diet. This reasoning is based on the assumption that the diet does have some deficiencies. Cureton[2] states, "Studies at the University of Illinois Physical Fitness Research Laboratory indicate that wheat germ, or its derivative wheat germ oil, aids those who consume it under proper conditions over a long period of time to enable the body to build up its glycogen (muscle fuel) reserve." There is some indication that wheat germ contributes to low cholesterol levels, and low cholesterol has been associated with superior physical fitness. There is no evidence that harmful effects will result from consuming a reasonable amount of wheat germ on a regular basis.

### Meat Eaters vs. Vegetarians

The primary argument for eating meat (or fish) rather than only vegetables is that meat is a primary source of amino acids which are indispensable for life. However, vegetarians can get along without meat if they use a variety of vegetables to assure an adequate supply of these essential acids. Reports that vegetarians have greater endurance than meat eaters should be discounted because of lack of scientific evidence. In fact, there is no evidence that vegetarians are superior in any athletic event, and reasoning and observation indicate that unless vegetarians have a well-rounded diet, they may suffer from malnutrition.

### Fad Foods

Some fad foods such as sunflower seeds, kelp, raw meat, black strap molasses and other such substances are sometimes claimed to have miraculous properties for improving performance. In rare cases when a person is sincerely dedicated to the value of the food, a psychological effect may be present. But there is no evidence that such foods have any miraculous effects and are thus no more valuable than a large number of other more commonly accepted foods.

### Distribution of Food Intake

Physiologists agree that frequent, moderate-sized meals result in more efficiency, from both the psychological and physiological standpoints. The athlete should eat at least three meals per day.

It has been found that small weight losses due to starvation (5% of initial weight) do not cause appreciable changes in performance. On the other hand, the American Medical Association has advised that submitting to acute starvation or several days of dehydration in order to lose weight is inadvisable, especially for young people who are not physically mature. An underfed person cannot sustain hard work as well as a well-fed person, because a substandard diet causes a reduction in performance of the physiological systems, especially the mechanisms for the delivery of oxygen and the removal of metabolic wastes. Another argument against excessive starvation is the fact that as the demand for energy exceeds the supply, body tissues are consumed in the course of the activity. The depletion of body tissues beyond a certain point impairs the functions of the organism. Furthermore, physical efficiency is lowered when body tissues instead of stored energy are used as fuel for performance.

## EFFECTS OF DRUGS ON CONDITIONING AND PERFORMANCE

It is worthwhile for coaches and athletes to be familiar with the effects of drugs on the physiological functioning of the body and, more specifically, to know the effects of these substances on conditioning and performance.

### Narcotics

According to common usage, there are three classes of narcotics: *opium* and its derivatives, *cocaine* and *marijuana*. There is some support for the addition of barbiturates and alcohol to this list.

*Opium* relieves pain and produces a sense of false well-being. It produces depression of the central nervous system, dulls pain and induces sleep. (It may cause very temporary excitement of the nervous system but this soon wears off.) It reduces body secretions except those of the skin. A large dose can depress respiration and cause death. Morphine, codeine and heroin are all derivatives of opium. Morphine causes body reactions similar to those caused by opium. Heroin also causes effects similar to those of opium. Heroin is the most dangerous in terms of producing drug addiction. Probably three-fourths of all confirmed drug addicts use heroin.

*Cocaine* is a powerful, quick-acting drug that is capable of producing strong addiction. Unlike most narcotics which act as sedatives, a moderate dose of cocaine stimulates the central nervous system, accelerating respiratory and circulatory rates. Taken in excess, cocaine can produce psychotic symptoms of great excitement and peculiar sensations of creatures crawling on the skin, commonly referred to as cocaine bugs.

*Marijuana* is a mild and intoxicating drug to which people become addicted psychologically rather than physiologically. The use of this drug might lead toward the use of more harmful drugs.

There is no argument in favor of athletes using narcotics, and there are very strong arguments against their use by people in general, and especially by athletes. Therefore, it should be firmly concluded that there is no place for the use of narcotics in athletic conditioning or performance.

### Sedatives

Sedatives reduce nervous system activity, produce a state of relaxation and depress the actions of the vital organs. They are basically sleep-producing drugs. The most commonly used of this group are barbiturates, of which there are at least 20 different drugs. Under proper medical supervision, the barbiturates serve a useful medical purpose. However, to use these drugs indiscriminately as an easy, quick method of reducing conscious activity of the brain is very unwise. The danger lies both in developing a dependency upon them and the possibility of overdosage. There is no argument in favor of using sedatives in connection with athletics except under medical supervision.

### Amphetamines

Amphetamines (trade names: Benzedrine, Dexedrine, Desamine and Methedrine) produce effects similar to those caused by the activity of the sympathetic nervous system.  For most people the immediate effect is increased alertness and quicker reactions.  Because of the stimulating effect of amphetamines, there has been some interest in determining whether athletic performance can be improved by their use.  Medically speaking, the practice of using stimulating drugs is not recommended.  The best evidence presently available indicates that amphetamines do not produce superior performance but tend to cause the participant to perceive that he is performing unusually well.

### Caffeine

Caffeine is the alkaloid consumed daily by millions of people in coffee, tea, cocoa and cola.  It is known for its mild stimulating effects.  When used in moderation, caffeine beverages are apparently harmless.  However caffeine is a toxic drug and, if injected into the bloodstream, a small amount can be fatal.  If injected into a muscle, caffeine causes temporary paralysis, and even a drop of the substance injected directly into the brain can cause severe convulsions.  With all of these reactions one would assume that caffeine beverages are dangerous.  However, toxic effects do not occur in an individual who drinks such beverages because caffeine diffuses into the bloodstream and then is removed from the blood to the kidneys where it is excreted.

Caffeine primarily acts upon the blood vessels, heart and nervous system.  Mild doses cause general vasoconstriction with simultaneous dilation of the coronary artery and increase the heart rate and the contractile force of the heart.  The temperature of the stomach increases along with an increase of hydrochloric acid secretion.  Mild doses may cause an increase in metabolic rate, may stimulate the central nervous system and may accelerate the respiratory rate.  In small doses caffeine increases the thought processes.

Exercise physiologists and other experts on conditioning generally agree that caffeine beverages are not ergogenic aids.  However, they also generally agree that moderate consumption of caffeine beverages has no detrimental effects on conditioning and performance provided such beverages do not interfere with a well-balanced diet and adequate sleep.

### Alcohol

It has been the general practice to exclude alcoholic beverages from the diet of athletes.  Strict adherence to this rule has been difficult to enforce, especially among professional athletes because they may argue that there is no evidence that moderate drinking causes disease, injures the general health or shortens life. In spite of this argument it has been demonstrated that reactions and neuromuscular coordinations are impaired by the consumption of alcohol, and that extensive habitual overuse often leads to poor eating patterns and malnutrition. These disadvantages, along with loss of sleep associated with the overuse of alcohol and the loss of normal social inhibitions, add up to making the prohibition of alcohol for athletes a logical and vital training rule. There is no doubt that strong alcoholic drinks can be detrimental to both conditioning and performance, and there are no arguments in favor of their use.

### Tobacco

The adverse effects of tobacco smoking on conditioning and performance have been well-established in recent years. As a rule, coaches are strongly against smoking, and rightfully so. According to the American Medical Association Committee on the Medical Aspects of Sports, it is unwise for a young man who has ambitions to excel in sports to begin smoking or to continue the habit if he has already started. The Committee noted that while the effects of tobacco vary with different people, the following conclusions seem warranted:

1. In smoking some carbon monoxide may be absorbed by the blood, thereby reducing temporarily the oxygen-carrying capacity of the blood. This restricts endurance.

2. Habitual smoking when the stomach is empty tends to produce digestive disturbances and distress.

3. Habitual smoking sometimes leads to an irritable nervous system, and this reaction is most likely in young people.

4. In certain persons the constricting effect of nicotine on the blood vessels may contribute to the development of circulatory disorders and circulatory inefficiencies.

5. Habitual smoking with inhaling irritates the delicate membranes of the throat and lungs and may induce "smoker's cough" and render the throat more susceptible to infections.

The role of tobacco smoke as a factor in lung cancer cannot be ignored by those professionally concerned with health and fitness. Statistically, it has been shown that a heavy smoker is 42 times as likely to develop lung cancer as a nonsmoker. Furthermore, smoking inhibits the flow of gastric juices and the onset of hunger pains and can thus interfere with nutritional patterns. It is also medically clear that smoking irritates the mucous membranes of the nose, throat and other respiratory passages. Since there is no good argument in favor of tobacco use and there are strong arguments against its use for athletes or nonathletes, it seems prudent for the coach to enforce vigorously a no smoking rule. Such a rule will be much more effective if the coach sets the example himself.

## PRECOMPETITION PROCEDURES

The rules which govern precompetition procedures are simple and rather well-established. They are as follows:

1. The food eaten during the 24 hours prior to competition should be high in carbohydrates in order to build a near-maximum supply of glycogen in the liver and the muscles. In order to avoid depletion of the glycogen supply, heavy work should be avoided during this period.

2. During the 24 hours prior to competition fatty foods and other slow-digesting foods should be minimized. Heavily spiced foods and foods that tend to cause indigestion should be avoided.

3. Training done during the 48 hours prior to competition should emphasize the fine points of the performance skills and should not involve extremely heavy work.

4. A normal amount of rest, or slightly more, should be obtained during the 48 hours prior to competition; however, excessive rest or other significant deviations from the normal living routine is not advised.

5. The competitor should occupy himself in pursuits that are interesting and relaxing, and which keep him from becoming too emotionally involved in the upcoming competition.

6. Without violating basically sound practices, the athlete should do those things which cause him to feel "ready" for the competition.

### Precompetition Meal

Much confusion and many misconceptions have existed relative to pre-meet meals, and today there is still much disagreement about this matter. There are two aspects to the precompetition meal: physiological and psychological. From the physiological standpoint the content, quantity and timing of the meal are all-important factors. From the psychological viewpoint the performer must feel that the meal was "right" to prepare him for his best effort. For track and field athletes the following guides are valid and should be helpful. Even within the framework of these guides there is much flexibility as to the exact content of the meal.

1. A substantial but not large meal should be eaten three to four hours before competition. A small amount of carbohydrates which are digested quickly may be eaten without harm as close as one hour before competition.

2. The precompetition meal, and also the meal preceding it, should consist mostly of carbohydrates with some protein and only a small amount of fats. This is because carbohydrates are digested rapidly and they replenish the supply of glycogen, thus providing quick energy.

3. Foods that are distasteful or which tend to cause stomach disturbance should be avoided.

4. Foods that are irritating to most people, such as roughage and highly spiced foods, should be avoided.

5. Gas-forming foods such as cabbage, beans, apples and onions, should be minimized.

6. Liquids are essential in the precompetition meal because the digestion and absorption of foods is dependent upon an adequate supply of liquid.

7. Milk, which has been taboo on training tables in the past, is now considered acceptable and even valuable in the regular diet, and also in the precompetition meal. Recent research indicates that no harmful effects result from drinking a moderate amount of milk three to four hours prior to competition.

8. The meal that has been traditionally recommended is similar to the following: eight-ounce broiled steak with fat removed, baked potato, green vegetable, toast and honey, fresh fruit, and two to three glasses of fluid. This is not a bad precompetition meal. The main criticism of it is that it might be too heavy on protein (meat) and too light on carbohydrates. However it has been argued that perhaps the psychological benefits outweigh any physiological deficiencies of the meal, because it is tasty and satisfying.

## WARM-UP

Several points of argument in favor of warm-up have been stated by people who are specialized in the study of athletic performance. They believe:

1. Warm-up increases the rate and strength of muscular contraction.

2. Warm-up related to the particular performance increases the necessary coordinations.

3. Warm-up helps to prevent injury by preparing the muscles for all-out efforts.

4. In endurance activities, warm-up brings on second wind more readily.

Unfortunately, much of the research done in connection with warm-up has been done under poorly controlled conditions, and some of it has involved mild exercise routines which do not actually warm the body. However, some valuable information has resulted from those studies which were well-conducted.

Laboratory studies have shown that cooling of the body (reducing body temperature) causes a loss of reaction time, a slowing of the muscle speed, a loss of muscle excitability and an increase in the duration of the action potential in the muscles. Theoretically, warming of the muscles will reverse these ill effects. Hill[4] found that by increasing the temperature of a muscle, a corresponding increase resulted in both contractile force and contractile speed. DeVries[3] reasoned that a warm-up which results in increased blood and muscle temperature should improve performance through the following mechanisms:

1. Increased speed of contraction and relaxation of muscles

2. Greater efficiency of muscle contractions

3. Greater exchange of oxygen to the tissues because hemoglobin gives up more oxygen at higher temperatures

4. Increased metabolic processes throughout the body

It is commonly believed, and rightfully so, that the preliminary performance of the skills involved in the activity will sharpen the competitor's coordination and timing, and thus make him more ready for the performance. Practical experience tends to support this idea. However, the degree to which the sharpening of skills actually occurs as a result of warm-up is not well-established by research results.

Based on the available evidence, most coaches and athletes want to continue with warm-up until additional evidence is accumulated. The authors strongly advocate extensive warm-up on the idea that it does contribute to better performance and the prevention of injury. But it must be recognized that indiscriminate warm-up may waste energy and prove detrimental to performance. The warm-up should be specific to the activity being performed and should be increased in intensity as the performer becomes better conditioned. The timing of the warm-up in relation to the performance must be correct. Otherwise, the beneficial effects may be reduced or eliminated. Following are some important guides:

1. Warm-up should be intense enough to actually increase body temperature and cause mild perspiration, but not so intense that it causes partial fatigue.

2. Warm-up should include some general stretching and loosening exercises along with a limited amount of heavy work.

3. It should include movements that are common to the performance for which warm-up is being done. That is, runners should include running, hurdlers should include hurdling, shot putters should include putting, etc. However, maximum efforts should be avoided.

4. The warm-up routine should begin to taper off 10 to 15 minutes prior to performance, and end at least five minutes before performance. This will allow time to recover from any mild and temporary fatigue and still not lose the effects of the warm-up.

## WEIGHT CONTROL

It has been found that a high percentage of body fat is detrimental to health in general and often decreases a person's ability to perform. It causes awkwardness because of the excess weight and, since it requires a constant supply of blood, it reduces the ability of the cardiovascular system to supply oxygen to the working muscles, thus impairing endurance.

The means of losing weight, if this is desirable, is relatively simple. One must either increase the expenditure of energy (utilization of calories) through activity, or control the amount and kind of food he eats, or a combination of both of these. If this is done, the stored fat will be utilized for body fuel and literally be "burned off." In most cases a combination of decreased calories and increased exercise is the best approach. Generally, the best advice for an athlete with regard to weight control is to maintain normal body weight, provided normal weight is defined as a relatively fat-free body. The emphasis that needs to be placed on weight control varies considerably with the particular athletic event, and with different individuals.

## COACHING AND COMPETITIVE HINTS

Many young competitors are under the illusion that all they need to do to win is to have a certain amount of ability and train hard. This is false because there is often a great difference between training and competing well. The following is a list of hints relative to areas such as preparation for competition and strategy which coaches and athletes will want to consider.

### Body Maintenance

1. Most athletes in hard training require eight to nine hours of sleep each night. This amount varies with individuals but it is essential that an athlete receive an adequate amount of rest.

2. The use of tobacco, alcohol and drugs is harmful to an athlete's performance. Therefore these substances should be strictly prohibited. (See the section on drugs, pp. 29–31.)

3. Prompt attention to all injuries, however slight (e.g. blisters), may prevent the loss of valuable training time. An athlete has an obligation to himself and to the team to try to remain free of injuries and sickness.

4. A proper and well-planned warm-up before competition is very important because it raises body temperature to a more efficient level and produces other important benefits. (See the section on warm-up, p. 33.)

5. Research and practical experience show that the recovery time after vigorous competition can be shortened if the athlete goes through a warm-down routine. The routine should start immediately after competition. The athlete should put on his warm-up clothes, begin by walking and finish with easy jogging and light calisthenics.

### All Events

1. The athlete should be sure to give careful attention to all of the aspects of his living pattern during the day of competition and the day prior to competition to be sure he is ready when the time arrives.

2. In addition to the physiological preparation, the athlete should pay special attention to preparing himself mentally for his best effort. He should strive for both physiological and psychological readiness.

3. He should check all personal items needed for competition well ahead of time to be sure they are in top condition and available.

4. He should arrive at the site of competition in plenty of time to prepare himself thoroughly, but not so early that he becomes tired from waiting.

5. Since competition is often spread over a long period of time, it is important to use adequate clothing to keep the body warm between performances. Research indicates that muscles do not function as effectively when they are cool. Also, much energy can be wasted in trying to keep the body warm in the absence of adequate clothing.

6. Time spent lying in the sun the day before and day of competition can sap energy needed for the competition.

7. During the day of competition an athlete should not spend too much time sitting or lying. Some walking or light jogging will help to get all of the body processes working properly.

8. As a part of his preparation for competition, each athlete should try to develop within himself an iron-willed determination to succeed. The coach should assist in every way possible to develop this attitude.

9. In most cases a coach will have better results using praise rather than criticism. However, when he finds it necessary to criticize or make recommendations for improved performances, he will find his athletes more responsive after a victory. It is better to wait several hours after defeat before approaching a competitor with criticism. Criticism is usually more effective when done privately on a person-to-person basis.

10. Staleness is a factor which is highly controversial. Some say it is physical and others say it is a state of mind. It is well-established that staleness is caused by monotony and emotional stress. The best remedy seems to be changing the training schedule, taking a few days' rest, or participation in other activities which divert the athlete's interests. The cliché that "a change is as good as a rest" is a valuable remedy for staleness.

11. In setting up goals for an athlete, the coach should have a series of short-range goals, along with certain carefully selected long-range goals so the athlete does not become discouraged in his quest for success. The goals should not be too easily attained, yet they should not exceed the athlete's grasp. The coach and the athlete should never be completely satisfied.

### Field Events

1. In field events, loosening and stretching exercises prior to each trial are recommended because lack of looseness can affect one's stride and range of motion enough to cause inconsistencies.

2. The athlete should view every trial as a winning attempt. He cannot afford to waste trials due to lack of maximum concentration and effort.

3. In competition where the time between trials is long, the athlete must prepare himself anew both psychologically and physiologically for each trial.

4. In the jumping events, consistency in striking the takeoff point is fundamental to success. Thus, everything that influences the approach should be done with unusual care, such as: (A) a steel tape should be used to measure the checkpoint; (B) since each runway surface is slightly different than any other, it is wise to practice the approach several times to be sure that the check-marks function effectively on that runway; (C) it is important to start at exactly the same point on the runway every time; and (D) it is beneficial to run at the same speed in competition as in practice. It might be better to reverse the statement and say run at the same speed in practice as in competition.

### Running Events

1. Breathing should be as natural as possible, coming through both the nose and the mouth.

2. The head should be held in natural alignment with the rest of the body. When fatigue occurs, many runners throw the head backward causing a loss of drive and shortening of the stride.

3. Acclimation in terms of both temperature and altitude can be an important factor in competition. The coach and athlete should pay adequate attention to the need for acclimation in a given instance, and should strive to bring about the necessary adjustments to enhance performance.

4. A runner should become *relaxation conscious*. Whenever he feels his body tightening up, he should relax by telling himself that the tension causes his body to burn additional energy. Relaxation is essential for expert performance.

5. The coach should remind his distance runners that when the pace results in extreme discomfort, it is probably affecting the opponents the same. A good distance runner must develop the ability to ward off fatigue and tolerate a certain amount of pain.

6. A coach should instruct his team members to finish every race unless doing so would cause injury or harm. Dropping out of races can easily become a habit.

### Race Strategy

1. A coach should be positive and encourage his runners to think big and have positive attitudes about themselves and their team.

2. As a rule, the less speed an individual has the longer should be the race he runs. Speed is a hereditary characteristic and cannot be improved greatly. Endurance, however, can be developed with a good training program over long periods of time.

3. A coach can assist a runner by helping him plan his strategy. However, the runner should realize that this prerace plan is subject to change during the race due to circumstances. The athlete may have to contend

against an unexpected dark horse in the race or with other runners who may not perform as expected.

4. The following items should be considered when planning race strategy: (A) the runner's competitive condition at the time; (B) the competitive condition of the opposition; (C) the basic speed of the runner and his competitors; (D) the race strategy used by the opposition in previous races; (E) the importance of the particular meet; and (F) track and weather conditions that could affect performances. Many inexperienced runners will reach their peak condition too early in the season and will waste their energy on winning lead-up meets before the important meets are held. A well preplanned schedule can do much to prevent this from happening.

5. When a runner is preparing to start his kick for the finish line the best position is on the outside shoulder of the runner immediately in front. This helps to prevent the runner from getting boxed in and places him in a position to respond to a challenge from another runner.

6. When a runner has a slower basic speed than his competition he will need to go out in front and set a fast pace in the hope that he can destroy his opposition's finishing kick.

7. Occasionally a runner will find his competition much slower than himself. In this case he will need to take the lead from the start of the race and maintain it to the end if he expects to run a good time.

8. If during a race a strong wind is blowing, it is best to fall behind another runner and let him act as a windbreak.

9. A coach must learn that he can overcoach his boys by making them overly concerned about race strategy. An athlete can best learn from his own experiences.

10. In distance races the best results will be obtained when the runner moves at an even, relaxed pace. When a runner has the ability to run at an even pace for several laps he need not worry about the last lap because most experienced runners can muster enough energy and determination to carry them through the final leg.

11. Once a runner starts his kick for the finish line he must maintain it all the way. Many runners have lost races because they started the kick with a fast rhythm and then slowed down. When they tried to pick up the pace again their muscles failed to respond.

12. When passing another man it is wise for the runner to pick a time when his opponent least expects a challenge, and then to use enough speed to carry him well beyond the opponent.

13. It is wise strategy to avoid running wide on the turns. If a man runs in lane two around a quarter-mile track he runs eight yards farther than if he were to run in lane one. In a mile this would total 32 yards, if every lap is run wide. Most races are lost by much less of a margin.

14. Many a race has been lost because an athlete did not know exactly where the finish line was located; this caused him to misjudge his finishing

kick or to slow down a few yards before the finish. Be certain where the finishing line is located. This advice is especially important for indoor meets.

15. When tactical decisions need to be made late in the race, they should be decisive.

16. An athlete should drive hard beyond the finish line and not start to slow down before the race is completed.

17. A runner must guard his position on the track and should never let another runner put him off balance with an elbow or by a cut in front. He must refuse to yield ground.

18. Each runner must.learn for himself the point at which he is neither over- nor under-confident. He must learn to assess his opponents in terms of their speed, endurance and race strategy from their previous performances. Then he should plan his own race for the purpose of meeting or disrupting his opponent's abilities and tactics.

19. When being passed it is wise for a runner to move out slightly to prevent being boxed in.

20. Passing on a curve should be avoided except when absolutely necessary.

21. In the mile run it is wise to avoid any faltering on the third lap. This is the lap where most inexperienced runners are the weakest psychologically. If the opponent will take advantage of this by maintaining or setting a faster pace he can very often gain an advantage.

22. In the last stages of a race when a runner is really hurting he should not think of his own problems but rather the problems of his opponents. This kind of concentration will help carry him through the last part of the race.

23. Once a runner takes the lead he should search for rhythm, smoothness and relaxation.

24. A runner should not look back. It can interfere with rhythm and may cause him to step on the curb of the track or the heel of another runner. When other runners see someone look back they often become encouraged because this indicates a lack of confidence.

### SELECTED REFERENCES

1. Best, C. H. and Taylor, N. B.: *The Physiological Basis of Medical Practice.* Baltimore: Williams & Wilkins Co., 1966.
2. Cureton, T. K.: What about the wheat germ? *Scholastic Coach,* 24:30 (November), 1959.
3. DeVries, H. A.: *Physiology of Exercise for Physical Education and Athletics.* Dubuque: William C. Brown & Co., 1966.
4. Hill, A. V.: The mechanics of voluntary muscle. *Lancet,* 261:947, 1951.
5. Morehouse, L. E. and Miller, A. T.: *Physiology of Exercise.* 6th ed., St. Louis: The C. V. Mosby Co., 1971.

# Part II
# Running Events

CHAPTER 3

# Short Sprints

The initial distance of the sprint is lost in antiquity although the stadium race (one length of the stadium) at the ancient Olympics is believed to have been about 210 yards. Races of various distances were contested during the 1800s and early 1900s, but finally the 100 yard or 100 meter and the 220 yard or 200 meter distances became the standard short sprints.

To determine the world champion, eight Olympic finalists in the 100 meter sprint are called to their marks. The starter's command "on your mark" is heard by the contestants through speakers placed immediately behind the starting blocks. The starter commands "set" and holds the sprinters in position for 1.89 seconds, then fires the gun. Neither the starter nor the recall starter detects a false start. But the electronic system registers a false start in lane three. All sprinters are called back and the runner in lane three is charged with a false start. On the next try the sprinters get off to an even start and in less than 10 seconds the race is over. Immediately the 80,000 spectators see the time of each sprinter on an electric scoreboard registered to the nearest 0.01 second. Simultaneously officials are viewing photographs of the finish which show the exact times and order of finish. There is no guesswork and no room for argument.

It was not always like this. When man first started running sprint races, getting off to a somewhat even start was a major task, and attempts at measuring the times accurately left much to be desired. In the ancient Olympics it was recommended that any runner who took unfair advantage at the start of the race be given corporal punishment.

During the early part of the nineteenth century, getting a race started often resulted in long delays as the "mutual consent start" frequently led to contestants trying to outfox each other with various strategies. A gun was fired as a last resort when the "mutual consent start" failed. Finally the gunshot became standard procedure.

The standard sprint starting technique, as we know it today, and the starting blocks used with this technique are both of recent origin. Bobby MacDonald, a Maori living in Scotland, is credited as being the first person to use the crouch starting technique in 1884. Using this starting method, John Owen Jr. became the person to first break the 10-second barrier when he ran the 100 yard dash in 9.8 in 1890.

Ten seconds for the 100 and 22 seconds for the 220 are known among sprinters as even times. During the early years of the modern era it was the dream of many athletes to be able to run even times for these two races. In recent decades the performances of sprinters, like other athletes, have improved significantly and steadily. As a result, even times for the two sprints are no longer the goals of the expert sprinters although they are still worthy accomplishments at certain levels of competition.

The evolution of world records in the short sprint races gives a rather accurate indication of the progress sprinters have made during the past hundred or more years. The progress has been consistent over a long period of time, and there is no reason to believe that the best races have yet been run. Even though the present world records might seem insurmountable, there is little doubt that sometime in the near future athletes who are dedicated and who employ improved running and training techniques will establish new world standards in all of the sprint races.

### 100 Yard Dash

| Time | Record-holder and country | Year |
|------|---------------------------|------|
| 10.5s. | B. S. Darbyshire, Great Britain | 1864 |
| 10s. | J. P. Tennent, Great Britain | 1868 |
| 10s. | Horace Lee, U.S. | 1877 |
| 10s. | William Wilmer, U.S. | 1878 |
| 9.8s. | John Owen Jr., U.S. | 1890 |
| 9.8s. | W. T. MacPherson, Australia | 1891 |
| 9.8s. | John Hempton, New Zealand | 1892 |
| 9.8s. | Charles Stage, U.S. | 1893 |
| 9.8s. | John Crum, U.S. | 1895 |
| 9.8s. | C. A. Bradley, Great Britain | 1895 |
| 9.8s. | Bernard Wefers, U.S. | 1895 |
| 9.8s. | John Maybury, U.S. | 1897 |
| 9.8s. | Charles Burroughs, U.S. | 1898 |
| 9.8s. | John Rush, U.S. | 1899 |
| 9.8s. | Archie Hahn, U.S. | 1901 |
| 9.8s. | Edward Merrill, U.S. | 1901 |
| 9.8s. | William A. Schick, U.S. | 1902 |
| 9.8s. | Frank M. Sears, U.S. | 1903 |
| 9.8s. | Charles Blair, U.S. | 1903 |
| 9.8s. | William Eaton, U.S. | 1904 |
| 9.8s. | Charles Parsons, U.S. | 1905 |
| 9.6s. | Daniel Kelly, U.S. | 1906 |
| 9.6s. | Howard Drew, U.S. | 1914 |
| 9.6s. | Charles Paddock, U.S. | 1921 |
| 9.6s. | Cyril Coaffee, Canada | 1922 |
| 9.6s. | DeHart Hubbard, U.S. | 1926 |
| 9.6s. | Chester Bowman, U.S. | 1927 |
| 9.5s. | Eddie Tolan, U.S. | 1929 |
| 9.4s. | Frank Wykoff, U.S. | 1930 |
| 9.4s. | Daniel Joubert, South Africa | 1931 |
| 9.4s. | Jesse Owens, U.S. | 1935 |
| 9.4s. | Clyde Jeffrey, U.S. | 1940 |
| 9.4s. | Melvin Patton, U.S. | 1947 |
| 9.3s. | Melvin Patton, U.S. | 1948 |
| 9.3s. | H. D. Hogan, Australia | 1954 |
| 9.3s. | James Golliday, U.S. | 1955 |
| 9.3s. | Leamon King, U.S. | 1956 |
| 9.3s. | David Sime, U.S. | 1957 |
| 9.3s. | Bobby Morrow, U.S. | 1957 |
| 9.3s. | Ray Norton, U.S. | 1958 |
| 9.3s. | William Woodhouse, U.S. | 1959 |
| 9.3s. | Roscoe Cook, U.S. | 1959 |
| 9.3s. | Frank Budd, U.S. | 1961 |

| | | |
|---|---|---|
| 9.2s. | Frank Budd, U.S.. . . . | 1961 |
| 9.2s. | Henry Jerome, Canada. . | 1962 |
| 9.1s. | Robert Hayes, U.S. . . . | 1963 |
| 9.1s. | Henry Jerome, Canada. . | 1966 |

| | | |
|---|---|---|
| 9.1s. | Jim Hines, U.S.. . . . . | 1967 |
| 9.1s. | Charlie Greene, U.S. . . | 1967 |
| 9.1s. | John Carlos, U.S. . . . | 1969 |
| 9.1s. | Steve Williams, U.S.. . . | 1973 |

## 100 Meter Dash

| Time | Record-holder and country | Year |
|---|---|---|
| 12s | Thomas Burke, U.S. . . | 1896 |
| 10.8s | Frank Jarvis, U.S. . . . | 1900 |
| 10.6s. | Donald Lippincott, U.S. . | 1912 |
| 10.6s. | Jackson Scholz, U.S. . . | 1920 |
| 10.4s. | Charles Paddock, U.S.. . | 1921 |
| 10.4s. | Eddie Tolan, U.S.. . . . | 1929 |
| 10.3s. | Percy Williams, Canada . | 1930 |
| 10.3s. | Eddie Tolan, U.S.. . . . | 1932 |
| 10.3s. | Ralph Metcalfe, U.S. . . | 1933 |
| 10.3s. | Eulace Peacock, U.S. . . | 1934 |
| 10.3s. | Christian Berger, Netherlands . . . . . | 1934 |
| 10.3s. | Ryutoku Yoshioka, Japan | 1935 |
| 10.2s. | Jesse Owens, U.S. . . | 1936 |
| 10.2s. | Harold Davis, U.S. . . . | 1941 |
| 10.2s. | Lloyd LaBeach, Panama . | 1948 |
| 10.2s. | Norwood Ewell, U.S. . . | 1948 |

| Time | Record-holder and country | Year |
|---|---|---|
| 10.2s. | E. McDonald Bailey, Great Britain . . . . . | 1951 |
| 10.2s. | Heinz Futterer, Germany. | 1954 |
| 10.1s. | Willie Williams, U.S. . . | 1956 |
| 10.1s. | Ira Murchison, U.S.. . . | 1956 |
| 10s. | Armin Hary, West Germany . . . . | 1960 |
| 10s. | Henry Jerome, Canada. . | 1960 |
| 10s. | Horacio Estevez, Venezuela . . . . . | 1964 |
| 10s. | Robert Hayes, U.S. . . . | 1964 |
| 10s. | Jim Hines, U.S.. . . . . | 1967 |
| 10s. | Enrique Figuerola, Cuba . | 1967 |
| 9.9s. | Jim Hines, U.S.. . . . . | 1968 |
| 9.9s. | Ronnie Smith, U.S. . . . | 1968 |
| 9.9s. | Charles Greene, U.S. . . | 1968 |
| 9.9s. | Eddie Hart, U.S. . . . . | 1972 |
| 9.9s. | Rey Robinson, U.S. . . . | 1972 |

## 220 Yard Dash (Straightaway)

| Time | Record-holder and country | Year |
|---|---|---|
| 23.5s. | Horace Lee, U.S. . . . . | 1877 |
| 23s. | Fred Saportas, U.S. . . . | 1877 |
| 22.$\frac{7}{8}$s. | William Wilmer, U.S. . . | 1878 |
| 22.6s. | Henry Brooks Jr., U.S. . | 1882 |
| 22.4s. | Wendell Baker, U.S.. . . | 1884 |
| 22s. | Wendell Baker, U.S.. . . | 1885 |
| 21.8s. | C. G. Wood, Great Britain | 1886 |
| 21.8s. | Luther Cary, U.S.. . . . | 1891 |
| 21.2s. | Bernard Wefers, U.S. . . | 1896 |
| 21.2s. | Ralph Craig, U.S.. . . . | 1910 |
| 21.2s. | Donald Lippincott, U.S. . | 1913 |

| | | |
|---|---|---|
| 21.2s. | Howard Drew, U.S. . . | 1914 |
| 21.2s. | Wm. Applegarth, Great Britain . . . . . | 1914 |
| 21.2s. | George Parker, U.S. . . | 1914 |
| 20.8s. | Charles Paddock, U.S.. . | 1921 |
| 20.6s. | Roland Locke, U.S. . . . | 1926 |
| 20.3s. | Jesse Owens, U.S.. . . . | 1935 |
| 20.2s. | Melvin Patton, U.S. . . . | 1949 |
| 20s. | David Sime, U.S. . . . . | 1956 |
| 20s. | Frank Budd, U.S.. . . . | 1962 |
| 19.5s. | Tommie Smith, U.S.. . . | 1966 |

## 220 Yard Dash (Turn)*

| Time | Record-holder and country | Year |
|---|---|---|
| 20.5s | Peter Radford, Great Britain . . . . | 1960 |

| | | |
|---|---|---|
| 20.5s | Livio Berruti, Italy . . . | 1960 |
| 20.3s | Henry Carr, U.S. . . . . | 1963 |
| 20.0s | Tommie Smith, U.S. . . | 1966 |

## 200 Meter Dash (Straightaway)

| Time | Record-holder and country | Year |
|---|---|---|
| 22.2s. | Walter Tewksbury, U.S. . | 1900 |
| 21.6s. | Archie Hahn, U.S. . . . | 1904 |
| 20.8s. | Charles Paddock, U.S.. . | 1921 |
| 20.6s. | Roland Locke, U.S. . . . | 1926 |
| 20.6s. | Ralph Metcalfe, U.S. . . | 1933 |

| | | |
|---|---|---|
| 20.3s. | Jesse Owens, U.S. . . . | 1935 |
| 20.2s. | Melvin Patton, U.S. . . . | 1949 |
| 20s. | David Sime, U.S. . . . . | 1956 |
| 20s. | Frank Budd, U.S. . . . | 1962 |
| 19.5s. | Tommie Smith, U.S. . . | 1966 |

### 200 Meter Dash (Turn)*

| Time | Record-holder and country | Year | | | |
|------|---------------------------|------|------|------|------|
| 20.2s | Henry Carr, U.S.A. . . . | 1964 | 19.8s | Tommie Smith, U.S.A. . | 1968 |
| 20.2s | Tommie Smith, U.S.A. | 1965 | 19.8s. | Donald Quarrie, Jamaica. | 1971 |

## SPRINTING TECHNIQUE

"Sprinting ability is a God-given talent: either you've got it or you don't"—so says world record holder Charlie Greene. If ever a perfect example of this statement existed, it is in the person of Dr. Delano Meriwether, a research scientist, and an athlete who did not compete until after he had completed medical school at age 27. He then became national champion in the 60 and 100 yard sprints in 6.0 and 9.0 (wind-aided) respectively.

"Sprinters are born—not made." If ever a denial of this statement existed, it is in the person of Ben Vaughn, a man whose best high school 100 and 220 times were 10.1 and 23.5, and who ran 9.8 and 21.9 as a college freshman, 9.5 and 21.3 as a sophomore, and 9.4 and 20.9 as a junior, and 9.4 and 20.6 as a senior. *You decide which point of view is correct.*

Sprinting can be thought of as a series of jumps taken so smoothly and rhythmically that one does not usually think of sprinting in this sense. But the fact is that during a 100 yard dash, the sprinter is in the air more than he is in contact with the track. It is sometimes profitable to think of sprinting as a series of jumps because it helps to emphasize a basic component of sprinting, leg power. Increased power will increase the length of stride and if all else remains equal this will result in faster sprinting.

### Foot Touch Pattern

Frequently we see athletes turn out for track who run like football players on a rope grid, with each foot coming down several inches away from a center line. This style of running gives the football player additional stability and it makes him more maneuverable in a variety of directions. However, it does not enhance running speed in a straight line. Proper foot touch pattern for sprinters is shown in Figure 3–1. It is very important that the feet stay close to the center line in order that on each stride the center of gravity will be projected straight forward rather than in a diagonal direction. Fortunately, the foot touch pattern is not a problem with most potential sprinters, but occasionally a potentially good sprinter runs with an erroneous touch pattern which must be corrected if the person is to achieve his potential.

Another problem which relates to foot touch is toeing out. The toes should be straight ahead or slightly inward. Athletes who toe out should pay careful attention to foot alignment while walking and running. Over a period of time the alignment can be improved.

* The International Amateur Athletic Federation (I.A.A.F.) began to distinguish between records set on a straightaway and a curve in 1960.

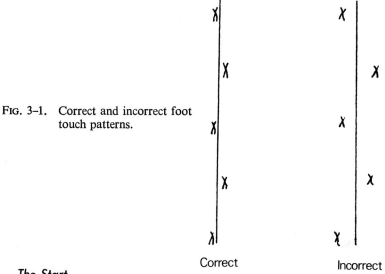

FIG. 3–1. Correct and incorrect foot touch patterns.

Correct                 Incorrect

### The Start

The crouch start is now universally accepted in sprinting and has proven to be the most effective starting position yet devised. The crouch ranges from an extreme bunch position (where the feet are placed close together) to an extreme elongated position (where the feet are far apart). Several research studies have been done comparing the relative effectiveness of the different foot positions. The research has produced conflicting results; however most of the information tends to favor the medium position. It is important to remember that each body structure differs from any other, and there is a variation in strength of the different muscle groups among individuals. Therefore, not all athletes will get their best results from an identical starting position.

Prior to being called to his mark, each sprinter ought to be sure that his blocks are secure and in the exact position he wants them to be. He should stand behind the starting line in a relaxed position and wait for the starter's command. At the command "take your mark" each runner should move into the "on the mark position" and work himself into a comfortable stance without wasting time or in any other way agitating his competitors. When the runner has reached his preferred position, he should so indicate by remaining motionless. At this time the runner should concentrate only upon his start. On the command "set," the runner shifts a greater portion of his weight to his arms and at the same time raising his buttocks. After reaching his preferred "set" position, he must remain steady until the gun is fired.

While waiting for the command "set," most sprinters breathe deeply once or twice. At the "set" command breathing ceases. The sprinter remains breathless and motionless until he makes his start. This breathing action is much the same as that of a marksman during the final seconds before firing.

At the report of the pistol, the arm opposite the lead leg is thrust directly forward, slightly flexed at the elbow. At the same time, the drive from both legs propels the body forward. The greater portion of the drive is given by the lead leg. A greater distance between the feet results in a greater portion of the drive from the lead leg, and lesser distance results in a more equalized drive. (See Figures 3–4b and 3–4c.)

The back knee moves forward in a straight line with the foot kept low to the ground. The foot is placed directly downward into a position that will allow the body to continue straight forward without deviating to either side. Forward lean must be maintained to the extent that the body weight pulls the runner forward and allows for maximum drive. As the sprinter gathers speed, his body gradually becomes more erect. He should reach erect running position only a short distance before he reaches top speed.

Good starts come as a result of intensive practice in which meet conditions are duplicated as closely as possible. Good starting requires absolute concentration on the fine points of the technique. Too often the starting practice is conducted in an atmosphere that is not conducive to adequate concentration. Experience has proven that the best starting practice consistently occurs with one or two athletes, or when all talk and other distractions are eliminated.

Attention should be given to the following characteristics of the start until they become automatic: 1) correct placement of feet in the blocks; 2) correct placement of the hands and arms; 3) correct speed in raising the body to the "set" position; 4) correct position of the head and eyes; 5) correct height of the hips in the "set" position; 6) optimum drive with the arms; 7) optimum drive with the legs; 8) correct angle of projection of the head and trunk; and 9) maximum concentration.

*Position in the Blocks.* The sprinter should feel comfortable in the blocks, but it should be remembered that comfort is associated with the old way of doing things and sometimes a comfortable position is mechanically incorrect. Most top-flight sprinters place the knee of the rear leg a few inches ahead of the lead foot. Pictures taken of the sprinters at the 1972 Olympics show that the distance between the front and back foot of each sprinter was between 12 and 18 inches. Most of the literature suggests that the back knee be even with the instep of the front foot. But in the 1972 Olympics all the finalists in the 100 meters had the knee ahead of the front foot. The placement of the back foot is determined by the desired angle of the back knee when in the set position. This in turn is influenced by the elevation of the hips. We think the hips should be slightly higher than the shoulders when the athlete is set.

When the starter calls the athlete to his mark, the athlete's weight is

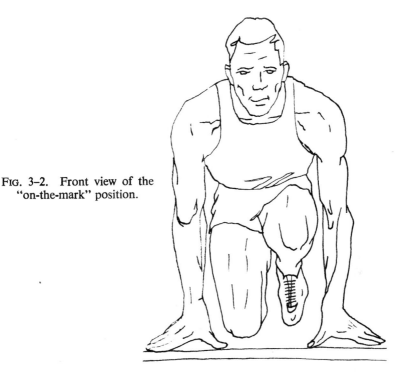

FIG. 3-2. Front view of the "on-the-mark" position.

supported on four points (Figure 3-2). Both feet touch the ground and the weight is supported on the hands, back knee and forward foot. His hands should be about shoulder width apart with the arms straight. The thumb and fingers are parallel to the starting line in a bridge position. The weight should be well forward with the shoulders out over the hands.

The head is held in a natural position, neither hanging nor held high; the eyes are focused on the track, two to three feet in front of the head. If the head is held too high, this tends to cause the sprinter to assume the erect running position prematurely and causes tightening in the neck and upper back.

*Set Position.* On the command "set," the sprinter should raise the hips to an elevation two to three inches higher than the shoulders. This will place the front knee at an angle of about 90°, and rear knee between an angle of 120° and 170°, depending upon the position of the foot. The hips should be brought up smoothly and slowly to a point where the thrusting action from the legs will drive the body straight forward. In the set position the shoulders will be slightly forward of the hands. The arms will be straight and the greater portion of the body weight will be resting upon the hands (see Figures 3-3 and 3-4a). The athlete must be able to hold this position in a relaxed state for at least two seconds.

*The Drive Out of the Blocks.* All too often inexperienced athletes listen for the sound of the gun. This is unfortunate because experiments have proven that athletes react faster when they concentrate on movement rather than on the sound of the gun. Concentration on movement will cause the movement to be an automatic reaction to the sound of the gun. Also, by concentrating on movement the athlete will be more likely to perform the movements correctly.

FIG. 3–3. Front view of the "set" position. The position is good except the head should be aligned with the trunk, meaning the face should be down and the eyes focused about three feet in front of the starting line.

The arms are fired forcefully into action by the sound of the gun.  The arm opposite the lead leg is thrust forward while the other arm is pumped backward (Figure 3–4c). Following these initial arm movements, some athletes tend to have a slight pause.  To overcome this, it is desirable to force the second action of the arms immediately.  The elbow should swing high on the back swing, and on the forward swing the hand should be driven vigorously to a position in front of the chest (Figure 3–4e).

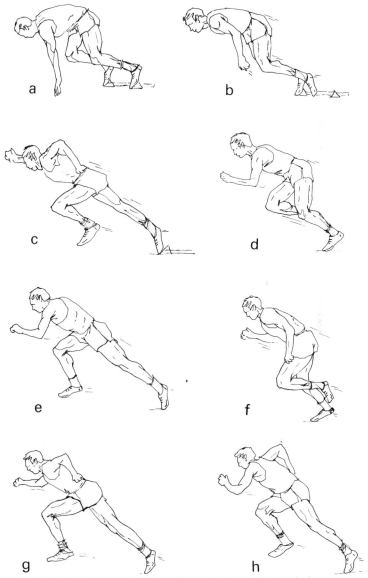

FIG. 3–4.  Sequence drawings of the sprint starting technique.

The maximum thrust from both legs is simultaneous to the initial arm action. Since the front leg is in contact with the blocks for a longer time, it provides the major part of the force. The back knee comes through fast and swings high while the foot stays very close to the ground so that it will touch down quickly as the leg starts its backward drive (Figure 3–4c).

The head remains in the normal position and the eyes continue to focus on the track just a few feet ahead of the face. As the back leg leaves the blocks and the lead leg straightens, a straight line should connect the shoulders, hips, knee and ankle. The angle of trajectory is kept low in order to maintain a driving position (Figure 3–4c). As the sprinter continues to drive, the shoulders get higher and higher so that by 15 to 20 yards out of the blocks, the sprinter is in an upright position. There is no separate movement of the head upward; it is simply elevated as the shoulders are elevated. At no time is there a sudden lifting of the head or upper body as the sprinter gradually assumes the upright sprinting position.

### Running Action

The transition from the driving start into the sprint should be gradual and smooth. The arms should move in perfect harmony with the legs, and the shoulders should be kept parallel to the track. There are four main aspects of running that deserve consideration—relaxation, running poise, arm action and leg action.

*Relaxation.* One of the most important steps towards success for a sprinter is learning to run relaxed. Relaxation in this case means the runner must coordinate his muscles in such a way that the mover muscles (agonists) contract with optimal force while the opposite muscles (antagonists) relax as completely as possible so as to not hinder the movement. A runner who runs with tense (unrelaxed) antagonistic muscles is comparable to an automobile being driven with the brake on—different parts of the machine work against one another. Make your running look easy and increase your chances of becoming a champion.

*Running Poise.* During the entire sprint, the head should be held in a straight line with the trunk of the body, meaning it should not be tilted forward or backward or inclined to the right or to the left. The forward-backward action of the legs should be in a straight line because any deviation from this results in a loss of time and energy. The arms should pump forward and backward in a manner that will add maximally to forward drive and help to maintain perfect balance.

*Arm Action.* There is a tendency to overlook the importance of arm action in sprinting. Most coaches recognize the harm done by improper action but do not seem to see the benefits obtained from correct action. The arms swing basically forward and backward as if hinged on the shoulders. The elbows are held at approximately a 90°-angle, and the hands come forward to about the height of the chin, and backward so

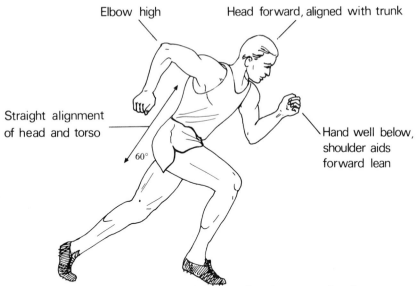

Elbow high          Head forward, aligned with trunk

Straight alignment
of head and torso

60°

Hand well below,
shoulder aids
forward lean

FIG. 3–5. Correct body position greatly enhances acceleration.

the elbow is about level with the shoulder. It is of particular importance that the arms swing on the shoulders rather than the shoulders rotating to initiate the arm swing. The shoulders should remain parallel to the track. Shoulder rotation may become a problem if sprinters do distance running such as cross country, because they may develop the natural easy rhythm of distance runners where the shoulders are rotated more than in sprinting.

One of the keys to relaxation lies in arm action. Vigorous action of the arms can increase body momentum provided it is not obtained at the expense of general body relaxation. The hands and arms should not be tensed. As a result of this danger some outstanding coaches rarely stress arm action except as an aid to balance and poise.

*Leg Action.* The legs should move straight forward and backward and should not deviate from this alignment. High knee lift is basic to good sprinting. Failure to get the knees up reduces the power the sprinter can exert on the driving leg and it shortens the length of the stride. The high knee lift has three basic advantages: A) it results in a longer stride, B) it places on stretch those muscles which will drive the leg backward causing the muscles to contract with greater force; and C) it takes advantage of the natural law that "for every action there is an equal and opposite reaction." This means that a powerful recovery of the swinging leg increases the power of the driving leg. Because one leg drives against the other, some coaches encourage a long reach as part of the high knee action. The intent probably is to increase knee lift and also increase length of stride.  Actually, careful observation of the sprinter or the study of slow motion films will show that the swinging leg is not completely extended at the knee and that the foot touches approximately underneath the center of gravity of the body.  Otherwise it would have a braking effect.

Powerful and complete extension of the driving leg and foot is essential to good sprinting.  It is important to keep the foot in contact with the ground as long as possible in order to continue the drive.  An important task of the coach is to help determine whether a sprinter is running with a stride so long that he loses velocity as a result of insufficient leg speed, or if his leg speed is so fast that he loses velocity as a result of a chopped stride.  What the coach really wants to accomplish is an increased stride without the loss of leg speed or increased leg speed without shortening the stride.

### Finish

It is no fallacy to say that the best finish is the winning finish.  Charles Paddock often used a flying leap, while Jim Hines won the 1968 Olympic

FIG. 3–6.  Two different styles of finish.

100 meter race in 9.9 and the photo finish showed him sprinting through the tape. His competitors were falling all over themselves—thrusting, leaning, etc., trying to win. There are three basic styles of finishing—the body lunge, the forward shrug with one shoulder and the straight ahead sprint. The lunge is when the sprinter exaggerates his forward lean, throws his arms back, and protrudes his chest in an effort to reach the finish at a time sooner than he otherwise would. The shrug is when the sprinter twists his upper extremity in an effort to hit the tape with the forward shoulder. Very little distance can be gained by either shrugging or lunging, but such action can produce a slight advantage if timed perfectly. We recommend that the sprinter finish what he started by sprinting a few yards past the finish line, and adding a slight lean if he can do so effectively.

## KEYS TO SUCCESS

There are several keys to success in sprinting. Among them are ability to relax, confidence you can win, adequate flexibility and power.

### Relaxation

Relaxation in this case means lack of unnecessary muscle tension which tends to retard speed of movement. A lack of relaxation is manifest by tense facial and neck muscles and by tightly gripped hands. The ability to relax while running at full speed can be taught, but the learner must make a conscious effort. In learning relaxation, the athlete should pay special attention to the hands, because he can see the hands whereas the face and neck are not visible to him. We like to see the runner compete with the hands loose—almost flapping. Forced relaxation of the hands will often cause a corresponding relaxation throughout most of the body. In turn this will result in less retarding effect by antagonistic muscles and will also contribute to the conservation of energy. When muscles are tense they work against each other and expend energy unnecessarily.

### Self-Confidence

When young athletes gather from throughout the country for top-flight competition, the need for self-confidence becomes apparent. Numerous sprinters have posted 9.4 or better for the 100 yard dash, but few run that time on any given day. When the competition is tight, the feeling that you can win is essential. Without it most athletes cannot relax adequately and will not concentrate on the important points of the race. Uncertainty about winning and lack of confidence result in many errors that would not otherwise occur and these errors pave the way to defeat. Self-confidence and emotional stability can aid an athlete in "willing" himself to victory.

### Flexibility

Many sprinters go through stretching routines more with the idea of getting through the routine than actually developing the desired flexibility.

Consequently, they do not possess the flexibility which will allow them easily to perform certain phases of the sprinting action.  The movements where adequate flexibility is essential are hip flexion and extension, ankle flexion and extension, and to a lesser degree, movements of the shoulder and shoulder girdle.  It is believed that increased freedom of movement in the hip region will increase the stride length without reducing the rate of leg movement.  If this is done it brings about a second advantage because when muscles are stretched to greater lengths they contract with greater force and thus produce more forceful movements.  Furthermore, it is known that when the antagonistic muscles stretch easily, they offer less resistance to the desired movements, thus making movements freer and more efficient.

### Power

Power is fundamental to sprinting, especially during the acceleration phase.  It is known that the rate of acceleration is proportional to the force causing it.  Therefore, acceleration is dependent directly upon the power with which the muscles contract.  If power is doubled then the rate of acceleration will be doubled; whereas if power is increased by half, then the rate of acceleration will increase by half.  Power is a combination of strength and speed of contraction.  Thus by increasing either of these components, power will be increased.  For detailed information on how to increase power refer to the sections on power, strength and speed in Chapter 1.

### Length of Stride and Leg Speed

Increase in top running speed is dependent mostly upon increasing propelling force (power) which increases the length of stride, and by eliminating noncontributing actions.  Increased power results in a harder forward thrust with each stride, and this combined with additional flexibility will cause a longer stride.  The longer stride increases the flexion of the knee on the back kick, which in turn contributes to a more powerful extension of the opposite leg.  This action is readily seen in horses and dogs.  As they move to top speed you can see them flatten out, get closer to the ground, and stretch out into a maximum sprint.

Good sprinters take four to five strides per second with the strides varying considerably in length among different sprinters.  If the sprinter can maintain his normal leg speed and increase stride length, then obviously he will cover more distance in a given amount of time.  However, the stride length should not be lengthened so much that the foot touches very far in front of the center of gravity, because this has a retarding effect on speed each time the foot strikes the ground.  If this occurs the sprinter is over-striding.

## VARIATIONS IN STYLE FOR THE 220 YARD SPRINT

It is important to recognize that some great sprinters slow down slightly during the last few yards of a 100 yard dash.  Obviously then, it is impossible to go 220 yards at an all-out sprint.  The race then must consist of an all-out effort at the start and for the first 40 to 50 yards,  This is followed by a fast, smooth striding sprint which is very close to full effort.

In the 220 relaxation is even more essential than in the shorter sprints because of the need to conserve energy.  By consciously relaxing the hands and lower arms, the runner sometimes actually experiences a removal of the weighted feeling (tiredness) in the legs and an overall feeling of increased freedom of movement.  Emphasis on smooth flowing strides which waste very little motion and conserve energy are essential to good running form in the 220.  (See Relaxation on page 55.)

Since 220 yard races ordinarily start on a turn, the runner should set his blocks in a position where he gets as much straight running distance as possible during the early part of the race.  This means the block should be near the outside of his lane at a slight angle pointing toward the inside. This affords the sprinter the opportunity to run along a straight line moving from the outside to the inside of his lane.  Due to the angle of the starting blocks, the left hand would be two to four inches from the starting line while the right hand would be immediately behind the line.

The starting technique in the 220 is the same as described earlier in this chapter.  However, after four or five strides, the runner must begin to negotiate the turn.  Teaching the athlete purposely to lean or dip the shoulder tends to create more problems than it solves.  By concentrating on good running form, staying close to the inside of the lane and practicing repeatedly around a turn, the sprinter will gradually make the necessary adjustment in his running form and learning to run the turn effectively.  If the athlete's attitude toward running a turn is highly positive, he will experience less difficulty than he would otherwise.

There are certain running faults which are magnified by running the turn.  The flailing of the lower leg which characterizes some sprinters affects balance on a turn.  This poor leg action sometimes becomes even more serious around the second turn of the 440 when the runner's form begins to deteriorate.

In summary it can be said that sprinting consists of three important components: A) fast reaction time at the movement of the start; B) fast acceleration; and C) great velocity at top running speed.

## APPLICATION OF SCIENTIFIC PRINCIPLES

Following are certain scientific principles and explanations of how these apply to sprinting:

1. *A body at rest tends to remain at rest whereas a body in motion continues in motion with consistent speed and in the same direction unless acted*

*upon by force.* In sprinting, muscle contractions provide the forces which overcome inertia. The rate at which inertia is overcome depends directly upon the amount of force applied. In order to put the body into rapid motion, or to change its rate of motion, muscles must contract with great force.

2. *The velocity of a body is increased only when acted upon by an additional force. The acceleration is proportional to and in the direction of the force.* The application of this principle is very important during the acceleration phase of the sprint. All else remaining equal, as a sprinter increases his ability to apply force, he will cause a proportionate increase in his rate of acceleration and thus will reach top speed sooner.

3. *The momentum of a segment of the body can be transferred to the total body.* In the sprint start, the vigorous forward driving actions of the arms contribute momentum to the total body and thus help to accelerate the body at a more rapid rate.

4. *All forces should be applied as directly as possible in line with the intended motion.* This means that a sprinter should reduce to a minimum all forces which do not directly contribute to forward progress. Unproductive muscular contractions resulting in head movements, throwing of the arms and swinging of the legs sideward are characteristic of unskilled performers. Further, if a runner points his toes outward, he misdirects the forces and reduces his running speed and efficiency. If he projects the body too vertically, he does too much up and down running at the expense of horizontal speed.

5. *Centrifugal force creates a tendency for an object to continue in motion in a straight line.* Because of this, a sprinter running around a curve must lean in the direction of the curve. The faster he runs, the more he must lean. Also, he must lean more if he is in the inside lane than if he were in the outside because the curve is sharper on the inside.

## COMMON FAULTS AND HOW TO CORRECT THEM

The following faults were identified by sprinting experts and the correction techniques were explained by coaches of champion sprinters.

### Start

Fault:      Dropping the head while in the set position.
Correction: The head should be aligned with the spine with the eyes focused on the track a few feet ahead of the face. This position helps to avoid coming to an erect running position prematurely. Concentrate on correct alignment of the head and, if necessary, place a mark on the track on which to focus the eyes.
Fault:      Slow reaction time to the gunshot.
Correction: Practice starting under conditions which permit great concentration. Practice under these conditions over and over until the starting action becomes automatic at the sound of the gun.

Fault: The back foot in the blocks coming through too high during the first stride.

Correction: Concentrate on keeping the foot low. It should barely skim the surface, in order that it will make fast contact upon completion of the stride. Drive the knee forward and not upward.

Fault: The arms crossing too much in front of the body instead of driving in the forward-backward direction.

Correction: This fault is sometimes due to too much rotation of the shoulders. Concentrate on keeping the shoulders square and driving the arms almost straight forward.

Fault: The footstep pattern is too wide, similar to a football player's foot pattern. (Figure 3–1).

Correction: Concentrate on driving the knee and foot straight forward out of the blocks. Also concentrate on placing the foot underneath the body upon contact with the track. Sometimes it is helpful to draw a line a few yards forward from the center of the blocks, then concentrate on touching the line with the inside of the foot with each step.

Fault: Placing the hips too high in the set position, causing the drive from the legs to go underneath the hips.

Correction: Purposely keep the hips lower so the leg drive is through the hips. As the leg extends during the driving action the body should tend to form a straight line (Figure 3–4).

### Stride

Fault: Incorrect forward lean causing the leg drive not to push through the hips.

Correction: Be sure that the body remains inclined forward enough to permit maximum forward drive. Rotate the pelvic girdle bottom forward to cause the hips to stay in line with the leg drive. To get the feel of the pelvic rotation stand with the back against the wall and attempt to flatten the small of the back by pushing the hips forward and rolling the top of the pelvic region backward. This is the position the hips should be in to enhance drive through the hips.

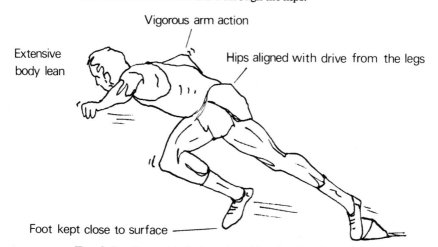

Vigorous arm action

Extensive body lean

Hips aligned with drive from the legs

Foot kept close to surface

FIG. 3–7. Correct technique in driving for the blocks.

Fault: Failure to run in a relaxed condition.
Correction: While running wind sprints concentrate on powerful, fast and relaxed movement. The best lead into a relaxed running style is to force the hands and the arms to remain loose.
Fault: Lack of sufficient vigor in the arm actions.
Correction: Concentrate on vigorous and forceful arm movements with practically all of the action at the shoulder joint and with the arms moving almost directly forward and backward.
Fault: Insufficient knee lift.
Correction: The knee of the lead leg should be lifted forward and upward forcefully. This action contributes to a powerful extension of the leg which is in contact with the track.
Fault: A poor finish.
Correction: Concentrate on sprinting to a point 10 yards beyond the tape. A lunge or a forward shrug with one shoulder may prove beneficial if perfectly timed at the tape, but if poorly timed these actions can prove costly

## THE TRAINING SCHEDULE

The following is a recommended training schedule for a mature sprinter. It can serve as an important guide for all sprinters but will need to be adjusted to fit the needs of a particular athlete because athletes differ in age, maturity and state of conditioning.

### Summer

During this season the sprinter should maintain a high level of general conditioning by participating regularly in activities that require extensive running. It is beneficial to participate in field games and fartlek running with emphasis on short acceleration sprints. These activities should be supplemented by specific exercises to maintain power in the muscles involved the most in sprinting. (See the recommended exercises at the end of this chapter.)

### Fall

The training schedule during the fall will be influenced by whether the athlete is preparing for the winter indoor season or the spring outdoor season. If he is preparing for the indoor season then the fall training schedule should be similar to the one described here for winter. If he is going to run in the outdoor season only, then the fall schedule should include a considerable amount of play type running and wind sprints along with continuation of the exercise program. The purpose is to maintain a high level of general conditioning and to keep the sprinting muscles especially well-conditioned. Also during this period running technique can be improved by concentrating on correct mechanics and relaxation while running wind sprints at near top speed. Ordinarily the sprinter will work out in the afternoon only, whereas distance runners usually work out twice daily during certain seasons of the year.

## Winter (Afternoon Workouts)

Monday:
1. Jog one-half mile.
2. Do stretching exercises for 10–15 minutes.
3. Run four 110s at near top speed.
4. Do 10 starts sprinting 30–40 yards each time.
5. Run three 440s in about 55 seconds each.
6. Jog one-half mile.
7. Weight train (see exercises at the end of this chapter).

Tuesday:
1. Jog one-half mile.
2. Do stretching exercises.
3. Run three to five miles of fartlek running emphasizing 50–200 yard pick ups.

Wednesday: Do the same as Monday, except run five 440s.

Thursday:
1. Jog one-half mile.
2. Do stretching exercises.
3. Run three 330s at about 39 seconds each.
4. Do three miles of fartlek running emphasizing short distance pick ups.
5. Jog one-half mile.

Friday: Do the same as Wednesday.
Saturday: Do the same as Tuesday.

## Spring (Early and Middle Portion)

Monday:
1. Jog one-half mile.
2. Do stretching exercises for 10–15 minutes.
3. Run four 110s at near full speed.
4. Run six 50 yard sprints.
5. Run two 150 yard sprints.
6. Jog one-half mile.
7. Weight train (see exercises at the end of this chapter).

Tuesday:
1. Jog one-half mile.
2. Do stretching exercises.
3. Run four 110s at near full speed.
4. Do 10 starts sprinting 30–40 yards each time (practice some starts on the turn for the 220).
5. Run six 110s at maximum speed.
6. Jog one-half mile.

Wednesday: Do the same as Monday except run two 330s instead of 50-yard sprints.

Thursday: Do the same as Tuesday except do only six starts.
Friday: Do light jogging and stretching or complete rest.
Saturday:
1. Competition—arrive at the meet in plenty of time to prepare for the race adequately. Have your race plan clearly in mind and follow it.
2. Weight train following competition.

## Late Season (May–June)

During this phase of the season the sprinter will ordinarily do the same kind of training as during the mid-season. Whether the program is intensified during the late season will depend on whether the athlete shows any signs of staleness.

## CONDITIONING EXERCISES

It is important for the sprinter to have a high level of power, especially in the legs.   Methods for developing power, which is a combination of strength and speed, are discussed in Chapter 1.   It is recommended that the appropriate sections of that chapter be studied carefully.

The specific exercises that should be included in the conditioning program are listed below and are illustrated in Appendix A.

Straight arm forward raise—exercise #1
Trunk flexion—exercise #14
Trunk extension—exercise #18
Trunk rotation (supine)—exercise #15
Leg raise (supine)—exercise #25
Leg press—exercise #20
Jumping jack—exercise #21
Heel raise—exercise #23
Quadriceps drill—exercise #24

CHAPTER **4**

# Quarter-Mile Sprint

Being one complete circle around the quarter-mile oval, the 440 yard (or 400 meter) sprint is one of the most spectacular of all track and field events. Initially, the best quarter-milers were fine 880 yard or mile runners who were gifted with speed. But through the years this interesting race has gradually evolved from an endurance run to a sprint. One of the greatest of the early quarter-milers was John H. Ridley of Great Britain, who broke the world record three different times and whose best time was 51.0 seconds in 1868. That same year, Edward H. Colbeck, also of Great Britain, recorded a 50.4 quarter-mile and on the same day he won the 880-yard run and was second in the 100 yard dash. It was not until 1879 that Lawrence Myers of the United States broke the 50-second mark when he ran the quarter in 49.2. Myers was a man of unusual achievement as he held every American record from the 50 yard dash through the mile run.

Aided by pacesetters, currently an illegal practice, Max W. Long of the United States recorded a remarkable 47.8 seconds for the quarter-mile in 1900. Ben Eastman of the United States, who proved to be in a class of his own in the quarter-mile during the early 1930s, moved the record down to an excellent 46.4 seconds in 1932. Adolph Plummer of the United States became the first person to break the 45-second mark when he did 44.9 in 1963. Currently, the world record is 44.5 set by John Smith of the United States in 1971. By comparison, Lee Evans of the United States ran a remarkable 400 meters in the 1968 Olympics posting a world record of 43.8 in the metric distance.

Following are chronological listings of world records for the 440 yard and 400 meter runs. Certainly these records are not the only important performances, but they do give a rather accurate indication of the trend that has existed relative to improved performances in these events. The trend toward improvement has been consistent over the years, and with the improved training and performance techniques now available, there is no reason to believe that this trend will be any different in the near future than it has been in the past.

### 440 Yard Run

| Time | Record-holder and country | Year |
|------|---------------------------|------|
| 56s. | B. S. Darbyshire, Great Britain | 1864 |
| 55s. | J. H. Ridley, Great Britain | 1866 |
| 52.75s. | J. H. Ridley, Great Britain | 1867 |
| 51s. | J. H. Ridley, Great Britain | 1868 |
| 50.4s. | E. H. Colbeck, Great Britain | 1868 |
| 49.2s. | Lawrence Myers, U.S. | 1879 |
| 48.6s. | Lawrence Myers, U.S. | 1881 |
| 48.2s. | H. C. D. Tindall, Great Britain | 1889 |
| 47.8s. | Maxwell Long, U.S. | 1900 |
| 47.4s. | James (Ted) Meredith, U.S. | 1916 |
| 47.4s. | Ben Eastman, U.S. | 1931 |
| 47.4s. | Victor Williams, U.S. | 1931 |
| 46.4s. | Ben Eastman, U.S. | 1932 |
| 46.4s. | Grover Klemmer, U.S. | 1941 |
| 46.3s. | H. McKenley, Jamaica, B.W.I. | 1947 |
| 46s. | H. McKenley, Jamaica, B.W.I. | 1948 |
| 45.8s. | Jim Lea, U.S. | 1956 |
| 45.7s. | Glenn Davis, U.S. | 1958 |
| 44.9s. | Adolph Plummer, U.S. | 1963 |
| 44.5s. | John Smith, U.S. | 1971 |

### 400 Meter Run

| Time | Record-holder and country | Year |
|------|---------------------------|------|
| 54.2s. | Thomas Burke, U.S. | 1896 |
| 49.4s. | Maxwell Long, U.S. | 1900 |
| 49.2s. | Harry Hillman, U.S. | 1904 |
| 48.2s. | Charles Reidpath, U.S. | 1912 |
| 47.6s. | Eric Liddell, Great Britain | 1924 |
| 47.4s. | James (Ted) Meredith, U.S. | 1916 |
| 47s. | Emerson Spencer, U.S. | 1928 |
| 46.2s. | William Carr, U.S. | 1932 |
| 46.1s. | Archie Williams, U.S. | 1936 |
| 46s. | Rudolf Harbig, Germany | 1939 |
| 46s. | Grover Klemmer, U.S. | 1941 |
| 45.9s. | Herb McKenley, Jamaica, B.W.I. | 1948 |
| 45.8s. | George Rhoden, Jamaica, B.W.I. | 1950 |
| 45.4s. | Lou Jones, U.S. | 1955 |
| 45.2s. | Lou Jones, U.S. | 1956 |
| 44.9s. | Otis Davis, U.S. | 1960 |
| 44.9s. | Carl Kauffman, Germany | 1960 |
| 44.9s. | Adolph Plummer, U.S. | 1963 |
| 44.9s. | Mike Larrabee, U.S. | 1964 |
| 44.5s. | Tommie Smith, U.S. | 1967 |
| 43.8s. | Lee Evans, U.S. | 1968 |

### QUARTER-MILE TECHNIQUE

For at least the past two decades the quarter-mile has been considered a long sprint and athletes have successively run it faster and faster. Currently some outstanding runners complete the first half of the race in times approximately equal to their best performances in the open 220 yard sprint.

It is not necessary to discuss starting technique and the acceleration phase of the quarter-mile sprint, because these phases of the race are the same as in the 100 and 220 (see Chapter 3). The major difference in running the quarter-mile is maintaining good sprinting form for the full distance.

The quarter-miler should give the same attention to starting technique as given by sprinters in shorter races (100 and 220). And he must accelerate himself at a maximum rate, thus reaching top running speed at 25–30 yards out of the blocks. There is no reason for anything other than maximum effort during this phase of the race. Shortly after reaching top sprinting speed, say 60 to 70 yards out of the blocks, the quarter-miler very cautiously wills himself into a relaxed running stride, which is so close to an all-out effort, that it is impossible for an observer to identify the transition. Many coaches and athletes refer to this running form as a "float." This term might be misleading in the sense that the quarter-miler does not float, at least not to the extent that he permits himself to decelerate. The relaxed sprint which characterizes the quarter-miler is used to avoid inefficient utilization of energy. His running style is devoid of the stress and strain characteristics seen in the 100 yard sprinter such as tense neck and facial muscles, clenched hands and the vigorous pumping action of the arms (Figure 4–1). This lack of tension is necessary for the conservation of energy. If such tension is not strictly avoided, running form will deteriorate badly toward the end of the race as a result of fatigue. Even among the

FIG. 4–1. Composed and relaxed running style during the final portion of the quarter-mile.

world's best quarter-milers some deterioration of form is evident during the last forty to fifty yards.

Because the quarter-miler must run near his top speed for the full distance of the race, one important question is, "How fast should he complete his first 220?" There is little agreement among the experts on this matter, and a close look at the 220 splits of the great quarter-mile runners does not furnish a definite answer. In establishing the world record, Lee Evans ran a very fast first 200 meters, just three tenths of a second off his best open 200 meter time. John Smith ran the first half of the 440 in just 0.5 second off his best 220 time and he established the world record for the 440 yard distance. A very fast opening 220, within about one second of the athlete's all-time best 220 yard time, characterizes a near maximum quarter-mile effort.

The following chart gives insight into the 220 yard splits of the world's best quarter-milers. The information in the chart indicates that the first 220 should be about one second slower than the athlete's best 220 time and the second 220 should be two to three seconds slower than his best 220 time. Thus, his quarter-mile time would be three to four seconds slower than his best 220 time doubled.

| Name | Country | 400 m | 200 m split | Best 200 m | Difference Between 400 m and Best 200 m Doubled |
|------|---------|-------|-------------|------------|------------------------------------------------|
| Lee Evans | U.S.A. | 43.8 | 20.7 | 20.4 | 3.0 |
| Larry James | U.S.A. | 43.9 | 20.9 | 21.0 | 1.9 |
| Curtis Mills* | U.S.A. | 44.4 | 21.8 | 20.4 | 3.6 |
| Ron Freeman | U.S.A. | 44.4 | 22.1 | 21.5 | 1.4 |
| John Smith | U.S.A. | 44.5 | 22.1 | 20.6 | 3.3 |
| Wayne Collett | U.S.A. | 44.7 | 21.3 | 20.6 | 3.5 |
| Adolph Plummer | U.S.A. | 44.9 | 21.7 | 20.7 | 3.5 |
| Otis Davis | U.S.A | 44.9 | 21.8 | 20.9 | 3.1 |
| Jean-Claude Nallet | France | 45.1 | 21.9 | 20.6 | 3.9 |
| Karl Kaufmann | West Germany | 44.9 | 21.8 | 21.0 | 2.9 |
| Mike Larrabee | U.S.A. | 45.1 | 22.6 | 21.0 | 3.1 |

* Convert from yards to meters, minus .3 seconds from 440 time minus 0.1 seconds from 220 time.

To get a truer reflection of how the 220 is related to the overall 440 yard time, let us examine the running feats of Lee Evans and Mike Larrabee. Both men ran enough open 220s to know how to run very near their best at that distance and they were both Olympic 400 meter champions. The 400 meter world record time of Lee Evans of 43.8 is exactly three seconds slower than his best 200 meter time doubled. Mike Larrabee's 45.1 time is

3.1 seconds slower than his best 200 meter time doubled. Evans ran his first 200 meters only 0.3 second slower than his all-time best for that distance, while his time for the second 200 meters was 2.7 seconds slower than his best 200 meter time. Larrabee ran at a more consistent pace, running the first 200 meters 1.5 seconds slower than his all-time best for that distance and then doing the second 200 meters only 1.6 seconds slower than his all-time best.

To run a slow first 200 meters, as Larrabee did in the Tokyo Olympics, requires extreme concentration on one's own race while paying little attention to his competitor. At age 31, Larrabee was a very seasoned competitor who had run many times against the world's best quarter-milers. Being behind the leader by 10-15 yards, as Larrabee was at the half-way mark, would seriously disrupt the race plan of less experienced competitors. Larrabee held to his plan, ignoring the pace set by other competitors, and the plan paid off.

Lee Evans explained that his concentration was excellent in his world record breaking race at the Mexico City Olympics as he maintained good form by thinking about getting his knees high and swinging his arms loosely but vigorously. This helped him to be only 0.3 second off his best mark when he completed the first 200 meters. Later in the Olympics, in the 1600 meter relay, he had hoped to run a 43 flat leg with splits of 21.0 and 22.0, but he lost his concentration due to the excitement of the competition and tied up toward the end of his leg. But he still finished the distance in a commendable time of 43.9.

It is interesting that the world caliber quarter-milers have emphasized a fast pace during the third 100 meters of the race. George Rhoden at Helsinki, Otis Davis at Rome, Mike Larrabee at Tokyo and Lee Evans at Mexico City, all won Olympic titles and they all ran unusually hard and fast in the third 100 meters. It was during this phase of the race that Larabee moved from eighth place to third and then passed the leaders with about 80 meters to go. Evans also purposely designed his race to run unusually fast during the third 100 meters. During this time he opened up a lead that was insurmountable for his competitors.

Conservation of effort and the proper expenditure of energy is so important that it needs to be illustrated by events which occurred in a recent 600 yard indoor race. The athletes were walked to the finish by the officials who pointed out the line. Then they walked half way around the track to the starting line. Soon after the race started the officials realized the start and finish were wrong so the finish line was moved some 40 yards further around the board track. As the athletes approached the finish line the frantic officials waved and shouted to continue running. The two athletes leading the race at this point, having started their kick to end at the original finish line, were already decelerating when they became aware that the officials were waving them on. But the lead runners were unable to respond with a new burst of speed. One athlete who had badly misjudged the race and saved far too much energy, sped by the faltering leaders to win easily. The winner ran 1:14 in this error-filled race, while the two leaders at the original designated finish, trailed far behind even though they had run 1:10 the week before.

The secret then, of running a properly paced 440 is to cross the finish line when deceleration has just begun. The athlete who finishes with a great closing rush is not running his best race, and neither is the athlete whose deceleration occurs many yards before the finish. Was it the properly paced race of Lee Evans in the 1968 Olympics that caused him to win over Larry James? Evans led by about three yards at 300 meters. James closed slowly over the last 100 meters but finished 0.1 second behind Evans' world record of 43.8. If James had run his third 100 meter a bit faster perhaps he would be the Olympic champ and world record holder. But he didn't and Lee Evans became champion because he ran the better race, using his energy to its maximum.

What race pace is best for an athlete, Mike Larrabee's even 200 meter splits or Lee Evans 200 meter splits of a fast first 200 (20.7) and a slower second 200 (23.1)? This is difficult to answer, but one tends to think that a steady pace should give the best results, and from the physiological viewpoint, this is logical reasoning. While a man is not simply a machine, an analogy between a man and a car will add meaning to a race plan. Poor gas mileage is obtained by speeding up and slowing down; good mileage is obtained by driving at a reasonable but constant speed. So it is in running a quarter-mile. The runner should set a fast but steady pace so that when the finish line is reached his energy is fully expended and deceleration has just started to become apparent.

Larrabee's splits were even, while Evans' splits were not even, but perhaps they are close enough to be considered a steady pace. Both men achieved a small difference between their 400 meter time and their best 200 meter time doubled, Evans 3.0 seconds and Larrabee 3.1 seconds.

Two things are certain about running a good quarter-mile race. The athlete must be highly conditioned both physiologically and psychologically, and he must have a sound race plan and follow it.

## APPLICATION OF SCIENTIFIC PRINCIPLES

All of the principles discussed in the previous chapter on sprinting apply to the quarter-mile, because it is a long sprint. It is suggested that those principles be reviewed.

## COMMON FAULTS AND HOW TO CORRECT THEM

Since the quarter-mile is a long sprint, common faults demonstrated by quarter-milers are essentially the same as those already discussed in the preceding chapter on sprinting. All of the common faults discussed there apply to the quarter mile. In addition, the quarter-miler needs to be especially cautious that he does not commit the following errors:

1. Many quarter-milers do not pace themselves properly. The most common error in pace is to run the third 110 yards too slowly. The quarter-miler should run a fast first half, then push himself hard during the next 110 yards, then finish the final quarter of the race with whatever is left in him. Many races have been lost unnecessarily as a result of running the third quarter of the race too slowly.

2. Since the quarter-mile is a sprint which taxes the maximum endurance of the athlete, it is very important to run relaxed and efficiently. Being able to sprint in a relaxed condition is fundamental to success in the quarter-mile.

3. Sprinting around a curve is somewhat different than sprinting a straightaway. It is important not to allow one's running form to deteriorate while running a curve. Two of the most common errors in running curves are: A) tightening up (loss of relaxation); and B) permitting the outside leg to swing wide during the recovery phase of the stride. The athlete should concentrate on maintaining essentially the same running form while running a curve as when running the straightaway.

## THE TRAINING SCHEDULE

The following is a recommended training schedule for an experienced quarter-miler. It should be adjusted to fit the needs of a particular athlete taking into account his age, maturity and state of conditioning.

### Summer

During this season the quarter-miler should maintain a high level of general conditioning by participating regularly in vigorous running activities. These might include field and court games in addition to play type cross-country running. The running activity should be supplemented by specific exercises to maintain power in the muscles involved the most in running. (See the recommended exercises at the end of this chapter.)

### Fall

The fall program would be influenced by whether the quarter-miler will compete during the indoor season or whether he is preparing for the outdoor season only. If he is preparing for the outdoor season only he should do a considerable amount of running involving a combination of cross-country and wind sprints for the purpose of increasing his general conditioning. Also, he should continue with the exercise program and increase its intensity. If the quarter-miler plans to compete during the indoor season then the fall schedule should be similar to the one described for winter.

The quarter-mile, being a very long sprint, requires that the athlete be in superb condition. For this reason some quarter-milers do two workouts a day during the pre-season, with the morning workout consisting mostly of long distance running. The main workout, however, is done in the afternoon, and that is the one described here.

### Winter (Afternoon Workout)

Monday:
1. Jog 880 yards.
2. Do 10–15 minutes of stretching exercises.
3. Run six 110-yard sprints concentrating on running form.
4. Run three to four acceleration 440s.
5. Jog one mile.
6. Weight train (see exercises at the end of this chapter).

Tuesday:
1. Jog 880 yards.
2. Do 10–15 minutes of stretching exercises.
3. Run six 110s concentrating on running form.
4. Run one 660 at near top speed.
5. Do three to four miles of cross-country running.

Wednesday:
1. Jog 880 yards.
2. Do stretching exercises for 10–15 minutes.
3. Run four 110s concentrating on form.
4. Run ten 220s.
5. Jog one mile.
6. Weight train.

Thursday:
1. Jog 880 yards.
2. Do 10–15 minutes of stretching exercises.
3. Run six 110s concentrating on form.
4. Run six to eight 330s at near top speed.
5. Jog one mile.

Friday:
1. Jog 880 yards.
2. Do 10–15 minutes of stretching exercises.
3. Run six 110s concentrating on form.
4. Run ten 50-yard sprints using a flying start.
5. Jog one mile.

Saturday:
1. Jog 880 yards.
2. Do 10–15 minutes of stretching exercises.
3. Run time trials.
4. Weight train.
5. Run three to four miles of cross-country.

### Spring (Early and Middle Portion)

Monday:
1. Jog 880 yards.
2. Do 10–15 minutes of stretching exercises.
3. Run four 110s concentrating on form.
4. Run three or four acceleration 440s.
5. Jog one mile
6. Weight train.

Tuesday:
1. Jog 880 yards.
2. Do 10–15 minutes of stretching exercises.
3. Run six 110s concentrating on form.
4. Run two 660s at near top speed.
5. Jog one mile.

Wednesday:   1. Jog 880 yards.
               2. Do 10–15 minutes of stretching exercises.
               4. Do six 220s at top speed.
               5. Jog one mile.
               6. Weight train.
Thursday:    1. Jog 880 yards.
               2. Do 10–15 minutes of stretching exercises.
               3. Do six 110s concentrating on form.
               4. Do ten 50-yard sprints using the flying start.
               5. Jog one mile.
Friday:        Do easy jogging or complete rest.
Saturday:    1. Competition—arrive at the meet in plenty of time for adequate preparation for the race.  Have your race plan clearly in mind and follow it.
               2. Weight train.

### Late Season (May–June)

During this phase of the season the quarter-miler will ordinarily do the same kind of training as during the mid season, except that the intensity might be increased.  This should depend on whether the athlete shows any sign of staleness.

## CONDITIONING EXERCISES

Like the participants in the short sprints the quarter-miler must have a high level of leg power.  A conditioning program which will develop power beyond the levels ordinarily developed by running is essential.  It is recommended that the reader study the sections on strength, speed and power found in Chapter 1.

Following are exercises which are beneficial for quarter-milers.  The exercises are illustrated in Appendix A.

Straight arm forward raise—exercise #1
Trunk flexion—exercise #14
Trunk rotation (supine)—exercise #15
Leg raise (supine)—exercise #25
Leg raise (high bar)—exercise #26
Leg press—exercise #20
Jumping jack—exercise #21
Heel raise—exercise #23
Quadriceps drill—exercise #24

# CHAPTER 5

# Distance Races

The history of distance races dates back at least to the era of the ancient Greeks. However, it was not until the modern era that these races became popular and the distances became standardized. The running of distance races around a quarter-mile track is of recent origin and it has added much to the standardization and popularity of these track events.

The standard distance races (including middle distance) are 880 yards (or 800 meters), one mile (or 1500 meters), three miles (or 5000 meters), six miles (or 10,000 meters), marathon and 3000 meter steeplechase. There are other distances for which records are kept, but those distances are run less frequently than those mentioned above.

Of all the distance races, the mile run is considered the most standard and most spectacular. It can be singled out as the representative race of all distance races, and thus is given some special attention. One of the first truly great milers was Walter George of Great Britain who in 1884 ran the mile in 4 minutes 18.4 seconds. Paavo Nurmi of Finland, who was the first to show mastery of a strong pace, lowered the world's standard to 4 minutes 10.4 seconds in 1923.

Skipping a generation of milers, in 1934 American Glenn Cunningham set a new world record of 4 minutes 6.8 seconds. As a child Cunningham was burned so badly that he was expected never to walk again but, driven by his strong personality, he fought against nature and became the first American to hold the world record in the mile.

Arne Andersson and Gunder Hagg both of Sweden were the first two runners to approach the 4-minute mark. Andersson ran 4 minutes 1.6 seconds in 1944 and Hagg did 4 minutes 1.4 seconds in 1945. Hagg's record stood until 1954 when Roger Bannister of England turned the magic trick and broke the 4-minute mile barrier, covering the distance in 3 minutes 59.4 seconds. Since then a host of runners have bettered the 4 minute mark, the most notable of which is Jim Ryun of the United States who currently holds the world record at 3 minutes 51.1 seconds.

The evolution of improved performances in the other distance races parallels that of the mile run rather closely. To help the reader visualize the patterns of improvement in the various distances, the listings of world records are presented for several of the distances.

### 880 Yard Run

| Time | Record-holder and country | Year |
|------|---------------------------|------|
| 2m. 7.5s. | Richard Webster, Great Britain | 1865 |
| 2m. 5s. | P. M. Thornton, Great Britain | 1866 |
| 2m. | A. E. Pelham, Great Britain | 1872 |
| 1m. 59s. | Walter Slade, Great Britain | 1876 |
| 1m. 57.5s. | F. T. Elborough, Great Britain | 1876 |
| 1m. 56s. | Lawrence Myers, U.S. | 1881 |
| 1m. 55.4s. | Lawrence Myers, U.S. | 1884 |
| 1m. 54.6s. | F. H. K. Cross, Great Britain | 1888 |
| 1m. 53.4s. | Charles Kilpatrick, U.S. | 1895 |
| 1m. 52.8s. | Emilio Lunghi, Italy | 1909 |
| 1m. 52.5s. | James (Ted) Meredith, U.S. | 1912 |
| 1m. 52.2s. | James (Ted) Meredith, U.S. | 1916 |
| 1m. 51.6s. | Otto Peltzer, Germany | 1926 |
| 1m. 50.9s. | Ben Eastman, U.S. | 1932 |
| 1m. 49.8s. | Ben Eastman, U.S. | 1934 |
| 1m. 49.6s. | Elroy Robinson, U.S. | 1937 |
| 1m. 49.2s. | Sydney Wooderson, Great Britain | 1938 |
| 1m. 49.2s. | Malvin Whitfield, U.S. | 1950 |
| 1m. 48.6s. | Mal Whitfield, U.S. | 1953 |
| 1m. 48.6s. | Gunnar Nielsen, Denmark | 1954 |
| 1m. 47.5s. | Lon Spurrier, U.S. | 1955 |
| 1m. 46.8s. | Tom Courtney, U.S. | 1957 |
| 1m. 45.1s. | Peter G. Snell, New Zealand | 1962 |
| 1m. 44.9s. | Jim Ryun, U.S. | 1966 |

### 800 Meter Run

| Time | Record-holder and country | Year |
|------|---------------------------|------|
| 2m. 11s. | Edwin Flack, Australia | 1896 |
| 2m. 1.4s. | Alfred Tysoe, U.S. | 1900 |
| 1m. 56s. | James Lightbody, U.S. | 1904 |
| 1m. 52.8s. | Melvin Sheppard, U.S. | 1908 |
| 1m. 51.9s. | James (Ted) Meredith, U.S. | 1912 |
| 1m. 51.6s. | Otto Peltzer, Germany | 1926 |
| 1m. 50.6s. | Sera Martin, France | 1928 |
| 1m. 49.8s. | Thomas Hampson, Great Britain | 1932 |
| 1m. 49.8s. | Ben Eastman, U.S. | 1934 |
| 1m. 49.7s. | Glenn Cunningham, U.S. | 1936 |
| 1m. 49.6s. | Elroy Robinson, U.S. | 1937 |
| 1m. 48.4s. | Sydney Wooderson, Great Britain | 1938 |
| 1m. 46.6s. | Rudolf Harbig, Germany | 1939 |
| 1m. 45.7s. | Roger Moens, Belgium | 1955 |
| 1m. 44s. | Peter G. Snell, New Zealand | 1962 |
| 1m. 44.3s. | Peter Snell, New Zealand | 1962 |
| 1m. 44.3s. | Ralph Doubell, Australia | 1968 |
| 1m. 44.3s. | Dave Wottle, U.S. | 1972 |

### 1 Mile Run

| Time | Record-holder and country | Year |
|------|---------------------------|------|
| 4m. 56s. | Charles Lawes, Great Britain | 1864 |
| 4m. 36.5s. | Richard Webster, Great Britain | 1865 |
| 4m. 29s. | Wm. Chinnery, Great Britain | 1868 |
| 4m. 28.8s. | W. C. Gibbs, Great Britain | 1868 |
| 4m. 26s. | Walter Slade, Great Britain | 1874 |
| 4m. 24.5s. | Walter Slade, Great Britain | 1875 |
| 4m. 23.2s. | Walter George, Great Britain | 1880 |
| 4m. 21.4s. | Walter George, Great Britain | 1882 |
| 4m. 19.4s. | Walter George, Great Britain | 1882 |
| 4m. 18.4s. | Walter George, Great Britain | 1884 |
| 4m. 18.2s. | Fred Bacon, Scotland | 1894 |
| 4m. 17s. | Fred Bacon, Scotland | 1895 |
| 4m. 15.6s. | Thomas Conneff, U.S. | 1895 |
| 4m. 15.4s. | John Paul Jones, U.S. | 1911 |
| 4m. 14.4s. | John Paul Jones, U.S. | 1913 |
| 4m. 12.6s. | Norman Taber, U.S. | 1915 |
| 4m. 10.4s. | Paavo Nurmi, Finland | 1923 |
| 4m. 9.2s. | Jules Ladoumegue, France | 1931 |
| 4m. 7.6s. | Jack Lovelock, New Zealand | 1933 |
| 4m. 6.8s. | Glenn Cunningham, U.S. | 1934 |
| 4m. 6.4s. | Sydney Wooderson, Great Britain | 1937 |
| 4m. 6.2s. | Gunder Hagg, Sweden | 1942 |
| 4m. 6.2s. | Arne Andersson, Sweden | 1942 |
| 4m. 4.6s. | Gunder Hagg, Sweden | 1942 |
| 4m. 2.6s. | Arne Andersson, Sweden | 1943 |
| 4m. 1.6s. | Arne Andersson, Sweden | 1944 |
| 4m. 1.4s. | Gunder Hagg, Sweden | 1945 |
| 3m. 59.4s. | Roger Bannister, England | 1954 |
| 3m. 58s. | John Landy, Australia | 1954 |
| 3m. 57.2s. | Derek Ibbotson, Great Britain | 1957 |
| 3m. 54.5s. | Herb Elliott, Australia | 1958 |
| 3m. 54.4s. | Peter G. Snell, New Zealand | 1962 |
| 3m. 53.6s. | Michel Jazy, France | 1965 |
| 3m. 51.3s. | Jim Ryun, U.S. | 1966 |
| 3m. 51.1s. | Jim Ryun, U.S. | 1967 |

### 1500 Meter Run

| Time | Record-holder and country | Year |
|------|---------------------------|------|
| 4m. 33.2s. | Edwin Flack, Australia | 1896 |
| 4m. 6s. | C. Bennett, Great Britain | 1900 |
| 4m. 5.4s. | James Lightbody, U.S. | 1904 |
| 4m. 3.4s. | Melvin Sheppard, U.S. | 1908 |
| 3m. 56.8s. | Arnold Jackson, Great Britain | 1912 |
| 3m. 55.8s. | Abel Kiviat, U.S. | 1912 |
| 3m. 54.7s. | J. Zander, Sweden | 1917 |
| 3m. 52.6s. | Paavo Nurmi, Finland | 1924 |
| 3m. 51s. | Otto Peltzer, Germany | 1926 |
| 3m. 49.2s. | Jules Ladoumegue, France | 1930 |
| 3m. 49.2s. | Luigi Beccali, Italy | 1933 |
| 3m. 49s. | Luigi Beccali, Italy | 1933 |
| 3m. 48.8s. | William Bonthron, U.S. | 1934 |
| 3m. 47.8s. | Jack Lovelock, New Zealand | 1936 |
| 3m. 47.6s. | Gunder Hagg, Sweden | 1941 |
| 3m. 45.8s. | Gunder Hagg, Sweden | 1942 |
| 3m. 45s. | Arne Andersson, Sweden | 1943 |
| 3m. 43s. | Gunder Hagg, Sweden | 1944 |

| | | |
|---|---|---|
| 3m. 43s. | Lennart Strand, Sweden . . . . | 1947 |
| 3m. 41.8s. | John Landy, Australia. . . . . | 1954 |
| 3m. 40.8s. | Sahdor Iharos, Hungary . . . | 1955 |
| 3m. 40.8s. | Laszlo Tabori, Hungary . . . | 1955 |
| 3m. 40.8s. | Gunnar Nielsen, Denmark . . . | 1955 |
| 3m. 40.6s. | Istvan Rozsavolgyi, Hungary . . . | 1956 |
| 3m. 38.1s. | Stanislav Jungwirth, Czechoslovakia . . | 1957 |
| 3m. 36s. | Herb Elliott, Australia. . . . | 1958 |
| 3m. 35.6s. | Herb Elliott, New Zealand . . . | 1960 |
| 3m. 33.1s. | Jim Ryun, U.S. . . . | 1967 |

## 3 Mile Run

| Time | Record-holder and country | Year |
|---|---|---|
| 14m. 17.6s. | Alfred Shrubb, Great Britain . . | 1903 |
| 14m. 11.2s. | Paavo Nurmi, Finland . . . . | 1923 |
| 13m. 50.6s. | Lauri Lehtinen, Finland . . . . | 1932 |
| 13m. 42.4s. | Taisto Maki, Finland . . . . | 1939 |
| 13m. 35.4s. | Gunder Hagg, Sweden . . . . | 1942 |
| 13m. 32.4s. | Gunder Hagg, Sweden . . . . | 1942 |
| 13m. 32.2s. | Fred Green, England | 1954 |
| 13m. 32.2s. | Chris Chataway, England . . . . | 1954 |
| 13m. 26.4s. | Vladimir Kuts, U.S.S.R. . . . . | 1954 |
| 13m. 14.2s. | Sandor Iharos, Hungary . . . | 1955 |
| 13m. 10.8s. | A. G. Thomas, Australia. . . . | 1958 |
| 13m. 10.0s. | Murray Halberg, New Zealand . . . | 1961 |
| 13m. 04.8s. | Michel Jazy, France . | 1965 |
| 12m. 52.4s. | Ron Clarke, Australia. . . . | 1965 |
| 12m. 50.4s. | Ron Clarke, Australia. . . . | 1965 |

## 5000 Meter Run

| Time | Record-holder and country | Year |
|---|---|---|
| 14m. 36.6s. | H. Kolehmainen, Finland . . . . | 1912 |
| 14m. 35.4s. | Paavo Nurmi, Finland . . . . | 1922 |
| 14m. 28.2s. | Paavo Nurmi, Finland . . . . | 1924 |
| 14m. 17s. | Lauri Lehtinen, Finland . . . . | 1932 |
| 14m. 8.8s. | Taisto Maki, Finland | 1939 |
| 13m. 58.2s. | Gunder Hagg, Sweden . . . . | 1942 |
| 13m. 57.2s. | Emil Zatopek, Czechoslovakia . . | 1954 |
| 13m. 51.2s. | Vladimir Kuts, U.S.S.R. . . . . | 1954 |
| 13m. 40.6s. | Sandor Iharos, Hungary . . . | 1955 |
| 13m. 36.8s. | Gordon Pirie, Great Britain . . . | 1956 |
| 13m. 35s. | Vladimir Kuts, U.S.S.R. . . . . | 1957 |
| 13m. 24.2s. | Kipchoge Keino, Kenya . . . . | 1965 |
| 13m. 13.6s. | Ron Clarke, Australia. . . . | 1966 |

## 6 Mile Run

| Time | Record-holder and country | Year |
|---|---|---|
| 29m. 59.4s. | Alfred Shrubb, Great Britain . . . | 1904 |
| 29m. 36.4s. | Paavo Nurmi, Finland . . . . | 1930 |
| 29m. 8.4s. | Ilmari Salminen, Finland . . . . | 1937 |

28m. 55.6s.  Taisto Maki, Finland  1939  
28m. 38.6s.  Viljo Heino, Finland.  1944  
28m. 30.8s.  Viljo Heino, Finland.  1949  
27m. 59.2s.  Emil Zatopek,  
         Czechoslovakia . . 1954  

27m. 43.8s.  Sandor Iharos,  
         Hungary  . . . . 1956  
26m. 47.0s.  Ron Clarke,  
         Australia. . . . . 1965  

### 10,000 Meter Run

| Time | Record-holder and country | Year |
|------|---------------------------|------|
| 30m. 58.8s. | Jean Bouin, France . | 1911 |
| 30m. 40.2s. | Paavo Nurmi, Finland . . . . | 1921 |
| 30m. 35.4s. | Willie Ritola, Finland . . . . | 1924 |
| 30m. 23.2s. | Willie Ritola, Finland . . . . | 1924 |
| 30m. 6.2s. | Paavo Nurmi Finland . . . . | 1924 |
| 30m. 5.6s. | Ilmari Salminen, Finland . . . . | 1937 |
| 30m. 2s. | Taisto Maki, Finland | 1938 |
| 29m. 52.6s. | Taisto Maki, Finland | 1939 |
| 29m. 35.4s. | Viljo Heino, Finland. | 1944 |
| 29m. 28.2s. | Emil Zatopek, Czechoslovakia . . | 1949 |
| 29m. 27.2s. | Viljo Heino, Finland. | 1949 |
| 29m. 21.2s. | Emil Zatopek, Czechoslovakia . . | 1949 |
| 29m. 2.6s. | Emil Zatopek, Czechoslovakia . . | 1950 |
| 28m. 54.2s. | Emil Zatopek, Czechoslovakia . . | 1954 |
| 28m. 30.4s. | Vladimir Kuts, U.S.S.R. . . . . | 1956 |
| 28m. 18.8s. | Pyotr Bolotnikov, U.S.S.R. . . . . | 1960 |
| 28m. 18.2s. | Pyotr Bolotnikov, U.S.S.R. . . . . | 1962 |
| 28m. 10.6s. | Gaston Roelants, Belgium . . . . | 1965 |
| 27m. 39.4s. | Ron Clarke, Australia. . . . . | 1965 |
| 27m. 38.4s. | Lasse Viren, Finland. | 1972 |

## ENDURANCE TRAINING

Because endurance is a primary factor in distance running, methods of increasing it are of paramount concern. To increase endurance, we must apply progressive overload regularly and we must employ a program which will develop the specific kind of endurance required. Overload for endurance simply means working the organism beyond previous endurance levels.

There are two basic kinds of endurance involved in athletics—*muscular* and *cardiovascular*. Development of the two kinds requires different approaches. Further, cardiovascular endurance can be divided into *aerobic* and *anaerobic*, and these two types require different training procedures.

Distance running requires a combination of muscular and cardiovascular endurance, and the cardiovascular endurance must be the correct combination of aerobic and anaerobic. However, the main limitation in distance running is *aerobic endurance*, because this is the form of endurance that determines the amount of oxygen that can be delivered to the tissues of the working muscles. Without an adequate supply of oxygen, anaerobic processes must be depended upon. These processes are very inefficient and are inadequate to sustain a runner for very long.

Pertinent information about how to develop the different forms of endurance is presented in Chapter 1. That information should be studied carefully and carefully applied to distance running.

## DISTANCE RUNNING TECHNIQUE

The technique of a distance runner differs from that of a sprinter in several ways (Figure 5-1). Furthermore, no two distance runners are alike. Therefore, running style is highly individual. A coach may make a serious mistake if he tries to change a runner's form too much. However, often there are some changes that can be made which will improve one's performance. Researchers and coaches have found there are certain characteristics which are commonly found among successful performers.

### Relaxation

The ability to maintain relaxation is of major concern because it is one of the secrets to conserving energy. Tight antagonistic muscles utilize energy themselves because they are in a partial state of contraction and they also cause a drag on the agonistic muscles which cause the movements. The runner must learn to *run easy* while moving at a fast pace. His movements should be free and well-coordinated.

Relaxation is a prime factor in running efficiency, but it is not the only consideration. The runner must also learn to avoid wasted motion. Any

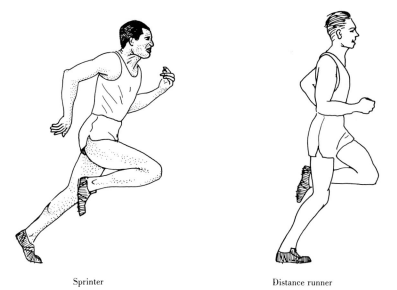

Sprinter    Distance runner

Fig. 5-1. Differences in running styles at different speeds. When compared with the sprinter, the distance runner typically runs with low strides, less vigorous and lower arm actions, a more upright body position, and more foot-surface contact.

movement which does not contribute to forward progress should be eliminated. All movements should be directed toward the objective of the runner—to project the body forward at the desired rate and with the least amount of energy.

Another important consideration in efficiency is pace. The faster a person runs, the more energy he uses to cover a given distance because as muscles contract at a faster rate they utilize more energy. Also, they work against greater forces of inertia, thus more energy is expended. Another important factor of pace is consistency. Additional energy is required to accelerate the body but very little energy is saved during the deceleration phase. Therefore, accelerating and decelerating will result in greater expenditure of energy. The runner should set the pace that he is capable of holding for the distance and vary as little as possible from that pace.

### Foot Action

The proper foot plant in distance running involves landing on the ball of the foot with the outer edge of the foot making contact first. The ball-to-heel action absorbs the shock of the landing. The knee should remain slightly bent upon landing to further cushion the action.

As the ball-to-heel action is completed the weight of the runner is momentarily supported by the whole foot. Then he glides smoothly forward into the next stride. As the body moves forward, the heel is lifted from the ground in a rock-up action and this is followed by the push-off as the leg and foot extend. The back leg is fully extended as contact with the track is broken. The proper foot action (ball-heel-toe) is illustrated in Figure 5–2.

It is very important for the feet to point straight forward for at least three reasons: a) if the foot points inward or outward at an angle, a certain amount of distance is lost on each stride; b) if the foot is angled outward, many of the muscles in the bottom of the foot are taken out of action because the runner rolls off the inside of the large toe; c) if the toes are angled outward or inward, the runner tends to project himself at a slight angle from the straight forward direction; this would result in a loss of distance on each stride. To illustrate in more detail the importance of the first reason, the following analysis is given: with the heel held in place and the toes pointing at a 20° angle outward, the front of the foot is about one-half

Fig. 5–2. The ball-heel-toe touch action of the distance runner.

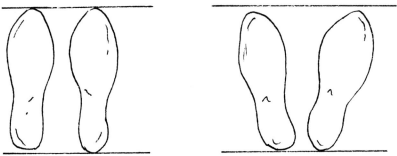

FIG. 5–3. Illustration of distance lost as a result of turning the feet outward.

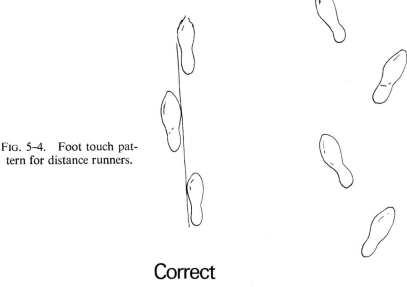

FIG. 5–4. Foot touch pattern for distance runners.

## Correct

## Incorrect

inch back of the straight-ahead foot position (Figure 5–3). Figuring a six-foot stride, a runner would lose over 12 yards in a mile if he lost a half inch on each stride. Obviously, this would make a big difference in the number of races won and lost.

### Stride

Length of stride is another important matter of efficiency. A distance runner should use a relatively short and economical stride, yet not so short that it disrupts rhythm or causes him to sacrifice the necessary speed.

The stride can be logically divided into three phases: recovery, support and drive. The recovery phase starts when the toe of the back foot breaks contact with the track and ends when the foot touches the ground again. In other words, it is the phase of the stride involving no contact between the foot and the surface. The support phase starts as the foot contacts the ground slightly in front of the runner's center of gravity and ends as the center of gravity passes over the foot. The conclusion of the support phase starts the beginning of the drive. During the drive the body is accelerated forward by the leg as the leg and foot extend. The runner initiates the drive as the body passes smoothly over the foot and the rock-up action of the foot begins. A runner with a good stride has a smooth and flowing appearance as he runs.

### Knee Lift and Back Kick Action

The knee lift required in distance running is less pronounced when compared with sprinting and middle distance running. This low knee lift is very popular with today's successful distance runners. The idea is to lift the knee only high enough for the foot to clear the ground and come forward in a nearly natural manner, as the rear leg is thrusting the body forward. In the recovery phase the knee reaches its highest point the moment the toe of the driving foot leaves the ground.

The rear leg kicks up behind (back kick) in a natural follow-through, after the drive against the ground has been completed. As running speed is increased, the back kick becomes higher because the driving force is greater and this causes a higher follow-through. A runner who uses a

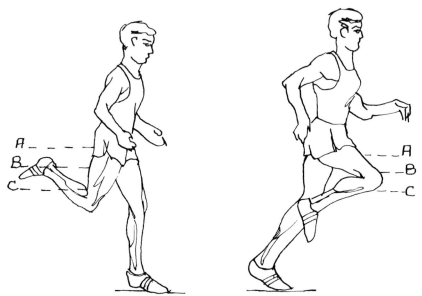

FIG. 5–5.   The height of the back kick and the knee lift of distance runners compared with middle distance runners and sprinters.

shorter stride will usually have less back kick than one who employs a longer stride due to the greater force applied during the driving phase of the longer stride (Figure 5–5).

### Posture

The correct amount of body lean is a topic of controversy among coaches. Traditionally it has been recommended that the distance runner lean slightly forward (10°–15°) in order to enhance the forward drive. However some excellent coaches of today contend that distance runners should run with the trunk and head erect. The authors agree that the distance runner should have only a slight amount of forward lean. The shoulders should be only barely forward of the center of gravity which is located in the middle of the pelvic region. The head should be aligned with the trunk and the eyes focused on the track 20–25 yards in front. This position is natural and should feel comfortable to the runner. As the distance runner enters his final sprint, the body lean will naturally increase a slight amount. Generally, the shorter the race, the longer will be the stride and the greater will be the body lean.

The runner must be sure that he does not lean backward, especially during the sprint phase of the race because this results in loss of drive.

The head should be held in a comfortable position that will not restrict breathing or cause tension in the neck, shoulders and arms. This is the natural head position and should result in relaxation of the neck muscles (Figure 5–6). The muscles of the face and neck should be consciously relaxed. This relaxed condition is exhibited when the face is expressionless or when the cheeks and lips have a bouncing action.

In distance running vigorous arm action wastes needed energy. The arms should move easily through a short range of motion. The faster the arms are swung, the faster the legs will move. While sprinting, the arms should be kept low and pumped hard and rapidly. In distance running

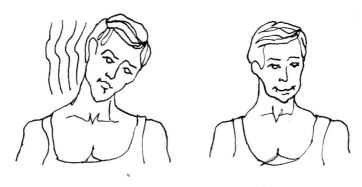

Incorrect        Correct

Fig. 5–6. Incorrect and correct head action during running.

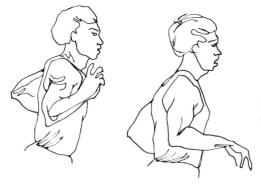

Fig. 5–7. Incorrect and correct arm action of the distance runner.

Faulty          Correct

the arms should be held higher and placed in a comfortable and restful position. At the high point of the swing, the hands should be at the height of the armpit but slightly toward the middle of the chest, and at the low point the hands should be near the hip pocket. The elbows should be kept close to the sides and flailing of the arms and hands should be eliminated. The arm action should consist of easy relaxed movements which are perfectly coordinated with the legs. The arms do not serve as a driving force, as they do in sprinting. On the other hand, it should be recognized that a runner whose legs have gone dead can often keep moving at the desired rate for a short distance by pumping the arms faster and harder. This is only an emergency measure and is not considered good form in distance running.

The hands should be relaxed and carried in a manner that is easy and comfortable. The fist should not be clenched and tensed. It is a good idea to cup the fingers causing the index finger and thumb to almost touch (Figure 5–7). Loose hands and loose face and neck muscles are the best indicators of relaxed running.

### Breathing

Breathing should be as steady and rhythmical as possible, without holding or forcing. The runner should inhale and exhale through both the mouth and nose. For inexperienced runners, it is often helpful to establish a pattern on a two-count beat. In other words, exhale every second time the right foot strikes the ground. It is vital for the runner to pay special attention to breathing because an adequate and consistent exchange of air is essential to good distance running.

Forced deep breathing is often done by distance runners just prior to the start of a race. The purpose is to build up a maximum store of oxygen in the blood and lungs. The value of this practice is highly questionable because it is known that it is impossible to store any significant amount of

FIG. 5–8. Sequence figure of good running form for a long distance runner.

oxygen. However, there is no disadvantage to the practice so long as it does not cause the runner to become dizzy. Some runners claim that it causes the lungs to feel expanded and more ready to carry on their functions.

## APPLICATION OF SCIENTIFIC PRINCIPLES

The same principles that apply to sprinting apply to distance running (see Chapter 3). However, their relative importance differs with races of various lengths. In addition to those principles, the following idea is very important in distance running:

*When efficiency is needed the body should be projected smoothly and at an even pace.* This means that in distance running the application of muscular forces should be consistent and as even as possible, so that the runner moves efficiently and economically at a constant speed. By this method he utilizes a minimum amount of energy to cover a given distance because energy is not wasted in combating the forces of inertia. This concept can be paralleled to driving a car where it is known that a car produces less mileage per gallon of gasoline when driven at varying speeds. Constant acceleration and deceleration wastes energy, whether the involvement is with the human body or an automobile.

## COMMON FAULTS AND HOW TO CORRECT THEM

The following common faults and their corrections were identified by experts in the field. The information was obtained through correspondence and personal interviews with nationally recognized coaches.

Fault:       Overstriding
Correction: Concentrate on a shorter and slightly faster arm swing. Consciously shorten the stride by shortening the forward reach of the foot. Also practice running up a gradual incline, because this forces a shorter stride.

Fault:          Failure to maintain the proper body angle, especially during ac-
                celeration.
Correction:     Concentrate on a fairly erect body position with slightly increased
                forward lean during acceleration. Any forward lean the runner
                assumes should be from the hips and not the result of simply tilting
                the head or rolling the shoulders forward. Running up a slight in-
                cline will tend to increase body lean, therefore, this practice should
                be followed if additional body lean is desirable.
Fault:          Carrying the arms too high and away from the body.
Correction:     Study the correct arm movements and concentrate on these actions
                during running. Also use wall pulley weights to practice correct arm
                movements, consciously rotating the palms of the hands inward and
                upward will help to bring the elbows in close to the sides where they
                belong. Concentrate on an arm action as if you were going to put
                the thumb in the hip pocket at the completion of each downswing.
Fault:          Tightness in the hands, arms and shoulders.
Correction:     Work on quick-step drills during warm-up. Concentrate on keeping
                the hands, arms and shoulders loose during the drills. Keeping the
                fingers loose and the thumb and index finger close together  Also,
                force relaxation while practicing over long distances.
Fault:          Unnecessary acceleration and deceleration.
Correction:     Be conscious of the inefficiency of this kind of running and emphasize
                a steady pace during practice. Any changes that are necessary in
                pace should be gradual and not abrupt.
Fault:          Running with too much bounce.
Correction:     Lengthen the stride to the back by concentrating on leaving the foot
                in contact with the ground longer, after it passes under the center of
                gravity. Also, land lower on the ball of the foot. Stress a reaching
                action with the arms rather than a pumping action. Increase body
                lean slightly. Stress lower knee lift, and concentrate on keeping the
                head on the same plane while running.
Fault:          Touching the ground with the inner part of the foot first.
Correction:     Concentrate on contacting the ground with the outside of the ball
                of the foot. Also do exercises which will straighten the foot and turn
                the sole of the foot slightly inward.

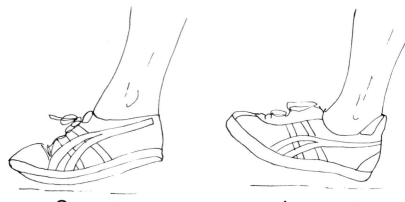

Correct                                    Incorrect
FIG. 5–9.   Correct and incorrect foot contact.

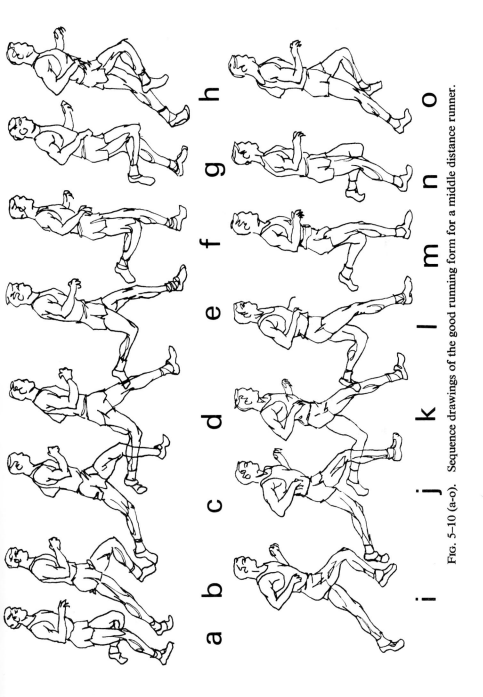

a    b    c    d    e    f    g    h

i    j    k    l    m    n    o

Fig. 5–10 (a-o).   Sequence drawings of the good running form for a middle distance runner.

85

Fault:          Toeing outward.
Correction:     Practice running a straight line concentrating on pointing the toes
                straight ahead.  During daily living while sitting and walking con-
                centrate on turning the foot slightly inward.  Do exercises which
                rotate the leg inward and thereby strengthen the muscles which cause
                inward rotation.  (NOTE: Most of the rotation which results in
                toeing outward occurs at the hip joint.  This should be taken into
                consideration in any attempts aimed at correcting the fault.)
Fault:          Landing on the heels (Figure 5–9).
Correction:     Be conscious of the error and concentrate during practice sessions
                on the correct foot-ground contact.  Shorten the stride slightly in
                order to avoid overreaching.  Also it might be beneficial to increase
                body lean slightly.
Fault:          Incorrect knee lift.
Correction:     Concentrate on lifting the knees just high enough for the feet to clear
                the ground during the recovery phase.  Knee lift higher than this
                results in wasted energy.  Long distance running tends to bring the
                knees down where they belong.  Knee lift should be concentrated
                on consistently to be sure that energy is not wasted as a result of
                excessive lift.

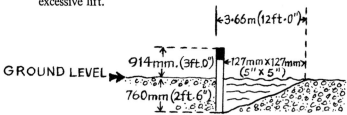

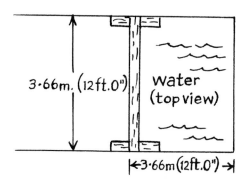

# WATER JUMP

FIG. 5–11.  Design of the water jump in the steeplechase.

## STEEPLECHASE

The steeplechase (two miles or 3000 meters) requires the endurance of a distance runner and certain qualifications of a hurdler. The rules state that there shall be five jumps (obstacles) including a water jump in each quarter-mile. The water jump shall be 12 feet in width and in length and the water 2′6″ in depth at the hurdle and shall slope to the level of the field at the other end. Each hurdle, of which there are four in each quarter-mile, is three feet high and at least 12 feet long. They must be built of heavy timber so they can be stepped upon by the runners without being over-turned. Each competitor must go over every hurdle and over or through

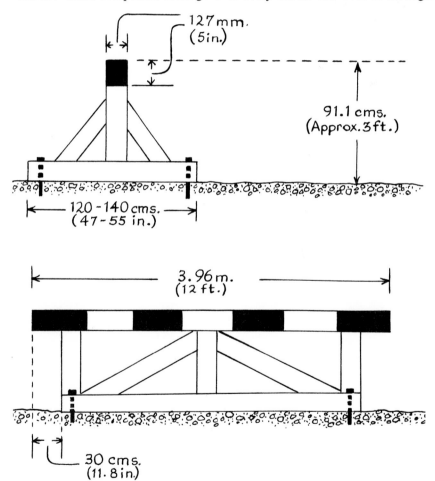

## STEEPLECHASE HURDLE

FIG. 5–12.  Design of a steeplechase hurdle.

the water jump. Anyone who steps to one side or the other of any obstacle shall be disqualified. Throughout the full distance of the race, each competitor goes over each of the four hurdles seven times (28 hurdles) and the water jump seven times, making a total of 35 obstacles in a race. Figure 5–11 shows the specifications of the water jump while Figure 5–12 gives the details of one of the hurdles.

### Steeplechase Technique

The running style and strategy of the steeplechaser should be the same as that of any other person running a distance race of the same length. (See previous section on distance running technique.) The main difference between the steeplechase and a flat distance race is the obstacles. The hurdles should be taken in a style similar to the technique explained in the chapter on intermediate hurdling, except the steeplechaser will be running at a slower speed than the quarter-mile hurdler; therefore, his hurdling technique will be somewhat more casual and he will cover less distance while going over the barrier. When the steeplechaser begins to fatigue,

Fig. 5–13. Recommended technique for taking the water jump in the steeplechase.

he might choose to step on top of the hurdle with one foot as he goes over. This is permissible. The technique recommended for clearing the water barrier is illustrated in Figure 5–13. Aside from the special work the steeplechaser does on the techniques of clearing the barriers, his training schedule is essentially the same as the one followed by athletes training for flat races of approximately the same length. See the training schedules at the end of this chapter.

## TRAINING SYSTEMS FOR DISTANCE RUNNERS

Following are descriptions of the standard training systems, along with various techniques that can be applied within each system. Many coaches combine the different systems to formulate programs they consider best for their particular athletes. In doing this, caution must be used to avoid cutting one system short before its beneficial effects have had time to develop.

### Interval Training

Major credit for the formulation of interval training is given to the coach-physiologist team of Gerschler and Reindall of Germany. It is a system of repeated efforts over a given distance in a specified time followed by a measured rest or recovery period. An example of this would be running six 220s at a 30–31-second pace with a 45-second rest or jogging period between. There are several important questions in interval training that a coach must consider. He needs to decide *what distance* should be run, *how many times* it should be repeated, *how fast* it should be run, *how much rest* should be taken between each run and *how often* this type of workout should be used. (Also study the section on anaerobic training in Chapter 2.)

*How many repetitions should be run?* There are many different views on the matter of repetitions but many coaches feel 10 to 12 is the optimum for speed development. Beyond this number the pace is slowed and only endurance is increased. However, this matter is influenced considerably by the length of each run.

*How fast should each repetition be run?* Speed will vary with each runner and his event. There should be a gradual buildup over a period of time until the athlete is running one or two seconds faster than racing pace. The workout should be demanding but not totally exhausting.

*How much rest between repetitions?* As a rule the longer the distance covered and the greater the speed, the longer the rest interval needs to be. Many coaches use the pulse rate as the determining factor. A basic rule to follow is that when the heart rate returns to 120 beats per minute the next repetition should be started. If a relaxed jog is used during the rest interval, the same principle should apply.

*How often should the workout be repeated?* Even the greatest advocates of interval training feel that every other day is sufficient to develop speed for the half-miler and miler. For longer races, speed intervals once a week are sufficient.

### Advantages of Interval Training

1. The runner can receive more attention from his coach.
2. It requires less time to complete a workout.
3. The individual's progress can be easily measured from week to week and month to month.
4. It is more demanding on the respiratory and circulatory systems.
5. Training at a pace which is slightly faster or equal to racing pace instills the running rhythm needed during competition.
6. Interval training is flexible in its application to time, length of run or place of run.
7. The runner develops judgement of pace.
8. It is the best method of developing aerobic endurance.
9. It can be highly motivating because it is challenging and provides variety.
10. More high quality work can be accomplished in less time.
11. It can be used to develop endurance and speed simultaneously.

### Disadvantages of Interval Training

1. It can become boring because it is repetitive.
2. If not used wisely it may cause a runner to peak out too early.
3. More injuries occur due to the faster, more intensive work.
4. The athlete may be obsessed with the challenge of the workout and lose sight of major goals.

### Fartlek Training (Speed Play)

Fartlek is a Swedish term which means "speed play." Although athletes throughout the ages have used this type of training in some form or another it remained for Gosta Holmer, the Swedish national coach, to give it a name. Fartlek is a method of endurance training which requires a mature, well-disciplined athlete to obtain its full value, because it is physically and mentally demanding. This form of training involves unrestricted running done over an undetermined distance for an indefinite time with some periods of running at a faster pace than others, dependent upon the athlete's physical and mental toughness.

This system gives best results when it is used only once or twice a week during the building phase of the program and no more than every other day during the sharpening phase. Ideally, the running should be done on a springy surface such as a forest floor, golf course, beach, park, etc. However, it can be done on a track or other such surfaces.

The athlete should be instructed to run in an area that is interesting, stimulating and easy on the legs. He should forget the stopwatch and run according to how he feels. A workout would be something like this: 5–10 minutes of calisthenics; jog 10–15 minutes; run at a fast, steady pace for 5–6 minutes covering about a mile; jog and sprint approximately one mile, taking 5–10 × 50–75 yard sprints during the distance covered; sprint uphill for 220–230 yards at full speed if a hill is available, if not available, run for 440–660 yards; jog 880 yards with intermittent short sprints, lifting the knees high; run four 220s at racing pace on the track; warm down with a 5-minute walk followed by 10 minutes of stretching exercises.

As can be seen from the sample workout, it could be very strenuous or a waste of time depending on the athlete's personal discipline. Many coaches feel there are few young runners who have the discipline necessary to get full value out of this system of training. For this reason a coach may want to have his workouts more structured until the athletes become mature enough to benefit from fartlek training.

### Advantages of Fartlek Training

1. It is physically and mentally stimulating.
2. It can build both aerobic and anaerobic endurance.
3. Its endurance development can be so structured as to meet the needs of all distance running events.
4. Runners may cover more miles at a faster pace because they are less aware of how fast and far they are running.
5. Uneven and uncertain footing will help to develop a shorter stride which is beneficial in distance running.
6. It provides variety and challenge.
7. It helps the athlete to know what his body is capable of doing.
8. It allows the athlete to get away from the pressures of the coach, track and stopwatch.
9. It encourages team spirit and fellowship when done in small groups.

### Disadvantages of Fartlek Training

1. Ideal training areas such as woods, golf courses, beaches, etc. may not be available.
2. When group running is done, not all runners will be worked to the degree of fatigue.
3. The immature and undisciplined runners may abuse this system by either working too hard or not hard enough.
4. It is very difficult to measure progress, due to the lack of exact times and distances.

## Lydiard System

This system of training was developed by Arthur Lydiard of New Zealand. It includes marathon training, speed-hill training and two phases of track training. Lydiard himself has been known to call his system marathon training. But his methods are more inclusive than what we normally regard as marathon training.

The first phase of the Lydiard system is the *marathon phase*, which includes running six or seven days a week and covering 100 or more miles per week. A novice runner will gradually increase his mileage as he develops. The extended distance should come only with an increase in stamina. The marathon phase lasts about 12 weeks.

Following the marathon phase, the runner goes into the strenuous *speed-hill phase*. This phase lasts for about six weeks and can be part of the cross-country season. If a gradual hill about one-half mile long can be found it is considered ideal. The runner sprints up the hill on his toes and exaggerates his knee action. High knee action is more important than the speed with which the hill is ascended. The runner then jogs to recover before descending the hill in a relaxed sprint. Following this the runner does repeat work such as three 330s and six 100s. These repetitions are increased in both number and speed as the runner's conditioning improves. A total of two to three miles is covered during ascending and descending the hill. When the warm-up short repeats and warm-down are included the total workout should be eight to ten miles. This phase builds upon the endurance base already gained in marathon training. It is very important that the coach not allow his athletes to become overly competitive with each other. Stiff competition would cause the speed to become too intense and the athletes would begin to peak out before the season starts.

From the speed hill training phase the runner advances to the *first track training phase* which lasts about six weeks. During this phase the runner will do over-distance at a steady pace or under-distance at a faster but controlled pace. This may include any one or a combination of the following: 30 to 40 220 yard runs, 15 to 20 440s or 8 to 10 880s. In this phase the coach is preparing the runner to advance to the final phase.

The *second track training phase*, which also lasts about six weeks, is designed to sharpen the speed of the runner. Distances of 100, 220, 330 and 440 yards are run at near maximum speed. The coach must supervise this phase very closely to make sure the training is not overdone and that attitude and competitive spirit are good. Seven to ten days before an important meet the runner should taper off, and on the last two days he should only jog two to three miles a day.

### Advantages of the Lydiard System

1. There are few weaknesses in Lydiard type training.
2. It prepares a competitor to become physically and mentally tough before competition starts.
3. It has a good balance between endurance and speed training.
4. It provides variety.

5. It allows a runner to progress steadily so there will be fewer injuries.

6. The various phases give the athlete a sense of direction.

*Disadvantages of the Lydiard Type Training*

1. It requires a long period to get into condition. It is designed to be a year-round program.

### Long Slow Distance

This form of running is valuable for developing an endurance base, but by itself it is not an effective method of preparing a runner for competition. The speed should be great enough to bring the heart rate to 150 beats per minute—usually a six- or seven-minute mile pace. A minimum of 10 miles seems to be required to achieve the desired effect, and distances up to 20 miles should be run regularly by experienced athletes.

This method of training is the first step in building the body to withstand the stresses and fatigue of running. It is a superior method of increasing the stroke volume of the heart and the capillarization of the muscles.

*Advantages of Long Slow Distance Training*

1. It is easy to administer.

2. It is less fatiguing to the runner than vigorous interval training.

3. Little pain and agony results from LSD running, not the extent encountered in some of the other methods.

4. It builds body relaxation and efficiency.

5. It is less likely to produce muscle and tendon injuries.

6. It builds cardiovascular, respiratory and circulatory systems.

7. It builds tenacity, determination and willpower.

*Disadvantages of Long Slow Distance Training*

1. It takes a lot of time.

2. Runners who lack self-discipline do not improve very rapidly with this system.

3. Runners may have a tendency to develop a slow rhythm and loss of speed if they stay on this system too long.

### Continuous Fast Running

During continuous fast running the person covers distances in excess of his racing distance. The pace should be fast enough to cause the heart to beat well in excess of 150 times per minute, and the rate should approach 180 during the later stages of the distance.

A half mile runner might run $\frac{3}{4}$ to one mile and repeat from two to four times. A six-miler might run eight miles at a fast, steady pace, or he might run four miles and repeat two or three times. Between each repeat he should walk or jog for five minutes.

*Advantages of Continuous Fast Running*

1. It is not as time-consuming as LSD training.

2. It conditions the athlete to tolerate the stresses encountered in running at faster speeds.

3. The training develops aerobic and anaerobic endurance.

*Disadvantages of Continuous Fast Running*

1. Because the pace is faster, fatigue is encountered sooner.

2. It may cause the athlete to peak out too soon.

### Training Techniques

The following are techniques of training, and not training systems. These techniques can be applied within the systems which have been described. Different techniques should be applied at different times in accordance with the needs of the athletes.

*Repetition of Sprints.* This involves the repetition of short sprints as a means of speed preparation for competition. Sprinting means running at maximum speed. Sprinting as a form of training is meant to improve leg power and racing speed.

*Slow Interval Training.* (See the description of interval training.) This technique develops aerobic endurance. The speed during each work bout is faster than in continuous fast running, thus adapting the athlete to running at a more intense effort. In this type of formal fast-slow running, the heart beats at the rate of approximately 180 beats per minute during the heavy work phase.

*Fast Interval Training.* (See the description of interval training.) This develops anaerobic endurance or speed-endurance. It develops the ability of the runner to withstand fatigue in the absence of an adequate oxygen supply. This method of training should be used after a basic amount of aerobic endurance has been developed. The heart should beat in excess of 180 per minute during the work phase.

*Repetition Running.* This differs from interval training in terms of the length of each run and the degree of recovery following each effort. It involves repetitions of comparatively longer distances with relatively complete recovery (usually walking) after each effort, during which time the heart rate reduces to below 120 beats per minute. Repetition running is concerned with repetitions of distances from one-half mile to two miles. Conversely, interval training usually includes repetitions of shorter distances (110 to 880 yards) with less complete recovery after each effort.

*Interval Sprinting.* In this technique the athlete sprints about 50 yards and jogs 10 yards for distances up to three miles. After the first few sprints, fatigue tends to inhibit the athlete from running top speed. Similarly, fatigue causes the athlete to reduce his recovery jogging to a very slow pace.

*Acceleration Sprinting.* This involves acceleration from jogging to striding to sprinting. For example, an athlete may jog 25 yards, stride 50 yards and sprint 50 yards, followed by 50 yards of walking, and repeat several times. This type of training emphasizes both speed and endurance, provided enough repetitions are performed to cause endurance overload.

*Hollow Sprints.* This involves two sprints joined by a *hollow* period of recovery jogging. Examples include sprint 50, jog 50, sprint 50, and walk 50 yards for recovery prior to the next repetition; sprint 110, jog 110, sprint 110, and walk 110 yards before the next repetition; sprint 220, jog 220, sprint 220, and walk 220 yards before repeating.

### Computerized Training Programs

A large number of computerized training programs have been developed by Gardner and Purty.* Through computer programming they have created many individualized workouts based upon the initial condition of the athlete. These programs have been tested on hundreds of track athletes and appear to be extremely accurate and highly useful for improving cardiovascular endurance.

### THE NEED FOR SPEED TRAINING

Training has as its purpose the covering of a given distance in shorter and shorter time limits. Any running which does not have speed as its goal cannot be classified as training but merely running for fun or health. Even though distance races are considered endurance contests, speed is of vital importance.

When we speak of speed training we are referring to the maximum speed that can be carried through a race. Naturally, it is relative to the length of the race. Speed training is an anaerobic function meaning that it takes place with an oxygen debt. In aerobic or endurance training the body replaces the oxygen as it is used. Since shorter races require more oxygen debt the proportion of speed training to endurance training is greater than for longer races where less oxygen debt is incurred. Experienced coaches will agree that speed is a commodity to be developed after a solid foundation of endurance has been built. Speed training, therefore, should be thought of as a supplement to endurance.

### Factors to Consider When Starting Speed Workouts

We recognize that speed training is essential, but it can also be dangerous because it increases stress and, therefore, the possibility for injury when the athlete can least afford it—during his racing season.

In order to minimize the dangers and maximize the benefits, the following cautions should be exercised:

* Gardner, J. B. and Purty, G. J.: *A Computerized Running Training Program.* Tafnews Press, P.O. Box 296, Los Altos, Calif. 94022, 1970.

1. Change gradually—slowly increase the proportion of speed work over a period of weeks.

2. Avoid violent running. Muscles and tendons are often torn during violent bursts of speed. Acceleration should be smooth.

3. Utilize rest. It is as important to rest after speed workouts as races. Every second or third day is often enough to do speed work.

4. Try to enjoy the workouts. Do all that can be done to keep speed training playful and enjoyable.

## SYMPTOMS OF OVERTRAINING

Often in an effort to obtain better times an athlete may train too frequently and with increased intensity. This is a pattern which is frequently followed by highly motivated distance runners. If staleness results performances begin to decline. The athlete often tries harder to improve, compounding the problem and adding to the overtrained state. Then he becomes frustrated and loses confidence in his coach and his own ability. This is a dangerous situation and one that is easier to prevent than cure.

From the very beginning the coach should have prevention of overtraining in mind. He should always be on the alert for symptoms of overtraining and act to combat them before they become serious.

The following is a list of overstress symptoms:
1. Frequent colds and mild sore throats
2. Poor appetite and loss of weight
3. Occasional headaches
4. Failure to sleep well
5. Loss of interest in training
6. Dark circles under the eyes and other symptoms of general fatigue
7. Persistent stiffness and soreness of muscles and joints
8. Sweating without previous exertion (slight temperature)
9. Swelling of the lymph glands (underarm and groin)
10. Irritability and nervousness
11. Nausea
12. Excessive depression
13. Slow recovery from colds and other infections
14. General weakness and fatigue after slight exertion
15. Loss of self-esteem (helplessness, uselessness, worthlessness)

At this point it is wise to remember that a good rapport between the coach and athlete is essential in order for the athlete to accept the coach's advice.

### Treatment

Preventing overtraining is a matter of recognizing the early symptoms of the syndrome and giving the matter appropriate attention. Many times the symptoms are not evident to the athlete but are apparent to an alert coach who knows what to watch for.

Ways to correct the situation are obvious—lower the activity level and provide variety in the training program until the athlete has regained his vitality. Remember that it is better to undertrain slightly than to overtrain and become stale.

## THE TRAINING SCHEDULE FOR THE HALF-MILE

The following is a sample workout program for half-milers. However, it would be a rare individual that could fit this program exactly without some modification. One mark of a good coach is the ability to sense the needs of his athletes and adjust their training schedules accordingly.

The following warm-up routine can be used throughout the season:

1. Jog two laps slowly using good form since this is where habits (good and bad) are formed.

2. Do limbering and stretching exercises.

3. Run wind-sprints for four laps.

    A. First two laps, run the straightaways and walk the curves. When running the straightaways, start slowly and accelerate.

    B. Second two laps, run the straightaways and jog the curves.

### Summer

During this season the distance runner should maintain a high level of general conditioning by participating regularly in activities that require extensive running. This could include certain court games and field games along with play-type running. These activities might be supplemented by specific exercises to maintain a high level of muscular endurance. (See the recommended exercises at the end of this chapter.)

### Fall

During the fall the emphasis should be on developing endurance strength and good form. Most good runners build this foundation by working out twice a day six days a week. This program is based on the assumption that no contests are scheduled.

Monday Through Saturday (Morning Workout):

> Three to six miles of light running ($\frac{1}{4}$ effort) on a soft surface if possible to save legs from excessive hard pounding.

Monday
Afternoon: 1. Run 30–50 minutes over hills, golf course, sand and a variety of terrains. Pace should be varied to fit the needs of each runner ($\frac{1}{2}$ effort).

    2. Stride six 110s ($\frac{3}{4}$ effort).

    3. Work on form and relaxation. (Cover 10–12 miles during both workouts.)

    4. Do weight training (see exercises at the end of this chapter).

Tuesday
  Afternoon: 1. Eight to ten miles over a flat surface ($\frac{1}{2}$ effort).
             2. Work on relaxation and form. (Cover 10–15 miles in two workouts.)
Wednesday
  Afternoon: 1. Five to six miles of fartlek. (Cover eight to twelve miles in both workouts.)
             2. Do weight training.
Thursday
  Afternoon:    Same as Tuesday.
Friday
  Afternoon: 1. Eight to ten miles with last two miles at $\frac{3}{4}$ effort on flat course. (Cover 12 miles in both workouts).
             2. Do weight training.
Saturday
  Afternoon:    Ten to fifteen miles on an easy cross-country course. (A total of 15–20 miles in both workouts.)
Sunday:         Rest.

### Winter

Weight training should be continued on a three-day-a-week basis. The running program is still based on covering distance and working on form and relaxation.

Monday Through Saturday (Morning Workout):

Three to five miles of light running

Monday
  Afternoon: 1. Warm-up (each afternoon workout should begin with a warm-up similar to the one described at the beginning of this section).
             2. 20–30 minutes of fartlek.
             3. Run six 440s in 70–75 seconds with a 440-yard jog between each.
             4. Stride six 110s ($\frac{3}{4}$ effort).
             5. Jog two to three miles.
             6. Do weight training. (Cover 10–12 miles in both workouts.)
Tuesday
  Afternoon: 1. Eight 220s in 31–33 seconds with two minutes rest between.
             2. Three 440s in 70–75 seconds with a 440-yard jog between each.
             3. Jog two to three miles. (Cover six to eight miles in both workouts.)
Wednesday
  Afternoon: 1. Two 660s in 1:40 seconds, jog 440 yards between.
             2. One 880 in 2 minutes 10 seconds.
             3. Jog two to three miles.
             4. Do weight training. (Cover six to eight miles in both workouts.)
Thursday
  Afternoon:    Same as Tuesday.
Friday
  Afternoon: 1. Do ten 440s in 70–75 seconds, two minutes rest between.
             2. Jog two miles.
             3. Do weight training. (Cover 8–10 miles in both workouts.)
Saturday
  Afternoon:    Five to ten miles of easy running. (Cover 10–15 miles in both workouts.)
Sunday:         Rest.

### Spring (Early and Middle Portion)

The runners should start into a speed training program with more emphasis on leg speed, pace and rhythm. It is important that the coach supervise each boy closely during this period to make sure he does not progress too quickly or too slowly.

Monday Through Friday (Morning Workouts):

Run three to four miles easy jogging.

**Monday**
Afternoon: 1. Warm-up (each afternoon session should start with a warm-up similar to the one described at the beginning of this section).
2. Do 10–20 minutes of fartlek ($\frac{4}{5}$ effort).
3. Run three 220s in 25–28 seconds, jog 220 in between.
4. Weight training.

**Tuesday**
Afternoon: 1. Do two 220s in 25–28 seconds, jog 220 in between.
2. Run eight 440s in 58–60 seconds with two minutes rest between.
3. Jog one to two miles.

**Wednesday**
Afternoon: 1. Run 660 yards for time.
2. Run 440 yards at first lap time for 880 competition.
3. Do two 220s in 24–26 seconds.
4. Do light weight training.

**Thursday**
Afternoon: 1. Light stretching.
2. Stride ten 100s on the grass.

**Friday**
Afternoon: Light jogging.
Saturday: Competition.

### Late Season (May–June)

During the late season the coach needs to be very careful that he does not allow his athletes to overtrain or do anything that would make them stiff and sore. Generally, if a boy is not in shape by the late season there is very little that can be done to improve his performance. The coach should be concerned with speed and keeping his boys sharp. The weight training workouts are discontinued.

Monday Through Friday (Morning Workouts):

Light jogging for three to four miles on Monday and Tuesday, one to two miles on Wednesday, Thursday, and Friday.

**Monday**
Afternoon: 1. Warm-up (the warm-up procedure described earlier should be followed at the beginning of each afternoon session).
2. Do ten 100-yard acceleration sprints.
3. Run six acceleration quarters; second 220 faster than first.
4. Jog two to three miles.

**Tuesday**
Afternoon: 1. Run ten 110-yard acceleration sprints.
2. Do one 660 for time.
3. Run two 220s in 24–25 seconds.
4. Jog two to three miles.

Wednesday
  Afternoon: 1. Run eight 110-yard acceleration sprints.
              2. Do three 440 yards in first lap time for 880 competition.
              3. Jog two to three miles easy on the grass.
Thursday
  Afternoon: 1. Run ten 100s easy on the grass.
              2. Do light jogging.
Friday
  Afternoon:    Do light jogging and stretching.
  Saturday:     Competition.

## THE TRAINING SCHEDULE FOR ONE MILE, THREE MILE, SIX MILE RUN AND MARATHON

To succeed in long distance running a runner must distribute his training over a longer period of time. We are finding that more distance runners are doing some kind of training 11–12 months a year. Many of them run twice a day and six to seven days a week. It should be kept in mind that the following is only a sample training schedule which can serve as an important guide.

### Warm-up

A warm-up routine similar to the following should be used every day before starting the workout.
  1. Jog one mile using good form since this is when habits (good and bad) are formed.
  2. Do limbering and stretching exercises.
  3. Jog a half mile.
  4. Run wind-sprints for four laps.
  A. First two laps, run the straightaways and walk the curves. When running the straightaways, start slowly and accelerate.
  B. Second two laps, run the straightaways and jog the curves.

### Summer

The runner should maintain a high level of general conditioning by participating regularly in activities that require extensive running. This could include certain court games and field games along with play-type running. These activities might be supplemented by specific exercises to maintain a high level of muscular endurance. (See the recommended exercises at the end of this chapter.)

### Fall and Winter

The fall and winter training program is basically the same for distance runners preparing for various distances. The major objective is to develop endurance, strength and good form. Distances from 60 to 100 miles a week are achieved by experienced, mature runners. For less experienced athletes the mileage will be proportionately less. The course should be varied to include such terrain as forests, hills, sand, golf courses, parks, etc. This adds variety and helps to prevent boredom. Following is a typical schedule, but if an athlete is participating in cross-country, the coach will need to take this into consideration and provide adequate rest before competition. Monday Through Friday (Morning Workout):

> Run six to eight miles ($\frac{1}{4}$ effort) on a soft surface if possible to save legs from excessive hard pounding.

Monday
Afternoon: 1. Warm-up (do the standard warm-up at the beginning of each afternoon session).
    2. Do six to nine miles of hill running. (Work on form and relaxation. Run hard uphill and at moderate speed downhill.)
    3. Weight training (see exercises at the end of this chapter).

Tuesday
Afternoon:     Run 40–50 minutes. Approximately 20 minutes of this time should be spent doing moderate fartlek running.

Wednesday
Afternoon: 1. Run 8–10 miles on the grass, golf course, park or forest. (Work on relaxation and good form.)
    2. Do weight training.

Thursday
Afternoon: 1. Run six to nine miles in the hills and on grass.
    2. Do 5–10 minutes of hard fartlek on the grass. (Work on keeping the body relaxed.)

Friday
Afternoon: 1. Do four 880s in 2 minutes 20 seconds—jog 440 yards in between.
    2. Run ten 440s in 70 seconds—jog 220 yards in between.
    3. Do weight training.

Saturday
Morning: Run 15–20 miles.
Saturday
Afternoon: Do light jogging.
Sunday: Rest

### Spring (Early and Middle Portion)—One Mile

During this period the demands of various individual events begin to emerge in the training programs. We now start to move into speed training with more emphasis on leg speed, pace and rhythm. It is very important that the coach supervise his athletes closely so they do not peak out too soon.
Monday Through Friday (Morning Workout):

> Morning workout should consist of running four to five miles at a relaxed pace.

Monday
Afternoon: 1. Warm-up.
    2. Do fartlek running for 30–40 minutes.
    3. Run four 440s at pace of first lap in mile run. Jog 220 yards in between.

4. Walk and jog one to two miles.
5. Do weight training.

Tuesday
  Afternoon: 1. Do fartlek running for 10–15 minutes.
            2. Do three 880s at two to three seconds slower than racing pace. Jog and walk five minutes in between.

Wednesday
  Afternoon: 1. Run one 660 for time.
            2. Do one 440 at first lap pace for one-mile race.
            3. Run one 220 in 26–28 seconds.
            4. Do light weight training.

Thursday
  Afternoon: 1. Light stretching
            2. Striding of ten 100s on the grass.

Friday
  Afternoon:    Light jogging
Saturday:       Competition
Sunday:         Rest

### Spring (Early and Middle Portion)—Three Mile and Six Mile

Monday Through Friday (Morning Workout):

Morning workout will vary from three to five miles of easy running, depending on when the next competition will be held and how important the meet is.

Monday
  Afternoon: 1. Warm-up
            2. Run eight 660s at about three-mile race pace—jog 440 yards in between.
            3. Jog and walk one mile.
            4. Do weight training (see exercises at the end of this chapter).

Tuesday
  Afternoon: 1. Run three miles striding the straightaways and jogging the curves.
            2. Do two 880s in 2 minutes 20 seconds—jog three minutes in between.

Wednesday
  Afternoon: 1. Run ten 440s in 70 seconds.  Jog 220 in between.
            2. Do light weight training.

Thursday
  Afternoon: 1. Run eight 220s in 32–25 seconds.  Jog 220 in between.
            2. Do light jogging on grass for 5–10 minutes.

Friday
  Afternoon:    Rest or light jogging
Saturday:       Competition
Sunday:         Rest

### Spring (Early and Middle Portion)—Marathon

Monday Through Friday (Morning Workout):

Morning workouts should consist of six to eight miles of steady running on a soft surface.

Monday
  Afternoon: 1. Run twenty-five 220s in 34–36 seconds.  Jog 110 yards in between.
            2. Do light jogging on grass for 15–20 minutes.

**Tuesday**
Afternoon: Do fartlek 6–10 miles. This should be run over different types of terrain such as hills, flat surface, roads, etc.

**Wednesday**
Afternoon: 1. Run four 1320 yards in 3 minutes 30 seconds to 3 minutes 45 seconds. Jog four minutes in between.
2. Do light jogging on the grass for 10–15 minutes.

**Thursday**
Afternoon: Do 10–12 miles steady running. Pick up the pace of the last two or three miles.

**Friday**
Afternoon: Do morning workout and rest in the afternoon.

**Saturday:** Compete in .some under-distance competition such as a 5- or 10-mile race.

### Late Season (May–June)—One Mile

During the late season the coach needs to be in close contact with his boys and make sure that they do not do anything that would cause them injury or make them unnecessarily stiff and sore. The majority of the work during this time is concerned with speed and helping the athlete stay sharp. The weight training workouts are discontinued.

Monday Through Friday (Morning Workout):

The morning workouts consist of easy jogging of two to three miles on a soft surface so as not to take the spring out of the legs. The intensity should lighten as the week continues.

**Monday**
Afternoon: 1. Warm-up.
2. Run ten 100-yard acceleration sprints.
3. Run fartlek for one to two miles with 75–100 yard-sprints en route.
4. Do three acceleration quarters; second 220 faster than first.
5. Jog two to three miles.

**Tuesday**
Afternoon: 1. Do ten 100-yard acceleration sprints.
2. Run one 880 in first two lap times for a competitive mile.
3. Do six 330-yard acceleration runs, picking up the pace for the last 110 yards.
4. Jogging on the grass for one to two miles.

**Wednesday**
Afternoon: 1. Run ten 100-yard acceleration sprints.
2. Do two 440s in first lap time for one-mile competition.
3. Jog on the grass for one to two miles.

**Thursday**
Afternoon: 1. Stride ten 100s on the grass.
2. Do light jogging.

**Friday**
Afternoon: Do light jogging and stretching.
Saturday: Competition
Sunday: Rest

### Late Season (May–June)—Three Mile and Six Mile

Monday Through Friday (Morning Workout):

Five miles of slow steady work on the grass or other soft surface to allow for the legs to recover their natural spring.

Monday
Afternoon: 1. Warm-up.
2. Do ten 100 yard acceleration sprints.
3. Do fartlek for two to three miles with bursts of speed for 100–200 yards.
4. Jog two to three miles on the grass.

Tuesday
Afternoon: 1. Do ten 100-yard acceleration sprints.
2. Run four to five miles of steady running, picking up the pace of the last mile.

Wednesday
Afternoon: 1. Do ten 100-yard acceleration sprints.
2. Run three 880s in 2 minutes 10 seconds to 2 minutes 15 seconds. Jog two minutes in between.
3. Jog two to three miles on the grass.

Thursday
Afternoon: 1. Run ten easy 100s on the grass.
2. Do light jogging.

Friday
Afternoon:    Do light jogging and stretching.
Saturday:      Competiton
Sunday:         Rest

### Late Season (May–June)—Marathon*

Monday Through Friday (Morning Workout):

Morning workouts should consist of five miles of steady running on a soft surface.

Monday
Afternoon: 1. Warm-up.
2. Do fifteen 330's at $\frac{3}{4}$ speed. Jog 110 in between.
3. Do light jogging on grass for 15 minutes.

Tuesday
Afternoon:    Do 10–15 miles of steady running.
Wednesday
Afternoon:    Run ten 880s in 2 minutes 30 seconds. Jog 220 yards in between.
Thursday
Afternoon:    Run 15–20 miles of steady running.
Friday
Afternoon:    Run eight miles. Pick up the pace to about $\frac{3}{4}$ effort on the last two miles.
Saturday:      Run the marathon distance at an even pace.
Sunday:         Rest

* If a marathon runner has competition coming up he should start on Wednesday afternoon with only light jogging up to the day of competition.

## CONDITIONING EXERCISES

For the distance runner the exercise program should develop muscle endurance and power in the legs, and endurance in the arm, shoulder and trunk muscles. The reader should study the sections on endurance and power in Chapter 1. Following are exercises which will help bring about the desired development. They are illustrated in Appendix A.

Arm curl—exercise #3
Straight arm forward raise—exercise #1
Trunk flexion—exercise #14
Trunk extension—exercise #18
Trunk rotation (supine)—exercise #15
Leg raise (supine)—exercise #25
Jumping jack—exercise #21
Heel raise—exercise #23
Quadriceps drill—exercise #24
Leg press—exercise #20

# CHAPTER 6

# High Hurdles

The 120 high hurdle race originated in England around the middle of the nineteenth century, and the first hurdles were solid sheep hurdles staked rigidly to the ground. Early hurdlers were as intent on getting over the barriers safely as they were in doing it rapidly. In clearing the hurdles the body was erect with the legs tucked under the body, hence passage over the hurdle was slow and the steps between hurdles were anything but uniform. By the beginning of the modern Olympics (1896) the world record was no faster than 15.4, held by Stephen Chase of the U.S.A.

The so-called father of modern hurdling was undoubtedly Alvin Kraenzlein who popularized the straight-leg lead and single-arm thrust. Kraenzlein ran 15.2 in 1898, and at the 1900 Olympics in Paris he showed his great versatility as he won the 60 meters (7.0), the 110 meter high hurdles (15.4), the 200 meter low hurdles (25.4) and the long jump (23′6″). He set a mark of 23.6 in the low hurdles in 1898 which stood for 25 years.

Earl Thomson, a Canadian, lowered the world mark significantly in 1920 when he ran the distance in 14.4. He was largely responsible for introducing the double-arm lead technique. Forrest Towns of the United States became the first person to break the 14-second barrier when he ran a remarkable time of 13.7 seconds in 1936. Other outstanding hurdlers gradually and consistently improved on the performances of the previous great hurdlers until finally in 1971 Rodney Milburn of the United States ran the 120 yard race in the remarkable time of 13.0 seconds.

The following list of official world records in the 120 yard and 110 meter high hurdle races indicate the progress that athletes have made since the event was originated a little more than 100 years ago.

## 120 Yard High Hurdles

| Time | Record-holder and country | Year |
|---|---|---|
| 17.75s. | A. W. T. Daniel, Great Britain | 1864 |
| 16.2s. | S. Palmer, Great Britain | 1878 |
| 16s. | C. F. Daft, Great Britain | 1886 |
| 15.8s. | Henry Williams, U.S. | 1891 |
| 15.75s. | Walter Henry, U.S. | 1892 |
| 15.6s. | Stephen Chase, U.S. | 1894 |
| 15.4s. | Stephen Chase, U.S. | 1895 |
| 15.2s. | Alvin Kraenzlein, U.S. | 1898 |
| 15s. | Forrest Smithson, U.S. | 1908 |
| 14.4s. | Earl Thomson, Canada | 1920 |
| 14.4s. | E. Wennstrom, Sweden | 1929 |
| 14.4s. | Stephen Anderson, U.S. | 1930 |
| 14.2s. | Percy Beard, U.S. | 1931 |
| 14.2s. | Tom Moore, U.S. | 1935 |
| 14.2s. | Philip Cope, U.S. | 1935 |
| 14.2s. | Roy Staley, U.S. | 1935 |
| 14.2s. | Alvin Moreau, U.S. | 1935 |
| 14.1s. | Forrest Towns, U.S. | 1936 |
| 13.7s. | Forrest Towns, U.S. | 1936 |
| 13.7s. | Fred Wolcott, U.S. | 1941 |
| 13.6s. | Harrison Dillard, U.S. | 1948 |
| 13.6s. | Richard Attlesey, U.S. | 1950 |
| 13.5s. | Richard Attlesey, U.S. | 1950 |
| 13.4s. | Jack Davis, U.S. | 1956 |
| 13.4s. | Milt Campbell, U.S. | 1957 |
| 13.2s. | Martin Lauer, Germany | 1959 |
| 13.2s. | Lee Calhoun, U.S. | 1960 |
| 13.2s. | Earl McCullouch, U.S. | 1967 |
| 13.0s. | Rodney Milburn, U.S. | 1971 |

## 110 Meter High Hurdles

| Time | Record-holder and country | Year |
|---|---|---|
| 15.4s. | Alvin Kraenzlein, U.S. | 1900 |
| 15s. | Forrest Smithson, U.S. | 1908 |
| 14.8s. | Earl Thomson, Canada | 1920 |
| 14.8s. | Sten Pettersson, Sweden | 1927 |
| 14.6s. | G. C. Weightman-Smith, South Africa | 1928 |
| 14.4s. | E. Wennstrom, Sweden | 1929 |
| 14.4s. | Bengt Sjostedt, Finland | 1931 |
| 14.4s. | Percy Beard, U.S. | 1932 |
| 14.4s. | Jack Keller, U.S. | 1932 |
| 14.4s. | George Saling, U.S. | 1932 |
| 14.4s. | John Morris, U.S. | 1933 |
| 14.3s. | Percy Beard, U.S. | 1934 |
| 14.2s. | Percy Beard, U.S. | 1934 |
| 14.2s. | Alvin Moreau, U.S. | 1935 |
| 14.1s. | Forrest Towns, U.S. | 1936 |
| 13.7s. | Forrest Towns, U.S. | 1936 |
| 13.7s. | Fred Wolcott, U.S. | 1941 |
| 13.6s. | Richard Attlesey, U.S. | 1950 |
| 13.5s. | Richard Attlesey, U.S. | 1950 |
| 13.4s. | Jack Davis, U.S. | 1956 |
| 13.2s. | Martin Lauer, Germany | 1959 |
| 13.2s. | Lee Calhoun, U.S. | 1960 |
| 13.2s. | Earl McCullouch, U.S. | 1967 |
| 13.0s. | Rodney Milburn, U.S. | 1971 |

## PROCEDURE

Like all other hurdle races, the 120 yard (or 110 meter) race includes 10 barriers. The first hurdle is 15 yards from the start and the last barrier is 15 yards from the finish. The hurdles are spaced 10 yards apart. The athlete starts from a sprint start position, takes either seven or eight strides to the first hurdle, clears the hurdle in the shortest time possible, then takes three strides between hurdles. The high hurdles must be considered a sprint race where the athlete clears 10 barriers during the 120 yard sprint. There is no penalty for hitting or knocking over hurdles.

## HIGH HURDLE TECHNIQUE

As in all sprint races, the start is very important. The starting technique is the same as used in other sprints (described in Chapter 4) except that in some cases the hurdler must adjust the position of his feet in the blocks in order to have a correct stride pattern to the first hurdle. The need for such adjustments can be determined only through experimentation by each individual athlete.

### To the First Hurdle

Most hurdlers use eight strides to the first hurdle, but a few are able to use only seven. Should the pattern be eight strides, the lead leg will be in the rear starting block whereas if seven strides are used the lead leg will be out front. During the acceleration phase, the hurdler must come to the erect position slightly sooner than he would if he were running a 100 yard dash, because he must be in the erect position in time to take the first hurdle, which is only 15 yards from the start. One of the difficult tasks is learning to accelerate all the way to the first hurdle. Otherwise, time is lost. This is not an easy task because most hurdlers have a tendency to stand up too soon after coming out of the starting blocks in anticipation of the first hurdle. The hurdler must force himself to stay low in a driving position as long as possible.

As pointed out in Chapter 4 the sprinter loses some of his drive if he snaps the head up too quickly after coming out of the blocks. Hurdlers have a tendency to do this because of the need to see the hurdle in preparation to clear it smoothly. The hurdler, like the sprinter, must spend many

FIG. 6–1.  Midway over the hurdle.

FIG. 6–2 (a–i). Sequence drawings of correct hurdling technique.

hours practicing the correct starting technique and the correct step pattern to the first hurdle.

As the hurdler comes close to the first hurdle he assumes the erect running position and readies himself to sprint over the hurdle (Figure 6–2a). The last step prior to the hurdle is a little shorter than the previous step. This enables the hurdler to shift the center of weight forward so that he can get the trunk of the body out over the lead leg while reaching with the leg to step over the hurdle.

### Over the Hurdle

High hurdles are run with three running strides between hurdles. The barrier is not taken in three strides and a jump, but rather in four running strides, the last of which is longer and accentuated. A relatively tall person with long legs has a mechanical advantage in high hurdling because he needs to travel a shorter distance through the vertical plane in order to clear the hurdle, thus he can get over the hurdle in less time.

The hurdler should leave the ground approximately seven feet in front of the hurdle and land about three and one-half feet behind it. In clearing the barrier, his forward leg, led by the knee, should be driven upward to clear the hurdle, then stretched forward to near maximum (Figure 6–2c, d, e). At the same time the upper body is brought forward to meet the upward driven leg. The arm opposite the lead leg (or sometimes both arms) is extended forward while the shoulders are kept level and parallel to each other. These movements are coordinated with the upward-forward drive from the takeoff leg (Figure 6–2e).

As the lead leg clears the hurdle it is driven downward. The upper body should still be well forward in order to aid in the downward drive of the leg. At the same time the trail leg is in rapid motion forward. As the lead leg approaches the ground the upper body becomes slightly more erect and the trail leg, with knee cocked and foot turned outward, clears the hurdle (Figure 6–2b). Upon contact with the ground the runner must maintain enough body lean to allow for maximum forward drive. At this point the trail leg is whipped forward and the next running stride is taken (Figure 6–2i).

When working for perfection in hurdling action, the athlete should keep these points in mind:

1. Clear each hurdle in the shortest possible time.

2. Let the hurdle interfere as little as possible with running rhythm, and stride pattern.

3. Maintain as near perfect balance as possible.

4. Try to come off each hurdle into perfect sprint position.

The following points deserve special emphasis:

1. A hurdler must be highly flexible in the movements required in hurdling. Without sufficient flexibility, proper hurdling form is impossible.

2. The thrust into the hurdle must be vigorous, as if the hurdler were *attacking* the hurdle.

3. The lean is from the hips straight forward with the shoulders kept near parallel to the track. It is as if the hurdler were reaching for the hurdle with the chest.

4. It is important to keep the hips square during the hurdling action in order that the lead leg is not pulled out of its correct alignment. If the hips are rotated, the lead leg will tend to cross over in front of the hurdler and the trail leg will drag too far behind. This results in a delayed pull through of the trail leg and throws the hurdler off balance, causing him to weave during the landing and the first stride after the hurdle.

5. The action of the trail leg should be continuous. There is no hesitation, just a smooth continuous drive from the time the foot leaves the track until the leg assumes the parallel position, and then continues on with the knee brought high almost to the armpit. The knee continues to pass high and the leg is swung through into the next running stride.

6. The foot of the trail leg should be pointed outward and turned upward as much as possible to avoid hitting the hurdle.

7. A forceful relaxed use of the arms is required in the approach as well as in the hurdling action. The lead arm goes forward with the lead leg and reaches toward the body's midline, with the elbow slightly flexed. The other arm moves part way forward and then moves farther forward as the hurdler comes off the hurdle with the arms in sprint position.

8. The hurdler must be able to step over the hurdle in proper balance and alignment and with enough forward lean to put him in perfect sprint position.

FIG. 6–3.  Front view of hurdling technique.

### Between Hurdles

It is imperative that the athlete *sprint* between hurdles. With the hurdles spaced 10 yards apart, the hurdler covers about 10.5' in clearing the hurdle and about 19.5' in the three strides between hurdles. The average of 6.5' per stride presents no problem to a mature athlete who is an experienced hurdler. But to many beginners this is a major problem.

One of the most difficult tasks for the beginner is to develop a correct and consistent step pattern between hurdles. Sometimes it is necessary for the coach to place obvious markers at the points where the feet should strike the ground. Some beginners have to use a loping rhythm between hurdles in order to cover the distance in three strides. This action is often helpful during the learning period but it must be replaced by an even three step sprint before the hurdler can perform well.

A point to be emphasized is that the trail leg, as it clears the hurdle, must be whipped forward into a full running stride. Otherwise the first stride after the hurdle will be shorter than the average of the three strides between hurdles (Figure 6–2i). In fact the first and second strides should be slightly longer than 6.5' in order that the third stride can be shortened slightly.

It is essential that the hurdler *drive* the total distance of the race. He must *drive* to the first hurdle, *drive* over the hurdles, and *drive* between hurdles.

### The Last Hurdle to the Tape

It is very important that the last hurdle be taken with the same form and precision as the other barriers. This means that the hurdler must come off the hurdle into good sprint position with sufficient forward lean (Figure 6–4). The remainder of the race is the same as the last portion of a short sprint.

Fig. 6–4. It is very important to come off the last hurdle in driving position for the final sprint.

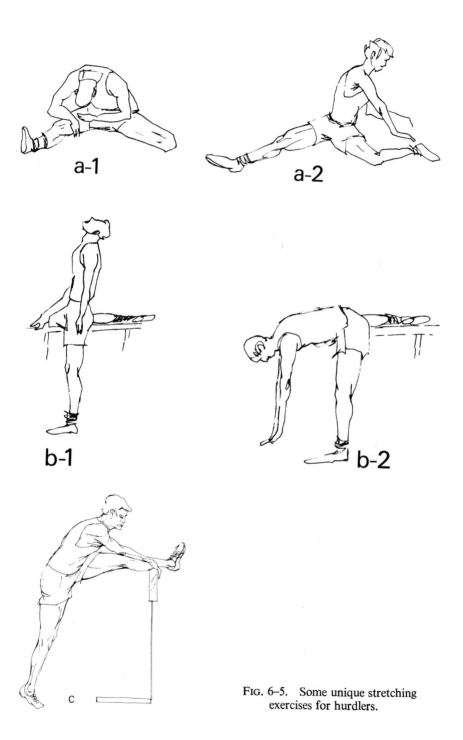

FIG. 6–5.   Some unique stretching
exercises for hurdlers.

It is recommended that the sprint continue to a point slightly beyond the tape. For more details about techniques of the finish, refer to the chapter on sprinting (Chapter 4).

## APPLICATION OF SCIENTIFIC PRINCIPLES

Since the high hurdle race is a sprint, the scientific principles stated in the chapter on sprinting would apply. In addition, there are certain other principles which are fundamental to correct hurdling technique. Following are explanations of how these principles apply.

Good hurdling is dependent upon three conditions: 1) shoulders and hips should remain square (not rotated excessively) while going over the hurdle; 2) the lead leg is led by the knee (knee comes up first); and 3) the body lean is straight forward from the waist and hips. It has been found that many other deviations in hurdling form can be traced back to one of these fundamental conditions. Therefore, in the process of attempting to perfect hurdling form, it is recommended that these three conditions be kept foremost in mind.

*The momentum of moving body segments can be transferred to the total body (transfer of momentum).* As the hurdler *attacks* the hurdle, he thrusts the arms, head and trunk forward and the momentum resulting from these thrusting actions is transferred to the total body to help pull the body over the hurdle faster.

*The length of time an object remains in flight depends upon the height it attains. The object remains in flight only as long as it takes to move through the vertical plane.* It is essential that the hurdler clear the hurdle in the shortest time possible in order that he can continue with his sprint. Thus the center of gravity of the body should raise a minimal amount and still permit the body to clear the hurdle. If the body is raised higher than is necessary the hurdler will lose time over each hurdle because he will remain in flight longer.

## COMMON FAULTS AND HOW TO CORRECT THEM

The following faults were identified by hurdling experts and the correction techniques were explained by coaches who have had extensive experience with superior hurdlers.

| | |
|---|---|
| Fault: | Opening up the hips on takeoff (the hips should be kept square to the direction of movement). |
| Correction: | Concentrate on straight-forward action of the various body parts. Also, do not let the trail leg lag too far behind during the hurdling action because this tends to open the hips. |
| Fault: | Twisting the shoulders during the early part of the hurdling action (the shoulders should remain almost parallel to the track). |
| Correction: | Concentrate on keeping the shoulders parallel when the trunk is in the forward position. Frequently hurdlers think of bringing the |

opposite shoulder to the knee while over the hurdle. This can cause undesirable rotation. The hurdler should think of bringing the chest to the knee.

Fault: Crossing the center line of the body with the arms.

Correction: This fault frequently occurs because the shoulders are rotated. Concentrate on keeping the shoulders square, leaning forward from the waist and hips, and thrusting the arms almost straight forward.

Fault: Leaning to the side away from the trail leg in an effort to lift the trail leg over the hurdle.

Correction: This indicates lack of dynamic flexibility (inability to move the trail leg through the correction motions). Spend more time on flexibility drills for the trail leg movement (follow the technique described under flexibility in Chapter 1). Also, work on hurdling drills which emphasize getting the trail leg over the hurdle.

Fault: Consistently hitting the ankle or foot of the trail leg on the hurdle.

Correction: The correction would be the same as for the previous fault. Also, concentrate on pointing the toe outward and lifting the foot upward at the ankle.

Fault: Drifting to the right or left from takeoff to landing.

Correction: The lead leg must come up in a straight-line direction and continue its straight-line movement. Sometimes it is helpful to place a marker on the track where the lead foot should land. This will guide straight-line movement. Also caution must be taken not to let the trail leg drag too far behind because this will cause the hips to open and shift the lead leg toward the inside.

Fault: Floating over the hurdle.

Correction: This fault results from lack of drive into the hurdle which is a failure to *attack* the hurdle. The problem may be related to fear of the hurdle or it might be that the hurdler does not recognize that the hurdle should be taken in an accentuated running stride and not a floating leap. Think of the hurdling action as a long and quick step. Some hurdlers are able to increase their confidence and their quickness over the hurdle by practicing the stepping action over low or intermediate hurdles.

Fault: Landing off balance.

Correction: This fault indicates 1) that the shoulders and hips are not kept square with the track; 2) that the body lean from the hips and waist is not in a straight-forward direction, or 3) that the lead leg is not kept in a straight line and is, therefore, out of alignment upon contact with the track. Through analysis of the hurdling action it is necessary to determine which of these errors is causing the loss of balance and then correct the error. Here again some hurdlers find it helpful to have a mark placed on the track at the point where the lead foot should make contact.

Fault: Landing on the heel.

Correction: This indicates insufficient body lean. Concentrate on driving into the hurdle and keeping the body weight well forward.

Fault: Trail leg coming through too high.

Correction: The problem here is that if the trail leg is brought through too high it tends to raise the trunk to a more erect position, whereas if the trunk is leaning well forward as it should be, the trail leg will tend to be flattened more. It is important to concentrate on sufficient body lean and not let the trail leg action disrupt this important part of hurdling technique.

Fault:           The lead leg is too straight.

Correction:   If this fault exists a slight checking of momentum will occur on the last stride prior to the hurdle, or there might be a slight backward lean which resembles a high jumper when he uses a straight leg left on his takeoff.  The hurdler must lead with a bent leg as if he were taking a running stride.  Then the knee straightens just in time to bring the foot over the hurdle.  In order to correct this fault, practice over low hurdles where emphasis can be placed on correct lead leg action.  Then do the same over intermediate hurdles, and finally apply the corrected form to the high hurdles.

Fault:           Failure to bring the lead leg down sufficiently fast.

Correction:   It is important to recognize that there is no floating action in hurdling.  This means that as soon as the lead leg clears the hurdle a sufficient amount, it must start its movement downward.  It is brought down quickly and forcefully as a result of an adequate amount of body lean.

Fault:           Consistently hitting the thigh of the lead leg on the hurdle.

Correction:   This indicates either insufficient height or premature driving of the lead leg downward.  If this fault occurs only during the latter part of the race it indicates poor conditioning or a lack of practice over a sufficient number of hurdles.  Through analysis try to identify the particular error which is causing this fault and then correct that error.

Fault:           Failure to take a full running stride with the trail leg following the hurdling action.

Correction:   This fault is usually caused by insufficient body lean which puts the hurdler in a poor sprint position as he comes off the hurdle.  The correction is to concentrate on keeping the body weight well forward.  A contributing factor is bringing the knee down too quickly after the foot passes over the hurdle, rather than swinging the knee high into a full running stride.  Poor body balance contributes to this problem.

## THE TRAINING SCHEDULE

The following is a recommended training schedule for the mature high hurdler.  It can serve as an important guide for all high hurdlers but will need to be adjusted to fit the needs of any particular person because of differences in age, maturity and state of conditioning among athletes.

### Summer

During this season the high hurdler should maintain a high level of general conditioning by participating regularly in vigorous running and jumping activities.  These activities might include field and court games in addition to play-type cross country running.  The athlete should also do a limited amount of work over hurdles.  The running activities should be supplemented by specific exercises to maintain power in the muscles involved the most in running and hurdling.  (See the recommended exercises at the end of this chapter.)

### Fall

The program during this season would be influenced by whether the athlete will compete during the indoor season or whether he is preparing only for the outdoor season. If he is preparing for the outdoor season only, he should do a considerable amount of cross country and wind-sprint running for the purpose of increasing his general conditioning, and in addition he should work consistently on hurdling form. Also he should continue with the exercise program and increase its intensity. If the hurdler plans to compete during the indoor season, the fall schedule should be similar to the one described for winter.

### Winter

Monday:
1. Jog one-half mile.
2. Do stretching exercises for 10–15 minutes (emphasize hurdling exercises).
3. Run four 110s at near top speed.
4. Work on hurdling form for 20 minutes over two or more hurdles.
5. Do 10–12 starts sprinting 30–40 yards each time.
6. Run four 440s in 54–56 seconds each.
7. Jog one-half mile.
8. Weight train (see exercises at the end of this chapter).

Tuesday:
1. Jog one-half mile.
2. Do stretching exercises for 10–15 minutes.
3. Do four to five miles of fartlek training, emphasizing pick up sprints of 50 to 220 yards each.

Wednesday:
1. Jog one-half mile.
2. Do 10–15 minutes of stretching exercises.
3. Run four 110s at near full speed.
4. Work for 20 minutes over two or more hurdles.
5. Do 8–10 starts sprinting 30–40 yards each time.
6. Run four 440s (emphasize several 50 yard pick ups during each 440).
7. Jog one-half mile.
8. Weight train.

Thursday:
1. Jog one-half mile.
2. Do stretching exercises.
3. Run three 330s in about 36 seconds each.
4. Work on hurdles for about 20 minutes.
5. Jog one-half mile.

Friday:
Do the same as Wednesday except no weight training.

Saturday:
1. Prepare for time trials.
2. Run time trials.
3. Do one to two miles of jogging.
4. Weight train.

### Spring (Early and Middle Portion)

Monday:
1. Jog one-half mile.
2. Do stretching exercises for 10–15 minutes.
3. Run four 110s at near top speed.
4. Do 20 minutes of work on the hurdles.

                5. Run six 50 yard sprints.
                6. Run two 150 yard sprints.
                7. Jog one-half mile.
                8. Weight train.
Tuesday:        1. Jog one-half mile.
                2. Do stretching exercises.
                3. Run four 110 yard sprints.
                4. Do 20 minutes of work over the hurdles.
                5. Do 10 starts sprinting 30–40 yards each time.
                6. Run four 150s at near top speed.
                7. Jog one-half mile.
Wednesday:      1. Jog one-half mile.
                2. Do stretching exercises.
                3. Run four 110 yard sprints at near top speed.
                4. Work for 20 minutes over the hurdles.
                5. Run two 330s at near top speed.
                6. Jog one-half mile.
                7. Weight train.
Thursday:       Do the same as Tuesday.
Friday:         Do a very light workout or rest.
Saturday:       1. Competition—arrive at the meet in plenty of time for adequate
                   preparation. Have your race plan clearly in mind and follow it.
                2. Weight train.

### Late Spring (May–June)

During this phase of the season the hurdler will ordinarily do the same kind of training as done at mid season. The intensity of the training might be increased depending on whether the athlete shows any signs of staleness.

### CONDITIONING EXERCISES

It is especially important for the hurdler to have a high level of power in the leg muscles, and to be highly flexible in certain areas of the body. The procedures for developing power, which is a combination of strength and speed, and for developing flexibility are explained in Chapter 1. It is recommended that the reader study the appropriate sections of that chapter.

The specific exercises which should be included in the conditioning program are listed below. The exercises are illustrated in Appendix A.

Straight arm forward raise—exercise #1
Trunk flexion—exercise #14
Trunk lateral flexion—exercise #17
Trunk extension—exercise #18
Trunk rotation (supine)—exercise #15
Leg raise (supine)—exercise #25
Leg raise (high bar)—exercise #26
Leg press—exercise #20
Jumping jack—exercise #21
Heel raise—exercise #23
Quadriceps drill—exercise #24
Hip flexion—exercise #27
Stretching exercises (see Figure 6–5)

CHAPTER 7

# Intermediate Hurdles

The intermediate hurdle race has a relatively short history. The first record of such a race being run was at Oxford University in 1860, with each competitor going over 12 hurdles. However the race did not appear on the program of major meets on a regular basis until well after the turn of the century. The event gained most of its popularity in France and appeared in the Olympics for the first time in Paris in 1900. In that race the hurdles consisted of 30-foot-long poles and there was a water jump between the last hurdle and the finish line. Walter Tewskbury of the United States finished the race in 57.6 seconds, to the disappointment of the French who had developed the race and had it placed on the Olympic program. It is interesting that Tewksbury also won the 200 meters, was second in the 100 meters and third in the 200 meter hurdles.

The 440 yard intermediate hurdles gained popularity slowly in the United States. The event was not included in the NCAA Championships except on Olympic years until 1959, and it was not until 1963 that the intermediate hurdles replaced the 220 low hurdles in college track meets. In spite of this lack of emphasis, Americans have dominated the event in world competition since its beginning.

The mid 1950s saw the rise of three great intermediate hurdlers, Glenn Davis and Eddie Southern of the United States and Gert Potgieter of South Africa. Davis and Southern dualed frequently and were the first competitors to break the 50-second barrier. In 1956 Davis barely beat Southern in a time of 49.5 at the United States Olympic trials, but both competitors were under the 50-second mark.

At the 1968 Olympics in Mexico City, it became evident that the finals of the 400 meter hurdles would be one of the most spectacular hurdle races in history. The spread of winning times of the four heats was less

119

than one second.  The fastest heat was won by American Ron Whitney in a record time of 49.0 seconds and the slowest heat was won by Italy's Roberto Frinolli in 49.9 seconds.  However, in the semifinals Frinolli had run 49.2 and Gerhardt Henninge of West Germany ran 49.1.  Thus all of the eight finalists had run 49.6 or better in the preliminary races.  When the final race was over a young American named Dave Hemery had established himself as the new Olympic champion and the world record holder with a remarkable time of 48.1 seconds for the metric distance.

Soon after the 1968 Olympics Ralph Mann and Wayne Collett of the United States became the top intermediate hurdlers.  They had dualed each other consistently since their high school days for supremacy in the various hurdle races.  This rivalry came to a climax in the NCAA finals in 1970 when Mann barely edged Collett at the tape to become national champion and the new world record holder for the 440 yard distance with a time of 48.8 seconds.  Collett finished in 49.2 seconds, also breaking the existing world record.

In the 1972 Olympics John Akii-Bua of Uganda became the world champion for the 400 meter distance when he won the race at the Olympics in a remarkable world record time of 47.8 seconds.  Ralph Mann of the United States was second.

To help the reader better visualize the evolution of progress made by intermediate hurdlers, listings of the world records are presented.

### 440 Yard Intermediate Hurdles

| Time | Record-holder and country | Year |
|------|---------------------------|------|
| 57.2s. | Godfrey Shaw, Great Britain | 1891 |
| 56.8s. | George Anderson, Great Britain | 1910 |
| 54.2s. | John Norton, U.S.A. | 1920 |
| 54.2s. | Lord Burghley, Great Britain | 1927 |
| 52.6s. | John Gibson, U.S.A. | 1927 |
| 52.2s. | Roy Cochran, U.S.A. | 1942 |
| 52.2s. | Richard Ault, U.S.A. | 1949 |
| 51.9s. | Armando Filiput, Italy | 1950 |
| 51.9s. | Charles Moore Jr., U.S.A. | 1952 |
| 51.6s. | Charles Moore Jr., U.S.A. | 1952 |
| 51.3s. | Yuri Lituyev, U.S.S.R. | 1954 |
| 50.7s. | G. C. Potgieter, South Africa | 1957 |
| 49.9s. | Glenn Davis, U.S.A. | 1958 |
| 49.7s. | Gert Potgieter, South Africa | 1958 |
| 49.3s. | Gert Potgieter, South Africa | 1960 |
| 48.8s. | Ralph Mann, U.S.A. | 1970 |

### 400 Meter Intermediate Hurdles

| Time | Record-holder and country | Year |
|------|---------------------------|------|
| 57.6s. | Walter Tewksbury, U.S.A. | 1900 |
| 55s. | Charles Bacon, U.S.A. | 1908 |
| 54s. | Frank Loomis, U.S.A. | 1920 |
| 53.8s. | Sten Pettersson, Sweden | 1925 |
| 52s. | Morgan Taylor, U.S.A. | 1928 |
| 52s. | Glenn Hardin, U.S.A. | 1932 |
| 51.8s. | Glenn Hardin, U.S.A. | 1934 |
| 50.6s. | Glenn Hardin, U.S.A. | 1934 |
| 50.4s. | Yuri Lituyev, U.S.S.R. | 1953 |
| 49.5s. | Glenn Davis, U.S.A. | 1956 |
| 49.2s. | Glenn Davis, U.S.A. | 1958 |
| 49.2s. | Salvatore Morale, Italy | 1962 |
| 49.1s. | Rex Cawley, U.S.A. | 1964 |
| 48.1s. | Dave Hemery, U.S.A. | 1968 |
| 47.8s. | John Akii-Bua, Uganda | 1972 |

### PROCEDURE

The 440 yard hurdler runs completely around a quarter mile track and clears 10 hurdles in the process. Each hurdle is 36 inches high. The first hurdle is placed 147'9" from the starting mark and the last hurdle is 139'6" from the finish line. There is a distance of 114'9" between hurdles. When the metric distance is run (400 meters) the first hurdle is 45 meters from the start, the last hurdle 40 meters from the finish line and the hurdles are 35 meters apart.

The hurdler starts from a crouched position the same as a sprinter. Ordinarily the hurdler will take 21 or 22 steps to the first hurdle and 13, 14 or 15 steps between hurdles. Mature hurdlers usually take 13 steps between the first five or six hurdles, then 14 or 15 steps between the remainder of the hurdles. A hurdler may knock over any number of his hurdles without being disqualified. Each contestant must run in his own lane the total distance of the race.

### INTERMEDIATE HURDLING TECHNIQUE

The intermediate hurdle race is similar to the flat 440 in the sense that it requires fast running speed and the ability to run at near top speed for the full distance of the race. However, it differs from the flat 440 in at least two respects. First, the hurdler must clear 10 barriers during the race and lose as little time as possible while doing so, and second he must adjust his step pattern to position himself correctly for each hurdle. The hurdler is not as free to alter his speed during the race as the flat 440 runner because the alteration of speed may disrupt the step pattern and prove disastrous for the hurdler.

The hurdling action used in going over an intermediate hurdle is essentially the same as that described for high hurdling (see Chapter 6), except in intermediate hurdling the actions are slightly less accentuated because the hurdle is six inches lower. Another difference is that the intermediate hurdler must learn to clear hurdles effectively while running around a curve. Relative to this there is some advantage to leading with the inside leg because while running around the curve the hurdler must lean into the curve to combat centrifugal force, and if he leads with the outside leg while doing this it is difficult for the trail leg to clear the hurdle.

#### To the First Hurdle

Most mature hurdlers use either 21 or 22 strides to the first hurdle. In the 1968 Olympics, six of the eight finalists used 21 strides. The other two used 22. It is interesting that the two taking 22 strides had the fastest times to the first hurdle. They were Frinolli with a time of 5.8 seconds and Vanderstock with a time of 5.9. The other six hurdlers had times ranging between 6.0 and 6.1. Ralph Mann, the current world record holder uses 22 strides, and on his record breaking effort he ran 5.9 seconds to the first

FIG. 7–1. World record holder Ralph Mann (440 yard hurdles) shows excellent form during the acceleration phase of the race.

hurdle. Among top-flight hurdlers it is usually considered that 6.5 is too slow while 6.2 or less is a possible record-breaking pace.

It is desirable for the hurdler to be able to use the starting technique of his choice and to start the same as he would if he were running a flat 440. However, this is not always possible because sometimes he must adjust the placement of his feet in the blocks and the length of his initial strides in order to place himself in the correct position to take the first hurdle. The placement of the feet in the blocks and the correct number of steps to the first hurdle can only be worked out by repeated starts from the blocks over the first one or two hurdles. It is not a difficult task but it does take much time and many repetitions. (See Figure 7–1.)

### Over the First Hurdle

The first hurdle is no more important than the other nine, but it usually requires more concentration to take the first hurdle with correct form because the hurdler is making the transition from the acceleration phase, and often has not hit a smooth and even stride prior to the hurdle. Taking the first hurdle is further complicated by the fact that the hurdle is on the turn, making it difficult for the athlete to clear the hurdle without losing balance. On the first hurdle it is especially important that the hurdler stay close to the inside of his lane, stay low on the hurdle, maintain good balance, and bring the trail leg through into a full running stride in order that he will not experience difficulty in his step pattern to the second hurdle (Figure 7–2).

### Strides Between Hurdles

Currently some of the world's best intermediate hurdlers are using 13 strides as far as possible (usually six hurdles) and then 15 strides between the remaining hurdles. The old pattern of 15 strides between hurdles throughout the race resulted in most of the better athletes chopping during the first half of the race. They were not able to stride out in a free and effortless fashion. It is believed that in the future some of the taller hurdlers will be able to develop enough endurance to take 13 strides between hurdles throughout the race, and that other good hurdlers will take 13 strides during the first part of the race, then use 14 strides during the latter part. (When 14, or any even number of strides are used between hurdles, the athlete must lead with right and left legs alternately.) The authors believe that when an athlete is learning to hurdle, he should use the fewest strides possible between hurdles. When an athlete is close to 13, 14 or 15 strides but cannot achieve it, and if he is fairly new in the event, he should be pushed toward fewer steps rather than allowing him to use the larger number which might be more convenient at the time. This approach was used with Ralph Mann and within a one-year period he was able to take the first six hurdles in 13 strides rather than 15.

FIG. 7–2 (a–h). Sequence drawings of correct hurdling technique for the intermediate hurdlers.

In summary it can be said that the athlete should learn to hurdle with as few strides as possible between hurdles and still run with a smooth and natural stride. He should not chop and neither should he overextend his stride. If possible, he should run with the same kind of stride that he would use in a flat 440. This might result in 13, 14 or 15 strides between hurdles. If it results in 14 strides then the hurdler must learn to alternate effectively.

### Changing Stride Pattern

Most mature hurdlers change their stride patterns after the sixth hurdle from 13 to 15 strides. This is prompted by fatigue which makes it impossible for the hurdler to continue with the same length stride as used during the early part of the race. The change in stride, combined with the onset of fatigue invariably results in a slowing down at that point in the race. However, the slowdown must be minimal and is often not apparent. It is very important that the hurdler try to maintain his speed during this transition.

### The Finish

Some hurdlers make the mistake of breaking their form over the last hurdle in an effort to enter into the sprint too soon. It is essential that the hurdler take the last hurdle in as near perfect form as possible and that he come off the hurdle into a good sprint position (Figure 7–3). He then sprints with all the energy that remains in him and continues the sprint through the tape.

## APPLICATION OF SCIENTIFIC PRINCIPLES

The same principles apply to hurdling action over the intermediate hurdles as over the high hurdle. Therefore, refer to the section on scientific principles in Chapter 6. The only additional principle that relates to intermediate hurdling has to do with centrifugal force, because several of the hurdles must be taken while running around a curve. Centrifugal force tends to cause the hurdler to drift to the outside of his lane while going over the hurdle and sometimes causes him to lose balance in the outward direction. To combat these tendencies the hurdler must go over the hurdle in a direction that will cause him to land close to the inside of his running lane, and at the same time he must lean into the turn a sufficient amount to combat the centrifugal force that would tend to pull him off balance in the outward direction. Because the body leans inward, it is an advantage for the hurdler to lead with the left leg because if he leads with the right leg it is difficult for the trail leg to clear the hurdle when the body is inclined inward.

## COMMON FAULTS AND HOW TO CORRECT THEM

The common faults stated in the chapter on high hurdling also apply to intermediate hurdling. Therefore, the reader should refer to the section on

FIG. 7–3. Ralph Mann clearing an intermediate hurdle in good form. His one fault in this case is that he is too high over the hurdle.

common faults in Chapter 6. In addition to the faults stated in that chapter, the following information is especially important about intermediate hurdling:

### Importance of Correct Hurdling Technique

Many coaches and athletes think that hurdling form is of only minor importance in the intermediate hurdles while speed for the 440 yard distance is the primary consideration. It is true that speed over 440 yards is fundamental to success, but the notion that hurdling technique is of minor importance is a serious error. Unless the hurdler is able to clear each hurdle quickly and smoothly causing little interference with his running stride, he will find it necessary to regain balance and to accelerate after each hurdle. It is the smooth flowing passage over the hurdle which allows the maintenance of rhythm and speed and the conservation of energy. Lack of expert hurdling form results in 1) too much time getting over the hurdle; 2) too much energy getting over the hurdle; and 3) loss of drive coming off the hurdle. If a hurdler loses 0.1 second due to poor technique, and if this is repeated over 10 hurdles, obviously the hurdler will run a second slower than he otherwise would.

A performer who has expert hurdling form should be able to run the intermediate hurdles within about two seconds of his best 440 yard time. Table 7–1 found near the end of this chapter shows that Ralph Mann has a differential of only 2.2 seconds between his best flat 440 time and his world record intermediate hurdle time. Of the other world-caliber hurdlers listed in that table one has even a smaller differential than Mann, while the others have slightly larger differentials.

The film of Mann's world record performance clearly illustrates his smooth flowing action over every hurdle. Wayne Collett, a super-speedster who ran second in that race, staggered badly coming off the fourth, fifth, and ninth hurdles and never totally regained his momentum after coming off the ninth hurdle. Simply stated, good form permits the athlete to maintain his speed, while bad form reduces the speed.

The best way to learn correct hurdling form is to work over high hurdles. High hurdles magnify all hurdling flaws and permit the athlete and coach to identify weaknesses in the hurdling form and then correct those weaknesses. Once good form is developed over high hurdles it is a simple matter to adjust to intermediate hurdling. Correct technique over the high hurdles is explained and illustrated in Chapter 6.

### Standardized Step Patterns are Essential

A second common error is to assume that running speed is of paramount importance while standardized step patterns do not require serious attention. Expert hurdlers and knowledgeable coaches know that a hurdler must have a definite plan relative to step patterns and that he must consistently follow the plan. The number of steps to the first hurdle and between hurdles will be determined by the length of stride of the athlete. Even though many mature hurdlers are able to run the first part of the race with 13 strides between hurdles and the latter part with 14 or 15 strides, younger and less experienced hurdlers will need to use a larger number of strides. Most inexperienced hurdlers use 15 strides during the first part of the race, then switching to 17 during the latter part. They work toward reducing their strides to 13 and 15. Regardless of the number of steps used, it takes much concentration and practice to perfect the pattern.

### The Hips Must Be Kept Square

Another error unique to intermediate hurdling is failure to keep the hips square with the hurdle while hurdling around a curve. This error is magnified by hurdlers who lead with the left leg. If the hips are not kept square, it causes the hurdler to head in the wrong direction as he goes over the hurdle and he lands in the outside of his lane. Correction of this error requires concentration on keeping the hips square and forcing the lead leg to land close to the inside of the lane. Sometimes it is helpful to place a spot on the track where the lead foot should land. This gives the hurdler a target to shoot at.

### Good Form Must Be Maintained

Often too little attention is given to the development of good form over the last two or three hurdles when fatigue becomes a serious factor. Since it is neither convenient nor feasible to run full flights of 440 yard hurdles during practice, it is recommended that the athlete run 440, 550 or 660 yard runs with two or three hurdles to be cleared during the last phase of each run. This can be done repeatedly during a single workout. This procedure teaches the hurdler to hold good hurdling form when fatigued, and it gives him a chance to concentrate on running in a relaxed fashion during the first portion of the run and then practice going over hurdles during the last portion. Running relaxed is extremely important to a 440 yard hurdler because it helps him to run with a minimal amount of energy. As the hurdler begins to experience fatigue his form tends to deteriorate so that the smooth, flowing action over the hurdle is lost. He tends to go higher over the hurdle in order to clear it, and he tends to land with a jarring action, causing a loss of momentum and balance. The body tends to have insufficient forward lean. All of these conditions result in loss of acceleration, which the athlete must attempt to regain between hurdles. Thus, it is apparent that maintaining good hurdling form is essential even when the athlete is fatigued.

## THE RACE PLAN

Regardless of how strong or weak the competition might be in a particular race, it is recommended that the first half of the race be run at or near top racing speed. Should the hurdler desire to ease up in order to save energy for subsequent races, this should be done over the second half of the race. Also, by running the first half of the race at or near maximum racing speed there is little chance that he will be behind a weaker opponent at this point who might be running a better race than expected. Conditioning, hurdling skill and stride pattern tell the difference from this point on.

It must be emphasized here that failure to concentrate on one's own race and being overconcerned about the other runners can be disastrous because lack of concentration can result in irregular step patterns and poor hurdling form. This is especially true toward the end of the race as fatigue increases. In summary the hurdler should:

1. Concentrate on getting a fast start and hitting the first hurdle in the prescribed time.

2. Run relaxed but at near maximum racing speed past the 220 yard mark.

3. During the second half of the race concentrate even more on relaxation in order to conserve energy and to keep from tying up.

4. Toward the end of the race, as the feeling of fatigue becomes more intense, concentrate even more on the correct step pattern and good hurdling form. It is essential that the hurdler maintain good form throughout the race.

5. Make a point to come off the 10th hurdle in good sprint position and then make an all-out effort, if such effort is desired and necessary, from there to a point beyond the tape.

## STRIDE PATTERN

Any serious consideration of intermediate hurdling must include a review of the stride patterns between hurdles by former champions. Unfortunately the records are very incomplete but some light can be shed on the subject by reviewing the information that is available. Following Hemery's world record at the 1968 Olympics in Mexico City, athletes, coaches and sports writers seemed amazed at the fact that he took the first six hurdles in 13 strides and the remainder in 15 strides. Some writers praised his bravery to employ such daring and novel strategy. But, his stride pattern was not as novel as many believed, because other outstanding hurdlers had experimented frequently with various patterns.

In 1950 Armando Filiput, an Italian, broke the world record for the 440 yard hurdles with a time of 51.9. The amazing Italian is credited with using 17 strides all the way. It seems reasonable that Filiput would have run a faster race if he had used 15 strides during the first portion of the race and 17 during the latter portion.

Charles Moore, the 1952 Olympic champion, employed 13 strides all the way in recording a 50.8 victory. Some authorities have suggested that he might have been more relaxed using 15 strides and could possibly have run the race faster. Second to Moore at Helsinki was a Russian, Yuri Lituyev, who employed 13 strides to the eighth hurdle and 15 strides from there on. In 1953 he used this pattern to set a world record of 50.4. It is interesting that beginning in 1954 he used 13 strides throughout all of his races.

The two Olympic wins by Glenn Davis in 1956 and 1960 provided an interesting contrast. In 1956 he used 13 strides up to the seventh hurdle, then 17 strides from there on. His 200 meter splits were 22.7 and 27.4. At the Rome Olympics in 1960 he ran 15 all the way and recorded a victory of 49.3. His splits were 24.0 and 25.3. In 1958 he raced to a world record at Budapest with a time of 49.2, using 15 strides all the way. A combination of strides which David never did emphasize is 13 strides during the first portion of the race and 15 during the last part. Based on the other combinations which he used, it seems that he could have done the 13–15 combination, and this might have produced better results for him than any other stride pattern.

Gert Potgieter of South Africa showed a different step pattern in setting his world mark in 1960. Although he was only 5′11″ tall, he ran 13 steps to the third hurdle and 14 steps thereafter. He strongly advocated that mature hurdlers should learn to alternate, but to date few of the other champions have taken his advice. The authors agree strongly with Potgieter's suggestion that intermediate hurdlers learn to alternate. John Akii-Bua proved the value of this when he alternated very effectively while setting a new world record in the 1972 Olympics.

Probably one factor that has influenced the stride pattern during recent years is the consistency of synthetic tracks which are now used for practically all large meets. A hurdler can now train to use 13 strides, at least during a portion of the race, with more assurance that he will be running on a track where his footing will be firm and his stride will not become disrupted as a result of the track surface.

Of the eight Olympic finalists at Mexico City in 1968, six used 13 strides for the first six hurdles and 15 for the remainder of the race, while the other two used 15 strides all the way. Wes Williams of San Diego State University has used 13 strides throughout his racing career. At the NCAA Championships in 1969 he was second in 49.7, and in 1970 he was third in 50.4. At the AAU Championships in 1971 he was second in 49.3. All of these races were won by Ralph Mann who employed 13 strides for six hurdles and 15 thereon. Films show that during 1969 and 1970 Williams had to overstride during the last three or four hurdles, but by 1971 he improved his striding technique so that he could take 13 strides throughout the race more conveniently. During the 1971 AAU Championships, Mann led by five yards at the seventh hurdle. Mann changed to 15 strides between the sixth and seventh hurdle and from that point on, Williams, who maintained 13 strides, cut into the five-yard lead. At the tape they were so even that the announcer called Williams the winner. But the photo finish showed that Mann won the race even though both competitors had a time of 49.3

In intermediate hurdling one thing is certain: maintaining momentum is of paramount importance. Both overstriding and chopping tend to slow the runner. Therefore, it is essential that the correct step pattern be worked out and consistently followed. Because hurdlers vary in length of stride, running power and endurance, it is not possible to recommend a best step pattern for all hurdlers. This is an individual matter which must be worked out as a result of much practice and experimentation. Also, it is not sound to assume that a particular step pattern will be best for any hurdler indefinitely. As a hurdler experiences changes in the length of stride, running power and endurance, his step pattern should be adjusted accordingly. It is very important that at any given time in the hurdler's development his step pattern be the one that will produce the best results; it is known that the pattern will need to be adjusted as he develops from a beginning to a seasoned and mature hurdler. Even after he has matured he must continue to experiment with minor changes in step patterns and hurdling form.

### 220 Yard Splits

Physiologically the best way to run an intermediate hurdle race is with an even effort throughout the total distance of the race, and evidence indicates that many of the outstanding intermediate hurdlers are coming close to doing this. The differentials between the first and second 220 for many of the world caliber hurdlers is 1.6 seconds or less. This is probably close enough to be considered an even effort throughout the race. The closest splits have been turned in by Ron Whitney and Clifford Cushman who had differentials of 0.6 seconds, and both used 15 strides throughout the race. There is evidence that they both ran the first 220 too slowly because the 15 strides caused them to chop during the first part of the race. Probably this accounts for the small differential between the first and second 220s.

It is known that the differential between the 220 splits is influenced significantly by 1) the stride patterns; 2) the endurance of the athlete; and 3) his ability to hold good hurdling form during the latter part of the race. Also it is known that when a hurdler changes from 13 to 15 strides this will slow him down, thus increasing the differential between the splits. Because of these facts it is theorized that the more successful hurdlers in the future will have small differentials between the splits, and they will achieve this by running either 13 strides all the way or 13 strides during the first portion of the race and 14 strides (requiring alternation) during the latter portion. It is strongly recommended that mature hurdlers who are using the 13–15 stride combination develop the ability to alternate and change to a 13–14 stride combination. Some of the hurdlers who have unusual power and

## TABLE 7–1
### Comparative Facts About Ten Outstanding Intermediate Hurdle Racers

| Name and Country | Step Pattern | IH Time | 1st Half Time | 2nd Half Time | Best Quarter-mile Time | Differential IH and 440 |
|---|---|---|---|---|---|---|
| Ralph Mann, U.S.A. | 13×6* | 48.8† | 23.7 | 25.1 | 46.6† | 2.2 |
| Wayne Collett, U.S.A. | 13×5 | 49.2† | 23.5 | 25.7 | 44.7† | 4.5 |
| Wes Williams, U.S.A. | 13 all | 49.3† | 23.5 | 25.8 | 46.8† | 2.5 |
| Rainer Schubert, Germany | 13×6* | 49.2 | 23.7 | 25.5 | 46.3ᴿ | 2.9 |
| Ron Whitney, U.S.A. | 15 all | 49.2 | 24.3 | 24.9 | 46.8 | 2.4 |
| John Sherwood, England | 13×6* | 49.0 | 23.7 | 25.3 | 46.0ᴿ | 3.0 |
| Gerhard Hennige, Germany | 13×6* | 49.0 | 23.8 | 25.2 | 46.5 | 2.5 |
| Dave Hemery, England | 13×6* | 48.1 | 23.3 | 24.8 | 45.1ᴿ | 3.0 |
| Glenn Davis, U.S.A. | 15 all | 49.3 | 24.0 | 25.3 | 45.5 | 3.8 |
| Salvatore Morale, Italy | 15 all | 49.2 | 23.9 | 25.3 | 47.6 | 1.6 |

* 13×6 means that 13 strides were taken between hurdles through the 6th hurdle.  It is understood that the hurdler then changed to 15 strides.
† 440-yard race—all others 400 meter hurdles
ᴿ Relay

132

endurance should strive for 13 strides throughout the race, as has been done by Wes Williams.

The following table illustrates some details of the running fetes of some of history's greatest intermediate hurdlers. It shows the flat running speed of such sprinters as Wayne Collett and Jean-Claude Nallet (20.6 seconds for 200 meters) as compared with Ralph Mann, who has a best of 21.8 for that distance. Their 400 meter times show similar advantages over the 400 meter time by Mann.

Collett and Nallett achieved their intermediate hurdling excellence as a result of their superior speed, while Mann achieved his excellence primarily as a result of his running power, his endurance and his excellent form over the hurdles. Some day someone will combine the speed of Collett and Nallett with the strong points of Mann and run the intermediate hurdles in 46 seconds or better. In order to accomplish this, the first 220 will have to be completed in about 22.7 seconds, and the differential between the 220 splits would have to be unusually small.

## THE TRAINING SCHEDULE

The following is a recommended training schedule for a mature and experienced hurdler. It can serve as an important guide but will need to be adjusted to fit the needs of a particular athlete because of differences in age, maturity and state of conditioning among athletes.

### Summer

During the summer the intermediate hurdler should maintain a high level of general conditioning by participating regularly in vigorous running and jumping activities. These activities might include field and court games in addition to play-type (fartlek) running. The athlete should also do a limited amount of work over hurdles. The running activities should be supplemented by specific exercises to maintain power in the muscles involved the most in running and hurdling. (See the recommended exercises at the end of this chapter.)

### Fall

During the fall the intermediate hurdler should do a considerable amount of running involving both cross country and wind-sprints. Also, he should spend some time working on hurdling technique. The exercise program should be continued and the intensity should be increased.

### Winter

Monday:
1. Jog one-half mile.
2. Do 10–15 minutes of stretching exercises emphasizing hurdling actions.
3. Run eight 100-yard acceleration sprints.
4. Run six 110s at near full speed.

5. Work over the hurdles for 15 minutes leading with both the left and right leg.
6. Jog one mile.
7. Weight train (see exercises at the end of this chapter).

Tuesday:     1. Jog one-half mile.
2. Do stretching exercises.
3. Run eight 100-yard acceleration sprints.
4. Run four 110s at near top speed.
5. Work over the hurdles for 15 minutes.
6. Run five 660s.
7. Jog one mile.

Wednesday:   Do the same as Monday.

Thursday:    1. Jog one-half mile.
2. Do 10–15 minutes of stretching exercises.
3. Run eight 100-yard acceleration sprints.
4. Run six 110s at near full speed.
5. Work on hurdling form.
6. Run eight 330s in 39–40 seconds each.
7. Do two to three miles of cross country.

Friday:      1. Jog one-half mile.
2. Do stretching exercises.
3. Run eight 100-yard acceleration sprints.
4. Run six 110s at near top speed.
5. Work on hurdling form.
6. Run ten 220s at 26–27 seconds each.
7. Jog one mile.

Saturday:    1. Run four to six miles of cross country.
2. Weight train.

### Spring (Early and Middle Portion)

Monday:      1. Jog one-half mile.
2. Do 10–15 minutes of stretching exercises emphasizing hurdling actions.
3. Run ten 100-yard acceleration sprints.
4. Run four 110s at near top speed.
5. Work on hurdling form with emphasis on leading with both the right and left legs.
6. Run five acceleration quarters (second 220 faster than the first).
7. Jog one mile.
8. Weight train.

Tuesday:     1. Jog one-half mile.
2. Do stretching exercises.
3. Run ten 100-yard acceleration sprints.
4. Run six 110s at near top speed.
5. Work on hurdling form.
6. Run three 600s.
7. Jog one mile.

Wednesday:   1. Jog one-half mile.
2. Do stretching exercises.
3. Run six 100-yard acceleration sprints.
4. Run six 110s at near top speed.
5. Work on hurdling form.

Thursday:
    6. Run eight 220s in about 26 seconds each (the first three over hurdles).
    7. Jog one mile.
    8. Weight train.

Thursday:
    1. Jog one-half mile.
    2. Do stretching exercises.
    3. Run eight 100-yard acceleration sprints.
    4. Run four 110s at near top speed.
    5. Work on hurdling form.
    6. Run six 150s at near top speed around the curve.
    7. Jog one mile

Friday:     Easy workout involving jogging and exercises, or complete rest.

Saturday:
    1. Prepare for competition—arrive at the meet in plenty of time for adequate preparation. Have your race plan clearly in mind and follow it.
    2. Weight train.

### Late Spring (May–June)

During this phase of the season the hurdler will ordinarily do the same kind of training as mid-season. The intensity of the training schedule might be increased depending on whether the athlete shows any signs of staleness.

## CONDITIONING EXERCISES

Like the high hurdler, the intermediate hurdler must have a high level of power, especially in the leg muscles, and he must be highly flexible. The procedures for developing power and flexibility are explained in Chapter 1.

The recommended exercises are listed below, and they are illustrated in Appendix A.

Straight arm forward raise—exercise #1
Trunk flexion—exercise #14
Trunk lateral flexion—exercise #17
Trunk extension—exercise #18
Trunk rotation (supine)—exercise #15
Leg raise (supine)—exercise #25
Leg raise (high bar)—exercise #26
Leg press—exercise #20
Jumping jack—exercise #21
Heel raise—exercise #23
Quadriceps drill—exercise #24
Hip flexion—exercise #27

CHAPTER **8**

# Relay Races

The origin of relay racing is uncertain but probably it was practiced on a limited basis as early as the ancient Greek era. During modern times relay racing became popularized late in the nineteenth century.

The oldest continuous relay carnival still in existence is the Penn Relays held annually at historic Franklin Field in Philadelphia. The carnival started in 1895 with a meet consisting of nine relays alternated with the regular program of track and field events. These nine relays were each one mile with only two teams in each race.

Relays first became a part of the Olympic program at London in 1908 in the form of a medley relay where the four men on each team ran the following distances: 220, 220, 440 and 880 yards. In the 1912 Olympics at Stockholm the 400 meter relay and the 1600 meter relay (one mile when run in yards) were added, while the medley relay was dropped from the program.

Originally each runner had to be touched off from a stationary start. A closed exchange zone was first introduced in 1926. Since then it has been required that the baton be exchanged inside the 22 yard zone.

The most popular relays today are the 440 yard (400 meter) relay and the mile relay (1600 meters), and these are the only two relays included in the Olympic program. However, other relays are included in relay carnivals and as special events in certain track meets. The evolution of world records, which is presented here for certain relays, will help the reader to better understand the progress that has been made in relays in the past several decades.

### 440 Yard Relay

| Time | Record-holder and country | Year |
|---|---|---|
| 42.8s. | United States National Team . . . . . . . | 1919 |
| 42.4s. | New York A.C., U.S.A. . | 1921 |
| 42.4s. | U. of Illinois, U.S.A.. . . | 1923 |
| 42s. | U. of California, U.S.A. . | 1925 |

| 41s. | Newark A.C., U.S.A. . . . 1927 |
| 40.8s. | U. of Southern California, U.S.A.. . . . . . . . 1931 |
| 40.5s. | U. of Southern California, U.S.A.. . . . . . . . 1938 |
| 40.2s. | U. of Texas, U.S.A. . . . 1955 |

| 39.9s. | U. of Texas, U.S.A. . . . 1957 |
| 39.7s. | Abilene Christian College, U.S.A.. . . . . . . . 1958 |
| 39.6s. | U. of Texas, U.S.A. . . . 1959 |
| 39.6s. | Southern U., U.S.A. . . . 1966 |
| 38.6s. | U. of Southern California, U.S.A. . . . . . . . 1967 |

## 400 Meter Relay

| Time | Record-holder and country | Year |
|---|---|---|
| 42.3s. | German National Team | 1912 |
| 42.2s. | United States National Team . . . . . . . . | 1920 |
| 42s. | British National Team . . | 1924 |
| 42s. | Dutch National Team . . | 1924 |
| 41s. | United States National Team . . . . . . . . | 1924 |
| 41s. | United States National Team . . . . . . . . | 1924 |
| 41s. | Newark A.C., U.S.A. . . . | 1927 |
| 41s. | Sp. C. Eintracht, Germany | 1928 |
| 40.8s. | German National Team . | 1928 |
| 40.8s. | Sp. C. Charlottenburg, Germany . . . . . . | 1929 |
| 40.8s. | U. of California, U.S.A. . | 1931 |

| 40s. | United States National Team . . . . . . . . 1932 |
| 39.8s. | United States National Team . . . . . . . . 1936 |
| 39.5s. | United States National Team . . . . . . . . 1956 |
| 39.5s. | German National Team . 1958 |
| 39.5s. | German National Team . 1960 |
| 39.5s. | German National Team . 1960 |
| 39.1s. | United States National Team . . . . . . . . 1961 |
| 39s. | United States National Team . . . . . . . . 1964 |
| 38.2s. | United States National Team . . . . . . . . 1968 |
| 38.2s. | United States National Team . . . . . . . . 1972 |

## 1 Mile Relay

| Time | Record-holder and country | Year |
|---|---|---|
| 3m. 18.2s. | United States National Team . . | 1911 |
| 3m. 18s. | U. of Pennsylvania, U.S.A.. . . . . . | 1915 |
| 3m. 16.4s. | American Legion, Pennsylvania, U.S.A.. . . . . . | 1921 |
| 3m. 13.4s. | United States National Team . . | 1928 |
| 3m. 12.6s. | Stanford U., U.S.A. . | 1931 |
| 3m. 11.6s. | U. of California, U.S.A.. . . . . . | 1936 |

| 3m. 10.5s. | Stanford U., U.S.A. . | 1940 |
| 3m. 9.4s. | U. of California, U.S.A.. . . . . . | 1941 |
| 3m. 8.8s. | United States National Team . . | 1952 |
| 3m. 7.3s. | United States National Team . . | 1956 |
| 3m. 5.6s. | United States National Team . . | 1960 |
| 3m. 4.5s. | Arizona State, U.S.A. | 1963 |
| 3m. 4.5s. | Southern T.C., U.S.A. | 1965 |
| 3m. 2.8s. | Trinidad National Team . . . . . | 1966 |

## 1600 Meter Relay

| Time | Record-holder and country | Year |
|---|---|---|
| 3m. 18.2s. | United States National Team . . | 1911 |
| 3m. 16.6s. | United States National Team . . | 1912 |
| 3m. 16.4s. | American Legion, Pennsylvania, U.S.A.. . . . . . | 1921 |

| 3m. 16s. | United States National Team . . | 1924 |
| 3m. 14.2s. | United States National Team . . | 1928 |
| 3m. 13.4s. | United States National Team . . | 1924 |
| 3m. 12.6s. | Stanford U., U.S.A. . | 1931 |
| 3m. 8.2s. | United States National Team . . | 1932 |

| 3m. 3.9s. | Jamaican National Team . . . . . 1952 | 3m. 00.7s. | United States National Team . . 1964 |
| 3m. 2.2s. | United States National Team . . 1960 | 2m. 59.6s. | United States National Team . . 1966 |
| 3m. 1.6s. | Great Britain-Northern Ireland National Team . . 1964 | 2m. 56.1s. | United States National Team . . 1968 |

## RELAY TECHNIQUE

In 1965 at Fresno, California, a Stanford University team set a world record of 39.7 in the 440 yard relay. It was described as the most perfect series of exchanges ever witnessed. Eric Frische, Dale Rubin, Bob Mac-Intyre and Larry Questad left nothing to be desired as they ran a near perfect race. Each exchange achieved maximum advantage and with such perfection it was inevitable that the record would fall. This race illustrated the essence of effective baton exchanges in relay racing, especially in the sprint relays. Stanford had only one great sprinter, Questad, who ran 9.3 earlier in the evening in the open 100. The other three members of the team were adequate sprinters but not superior. Their life-time bests were: Frische—9.5, Rubin—9.6 and MacIntyre—9.8. Earlier in the evening they had run the flat 100 in 9.7, 9.8 and 9.9 respectively. The sum of their times in the flat 100 equalled 38.7 (for 400 yards). The additional 40 yards would take about 3.6 seconds for a total of 42.3 for the quarter. Add 0.3 second each for the two legs run on a curve for a total of 42.9. Then subtract 0.3 second for the distance gained on the three near-perfect exchanges and subtract 0.9 second for each of the three running starts and this gives a net of 39.6. They achieved 39.7, and thus came very close to their maximum potential. The components used in this analysis are not exact, but they are close enough to illustrate the fact that the Stanford University team ran a near-perfect race.

Using a similar analysis, it can be seen that the American Olympic team which set a 400 meter relay record at the 1968 Olympics in 38.2, did not come nearly so close to their potential. All four members of that team had recorded their lifetime best marks for the 100 meter distance either in the games or just prior to the games. Their individual times were as follows: Charlie Greene—9.9, Mel Pender—10.0, Ronnie Ray Smith—10.0, Jim Haines—9.9 (100 meter distance). The sum of their four times was 39.8 for 400 meters. By adding 0.3 second for each leg run on the curve, subtracting 0.3 second for the distance gained on each of three near-perfect passes and subtracting 0.9 second for each of the three running starts, the team had a potential of 37.1. Their world record effort was well off their potential at 38.2.

The Cuban team, which was second in that race at 38.3, had a theoretical potential of 37.9, which means the Cubans ran closer to their potential than the Americans. On that same occasion the French team was third in 38.4

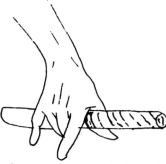

Fig. 8–1. Correct technique of holding the baton during the start.

as they ran the most perfect sprint relay on record. Based on the analysis, their potential was 38.4, the same time that they achieved.

It can be seen that baton exchanges can easily determine which team wins the race. This is especially so in short relays. As a result of efficient baton passing, teams with inferior sprinters are often able to beat other teams that have more inherent speed.

## BATON PASSING TECHNIQUE

According to the rules, the baton must be passed, it cannot be thrown, and the exchange must take place within a 20 meter (22 yard) passing zone. The international exchange zone allows the waiting member to stand 10 meters (11 yards) in front of the passing zone in both the 440 and 880 yard relays.

It is recommended that the leadoff man starts the race holding the baton in his right hand (Figure 8–1). He runs as close along the inside of his lane as possible and exchanges to the left hand of the second man. The second man passes the baton to the right hand of the third man who runs the inside of the lane to exchange to the left hand of the anchor man, who is in the outside of the lane during the exchange. Following the exchange, the baton should not be changed from one hand to the other by the carrier. If possible, the necessity of adjusting the baton in the hand should be avoided because such adjustments require both hands and this interferes with the rhythm of the sprint.

Basic to a proficient exchange is a *set line*, a *go line* and a *voice command*. The receiving runner places two marks on the track. The first is the set line and the second is the go line. When the incoming runner hits the set line the receiver prepares for his start, and when the runner reaches the go line the receiver begins his sprint. When the receiver goes into motion he should sprint with an all-out effort. Anything less than this will result in variations which cause the exchange to be inconsistent and unpredictable. It is essential to get into high gear as quickly as possible.

The baton exchange is completed in one stride, and the incoming runner is responsible for determining the moment of exchange. When he sees that he is close enough to hand off he gives the voice command *"hand."* The receiving runner on the next backward swing of the arm aims the hand directly backward, turning the palm upward so that the thumb is toward the inside. With deliberate action the incoming runner places the baton downward into the open hand of the receiver (Figure 8–2). The exchange is completed, and the hand with the baton goes forward with the next running stride.

If the exchange is missed, time will undoubtedly be lost, but the exchange is attempted again on the next backward movement of the receiver's hand. It is of utmost importance that the exchange not be missed on the first attempt. Adequate practice will safeguard against this. The incoming runner must focus his sight on the hand of the receiver and deliberately place the baton firmly in the receiver's hand.

Another popular method of exchange is for the receiver to place his hand so that the palm is facing back and the thumb and fingers are pointing downward (Figure 8–3). At just the right moment the incoming runner brings the baton upward, placing it between the thumb and first finger of the receiver. The disadvantage of this method is that the receiver has hold of the wrong end of the baton for passing off. Thus, he must adjust his grip on the baton while he is sprinting.

It is imperative that the passer run all the way through the passing zone. Bad habits creep in when speed is reduced at the exchange. There is a tendency for the passer to slow down just prior to the exchange and this malpractice must be strictly avoided. If this happens, it is apparent that the receiver is not leaving soon enough to attain full speed, or he is coasting until he receives the baton. Sufficient practice, along with increased confidence in the exchange, will eliminate these errors.

Baton passing drills at jogging speed can be effective for developing the mechanics of the exchange. But the timing of the exchange must be perfected while practicing the exchange at racing speed. It is well to time the baton through the exchange zone. If a team can move through the zone in 1.7 to 1.8 seconds, they have developed a very proficient exchange.

### Variations in Exchanges for Longer Relays

In longer relays the exchange method sometimes varies from that described. In the longer races there is a tendency to concentrate less on proficient exchanges. This is a great error because regardless of how fast the athletes run between exchanges, the race will always be slower than it would have been if the exchanges had been more proficient. Lost time can never be recovered. In longer races, many runners prefer to carry the baton in the right hand and, therefore, they want to receive it in that hand.

In the mile relay and longer races, fatigue is an important factor in baton

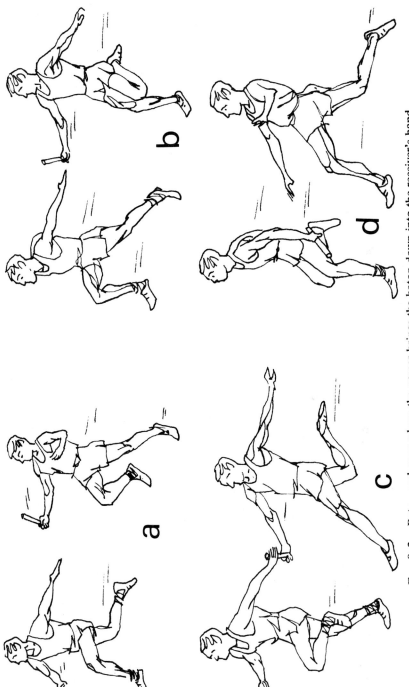

FIG. 8–2. Baton exchange where the passer brings the baton down into the receiver's hand.

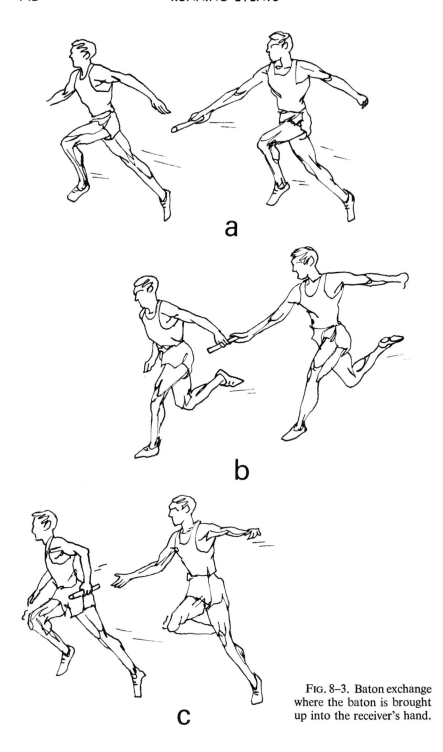

a

b

c

FIG. 8–3. Baton exchange where the baton is brought up into the receiver's hand.

exchanges. Because of fatigue, the speed at which the incoming man is running is more difficult to predict and there is a greater chance that the receiver will run away from him. Also, the accuracy of the pass-off might be affected by fatigue, and there is an increased chance that the incoming runner will fall or pass out. Because of these circumstances, in the longer races the receiver often looks back to keep a watching eye on the incoming runner until the exchange is made. This procedure always results in a loss of time, but it is often considered the safe thing to do. Whether or not this method is advisable is influenced by the runners involved, the amount of fatigue that can be expected in each runner, and the amount of practice the runners have had in exchanging the baton under race conditions. Well-conditioned athletes who have competed on relay teams with each other repeatedly can successfully use the blind exchange described in the section on the 440 yard relay. This minimizes the loss of time and eliminates the twisting and turning of the body which is characteristic of the visual exchange. It is important to recognize that proficiency in the exchange can make the difference between victory and defeat, and that if a second is lost on an exchange it can never be recovered. The final time of the race will be one second slower than it otherwise would have been.

## ORDER OF RUNNING

In the 440 yard relay the following should be considered with regard to the order the team members run: 1) The first man must be a fast starter and a good curve runner; 2) the fastest man should run last, unless there is good reason to do otherwise; and 3) it makes little difference which of the remaining two men runs second and which one runs third, except that the third man should be a good curve runner.

In the 880 yard relay the order of runners could be altered from what they are in the 440 depending on how the 880 yard relay is run. If the second runner is permitted to cut for the pole (inside lane), then it is wise to run the two fastest men first, with the slowest man running last. This provides a greater chance for the second man to be out front when he cuts for the pole and will aid in gaining the pole position. The pole position is a distinct advantage because other runners must go to the outside to make the exchange, and in addition, many runners are not able to hold their poise very well when they are behind.

In the mile relay it is usually an advantage to have the fast man run last. The second fastest man usually runs first, provided he is a fast starter, and the third fastest man usually runs the second leg with the slowest man in the third position.

# Part III
# Jumping Events

CHAPTER **9**

# High Jump

There is no reference to competitive high jumping in the ancient Olympic games. However, the Irish included this event in their Tailteann games which were first held prior to the Christian era. In the British Isles high jumping has been done for many centuries.

One of the earliest available records of an official jump is a 5′5″ performance which won the event in a meet between Oxford and Cambridge Universities in 1864. The first documented clearance of the magic height of 6′ occurred in 1876, when Marshall Brooks, an Oxford student, went over the bar at 6′½″. His lifetime best was a jump of 6′2½″ done that same year. The first great American jumper was William Page who cleared 6′4″ in 1887.

Up to that time, high jumpers had shown little concern for form. But in the last decade of the nineteenth century jumping form received considerable attention. During that period, the eastern cutoff style was introduced by Michael Sweeney, an Irish immigrant to America. In 1892, he raised the world mark to 6′4¼″, and in 1895, he mastered 6′5⅝″. At the first modern Olympics in 1896, Ellery Clark of the United States won the high jump with a leap of 5′11¼″.

George Horine did much experimentation with different jumping forms and finally in 1912, using an unorthodox roll style, he set a new American record of 6′4¾″. Later in the year he set the world record at 6′7″. He is credited with developing the style known as the western roll.

By the end of 1932, 20 years after Horine's 6′7″ (2 meter) effort, only 10 men had jumped two meters or higher. The only non-American in that group was Simeon Toribio of the Philippines, who cleared exactly that height in 1930.

During the early and mid 1950s Walter Davis and Ernie Shelton flirted consistently with the 7′ mark, but neither of them ever succeeded at that height. Consequently, Charles Dumas of the United States became the first person ever to clear 7′ when at the Olympic trials in 1956 he did 7′⅝″ using the straddle roll style.

The following year, 1959, marked the beginning of a great surge in high jump emphasis by the Russians. That year, Yuri Stepanov worked his way up to the seven-foot mark and late in the year, set a new world record of 7′1″. During the same year, two other Russians, Vladimir Sitkin and Igor Kashkarov established marks of 7′¾″ and 7′¼″ respectively.

During the early 1960s Valery Brumel of Russia established himself as the world's greatest high jumper to date, as he consistently cleared heights beyond 7′. His best effort was 7′5¾″ in 1963. In 1971 Pat Matzdorf of the United States became the first to break the seven and one-half foot-barrier when he cleared the bar at 7′6¼″. The following list of world records indicates the steady and significant improvement that has occurred in this interesting athletic event.

| Height | Record-holder and country | Year |
|---|---|---|
| 5ft. 6in. | F. H. Gooch, Great Britain | 1864 |
| 5ft. 9in. | T. G. Little, Great Britain | 1866 |
| 5ft. 9in. | J. H. S. Roupel, Great Britain | 1866 |
| 5ft. 9½in. | R. J. C. Mitchell, Great Britain | 1871 |
| 5ft. 10in. | M. J. Brooks, Great Britain | 1874 |
| 6ft. ½in. | M. J. Brooks, Great Britain | 1876 |
| 6ft. 2½in. | M. J. Brooks, Great Britain | 1876 |
| 6ft. 2¾in. | Patrick Navin, Ireland | 1880 |
| 6ft. 3½in. | William Page, U.S.A. | 1887 |
| 6ft. 4in. | William Page, U.S.A. | 1887 |
| 6ft. 4¼in. | Michael Sweeney, U.S.A. | 1892 |
| 6ft. 4½in. | J. M. Ryan, Ireland | 1895 |
| 6ft. 5in. | Michael Sweeney, U.S.A. | 1895 |
| 6ft. 5⅝in. | Michael Sweeney, U.S.A. | 1895 |
| 6ft. 6⅛in. | George Horine, U.S.A. | 1912 |
| 6ft. 7in. | George Horine, U.S.A. | 1912 |
| 6ft. 7 5/16 in. | Edward Beeson, U.S.A. | 1914 |
| 6ft. 8¼in. | Harold Osborn, U.S.A. | 1924 |
| 6ft. 8⅝in. | Walter Marty, U.S.A. | 1933 |
| 6ft. 9⅛in. | Walter Marty, U.S.A. | 1934 |
| 6ft. 9¾in. | Cornelius Johnson, U.S.A. | 1936 |
| 6ft. 9¾in. | Davie Albritton, U.S.A. | 1936 |
| 6ft. 10⅝in. | Melvin Walker, U.S.A. | 1937 |
| 6ft. 11in. | Les Steers, U.S.A. | 1941 |
| 6ft. 11½in. | Walt Davis, U.S.A. | 1953 |
| 7ft. ½in. | Charles Dumas, U.S.A. | 1956 |
| 7ft. 1in. | Yuri Stepanov, U.S.S.R. | 1957 |
| 7ft. 3¾in. | John Thomas, U.S.A. | 1960 |
| 7ft. 4½in. | Valery Brumel, U.S.S.R. | 1961 |
| 7ft. 5in. | Valery Brumel, U.S.S.R. | 1962 |
| 7ft. 5½in. | Valery Brumel, U.S.S.R. | 1962 |
| 7ft. 5¾in. | Valery Brumel, U.S.S.R. | 1963 |
| 7ft. 6¼in. | Pat Matzdorf, U.S.A. | 1971 |

## PROCEDURE AND RULES

The athlete may run any distance and from any direction he chooses during the approach, then he leaps from *one* foot in an effort to clear the cross bar and land in the pit. He may use any jumping technique he desires so long as it does not violate any specific rule (see official rule book). He may not carry weights in the hands or use any artificial device. The jumper remains in competition until he commits three consecutive misses. The height of a jump is measured along a perfectly vertical line from the top of the cross bar, midway between the two standards, to the surface directly below.

## STRADDLE ROLL TECHNIQUE

The straddle roll is the technique used by almost all outstanding high jumpers (Figure 9-1). The high jumper is concerned primarily with two factors, lifting the body to maximum height, and clearing the bar as effectively and efficiently as possible. In order to achieve success, the jumper must perfect the several aspects of the jump, which are, 1) the *approach*, including the *run* and the *gather*, 2) the *foot plant* and *takeoff*, 3) *action of the lead leg and arms*, 4) *action in the air*, 5) *clearance of the bar*. and 6) the *landing*.

### Approach

The run should be relaxed, with a bouncy but smooth stride, and with arm actions that are free and smooth. The first four or five strides should be about the same length, while the last three or four strides should be

FIG. 9-1. Straddle roll technique.

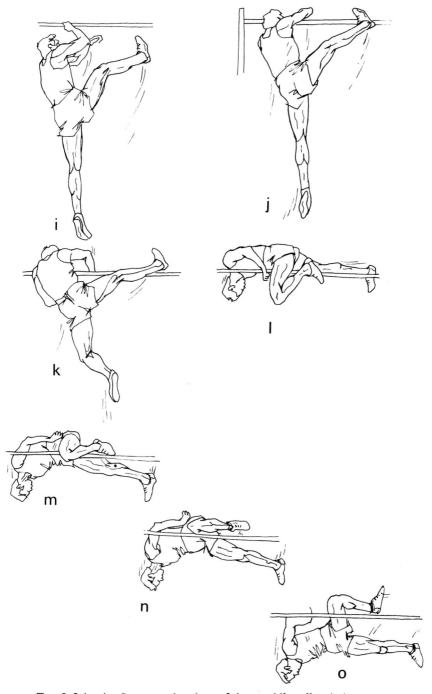

FIG. 9–2 (a–o). Sequence drawings of the straddle roll technique.

longer and accelerated. The key to success in the approach lies in the jumper's ability to obtain smoothness and control of his speed. The athlete should use as much speed as he is able to control, because the greater the speed of the run, the greater will be the momentum that can be converted upward.

Most jumpers approach the cross bar at angles that range between thirty and forty degrees from the long horizontal axes of the cross bar. Each athlete will have an angle that is best for him. The smaller the angle of approach, the more time the jumper will spend over the cross bar because he will move more parallel to the bar while in flight. Conversely, the greater the angle, the more the cross bar forces the jumper to jump vertically, but the harder it is for him to drive a straight leg up from a close takeoff. The athlete must experiment until he finds the angle of approach that works best for him.

To determine the approximate position of the takeoff, the jumper should stand next to the bar with his left side toward it (jumping from the left side) in a position where the finger tips of the left hand touch the bar when the arm is extended to the side. The position of his left foot is the approximate point of takeoff. This point is only an estimate; the exact point must be determined by experimenting with actually jumping.

Once the takeoff point and the length of the run have been determined, check-marks can be established. A jumper must have an accurately placed mark from which he starts his approach. Some athletes prefer to use a second check-mark three to four steps from the takeoff. However, as the approach is perfected the second check-mark will become less important. The approach should be practiced until the jumper can accurately strike the takeoff each time he jumps.

The conversion of horizontal momentum to vertical momentum requires that a jumper have great power in the "jumping muscles," (especially the extensors of the takeoff leg, and hip flexors of the lead leg) and he must position the body to permit those muscles to act effectively. This positioning is known as the "gather," and it results in the jumper lowering his center of gravity as he goes into the last step and placing the body in correct jumping position (Figure 9–2b, c, d). The jumper should consciously lower the hips, shoulders and arms while keeping the head and chest up and the back slightly arched.

### Foot Plant and Takeoff

The foot plant is the final part of the last stride. The foot, which is planted heel first, remains flat on the surface until the body is pulled over the foot, then the leg and foot extend vigorously. The foot plant also serves as a brake to the forward momentum by converting it to the vertical direction. It is very important to convert the momentum to the vertical direction with as little loss as possible (Figure 9–2e, f).

The takeoff is the heart of the jump. It results from a combination of co-ordinated forces, of which the extension of the jumping leg is only one. Upward lift at takeoff is accomplished by: 1) conversion of horizontal momentum to vertical momentum; 2) a powerful extension of the jumping leg; 3) vigorous forward and upward action of the lead leg; and 4) the upward lift of the arms and shoulders (Figure 9–2h, i).

*Conversion of Horizontal Momentum to Vertical.* On the last stride the foot is planted well in front of the body's center of gravity. The leg is held somewhat rigid, causing the body to rock forward and upward on to the leg, much like a pole vaulter rocks on the pole after planting it in the vaulting box (Figure 9–2f). The rocker action is the key movement in converting the momentum of the run to the vertical lift.

*Extension of the Jumping Leg.* As the body rocks up and over the planted foot the leg and foot extend vigorously, lifting the body directly upward with great force (Figure 9–2i).

*Lead Leg Action.* Near the completion of the rocker action of the body, the free leg is swung through and thrust vigorously upward. It should swing toward the far jump standard and in a direction almost parallel to the bar (Figure 9–3). It is important for the jumper to drive the leg mostly upward rather than forward. This will result in maximum vertical lift from the leg action. The higher the leg is kicked, the higher will be the center of gravity of the body, and the greater will be the lifting action of the leg. It is an advantage to keep the leg straight at the knee, or nearly so, because this results in greater lifting force (Figure 9–2h, i, j).

FIG. 9–3.   High jump takeoff with a straight leg.

FIG. 9–4. High jump take-off with a slightly bent lead leg.

*Arm and Shoulder Action.* During the last step of the approach the arms are swung backward well behind the line of the body. Then, in one continuous action, the arms are brought forward and thrust upward to aid in the vertical lift. Near the completion of the upward thrust of the arms, the shoulder girdles are thrust upward to add to the lifting force (Figure 9–2h, i).

### Action in the Air

The jumper should not start the layout until he is completely in the air (takeoff foot off the ground). Also, he should delay the turn into the layout until the head and shoulders have risen above the bar.

As the athlete nears the peak of his jump and is going into the layout position, he must bring his inside arm close to the body and keep it there (Figure 9–2k, l, m). This will help prevent catching the bar between the arm and the body. Some jumpers place the arm on the abdomen, while others place it on the front of the thigh as a precaution against hitting the bar.

### Clearance of the Bar

The first part of the body over the bar is the outside arm, which becomes the lead arm. The arm is followed by the shoulder and head. As soon as these body parts clear the bar they should be dropped as low as possible to help raise the center of gravity of the total body. The lead leg crosses the bar at about the same time as the head, and it is followed by the trunk. The lead leg also drops low as soon as it clears the bar to help raise the body's center of gravity (Figure 9–2m).

At this stage in the jump the only body part that is not across the bar is the trail leg, and this is what causes jumpers the most problems. The following two important actions will help get the trail leg over. 1) Thrust the lead arm backward and upward; this causes a countertwist of the trunk which will lift the trail leg. The counter twist can be demonstrated by having an athlete stand on a turntable (this simulates being free in the air) and instruct him to rotate his arms and shoulders in one direction. The hips and legs will automatically rotate in the opposite direction. 2) Turn the toes of the trail leg toward the sky. This pointing action of the toes, together with the upward movement of the trail leg resulting from the sweeping action of the lead arm, will allow the trail leg to clear the bar (Figure 9–2n, o).

### Landing

The landing, which is the follow-through of the jump, must be done in a way that will not distract the attention of the jumper from correct jumping technique. The athlete should be able to relax and "give" with the landing pit so he is not jarred by the landing. It is important for him to be disconcerned about the landing until after he has cleared the bar.

## APPLICATION OF SCIENTIFIC PRINCIPLES

The following are explanations of how certain laws and principles apply to the high jump.

*When a force is applied to a body the body develops greater velocity as the distance of force application is increased.* During the projection phase of the jump it is important to keep the foot in contact with the surface until the leg and foot have completed their extension. Some inexperienced jumpers tend to break contact with the surface too soon.

*All forces should be applied as directly as possible in the direction of intended motion.* The objective of the high jumper is to raise the body vertically as high as possible and to be able to cross over the bar. It is important that the several contributing forces be directed mostly vertically in order to lift the body to the maximum height, with just enough horizontal force to carry the body across the bar. Forces that are misdirected lose all or part of their effectiveness (Figure 9–5).

*The final velocity is the result of the sum of the velocities of body segments contributing to the act, provided the movements are done in correct sequence and timing.* In the high jump the final velocity is the speed at which the body is moving at the moment it breaks contact with the surface. This is a result of a combination of the velocities of the different body movements that contribute to the act. An increase in the speed of any contributing movement will increase the final velocity of the body, and this will result in greater height.

*Momentum of moving body segments can be transferred to the total body.* In high jumping, the momentum from the swinging actions of the arms and free leg is transferred to the total body to help lift the body. The greater the momentum of these body segments, the greater will be their lifting effect (Figures 9–4 and 9–5).

*The force of muscular contraction may be increased by putting the muscles on sudden stretch.* In the high jump, the sudden stretch of the muscles results from the actions just prior to the takeoff—the flexion of the takeoff leg, backward swing of the arms, etc. (Figure 9–2e, f).

*When executing a performance where consecutive motions contribute to movement in the same direction, there should usually be no pause between the motions.* In the high jump it is important that all of the different movements blend smoothly toward lifting the body upward. Any break in sequence or timing of the movements will cause a loss of upward momentum.

*When the body is suspended in space, movement of body parts may cause rotation about the body's center of gravity, but the flight path of the total body will not change.* The most obvious application of this principle in the high jump is the upward-backward movement of the lead arm and the head after

FIG. 9–5. The high jumper swings his arms and free leg vigorously using them to pull the total body upward. This is known as transfer of momentum from swinging body parts.

they have cleared the bar. This results in a counter action of the trail leg, causing it to raise upward to clear the bar.

## COMMON FAULTS AND HOW TO CORRECT THEM

The following faults were identified by high jump experts, and the correction techniques were stated by coaches who have produced outstanding high jumpers.

### The Approach

Fault: The run is either too long or too short.

Correction: Experiment with the run until it seems to be of optimum length. Experience shows that optimum length is eight strides for most jumpers. However, some use nine or ten strides.

Fault: The run is too slow.

Correction: Emphasize accelerating steadily from the beginning to the end of the run, with the most acceleration taking place during the last four strides. Run short sprints to help build acceleration speed.

Fault: Failure to acclerate during the last three or four strides.

Correction: Lengthen the last four strides. This tends to force increased acceleration. Also, concentrate on optimal acceleration.

Fault: Angle of approach is wrong, or inconsistent.

Correction: Experiment until the optimum angle of approach is determined, then a chalk line can be placed on the runway to be followed during practice. Also, markers indicating the placement of each foot during the approach can be used.

Fault: Failure to "gather" prior to the takeoff.

Correction: During practice concentrate on gathering at the correct time, and force the gather. While practicing with the bar at a low height, overemphasize the gather.

### Foot Plant and Takeoff

Fault: The takeoff mark is too close or too far from the cross bar.

Correction: As a result of practice and analysis of the jump, determine whether the takeoff point needs to be adjusted, then adjust the takeoff and the approach as needed. The point can be marked with a spot of lime, chalk dust or tape.

Fault: The foot plant is not in line with the direction of the run.

Correction: Place a line at the takeoff point running in the direction that the foot should point and attempt to step exactly on the line. Practice running through the approach without actually jumping and concentrate on the placement of the foot.

Fault: Failure to plant the takeoff foot forcefully prior to the rocker action.

Correction: While going through the approach without jumping, practice a full plant of the takeoff foot in the correct position. Using a short approach, and with the bar at a low height, emphasize a forceful foot plant.

Fault: The takeoff leg is extended too early, before the rocker action is completed.

Correction: Hesitate the leg extension long enough to complete the rocker action and permit the center of gravity to come over the takeoff foot.

Fault:            Failure to extend the leg and foot completely at takeoff.
Correction:       Go through the approach many times and practice leaping high into
                  the air without going over the bar.  This provides opportunity to
                  concentrate on full extension of the leg and foot.
Fault:            Failure to plant the takeoff foot well ahead of the center of gravity.
Correction:       Force a long last stride, placing the takeoff foot well ahead of the
                  center of gravity.  Also place marks on the ground for the final two
                  strides in positions that will force a long final stride.

### Actions of the Lead Leg and Arms

Fault:            Failure to kick the lead leg high enough and with enough force.
Correction:       Without going over the bar, practice taking a few steps followed by
                  a hard high kick.
Fault:            Failure to use the arms and shoulders sufficiently to aid in the vertical
                  lift.
Correction:       Practice leaping into the air without going over the bar and emphasize
                  the lifting action of the arms and shoulders.

### Clearing the Bar

Fault:            Turning into the bar too soon after takeoff.
Correction:       Practice kicking the lead leg in line with the angle of approach.
                  Swing the opposite arm across in front of the chest as it moves up-
                  ward, to compensate for the twisting action caused by the swing of
                  the lead leg.
Fault:            Failure to lower the lead arm and the head immediately after they
                  cross the bar.
Correction:       Jump over the bar at a low height many times and concentrate on
                  getting the arm and head as low as possible after they cross the bar.
Fault:            Failure to throw the lead arm backward and upward to aid in lifting
                  the trail leg over the bar.
Correction:       Practice the jump many times at a low height and concentrate on the
                  correct action of the lead arm and the corresponding action of the
                  trail leg.

## THE FOSBURY TECHNIQUE

In 1962, Dick Fosbury, a Medford, Oregon high school sophomore
jumped less than six feet with a conventional layout technique.  Dissatis-
fied, he started experimenting with his style.  Turning his back to the bar
as he jumped, Fosbury cleared $6'3\frac{1}{4}''$ as a junior and went over the bar at
$6'7''$ as a high school senior.

Entering Oregon State University in 1966, Fosbury attempted to drop
his unorthodox style in favor of the straddle roll.  The result was a best of
$5'11''$ and a discouraged athlete.  Yet returning to his "flop," Fosbury
cleared $6'7\frac{1}{4}''$ in competition at the end of his freshman track season.  He
leaped into success as a sophomore at $6'10\frac{3}{4}''$, then really took off as a junior,
winning the NCAA indoor title at $7'1\frac{1}{4}''$, the NCAA outdoor championship
and setting a new collegiate record at $7'2\frac{1}{4}''$.

Then came the Olympic Games in Mexico and world fame as Dick Fosbury won the Gold Medal with a record shattering flight of $7'4\frac{1}{4}''$ and came within a fraction of clearing $7'6''$.

Fosbury's approach begins $47'6''$ from the left bar standard, and $19'6''$ to the left of this standard. He takes an eight-step run and takes off from his right foot. His curved approach differs from any previous jumping style, and it enables the jumper to take advantage of centrifugal force.

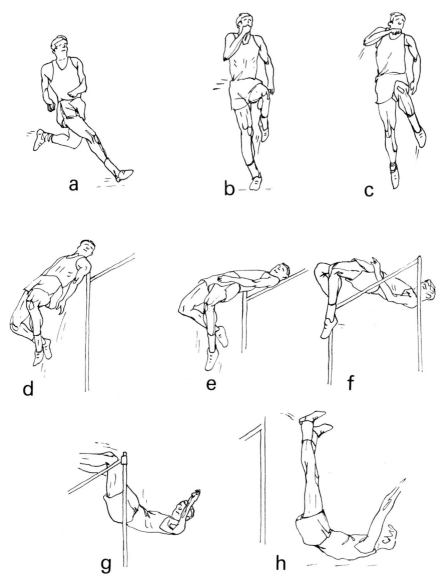

FIG. 9–6 (a–h). Sequence drawings of Fosbury technique.

The jumper uses force to hold his body in the circular approach path. When this force is released at takeoff, the jumper's body is thrown in a line tangent to his circular approach, like whirling a stone in a sling, then letting go. The momentum throws the jumper toward the bar without any waste of his jumping force.   Other styles force the jumper to control his speed and "gather" before leaping.   The Fosbury technique allows the jumper to approach the bar at nearly full speed (Figure 9–6b, c).

The body leans backward as the takeoff foot is planted.   Then, the force keeping the body in the circular approach path is released to throw the body across the bar (Figure 9–6d).

The jumper adds an upward force at takeoff, by pushing against the ground as hard as possible with the right takeoff foot.   This push-off is accompanied by a transfer of momentum, achieved by sharply raising the right arm and left leg (Figure 9–6c).   This combines upward force with the momentum, throwing the body across the bar.   A final, very slight force is added for rotation as the jumper turns his back to the bar by twisting the left knee to the right as it is lifted up.

The danger in the backward landing style is minimized because to clear his legs over the bar, the jumper flexes his hips and straightens his knees. This action causes a reaction that raises the body's trunk toward the legs. Thus the jumper lands safely on his upper back.   Of course, the jumping pit should always contain some form of foam pads for a soft landing surface (Figure 9–6f, g, h).

### THE TRAINING SCHEDULE

This recommended training schedule is for an experienced and mature high jumper.   It can serve as a guide for all high jumpers but should be adjusted to fit a particular athlete's needs because of variation in maturity, age and condition.

#### Summer

During the summer the jumper should maintain a high level of general conditioning by participating regularly in activities which involve at least moderate amounts of running and much jumping.   Such activities are basketball, volleyball and play-type (fartlek) running. These activities should be supplemented by specific exercises to keep a high level of power and endurance in the muscles used in the high jump. (See the recommended exercises at the end of this chapter.)   Summer employment that involves heavy work is generally beneficial.

#### Fall

During the fall months the jumper should do weight training on Monday, Wednesday and Friday with emphasis on exercises which develop power in the legs.   Also he should do a considerable amount of running, mostly short distances at near top speed.  In addition he should work regularly on jumping form and jump for height occasionally.

### Winter

This program is based on the assumption that the jumper is preparing for the spring season.  If he is preparing for the winter (indoor) season, then this program should be followed during the late fall instead of the winter.

During the winter the jumper should do a considerable amount of running including some sprinting, and he should increase the intensity of the exercise program.  Also, he should participate regularly in high jump drills with emphasis on the improvement of technique.  Occasionally during this period he should jump for maximum height.

Monday:
1. Jog one-quarter mile.
2. Run wind-sprints for one mile.
3. Do stretching exercises.
4. Jump 15–25 times, concentrating on the approach and takeoff.
5. Run three flights of 80-yard low hurdles.
6. Weight train (see exercises at the end of this chapter).

Tuesday:
1. Jog one-quarter mile.
2. Do stretching exercises for 15 minutes.
3. Run wind-sprints for one mile.
4. Do "bounding exercises" by springing off one foot and then the other for 10 minutes.

Wednesday:
1. Jog one-quarter mile.
2. Do stretching exercises.
3. Run wind-sprints for one-half mile.
4. Jump 15–25 times working on the takeoff and bar clearance.
5. Run three flights of 80-yard low hurdles.
6. Weight train.

Thursday:
1. Jog one-quarter mile.
2. Do stretching exercises.
3. Run wind-sprints for one half-mile.
4. Work on jumping form.

Friday:
1. Jog one-quarter mile.
2. Do stretching exercises.
3. Run wind-sprints for one-quarter mile.

Saturday:
1. Warm up.
2. Jump for height.
3. Weight train.

### Spring (Early and Middle Portion)

Monday:
1. Jog one-quarter mile.
2. Do stretching exercises.
3. Run wind-sprints for one-half mile.
4. Jump 10–15 times.  Practice on the run and the jump.  Concentrate especially on the last three steps and the takeoff.
5. Run three flights of 80-yard low hurdles.
6. Weight train.

Tuesday:      1. Jog one-quarter mile.
              2. Do stretching exercises.
              3. Run wind-sprints for one-half mile.
              4. Work on jumping form.
Wednesday:   1. Jog one-quarter mile.
              2. Do stretching exercises.
              3. Run wind-sprints for one-quarter mile.
              4. Jump 10 times at maximum height.
              5. Weight train.
Thursday:     1. Jog one-quarter mile.
              2. Do stretching exercises.
              3. Run wind-sprints for one-half mile.
              4. Work on jumping form.
Friday:        Rest or study high jump movies.
Saturday:     1. Day of meet—arrive at the field early enough to place marks, etc. Check your approach four or five times. Jump three or four times at medium height. Be confident and relaxed.
              2. Weight train.

### Late Spring (May–June)

During the late season the high jumper will ordinarily do the same kind of training as during the mid season. However, he should increase his volume of training somewhat, depending on how close he is to his peak, and should do a considerable amount of work on the fine points of the jumping technique.

## CONDITIONING EXERCISES

The main objective of the conditioning program for high jumpers is to develop maximum power in the muscle groups which thrust the body upward. The following exercises will assist in developing powerful movements in the proper muscles. The exercises are illustrated in Appendix A.

Straight arm forward raise—exercise #1
Trunk flexion—exercise #14
Jumping jack—exercise #21
Half squat—exercise #22
Heel raise—exercise #23
Quadriceps drill—exercise #24
Vertical jump drill—exercise #28
Hip flexion (lead leg)—exercise #27

CHAPTER **10**

# Long Jump

Even though the long jump was the only jumping event included in the ancient Olympic Games, the earliest recorded jump of significance was an 18′ effort by Franklin H. Gooch of England in 1864.

The 25-foot mark was not exceeded until 1921 when Edward Gourdin of the United States jumped 25′3″. In 1928 Silvio Cator of Haiti surpassed the 26-foot mark by 1/8 inch. The 27-foot mark fell to Ralph Boston of the United States when he did a jump of 27′2″ in 1960. Then, in 1968, Bob Beamon of the United States accomplished what seemed to be an impossible task when he established a new record at 29′2¼″. The following complete list of world records in the long jump demonstrates the evolution of progress that has occurred in this athletic event since Gooch jumped 18′ in 1864.

| Distance | Record-holder and country | Year |
|---|---|---|
| 18ft. | F. H. Gooch, Great Britain | 1864 |
| 22ft. 7in. | E. J. Davies, Great Britain | 1872 |
| 23ft. 1½in. | J. Lane, Ireland, | 1874 |
| 23ft. 2in. | Patrick Navin, Ireland | 1883 |
| 23ft. 3in. | Malcolm Ford, U.S.A. | 1886 |
| 23ft. 3⅛in. | Alfred Copland, U.S.A. | 1890 |
| 23ft. 6½in. | Charles Reber, U.S.A. | 1891 |
| 23ft. 7½in. | Matthew Rosengrave, Australia | 1896 |
| 24ft. ½in. | W. J. M. Newburn, Ireland | 1898 |
| 24ft. 3½in. | Alvin Kraenzlein, U.S.A. | 1899 |
| 24ft. 4½in. | Alvin Kraenzlein, U.S.A. | 1899 |
| 24ft. 7½in. | Myer Prinstein, U.S.A. | 1900 |
| 24ft. 11¾in. | Patrick O'Connor, Ireland | 1901 |
| 25ft. 3in. | Edward Gourdin, U.S.A. | 1921 |
| 25ft. 5¾in. | Robert Legendre, U.S.A. | 1924 |
| 25ft. 10⅞in. | DeHart Hubbard, U.S.A. | 1925 |
| 25ft. 11⅛in. | Edward Hamm, U.S.A. | 1928 |

| | | |
|---|---|---|
| 26ft. $\frac{1}{8}$in. | Silvio Cator, Haiti. . | 1928 |
| 26ft. $2\frac{1}{8}$in. | Chuhei Nambu, | |
| | Japan . . . . . | 1931 |
| 26ft. $8\frac{1}{4}$in. | Jesse Owens, U.S.A. . | 1935 |
| 26ft. $11\frac{1}{4}$in. | Ralph Boston, U.S.A. | 1960 |
| 27ft. 2in. | Ralph Boston, U.S.A. | 1960 |
| 27ft. $3\frac{1}{4}$in. | Igor Ter-Ovanesyan, | |
| | U.S.S.R. . . . . . | 1962 |
| 27ft. $4\frac{3}{4}$in. | Ralph Boston, U.S.A. | 1965 |
| 27ft. $4\frac{3}{4}$in. | Igor Ter-Ovanesyan, | |
| | U.S.S.R. . . . . | 1967 |
| 29ft. $2\frac{1}{4}$in. | Bob Beamon, U.S.A. . | 1968 |

Fig. 10–1. A jumper landing with just enough momentum to bring the body between the knees and over the feet.

PROCEDURE

The athlete runs at near top speed, then jumps and covers as much horizontal distance as possible.  The rules permit the performer to run as far
as he desires during the approach.  He must jump from behind the scratch
line (the forward edge of the takeoff board) and land in the pit.  He may
not carry weights in the hands or use other devices to aid his jump.  The distance of the jump is measured along a straight line from the scratch line to
the nearest point of contact with the surface of the sand-filled pit.

LONG JUMP TECHNIQUE

The running long jump is one continuous action from the beginning of
the run to the landing in the pit.  Three important factors are fundamental
to the distance of the jump: 1) running speed at the moment of takeoff;
2) the force with which the body is projected; and 3) the angle of projection.
For purposes of analysis, the event may be divided into four phases: the
*approach*, the *gather* and *takeoff*, *action in the air* and the *landing*.

### Approach

The purpose of the approach is to gain near maximum running speed,
and to arrive at the desired point of takeoff on the correct foot and in
perfect jumping position.  Most jumpers run between 110 and 130 feet.
To determine the optimal distance of the run, the athlete must experiment
with various lengths, noting how he feels when he reaches the board.  If he
feels tired or tense, then the run is too long; whereas, if he is unable to attain near maximum speed prior to the gather, the run is too short.

How fast should the jumper run?  He should run as fast as possible and
still be able to relax and obtain maximum lift off the board.  He should
accelerate gradually during the initial strides, and should be at about 95%
maximum speed during the final strides.

The jumper's step pattern during the run must be consistent in order that
he will step just short of the front edge of the takeoff board.  When he is
able to do this consistently, he can concentrate more on maximum relaxed
speed and jumping technique.

To add accuracy to his approach, the athlete should use at least two
check-marks, one to mark the beginning of the approach and one about
60′ from the takeoff board.  The check-marks can be established by measuring the distance of the run (say 120′) on the running track.  Starting with
both feet together on the first mark, the athlete steps off with the takeoff
foot and runs down the track.  At the end of the measured distance the
coach determines the point where the takeoff foot struck the ground and
marks that point.  The run should be repeated several times to check the
consistency of the step pattern.  To determine the second check-mark, the
athlete runs through the approach again, and the coach checks the spot
where the takeoff foot struck the track at approximately 60′ from the

Fig. 10–2. Heel protection cup.

takeoff. The second check-mark is used as a green light signal, and tends to give the jumper increased confidence in his approach. The jumper should not attempt to change the approach if he hits the second check-mark correctly. When the athlete and the coach are satisfied that the check-marks are correct, the marks can be measured and placed on the runway.

Some jumpers use a third checkpoint closer to the board, and a few jumpers place it only two strides away from the takeoff.

### Gather and Takeoff

The key to a good jump is an effective takeoff. Everything the jumper does during the approach is designed to facilitate this phase of the jump. The takeoff is the part of the jump where the forward momentum from the run is combined with all of the jumping forces to drive the body in the upward-forward direction. Problems that occur later in the jump can often be traced to a poor takeoff.

To allow the optimum transfer of forward momentum to the upward-forward direction, the jumper must "settle" or "gather" slightly near the end of the run. This enables him to assume control of his speed and concentrate on the jump. The "gather" starts two or three strides before the takeoff. During this time, four adjustments occur (Figure 10–3a, b):

1. The body settles slightly in preparation for the upward lift.

2. The trunk assumes a more erect position, which permits a heel-ball-toe action of the takeoff foot and allows more forward placement of the takeoff leg.

3. The last stride is shortened slightly. The jumper must not reach for the board, because this will cause him to lose his ability to spring vigorously from the takeoff leg.

4. The takeoff foot is shifted slightly inward to a position directly under the center of the body weight. This is necessary for balance as well as for full benefit from the powerful extension of the body during the takeoff.

The foot plant at the board should not be a vigorous "stamp" as is often advocated, because this reduces the springing action of the leg and foot and tends to cause injury to the foot. The plant should be a firm relaxed placement of the foot with the toes pointing directly forward. The foot should go through a heel-ball-toe motion during the takeoff, and it should remain in contact with the board as long as possible. The takeoff foot should strike the board in advance of the body, then the center of gravity moves more directly over the foot as the knee flexes. As the *rocker action* of the foot continues, the center of gravity will move over the foot, then ahead of it, and will be well out in front as the foot leaves the board (Figure 10-3b, c).

As the body passes over the takeoff foot, the leg extends vigorously, and the foot completes the heel-ball-toe action. At the same time, the free leg is swept forward and upward to assist in the lift. The jumper should experience a feeling of "running off the board" (Figure 10–3c, d).

Other body parts also aid in the lifting action. Both arms are swung vigorously upward, the head and chest are raised sharply, and the back is well arched to aid in the lifting of the hips.

### Action in the Air

Once the athlete leaves the ground, there is nothing he can do to increase his momentum. The objective during the flight is to maintain balance and to position the body for the most effective landing. There are three styles of flight: the *hang*, the *hitch-kick*, and the *run*. The hang is a simple style, but it is less effective than the hitch kick or run.

In the *hang* style the legs follow the hips in a semirelaxed fashion until the athlete approaches the high point of the jump. The chin and chest are up with the back slightly arched, and the feet trailing behind the rest of the body. The arms are slightly forward and out beyond shoulder width. At the crest of the flight the hips are swung more forward to aid in lifting the legs. Then the legs are flexed at the hips to bring the knees and feet forward so the heels are about level with the hips. Simultaneously the arms are swung forward as the head and trunk are lowered toward the knees. This puts the jumper in a sitting position for the landing, with the arms and trunk reaching forward, and the feet forward and at about shoulder width apart.

The preferred style of flight for many expert jumpers is the *hitch-kick*. This style enhances aerial balance and permits a vigorous takeoff from the board with a natural follow-through action after takeoff. It also leads to an easier and more complete lifting of the legs for the landing, due to the following: 1) the trunk is erect in flight and is not drawn down by the early lifting of the legs; and 2) during the last phase of the action the back leg swings like a pendulum to aid the muscles in thrusting the legs high and forward for the landing.

The hitch-kick involves two strides in the air. The action starts as the jumper drives the free leg upward at the takeoff. At the peak of the jump, the free leg steps down as though the jumper were stepping onto an imaginary box. At the same time the other leg (takeoff leg) swings forward, knee first. With the takeoff leg now out front the final phase of the action starts. The back leg comes up to the takeoff leg, which has been extended to a position in front of the hips.

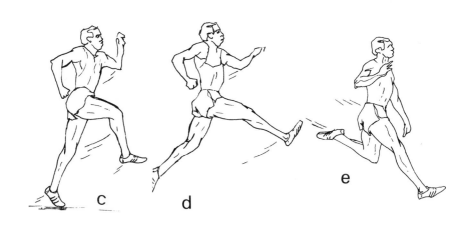

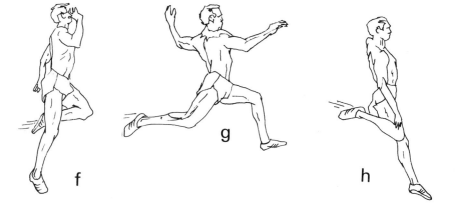

Fig. 10–3 (a–m). Sequence drawings of correct technique in the long jump.

The action of the legs during the hitch-kick can be summarized as follows: the free or kicking leg swings forward as the jumper leaves the ground. Then it drops down to counterbalance the forward motion of the takeoff leg. The free leg than swings forward again and reaches out front, parallel with the takeoff leg as both legs extend for the landing (Figure 10–3d–1).

Throughout the entire flight, the arm actions are synchronized with the legs as in running. When the right leg is forward, the left arm is up and forward. This aids in aerial balance. On the last step (when the takeoff leg is brought through the second time) the trailing arm comes forward quickly to enable both arms to reach forward for the landing.

The *run* style is used frequently by top-flight jumpers. It is similar to the hitch-kick except with the run style the jumper takes more strides while in the air. As he leaves the board, he continues his running action but at an accelerated rate. Some jumpers will complete four or five strides before landing. The run style provides a natural follow-through after takeoff, and it is effective in maintaining balance while in flight.

### Landing

The objective of this phase is to gain maximum distance by reaching forward as far as possible with the feet and still having enough momentum to carry the center of gravity to a position between the knees and over the feet. Three specific movements are necessary to help prevent the jumper from falling back into the pit. As soon as the heels touch the pit, with the feet placed 12–15″ apart, the jumper must: 1) drop the chin to the chest; 2) allow controlled flexing of the knees; and 3) swing the arms downward and backward vigorously to help thrust the trunk forward (Figures 10–4 and 10–5).

If the jump is well-performed, the athlete will experience a landing which is smooth and not jarring. One indication of a good jump is when the jumper feels like he landed on feathers. This indicates that nearly all of the forward momentum was used in the jump, a necessary factor for a maximum effort.

## APPLICATION OF SCIENTIFIC PRINCIPLES

Following are explanations of the application of certain laws and principles which are fundamental to effective performance in the long jump.

FIG. 10–4. Body position just prior to the landing.

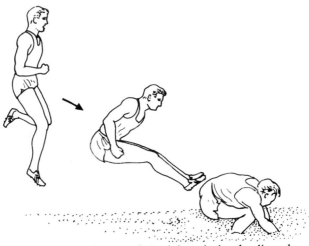

FIG. 10–5. Controlled flexion of the joints during landing absorbs the force over a longer time, thus reducing the chance of injury. A soft landing surface, such as a sand pit, also causes absorption of force over a longer time.

*When a force is applied to a body, the body develops greater velocity as the distance of force application increases.* During the jump it is important to keep the takeoff foot in contact with the surface until the leg and foot are fully extended, thus providing the thrusting force over as much distance as possible. Some inexperienced jumpers make the mistake of breaking contact with the board before the extension is completed.

*All contributing forces should be applied as directly as possible in the direction of the intended motion.* In the long jump the several contributing forces must be correctly combined in such a way that the body is projected at the optimum angle and with maximum velocity. All the possible forces should be used maximally, including the run, the thrust from the takeoff leg, the swing of the arms and free leg and the extension of the trunk.

*The final velocity is the result of the sum of the velocities of all the body segments contributing to the act.* The final velocity of the jumper is the speed at which he is moving at the moment he breaks contact with the board. An increase in the speed of any of the contributing movements would increase the final velocity.

*The momentum of moving body segments can be transferred to the total body.* In the long jump, momentum from the vigorous swinging movements of the arms and the free leg, along with the lifting action of the shoulder and trunk, is transferred to the total body at takeoff. This transfer is very important to the height and distance of the jump (Figure 10–3c).

*When the body is unsupported, movements of body segments may cause the body to rotate about its center of gravity, but its flight path will be unaffected by the movements.* The action taken by a jumper while in flight is important as a follow-through after the takeoff, as an aid in maintaining balance while in the air, and to position the body for an effective landing. But the movements do not change the course of flight of the total body, because this course is determined at the time of takeoff.

*A correct follow-through is essential to a maximum effort performance.* In the long jump the follow-through is the action in the air immediately following the takeoff. This action permits the jumper to continue maximum drive until contact is broken. Without such follow-through the jumper would tend to diminish his velocity prior to takeoff (Figure 10–3).

*The length of time an object remains in flight is dependent upon the height it attains.* The jumper will remain in flight only as long as it takes for him to move up and down through the vertical plane. The horizontal distance he travels has no influence on his time in flight. If all other factors remain constant, the higher he jumps the longer he will remain in flight, thus the farther he will jump. This explains why optimal height is essential.

*In jumping activities where maximum distance is the goal, final velocity in the intended direction is fundamental to success.* Since a long jumper will remain in flight only a given length of time, dependent upon the height of the jump, the distance he covers during that time is directly related to his horizontal speed at takeoff (Figure 10–3c, d).

*A force can be more gradually diminished by distributing the force over a greater time or body area.* As a person lands after jumping, the shock-absorbing joints move through flexion in order to distribute the force over a longer time, thus reducing the chance of injury. The sand-filled pit also contributes toward absorbing the force over more time (Figure 10–5).

## COMMON FAULTS AND HOW TO CORRECT THEM

In discussing the methods of correcting errors in the long jump, reference is made to the term *pop-up*. The pop-up is simply a jump at reduced speed in which the board is ignored, and the takeoff is close to the pit. The reduced running speed permits greater control and better concentration on the technique.

The common faults and the correction techniques were stated by coaches who have produced outstanding long jump performers.

### The Approach

Fault: Failure to strike the check-marks accurately.

Correction: Practice the approach several times each workout, concentrating on striking the check-marks. Also practice wind-sprints at the speed of the approach. Run low hurdles during practice sessions to help develop a consistent stride.

Fault: Too much tension during the final strides and the takeoff. (The final portion of the run should be at top floating speed, but the athlete should not sprint so hard that he must strain.)

Correction: The correction is obvious—slow down slightly, to a relaxed sprint.

Fault: Not enough speed at the moment of takeoff. (At this moment speed is of prime importance, while speed at any other time is irrelevant.)

Correction: The approach run might be too short to allow the buildup of sufficient speed. If so, the run should be lengthened. The running of wind-sprints will help increase running speed.

Fault: Either stretching the last step before takeoff or shortening it too much.

Correction: Practice the approach until the board can be hit consistently without concentrating on the board. This will permit undivided attention devoted to the jumping action. Run through the approach several times each day to develop a smooth, uniform stride and to develop confidence in the check-marks. The check-marks might need to be adjusted periodically.

Fault: Slowing down before the takeoff.

Correction: If the slowing down is a result of an approach that is too long, then the approach must be shortened accordingly. If the slowing down is done in order to hit the takeoff board, then the check-marks should be adjusted.

### The Takeoff

Fault: Failure to "gather" in preparation for the takeoff.

Correction: Run through the approach several times each day emphasizing the gather. Practice the pop-up with emphasis on the gather.

Fault: Failure to obtain sufficient lift from the takeoff.

Correction: Do several pop-ups each day with emphasis on obtaining height.

Also a cross bar can be placed at an appropriate height between the takeoff board and the pit to force adequate height.

Fault:        Stomping flat-footed on the takeoff board rather than using a smooth heel-ball-toe action.

Correction:   Do pop-ups, emphasizing a smooth rocker action, then concentrate on carrying this over into maximum effort jumps.

Fault:        Failure to straighten the takeoff leg completely prior to breaking contact with the board.

Correction:   While doing pop-ups at a slow speed attempt to gain as much height as possible by arching the back, pushing the chest high into the air and extending the takeoff leg vigorously and completely.

Fault:        Failure to utilize fully the potential of the swinging action of the free leg.

Correction:   Hang on a high bar and practice the action of the leg swing. Also, while doing pop-ups, accentuate the upward thrust of the lead leg.

Fault:        Failure to utilize fully the upward thrust of the arms and shoulders to lift the body at the takeoff.

Correction:   While doing pop-ups, emphasize the lifting action of the arms and shoulders.

### During Flight

Fault:        Failure to maintain balance and control while in the air.

Correction:   Practice pop-ups emphasizing balance and control during flight.

Fault:        Starting the hitch-kick or running action too soon after takeoff.

Correction:   Practice pop-ups with emphasis on gaining height and allowing the legs to drag momentarily before the leg action is started.

Fault:        Continuing the running action too far into the jump.

Correction:   Practice pop-ups to learn when to stop the running action and bring the legs forward in preparation for the landing.

### The Landing

Fault:        Failure to lift the knees high enough in preparation for the landing.

Correction:   Practice pop-ups and concentrate on bringing the knees to the desired position near the end of the flight. Also, while hanging on a high bar practice the hitch-kick, bringing the knees high toward the chest at the completion of the action.

Fault:        Extension of the legs too far forward during the landing. If the jumper does this, he will fall back into the pit.

Correction:   Jump many times, using both pop-ups and the full approach, until it is known where to place the feet to get maximum distance.

Fault:        Failure to swing the arms backward as the heels touch the landing area.

Correction:   Practice the standing long jump to learn to use the arm actions to prevent falling back into the pit.

Fault:        Landing with the legs stiff and not allowing the legs to "pull" the body forward.

Correction:   Pop-ups can be used to aid in the correction of this error. As the heels touch the sand, lean forward, begin to flex the knees, swing the arms downward and backward, and attempt to glide up and over the feet.

## THE TRAINING SCHEDULE

Track and field athletes vary considerably in age, maturity and condition. Thus it is not possible to prepare a single training schedule that will fit the needs of all athletes in the long jump. The following is a recommended schedule which can serve as an important guide and which can be adjusted to fit a particular performer.

### Summer

During the summer the long jumper should maintain a high level of general conditioning by participating in vigorous activities which involve a considerable amount of running and jumping. Among such activities are basketball, volleyball, soccer and play-type (fartlek) running. These activities should be supplemented by selected exercises to keep a high level of strength and endurance. (See the recommended exercises at the end of this chapter.)

### Fall

During the fall the jumper should do weight training on Monday, Wednesday and Friday, with emphasis on the development of power in the legs. Also, he should do a considerable amount of running, mostly at near top speed. In addition he should work regularly on running low hurdles to increase the consistency of his stride, and should work to improve his jumping form.

### Winter

This program is based on the assumption that the jumper is preparing for the spring season. If he is preparing for the winter indoor season, then this program should be followed during the late fall.

During the winter months the long jumper should do a considerable amount of sprinting in order to improve his running speed, develop a more consistent stride and improve endurance. The running of low hurdles is recommended as a method of improving stride consistency. Also he should increase the intensity of the exercise program in order to improve power. He should do some jumping at less than maximum effort, emphasizing technique and the coordinations involved in the performance. A limited amount of maximum effort jumping should be done.

Monday:
1. Jog one-quarter mile.
2. Do stretching exercises such as: hurdle exercises from a sitting position; touch the toes from a standing position keeping the knees stiff; vertical sit-ups, raising the feet and touching the toes in an inverted jackknife action; inverted bicycle exercise.
3. Run wind-sprints for one-half mile.
4. Go through the "run-up" five times at full speed.
5. Take 10 jumps (pop-ups).

6. Run three flights of 80-yard low hurdles.
7. Weight train (see exercises at the end of this chapter).

Tuesday:
1. Jog one-quarter mile.
2. Do stretching exercises.
3. Run one-half mile of wind-sprints.
4. Take eight jumps (pop-ups).
5. Run three flights of 80-yard low hurdles.
6. Take five starts from the blocks, running 50 yards each time.

Wednesday:
1. Jog one-quarter mile.
2. Do stretching exercises.
3. Run one-half mile of wind-sprints.
4. Take five jumps (pop-ups).
5. Take 10 jumps using full run; five jumps at half-speed and five jumps at three-quarter speed.
6. Weight train.

Thursday:
1. Jog one-quarter mile.
2. Do stretching exercises.
3. Run one-half mile of wind-sprints.
4. Take six starts from the blocks, running 50 yards each time.
5. Run three flights of 80-yard low hurdles.

Friday:
1. Jog one-quarter mile.
2. Do stretching exercises.
3. Run one-half mile of wind-sprints.
4. Run through a full run checking accuracy of the stride with the check-marks three times.

Saturday:
1. Warm up as on the day of competition.
2. Jump for distance.
3. Run wind-sprints.
4. Weight train.

## Spring (Early and Middle Portion)

Monday:
1. Jog one-quarter mile.
2. Do stretching exercises.
3. Run one-half mile of wind-sprints.
4. Go through the run five times at full speed.
5. Take eight jumps (pop-ups).
6. Take five jumps using the full run at three-quarter speed; work on "gather" for the takeoff and on lifting off the board.
7. Weight train (see exercises at the end of this chapter).

Tuesday:
1. Jog one-quarter mile.
2. Do stretching exercises.
3. Run one-half mile of wind-sprints.
4. Run three flights of 80 yard low hurdles.
5. Take three starts from the blocks running 50 yards each time.

Wednesday:
1. Jog one-quarter mile.
2. Do stretching exercises.
3. Run one-half mile of wind-sprints.
4. Take eight jumps (pop-ups).
5. Take five jumps using full run at full speed each time.
6. Weight train.

Thursday:
1. Jog one-quarter mile.
2. Do stretching exercises.

              3. Run one-half mile of wind-sprints.

              4. Take five starts from the blocks, running 50 yards each time.

              5. Go through the "run-up" three times.

Friday:      Rest or do light work, with emphasis on technique and coordination.

Saturday:   1. Day of meet—arrive at the field early enough to place check-marks, etc. Run through the approach four or five times. Be confident and relaxed.

              2. Run wind-sprints after competition.

              3. Weight train.

### Late Spring (May–June)

During the late season the athlete will do the same kind of training as during the mid season. The volume of work should usually be increased to peak the athlete out at the end of the season. How much the volume increases will be determined by the athlete's state of conditioning and whether he shows signs of staleness. Increased emphasis should be placed on the fine points of correct technique, and on attaining peak condition.

## CONDITIONING EXERCISES

The long jump is primarily a power event, and power is a combination of speed and strength. In the first place, it is important that the long jumper be able to run with great speed in order to add to the horizontal component of the jump. Secondly, it is imperative that he spring from the takeoff board with tremendous force in order to project the body upward and forward. Both of these aspects of the jump are based on power. The following exercises will help to develop power in the muscle groups that contribute the most to long jumping. The exercises are illustrated in Appendix A.

Straight arm forward raise—exercise #1
Trunk flexion—exercise #14
Jumping jack with weight on shoulders—exercise #21
Half squat with heavy weight—exercise #22
Heel raise with heavy weight—exercise #23
Quadriceps drill—exercise #24
Vertical jump drill—exercise #28
Hip flexion—exercise #27

CHAPTER **11**

# Triple Jump

There are no records of the triple jump (hop, step and jump) in the programs of ancient athletic contests. The Irish of the modern era are acknowledged as being the inventors of the activity. The leading Irish exponent of this event was John Purcell whose best jump of 48′3″ stood as the world record in 1887. The Japanese dominated the event during the early 1930s when Mikio Oda, Chuhei Nambu and Naoto Tajima all held the world record at different times between 1930 and 1936. During the 1950s Adhemar da Silva of Brazil stood alone as the one in command of world level competition in this event. His best mark was 53′3¾″ set in 1955. During the late 1950s and the 1960s athletes from Russia and Poland dominated the event. Then, in 1971 Pedro Perez of Cuba set the world record at 57′1″. Following is a list of world records in this unique event.

| Distance | Record-holder and country | Year |
|---|---|---|
| 42ft. 10in. | John Purcell, Ireland | 1884 |
| 46ft. 8in. | John Purcell, Ireland | 1885 |
| 46ft. 9in. | John Purcell, Ireland | 1886 |
| 48ft. 3in. | John Purcell, Ireland | 1887 |
| 48ft. 6in. | Edward Bloss, U.S.A. | 1893 |
| 48ft. 11¼in. | Timothy Ahearne, Ireland | 1908 |
| 50ft. 11in. | Daniel Ahearn, U.S.A. | 1909 |
| 50ft. 11¼in. | Anthony Winter, Australia | 1924 |
| 51ft. 1⅜in. | Mikio Oda, Japan | 1931 |
| 51ft. 7in. | Chuhei Nambu, Japan | 1932 |
| 51ft. 9⅜in. | John Metcalfe, Australia | 1935 |
| 52ft. 5⅞in. | Naoto Tajima, Japan | 1936 |
| 52ft. 5⅞in. | Adhemar da Silva, Brazil | 1950 |
| 52ft. 6¼in. | Adhemar da Silva, Brazil | 1951 |
| 52ft. 10½in. | Adhemar da Silva, Brazil | 1952 |
| 53ft. 2½in. | Adhemar da Silva, Brazil | 1952 |

177

| | | | | |
|---|---|---|---|---|
| 53ft. 2¾in. | L. Scherbakov,<br>U.S.S.R. . . . . 1953 | | 54ft. 9½in. | Oleg Fedoseyev,<br>U.S.S.R. . . . . 1959 |
| 53ft. 3¾in. | Adhemar da Silva,<br>Brazil . . . . . 1955 | | 55ft. 10¼in. | Josef Schmidt,<br>Poland . . . . . 1960 |
| 54ft. 5in. | O. Ryakhovsky,<br>U.S.S.R. . . . . 1957 | | 57ft. 1in. | Pedro Perez, Cuba . 1971 |

### PROCEDURE

The athlete runs at near top speed, then jumps off one foot from behind the scratch line and covers as much total distance as possible in a hop, step and jump. He lands on the same foot (the hop), then leaps again and lands on the opposite foot (the step), then leaps again and lands on both feet in the pit (the jump). The performer may run as far as he desires during the approach. He may not carry weights in the hands or use other devices to aid him. The distance of the triple jump is measured along a straight line from the scratch line to the nearest point of contact with the surface of the sand-filled pit in which the performer lands at the completion of the jump.

### TRIPLE JUMP TECHNIQUE

The triple jump can be logically divided into the following: 1) the *approach*; 2) the *hop*; 3) the *step*; and 4) the *jump*. None of the phases should be emphasized to the point that it affects another phase negatively, because success is dependent upon excellence in all phases.

Ordinarily the hop and the jump are about equal length, while the step is somewhat shorter. The height of the hop and step must be minimized to maintain the horizontal momentum necessary for a long jump. The relative angles of the three parts of the triple jump are represented on the following diagram.

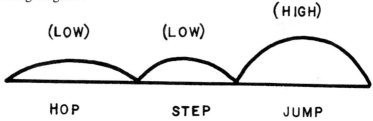

### The Approach

The length of the run will depend upon the distance that it takes for the athlete to gain near maximum speed. Typically the approach is about 120′ long. The length of the run and the check-marks can be determined in the same manner as for the long jump (see Chapter 10).

The approach run should be at maximum controllable speed, which is only slightly less than an all-out sprint. The jumper should not strain, but he should run at near top speed, because as long as the run is relaxed and in good control, then the greater the speed at takeoff the greater will be the distance of the jump.

During the final phase of the approach the jumper must concentrate on horizontal momentum, and use no more lift than is necessary to achieve a successful hop and step. Only after the jumper has completed the hop and step should he attempt to gain vertical lift with a maximum effort.

### The Hop

In the hop the takeoff foot is also the foot on which the athlete lands. The objectives of the hop include: 1) obtaining adequate distance without losing horizontal momentum; 2) controlling and maintaining body balance, and 3) landing in correct position to effectively perform the next phase, the step.

To perform a good hop the jumper should settle back slightly on his heels and run more flat-footed during the last few strides of the approach. He should not rear back on the board as the long jumper does, because he does not want too much height during the hop. His eyes should be focused straight ahead and he should not look up or down as he hops, for this will tend to destroy his balance. The jumper should take off at an angle no more than 20°, because a low angle is necessary to retain horizontal momentum, and still get good distance on the hop (Figure 11–1a, b, c).

Most jumpers use their stronger leg for the takeoff of the hop. This enables them also to use the strong leg for the first landing and for the takeoff of the step.

As the jumper leaves the board, he swings the lead knee forward and upward almost to hip level so the thigh is nearly parallel to the ground. This action should be more forward than upward (Figure 11–1b, c). After the body leaves the ground, the lead leg swings back to the straight position, and the takeoff leg is brought through, bent at the knee, and is positioned for the landing.

In the landing of the hop, the leg—with the foot ahead of the knee—is swung down to the ground. The foot must strike the ground and then "pull" the body forward. It must not be planted too far in front of the body in an attempt to gain distance, because this will result in a loss of the momentum needed for the step and the jump (Figure 11–1e, f).

The arm action is very important. The forward, upward thrust of the arms should be coordinated with the movements of the free leg in order to create inertia to complement the springing action of the takeoff leg. The jumper must hold the arms high and away from his sides and avoid dropping the arms below the waist, because dropping the arms too low will cause him to partially buckle at the waist.

The body should remain tilted slightly forward, with the chest up. This provides a posture that allows the jumper to utilize his speed effectively through all three phases of the jump.

a

b

c

d

e

f

g

h

Fig. 11–1 (a–n).   Sequence drawings of correct technique in the triple jump.

### The Step

Too many triple jumpers make the mistake of failing to drive after landing from the hop.   At the completion of the hop the landing foot should touch flat, with the foot moving backwards as the leg pulls the body forward in an effort to retain momentum.   As the center of gravity comes over the contact foot, the jumper begins a vigorous thrust of the free leg.   The knee is driven forward and upward almost to hip height. The knee is swung high for position as well as to give added lift.   The foot of the free leg should be flexed with the toes up and directly below the knee (Figure 11–1e, f).   The trail leg should flex slightly at the knee and remain behind the hips.

The jumper holds this position and "rides out the step."   Just before he completes the step, the jumper extends the lead leg slightly as he makes the landing (Figure 11–1h).   Again the jumper must not reach too far forward with the foot at the landing or he will lose momentum.

*The Jump*

In the jump the athlete must put all of his remaining power into an effort to gain height and distance. If adequate momentum has been maintained through the hop and step, then the final phase should be highly successful.

The drive is made from the takeoff foot, with the free leg thrust vigorously forward and upward (Figure 11–1j). From a position behind the body, the arms swing forward and upward to aid in the lift. The head and chest should be held high.

As the athlete approaches the peak of his jump he should bring his trailing leg up to join the lead leg. Then both legs are brought farther forward (Figure 11–1m).

In the landing, the feet should be placed about 10″ apart. As the feet contact the sand, the knees bend and the hips pass forward between the knees. The arms should be driven down and back as the knees bend. This will help to drive the body up and over the feet and prevent the jumper from falling back into the pit. (See also the section on landing in Chapter 10.)

## JUMPING RATIOS

An athlete should not slavishly copy the ratios of another jumper but should develop the jumping pattern that seems to suit his ability best. However, the following list of distances can serve as a useful guide (recorded in feet).

| Total Distance | Hop | Step | Jump |
|---|---|---|---|
| 40 | 14–9 | 10–6 | 14–9 |
| 42 | 15–6 | 11–0 | 15–6 |
| 44 | 16–1 | 11–10 | 16–1 |
| 46 | 16–9 | 12–6 | 16–9 |
| 48 | 17–4 | 13–4 | 17–4 |
| 50 | 18–0 | 14–0 | 18–0 |
| 52 | 18–6 | 15–0 | 18–6 |
| 54 | 18–10 | 16–4 | 18–10 |

## APPLICATION OF SCIENTIFIC PRINCIPLES

The following are explanations of how certain scientific laws and principles apply to the triple jump.

*If a force is applied to a body or object, the body develops greater velocity as the distance of force application is increased.* In each leap of the triple jump it is important that the leg be flexed to the optimum angle and that the foot remain in contact with the surface until the leg and foot are fully extended.  Some jumpers tend to break contact with the surface prematurely.

*In general all forces should be applied as directly as possible in the direction of the intended motion.*  Correct direction of force application is especially important in the triple jump.  The forces should be mostly horizontal with only enough vertical component to raise the body to the optimum height in each leap.  Misdirected forces will result in the wrong angle of projection and loss of the momentum necessary to carry the athlete through the three leaps.

*The momentum of moving body segments can be transferred to the total body.*  In the triple jump the momentum from the swinging action of the free leg and the arms is transferred to the total body to help lift the body upward and thrust it forward.  These actions are very important to the performer's success (Figure 11–1j).

*When performing activities in which two or more consecutive motions contribute to movement in the same direction, there should usually be no pause between the motions.*  This principle is especially important in the triple jump where the athlete must cover as much distance as possible in three successive leaps.  Any pause that causes a reduction of body momentum will detract from success.

*In throwing or jumping activities where maximum distance is the goal, final velocity in the intended direction is fundamental to success.*  With each leap the triple jumper will remain in flight a given length of time depending on the height he attains.  The distance he covers during the time in flight is determined by his horizontal speed at the time of takeoff.  The faster he is moving the farther he will go.

## COMMON FAULTS AND HOW TO CORRECT THEM

These common faults were identified through correspondence with coaches and outstanding performers.  The suggested corrections were provided by experts on triple jumping.

### The Approach and Takeoff

Fault:        Failure to strike the check-marks correctly.
Correction:  Run wind-sprints and low hurdles to develop an even and smooth stride.  Also, run through the approach several times each day.
Fault:        Slowing down just prior to the takeoff.
Correction:  It might be that the approach is too long.  If this seems to be the case, the run must be shortened accordingly.  Run through the approach several times each day and concentrate on maintaining optimal speed through the takeoff.
Fault:        Lengthening the last two or three steps before the takeoff.
Correction:  Adjust the check-marks so that stretching to hit the takeoff board is not necessary.  If the final check-mark is hit correctly, concentrate on the technique and not on hitting the board.

### The Hop

Fault:          During the flight of the hop, the jumper tends to lean back. This is a carry-over habit from the long jump.
Correction:     A marker to focus the eyes on should be placed beyond the pit. This will help to keep the head forward, and the body canted forward at the correct angle (Figure 11–1b).
Fault:          The hop is too high and too long.
Correction:     This is usually a result of stretching for the board at the takeoff, and thus placing the body weight too far behind the takeoff leg. The last step should be shortened so the body weight is over the takeoff leg when the takeoff foot is planted.
Fault:          Landing on a straight leg after the hop.
Correction:     Allow the leg to bend slightly at the knee. If the leg is kept too straight during the landing, it tends to retard the forward momentum.

### The Step

Fault:          Too much height during the step.
Correction:     This fault usually lies in the attempt to reach too far upon landing from the hop, which in turn tilts the body backward. To overcome this fault place the foot closer to the body upon landing from the hop and emphasize pulling the body forward over the foot.
Fault:          Raising the lead knee too high or not high enough going into the step.
Correction:     While doing pop-ups practice driving the lead knee to the correct height. A pop-up in this case means a short approach, and a short hop prior to the step.

### The Jump

Fault:          Insufficient momentum to achieve enough distance during the final phase, the jump.
Correction:     This is caused by either too much height or lack of drive during the hop or step or both. Analyze the hop and step to determine the cause of the problem, then work to correct it.
Fault:          Not enough height during the jump.
Correction:     After staying relatively low during the hop and step, it is important to project the body at the optimum angle during the jump. The problem here is essentially the same as in the long jump. It is recommended that the content of the chapter on long jumping be applied to this phase of the triple jump.

### Other Faults

Fault:          Poor rhythm—the rhythm should be even: *dah-dah-dah*, and not *dah-dit-dah*.
Correction:     The correct rhythm can be developed by using the standing hop, step and jump, and gradually increasing the distances while concentrating on an even rhythm.
Fault:          Failure to emphasize equally the hop, the step and the jump.
Correction:     Set challenging goals for each phase in order to have equal incentive to improve each of the phases. But be cautious about getting any phase out of correct proportion at the expense of the other two phases.

## THE TRAINING SCHEDULE

The following schedule can serve as an important guide for triple jumpers. It can be adjusted to fit the needs of any particular athlete depending upon his age, maturity and state of conditioning.

### Summer

During the summer months the triple jumper should maintain a high level of general conditioning by participating in vigorous activities which involve a considerable amount of running and jumping. These activities should be supplemented by selected exercises to keep a high level of muscular strength and endurance. (See the recommended exercises at the end of this chapter.)

### Fall

During the fall months the triple jumper should do weight training on Monday, Wednesday and Friday with emphasis on the development of power in the legs. Also he should do a considerable amount of running, mostly at near top speed. In addition, he should work regularly over low hurdles to increase the consistency of his stride and should work to improve his jumping form.

### Winter

This program is based on the assumption that the jumper is preparing for the spring season. If he is preparing for the winter (indoor) season, then this program should be followed during the late fall. During the winter months the long jumper should do a considerable amount of sprinting in order to improve his running speed, to develop a more consistent stride and to improve endurance. The running of low hurdles is recommended as a method of improving the consistency of the stride. Also, he should increase the intensity of the weight training program in order to further improve power. He should do some jumping at less than maximum effort, emphasizing technique and the coordinations involved in the performance. A limited amount of maximum effort jumping should be done.

Monday:
1. Jog one-quarter mile.
2. Do stretching exercises such as: hurdle exercises from the sitting position; touching the toes from a standing position, keeping the knees stiff; vertical sit-ups, raising the feet and touching the toes in an inverted jackknife position; and inverted bicycle exercises, etc.
3. Run wind-sprints for one-half mile.
4. Go through the run-up five times at full speed.
5. Take ten jumps (pop-ups) doing the hop, step and jump.
6. Run three flights of 80-yard low hurdles.
7. Weight train (see exercises at the end of this chapter).

Tuesday:
1. Jog one-quarter mile.
2. Do stretching exercises.
3. Run one-half mile of wind-sprints.
4. Take eight jumps (pop-ups) doing the hop, step and jump.
5. Run three flights of 80-yard low hurdles.
6. Take starts from the blocks running 50 yards each time.

Wednesday:
1. Jog one-quarter mile.
2. Do stretching exercises.
3. Run one-half mile of wind-sprints.
4. Take five jumps (pop-ups).
5. Take ten jumps using the full run; five jumps at half-speed and five jumps at three-quarter speed.
6. Weight train.

Thursday:
1. Jog one-quarter mile.
2. Do stretching exercises.
3. Run one-half mile of wind-sprints.
4. Take ten jumps (pop-ups).
5. Take six starts from the blocks, sprinting 50 yards each time.
6. Run three flights of 80-yard low hurdles.

Friday:
1. Jog one-quarter mile.
2. Do stretching exercises.
3. Run one-half mile of wind-sprints.
4. Go through the run three times at full speed, checking the accuracy of the check-marks.

Saturday:
1. Warm up as on the day of competition.
2. Jump for distance.
3. Run wind-sprints.
4. Weight train.

## Spring (Early and Middle Portion)

Monday:
1. Jog one-quarter mile.
2. Do stretching exercises.
3. Run one-half mile of wind-sprints.
4. Go through the full run five times at full speed.
5. Take eight jumps (pop-ups), doing the hop, step and jump.
6. Take five jumps using the full run at three-quarter speed. Work on the "gather" and on lifting off the board.
7. Weight train (see exercises at the end of this chapter).

Tuesday:
1. Jog one-quarter mile.
2. Do stretching exercises.
3. Run one-half mile of wind-sprints.
4. Run three flights of 80-yard low hurdles.
5. Take five starts from the blocks, sprinting 50 yards each time.

Wednesday:
1. Jog one-quarter mile.
2. Do stretching exercises.
3. Run one-half mile of wind-sprints.
4. Take eight jumps (pop-ups).
5. Take five jumps using the full run at full speed each time.
6. Weight train.

Thursday:
1. Jog one-quarter mile.
2. Do stretching exercises.
3. Run one-half mile of wind-sprints.

|        |                                                                          |
|--------|--------------------------------------------------------------------------|
|        | 4. Take five starts from the blocks and sprint 50 yards each time.        |
|        | 5. Go through the approach run at full speed five times.                  |

Friday:      Rest or do light work with emphasis on technique and coordination.

Saturday:      1. Day of meet—arrive at the field early enough to place checkmarks, etc. Run through the approach four or five times. Be confident and relaxed.

                   2. After competition, run wind-sprints.

                   3. Weight train.

### Late Spring (May–June)

During the late season the triple jumper will do the same kind of training as during the mid season. The volume of work should usually be increased to peak the athlete out at the end of the season. How much the volume increases will be determined by the athlete's state of conditioning and whether he shows signs of staleness. Increased emphasis should be placed on the fine points of correct technique and on attaining peak condition.

### CONDITIONING EXERCISES

Like the long jump, the triple jump is primarily a power event. Both running speed and spring from the takeoff board are fundamental to triple jumping. The following exercises will help develop power in the muscle groups that contribute the most to the triple jump. The exercises are illustrated in Appendix A.

Straight arm forward raise—exercise #1
Trunk flexion—exercise #14
Jumping jack—exercise #21
Half squat—exercise #22
Heel raise—exercise #23
Quadriceps drill—exercise #24
Vertical jump drill—exercise #28
Hip flexion (lead leg)—exercise #27

CHAPTER **12**

# Pole Vault

The origin of the pole vault is connected with survival and war activities of early man.  Athletically speaking, an event called *pole jumping* figured in the program of the ancient Tailteann games of Ireland.  However, it did not appear in the program of the ancient Olympic games.  In the modern era of athletics, pole vaulting appeared in Germany around the middle of the nineteenth century.  Initially, the event was vaulting for distance rather than for height.  Some pole vaulting for height was done in England during the 1850s and 1860s.  Sometime in the 1870s the event began to appear in track and field meets in America and Japan.  The Americans ruled out the practice of climbing the pole and thus laid the foundation for the modern vaulting technique.

Results in the early editions of the world Olympics were generally unimpressive, and it was not until the third modern Olympic games in 1908 that 12' was surpassed in the games.  During that same year, Walter Dray of the United States raised the world record to $12'9\frac{1}{2}''$.

History's first 13-foot vaulter was another American named Robert Gardner who achieved 13'1" in 1912.  And in 1927, American Sabin Carr equalled the 14' barrier.  The 15-foot mark was not surpassed until 1940 when Cornelius Warmerdam of the United States did $15'1\frac{1}{8}''$.  His best vault was $15'7\frac{3}{4}''$ in 1942, a mark which stood as a world record for 15 years.

Around 1960 the fiberglass vaulting pole came into being.  This started a revolution of pole vaulting marks throughout the world.  Using the fiberglass pole, John Uelses of the United States broke the 16' barrier in 1962 and, two years later, Fred Hansen of the United States broke the 17' barrier when he cleared 17'4".  Since that time numerous vaulters have exceeded the 17' mark and the current world record is $18'5\frac{3}{4}''$ held by Seagren of the United States set in 1972.  With the possibility of still further improvements being made in the vaulting pole and with improved training and performance techniques, it is difficult to project how high vaulters will go in the near future. Following is a list of the world records for the pole vault.

| Height | Record-holder and country | Year |
|---|---|---|
| 10ft. | J. Wheeler, Great Britain | 1866 |
| 10ft. 6½in. | R. J. C. Mitchell, Great Britain | 1868 |
| 10ft. 9in. | H. E. Kayall, Great Britain | 1877 |
| 10ft. 11in. | William Van Houten, U.S.A. | 1880 |
| 11ft. ½in. | Hugh Baxter, U.S.A. | 1883 |
| 11ft. 5in. | Hugh Baxter, U.S.A. | 1887 |
| 11ft. 5⅜in. | Walter Rodenbaugh, U.S.A. | 1892 |
| 11ft. 10½in. | Raymond Clapp, U.S.A | 1898 |
| 12ft. 1³⁄₁₀in. | Norman Cole, U.S.A. | 1904 |
| 12ft. 2in. | F. Gouder, France | 1905 |
| 12ft. 4⅞in. | LeRoy Samse, U.S.A. | 1906 |
| 12ft. 5½in. | Walter Dray, U.S.A. | 1907 |
| 12ft. 7½in. | Alfred Gilbert, U.S.A. | 1908 |
| 12ft. 9½in. | Walter Dray, U.S.A. | 1908 |
| 12ft. 10⅞in. | Leland Scott, U.S.A. | 1910 |
| 13ft. 1in. | Robert Gardner, U.S.A. | 1912 |
| 13ft. 2¼in. | Marc Wright, U.S.A. | 1912 |
| 13ft. 5in. | Frank Foss, U.S.A. | 1920 |
| 13ft. 6⅛in. | Charles Hoff, Norway | 1922 |
| 13ft. 9¾in. | Charles Hoff, Norway | 1923 |
| 13ft. 11⅜in. | Charles Hoff, Norway | 1925 |

| Height | Record-holder and country | Year |
|---|---|---|
| 14ft. | Sabin Carr, U.S.A. | 1927 |
| 14ft. 1½in. | Lee Barnes, U.S.A. | 1928 |
| 14ft. 4⅜in. | William Graber, U.S.A. | 1932 |
| 14ft. 5⅛in. | Keith Brown, U.S.A. | 1935 |
| 14ft. 6½in. | George Varoff, U.S.A. | 1936 |
| 14ft. 11in. | William Sefton, U.S.A. | 1937 |
| 15ft. 1⅛in. | Cornelius Warmerdam, U.S.A. | 1940 |
| 15ft. 5¾in. | Cornelius Warmerdam, U.S.A. | 1941 |
| 15ft. 7¾in. | Cornelius Warmerdam, U.S.A. | 1942 |
| 15ft. 8¼in. | R. A. Gutowski, U.S.A. | 1957 |
| 15ft. 9¼in. | Donald Bragg, U.S.A. | 1960 |
| 15ft. 10¼in. | George Davies, U.S.A. | 1961 |
| 16ft. ¾in. | John Uelses, U.S.A. | 1962 |
| 16ft. 2in. | David Tork, U.S.A. | 1962 |
| 16ft. 2½in. | Pentti Nikula, Finland | 1962 |
| 16ft. 10¾in. | M. Preussger, Germany | 1964 |
| 17ft. 4in. | Fred Hansen, U.S.A. | 1964 |
| 17ft. 6¼in. | John Pennel, U.S.A. | 1966 |
| 17ft. 7¾in. | Paul Wilson, U.S.A. | 1967 |
| 18ft. 5¾in. | Bob Seagren, U.S.A. | 1972 |

## PROCEDURES AND RULES

The vaulter runs at near top speed down the runway and attempts to clear the cross bar by use of the vaulting pole. The rules permit the athlete to run as far as he desires during the approach. He must plant the pole in the box, then ride the pole up and over the bar. The bar may not be displaced from the standards by either the body or the pole. The performer is allowed three consecutive misses before being eliminated. The height of a vault is measured along a perfectly vertical line from the top of the vaulting box (or an extension thereof) to the top of the cross bar.

## POLE VAULT TECHNIQUE

The pole vault is among the most complex events in sports. It is one unified and inseparable action which begins with the first step of the run and ends when the vaulter lands in the pit. There are four important aspects to achieving excellent performance in the vault. They are, 1) near maximum horizontal velocity during the final part of the approach; 2) effective conversion of the horizontal momentum to the vertical direction; 3) additional vertical lift coming primarily from the pull and push with the arms; and 4) effectively crossing over the bar. In order to cover the various aspects of vaulting, the subsequent discussion is divided into the following phases: *pole selection*, the *run*, *pole grip* and *carry*, *pole plant*, the *takeoff*, the *rock-back*, *pull-up* and *push-up*, *pole release* and *cross bar clearance* and the *landing*. The discussion applies to a right-handed vaulter. The directions would be reversed for a left-handed vaulter.

### Pole Selection

The fiberglass pole, which is now used universally among expert vaulters, has three distinct advantages:

1. It permits a vaulter to use a higher hand grip. Vaulters can hold as much as 12″–18″ higher on the fiberglass pole than on a steel pole.

2. The flexibility of the fiberglass pole causes a more efficient conversion of energy from the run to stored energy in the pole.

3. The flexibility of the fiberglass pole has taken away the terrific shock at the moment of takeoff experienced by vaulters using the less flexible steel pole. This tends to cause vaulters to run harder into the vault, and thus have greater speed at the moment of takeoff.

The vaulter should select a pole that is strong enough to hold him without breaking, and yet one that will bend a considerable amount as a result of the force placed upon it. One of the keys to success is to obtain a pole with just the right amount of stiffness for the particular vaulter, so that its release of stored energy is synchronized with the actions of the vaulter. The selection must be based on past experience and experimentation with different poles.

### The Run

The length of the run will vary with the amount of distance required by the vaulter to develop a comfortable and powerful stride with sufficient speed. The run should not be so long that the vaulter begins to tire near the end. On the other hand, it should be long enough to enable him to reach the optimum speed. It is better to run slower and perform the mechanics of the pole plant and takeoff with perfection than to run full speed and perform these movements poorly. However, as long as the vaulter is able to maintain proper control, then the more speed he has the higher he will vault.

Two check-marks on the runway are preferred by most vaulters, one placed at the start of the run (110–135′ from the box) and the other 70–80′ from the box. The second mark is used to check the accuracy of the stride at that point in the approach.

The exact position of the check-marks and the length of the run can be determined on the running track. To do this a distance of about 125′ is measured off on the track. The vaulter stands at the end of the measured distance with both feet on the first mark. He steps forward with the takeoff foot and runs down the track carrying the pole with a relaxed running style. The coach checks the point where the takeoff foot strikes the ground at the end of the run. The vaulter runs through again and the coach checks where the takeoff foot strikes the ground near the midpoint of the run, and this becomes the second check-mark. The run should be repeated several times until the vaulter and coach are satisfied that the check-marks and the length of the run are correct. Then the marks can be moved to the pole vault runway. The vaulter should test the distance of the run and the check-marks by practicing the vault. It may be necessary to adjust the check-marks slightly due to different runway surfaces. A vaulter should do a considerable amount of running with the pole in order that he will develop a smooth and consistent run while carrying the pole.

### Pole Grip and Carry

In carrying the pole, the left hand acts as a fulcrum and the main force is applied with the right hand, which pulls down on the pole. The pole should be carried in a manner that allows a comfortable and relaxed run. The pole should not be punched back and forth during the approach, because this action interferes with the smoothness of the run and makes an accurate pole plant difficult. The pole should be carried at an angle that will allow for ease and smoothness of the plant. The best height is with the tip of the pole at approximately eye level (Figure 12–1a,b).

A pole will bend more easily in one direction than in any other direction. This direction is referred to as the "bend direction." Most vaulters mark the pole near the bottom on the side opposite the direction the pole will bend. The vaulter carries the pole in such a way that when it is placed in the box the "bend direction" will be upward and to the left, away from the vaulter.

### Pole Plant

The pole plant is one of the keys to a successful vault. To achieve an optimum bend, an early, vigorous and near perfect plant is necessary. The planting action should start three strides before the takeoff, and the pole should be in the box before the takeoff foot strikes the ground.

As the plant starts, the right hand pulls toward the body to straighten the pole in line with the box. Then the hands push the pole forward toward the box with the pole kept close to the body. This action continues until the pole is in the box and the right hand is in front of and above the head. This is the position just before the takeoff foot reaches the ground. If the vaulter brings the pole around the body instead of straight forward, the

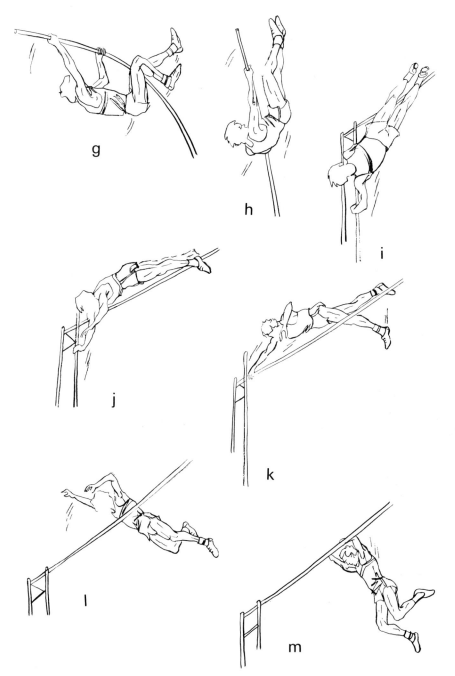

Fig. 12–1 (a–m). Sequence drawings of correct technique in the pole vault.

action will interfere with balance at the takeoff. A great amount of the imbalance seen in pole vaulting can be attributed to a poor pole plant (Figure 12–1c, d).

The hand spread during the plant should be about shoulder width. This enables the vaulter to control the bend of the pole, to keep the pole out ahead of the body (which is very important) and to speed up the rock-back and pull-up actions.

### The Takeoff

The placement of the takeoff foot must allow a smooth and powerful transition from the run to the vault. The correct takeoff point is perhaps the greatest single contribution to a successful vault. The takeoff foot should be placed in the middle of the runway directly under the top hand when the pole is in the box and the arm is extended fully overhead. If the vaulter places the takeoff foot too closely to the box, he will swing far ahead of the pole and will stall out. If the takeoff foot is too far away from the box, the vaulter will tend to "jump onto the pole" thus destroying any chance for a powerful drive forward and upward.

The pole-body alignment at the takeoff finds the pole bisecting the body when viewed from the front or rear. Poor pole-body alignment can cause the vaulter to swing off to one side during the vault.

During the takeoff, the vaulter springs off the ground much like the long jumper does. The lead knee is driven upward and toward the back of the pit as the left leg (takeoff) is vigorously extended. A driving action with

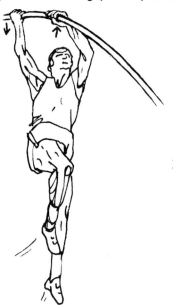

Fig. 12–2.   Body position at the time of takeoff.

the hands upward and forward will increase the vaulter's velocity in that direction (Figure 12–1d, e).

The vaulter should attempt to control the takeoff and swing by stiffening the left arm and maintaining a firm grip with the right hand. This helps keep the pole the correct distance away from the body and aids in the pole bend. This action also provides the vaulter with a pivotal axis around which to rotate the body on the flexing and moving pole (Figure 12–2).

### The Rock-Back

The rock-back phase of the vault is another critical phase. It is accomplished by a sweep of the right knee forward and upward toward the head. The trail (takeoff) leg is also swept upward immediately following the lead leg, and the head is dropped back sharply. This results in flexion of the hips and knees as the vaulter assumes the rock-back position.

The rock-back can be compared to a position of lying on the back on the floor with the hips flexed and the knees toward the chest. The eyes should be focused straight up or slightly backward. If the vaulter looks at the cross bar it will hinder the rock-back action (Figure 12–1g).

During the rock-back, the body tends to rush ahead of the pole. The vaulter must resist this by keeping the left arm fairly straight and stiff. This holds him behind the pole and permits him to take full advantage of the momentum of the swing. If it is properly timed, the rock-back will place the vaulter correctly into the third and last critical position, the pre-pull position.

In the pre-pull position, the hips are at least even with the shoulders, the back is parallel to the ground, and the legs are pointed upward and are parallel to the pole. When the vaulter has reached this position the pull-up starts.

### The Pull-up and Push-up

The pull-up-turn-push-up is one continuous and powerful movement. The vaulter should have no feeling of hesitation between these phases. When executing the pull-up, the vaulter must have his hips and legs traveling in a near vertical direction. If he fails to do this, the thrust of the pole will tend to push him toward or under the cross bar. The pull-up action can be supplemented by an upward driving action of the legs, resulting from partial straightening at the hips. This action is initiated during the swing-up, and comes in unison with the snap (straightening) of the pole (Figure 12–1h).

During the pull-up, the vaulter must not reach for the bar with his legs. This can be prevented by concentrating on getting the hips and legs high into the air. The vaulter must also prevent turning over too soon. The turn should be delayed until the vaulter has pulled himself into the optimal position for the push-up (Figure 12–1i)

FIG. 12–3. Body position at the time of pole release.

The push-up action is done while the hips and legs are still moving up-ward. If the vaulter attempts to push as the hips are falling, he fails to gain additional height and will likely push himself into the cross bar. The pull and the push must be very vigorous and perfectly timed in order to thrust the body as high as possible (Figure 12–1j).

### Pole Release and Cross Bar Clearance

Due to the spread of the hands, the lower hand releases first, followed immediately by a final upward push and release with the upper hand. During the push-up phase, the feet and legs are put over the bar, then dropped down as the vaulter assumes a partial pike (jackknife) position. At this point the hips are over the bar. This is followed immediately by a "fly-away" action where the vaulter makes the final push from the pole and throws the chest and arms upward and backward in an effort to get the upper portion of the body over the bar (Figures 12–1k and 12–3).

### The Landing

The use of the foam rubber pit has allowed the vaulter to land prac-tically any way he chooses. However, most faulters land on the middle and upper back, absorbing most of the shock over a large area, and with the hips and knees slightly flexed, and the arms generally outward from the body.

## BENDING THE POLE

Having a pole of the correct weight, and then getting maximum bend of the pole are both very important factors to vaulting. There are four essen-

FIG. 12–4.    Bend of the pole soon after takeoff.

tial considerations related to bending the pole: 1) the weight of the vaulter; 2) the height of the top hand on the pole in relation to the position of the bottom hand; 3) the force the vaulter applies at the time he plants the pole; and 4) the forces he applies upward with the left hand and downward with the right hand (Figure 12–4).    Improvement of any of these factors will result in more pole bend.

If a vaulter's pole does not bend far enough, there are several possible reasons: 1) the pole might be too stiff for the vaulter (incorrect weight of the pole); 2) the vaulter might be using an over-relaxed takeoff and fail to *drive* into the box; 3) he might fail to offer sufficient resistance on the pole with the left arm;  4) the hands might not be far enough apart;  5) the vaulter might hold the pole too closely to him at the takeoff instead of extending the arms and pushing the pole upward; 6) the vaulter might not rock-back on the pole soon enough; 7) he might fail to throw his head back sufficiently hard to assist in the rock-back action; 8) the takeoff point might be wrong, either too far forward or too far backward; 9) the vaulter might lack forcefulness in flexing the thighs and knees while rocking back.

## APPLICATION OF SCIENTIFIC PRINCIPLES

Certain scientific principles apply to pole vaulting.    They are stated and their applications are explained.

*If a force is applied to a body, the body develops greater velocity as the distance of force application is increased.*    In vaulting it is very important that the takeoff leg and foot move through full extension before the foot breaks contact with the ground.    During this same time it is important that the vaulter continue his drive into the box in order to get maximum bend of the pole. In other words, it is important that the vaulter not break contact with the ground prematurely.

*In general, all forces should be applied as directly as possible in the direction of the intended motion.* In the vault, misdirected forces can detract considerably from the vaulter's effectiveness. This is especially true during the pulling and pushing phases. If the forces are misdirected, it is likely they will result in too much horizontal and too little vertical movement of the body.

*If an implement has elasticity, it can temporarily store force and then return the force after a brief delay.* When the fiberglass vaulting pole is inserted in the vaulting box and the vaulter applies sufficient force against the pole, it bends and remains bent for a brief time, then springs back to its original shape thus releasing the force that has been temporarily stored. The amount of force that will be released is determined by how far the pole is bent, and the amount of elasticity it has.

*When performing activities in which two or more consecutive motions contribute to movement in the same direction, there usually should be no pause between the motions.* This principle applies especially to the pull-up and push-up actions of the vaulter. When he pulls himself upward, then reverses and pushes farther upward, there should be no pause. The pull and push must be a continuous action.

## COMMON FAULTS AND HOW TO CORRECT THEM

The common faults stated below along with the recommended correction techniques were identified by pole vault experts and coaches who have produced champion vaulters.

### The Approach

Fault:         Failure to maintain adequate momentum through the pole plant phase.

Correction:   Run wind-sprints with the pole, concentrating on driving into the last portion of the run. This will help the vaulter to become conscious of the importance of driving into the box. Also practice the run on the runway without the cross bar, and concentrate on driving into the box and then run through the pit.

Fault:         Failure to strike the check-marks accurately.

Correction:   Place the check-marks on the running track and practice the approach while carrying the pole until the check-marks are struck consistently. It might be that the marks need to be adjusted. Also practice a considerable amount of running at the speed used during the approach (relaxed sprint), and concentrate on a consistent stride. Some vaulters find it helpful to practice running low hurdles because a consistent stride is required in hurdling.

Fault:         Failure to use a relaxed sprint during the approach.

Correction:   Do a considerable amount of running on the track with the pole and concentrate on a relaxed sprint. It is important to have as much speed as possible and yet not strain. Try to develop a relaxed but powerful stride.

Fault: Insufficient speed at the end of the approach.

Correction: Run wind-sprints both with and without the pole in an effort to develop as much speed as possible while still running relaxed.

### The Pole Plant

Fault: Failure to start the plant soon enough.

Correction: Start about 20' from the box and run slowly through the pole plant, concentrating on starting the plant three strides from the box. A mark can be placed on the runway at the point where the plant should start.

Fault: The hands are moved too closely together during the plant.

Correction: If the bottom hand is being moved up too far during the plant, a piece of tape can be placed on the pole to mark the point where the left hand should grip the pole.

Fault: The pole is not raised directly over the vaulter's head during the plant.

Correction: Start four or five steps back and walk through the plant several times concentrating on pushing the pole directly over the head. The right arm should be fairly straight and the right hand should be directly above the head.

### The Takeoff

Fault: Failure to drive hard from the ground at the takeoff.

Correction: While using a short approach and reduced speed, practice springing off the ground much like the long jumper does. Drive the lead knee vigorously forward and upward.

Fault: Placing the takeoff foot too far forward, too far backward, or to the left or right of the correct takeoff point.

Correction: The check-marks might need to be adjusted to cause the foot to strike the correct takeoff point. Also a piece of tape can be placed at the desired position on the runway. This will serve as a guide as to where the takeoff foot should strike the runway. However, the vaulter must not look down as he prepares to take off; he should only be aware of the position of the marker.

### The Swing and Rock-Back

Fault: Failure to bring the knees—especially the knee of the trail leg—up fast toward the chest and simultaneously to drop the head back.

Correction: Hang on a high bar and practice the rock-back action by bringing the knees high toward the chest and dropping the head backward. Also practice this action while vaulting at a low height and with a short run.

Fault: Failure to hold the rock-back position long enough.

Correction: It is important to stay on the back until the pole begins to straighten. Through experimentation it can be learned how long this position should be held. Then it is important to force yourself to hold the position for just the right length of time.

Fault: Failure to "hang" on the pole during the swing.

Correction: It is important that the vaulter stay behind the pole and hang for a sufficient length of time. To accomplish this, keep the left arm fairly straight and rigid during the swing. It is important to keep the center of gravity far away from the grip during this phase in order to conserve momentum which will be used later to bring the body into correct position for the pull-up.

### The Pull-up and Turn

| | |
|---|---|
| Fault: | Beginning the pull-up before the pole has started to straighten. |
| Correction: | Force yourself to hold the rock-back position until the pole begins to straighten, then coordinate the initial phase of the pull-up with the initial response of the pole. |
| Fault: | Starting the turn too soon. |
| Correction: | The correction here is similar to the previous one. It might be necessary to force a delay in the turning action until the legs and hips are in a nearly vertical position, because once the turn has been started the vaulter is in no position to effectively continue the pull-up. |
| Fault: | Failure to reach a near handstand position at the crest of the vault. |
| Correction: | Here again it is important to delay the turn until the hips and legs are as high as possible. This will permit the vaulter to turn over into a near handstand position and push from that position. |

### Other Errors

| | |
|---|---|
| Fault: | The vaulter uses a pole which is either too flexible or too stiff. |
| Correction: | In this regard, it is important to receive guidance from a knowledgeable coach, and this must be combined with a certain amount of experimentation with poles before the proper one can be selected. |
| Fault: | Releasing the pole too soon at the crest of the vault. |
| Correction: | It is important to "stay on" the pole until the body has reached the handstand position and completed the final push. Force yourself to perform a complete push-off. |
| Fault: | Releasing the pole too late. |
| Correction: | It is important to let go of the pole at just the right time as you spring off of it during the fly away. It is necessary to concentrate on releasing at this time and to not hold onto the pole too long. |

## THE TRAINING SCHEDULE

Following is a recommended training schedule for an experienced vaulter. It can be adjusted slightly as needed to fit the requirements of any particular athlete.

### Summer

During the summer the pole vaulter should maintain a high level of general conditioning by participating in a variety of activities which involve the major muscle groups. The vaulter should emphasize running, along with activities which develop the arms and shoulders. Play-type (fartlek) running and gymnastics are especially recommended. These activities should be supplemented with exercises to keep a high level of strength and endurance in the muscle groups used the most in vaulting (see the recommended exercises at the end of this chapter). Summer employment which involves vigorous muscular work is generally beneficial.

### Fall

During the fall the vaulter should follow a sound weight training program on Monday, Wednesday and Friday, and should do an extensive amount of running. Much of the running should be at vaulting speed, and some of it should be done with pole in hand. Also, a considerable amount of vaulting should be done, with the emphasis on form rather than height.

### Winter

The training program during the winter will be influenced by whether the athlete competes in an indoor season. The following program is based on the assumption that the vaulter is preparing for the spring season. If he is preparing for a winter season, this program should be employed during the late fall.

The athlete should continue to do a considerable amount of running at near top speed, sometimes carrying the pole. He should increase the intensity of his exercise program in order to increase strength and power to near maximum levels. Also, he should do some work in gymnastics and practice vaulting mostly at less than maximum height but sometimes he should vault at maximum.

Monday:
1. Jog one-quarter mile
2. Do exercises that include: push-ups; walking on hands; high kicks; hurdle exercises from sitting position; and vertical sit-ups, raising feet and touching toes in an inverted jackknife position.
3. Run one-half mile of wind-sprints.
4. Work for 15 minutes on the run-up, giving special attention to check-marks and the takeoff points.
5. Take six to eight vaults using a run of 40–50'.
6. Take 10–14 vaults using a full run.
7. Work for 10 minutes on the horizontal bar. Do pull-ups and kick-ups.
8. Weight train (see recommended exercises at the end of this chapter).

Tuesday:
1. Jog one-quarter mile.
2. Do calisthenic exercises. (See number 2 above.)
3. Run one-half mile of wind-sprints.
4. Run four full straightaways with the pole, working on speed and relaxation.
5. Work for 30 minutes on parallel bars, horizontal bar and rope climb.

Wednesday:
1. Jog one-quarter mile.
2. Do exercises.
3. Run one-half mile of wind-sprints.
4. Work for 15 minutes on the hand shift and pole plant, doing the last four strides of the run only.
5. Take six vaults using a short run.
6. Take 10–15 vaults using a full run.
7. Take six starts running 25 yards each time.
8. Weight train.

Thursday:
1. Jog one-quarter mile.
2. Do exercises.
3. Run one-half mile of wind-sprints.
4. Run five straightaways with the pole.
5. Do 30 minutes of work on parallel bar, horizontal bar and rope.

Friday:
1. Jog one-quarter mile.
2. Do stretching exercises.
3. Run one-half mile of wind-sprints.
4. Practice a limited amount on vaulting form.

Saturday:
1. Warm-up.
2. Vault for maximum height as in competition.
3. Weight train.

### Spring (Early and Middle Portion)

Monday:
1. Jog one-quarter mile.
2. Do exercises.
3. Run one-half mile of wind-sprints.
4. Take five vaults using a short run.
5. Take 10–15 vaults using a full run.
6. Run three straightaways with the pole.
7. Weight train.

Tuesday:
1. Jog one-quarter mile.
2. Do exercises.
3. Run one-half mile of wind-sprints.
4. Take six starts running out of the blocks for 25 yards.
5. Do 30 minutes of exercises on parallel bars, horizontal bar and rope.

Wednesday:
1. Jog one-quarter mile.
2. Do exercises.
3. Run one-half mile of wind-sprints.
4. Work for 10 minutes on the hand shift and pole plant using only the last four strides of the run.
5. Do 10–15 vaults. The last six are to be done at maximum height.
6. Run three straightaways with the pole.
7. Weight train.

Thursday:
1. Jog one-quarter mile.
2. Do exercises.
3. Run one-half mile of wind-sprints.
4. Take six starts running out of the blocks for 25 yards each time.
5. Work for 30 minutes on the bars and rope.

Friday:
Rest or study movies of pole vaulting.

Saturday:
1. Day of the meet—be on the field early enough to place check marks, etc. Check your run at least four or five times. Vault at medium height four or five times before competition begins. Be confident and relaxed.
2. Weight train following competition.

### Late Spring (May–June)

Ordinarily the volume of work will be increased slightly during the late season in order to peak out the athlete. Increased emphasis should be placed on perfecting the technique and improving consistency. Perfection of coordination and timing deserves increased attention during this time.

## CONDITIONING EXERCISES

The pole vault requires a good deal of strength and power in all of the major muscle groups of the body because it involves a combination of running speed and vaulting action. Running speed is dependent upon powerful leg muscles while the vaulting action depends more upon the strength and power of the muscles of the upper body. The following conditioning exercises will assist in developing the desired levels of strength and power. The exercises are illustrated in Appendix A.

Hand stand push-ups—exercise #10
Supine pull-over—exercise #2
Hand grip—exercise #12
Pull-ups—exercise #9
Arm curl—exercise #3
Body curl—exercise #16
Trunk rotation (supine)—exercise #15
Jumping jack—exercise #21
Quadriceps drill—exercise #24
Heel raise—exercise #23
Leg raise (supine)—exercise #25

# Part IV
# Throwing Events

CHAPTER **13**

# Shot Put

Shot putting apparently started as a test of strength in the Scottish-Irish society. Originally a rock was used as the implement. The 16-pound iron ball appeared about the middle of the nineteenth century, and the seven-foot throwing ring became standard about the end of that century.

The first prominent figure in the modern era of shot putting was George Gray, who broke the world record six times. His best performance was 47' in 1893.

Ralph Rose of the United States was the first person to exceed 50' when he threw 51' even in 1909. This record stood for 21 years. Jack Torrance of the United States was the top shot-putter in the world during the 1930s breaking the world record three times and finally setting the mark at 57'1" in 1934. His record stood for 14 years. Charles Fonville, a relatively small shot putter, capitalized on superior technique and speed to set a world record of 58'$\frac{3}{4}$" in 1948. The pattern of speed and explosiveness introduced by Fonville was further developed by James Fuchs who had been state high school 100 yard dash champion in Illinois with a time of 9.9. Fuchs broke the world record four different times with his life-time best being 58'10$\frac{1}{2}$" in 1950. Parry O'Brien of the United States succeeded Fuchs as the leading shot putter in the world, and in 1954 he gained the distinction of being the first man to put the shot more than 60'. His throw went 60'10". Eventually he set a mark of 63'2" in 1956. Other potentially great shot putters adopted portions of O'Brien's superior technique and were subsequently able to exceed his performances.

William Nieder of the United States was the first person to exceed the 65-foot mark with a great effort in 1960. In 1965 Randy Matson of the United States exceeded 70'. Later he made a mark of 71'5$\frac{1}{2}$" accomplished in 1967. The tremendous upward trend in shot put performances during the past two decades is generally attributed to the broad use of the improved technique developed by O'Brien along with vastly increased muscular power resulting primarily from improved weight training methods. The following complete list of world records serves as a good indicator of the trend toward improvement in this event.

| *Distance* | *Record-holder and country* | *Year* |
|---|---|---|
| 30ft. 11$\frac{1}{2}$in. | J. M. Mann, U.S.A. | 1876 |
| 32ft. 5in. | Henry Buermeyer, U.S.A. | 1876 |
| 33ft. | Francis Larkin Jr., U.S.A. | 1877 |
| 37ft. 2in. | Henry Buermeyer, U.S.A. | 1877 |
| 37ft. 4in. | Henry Buermeyer, U.S.A. | 1878 |
| 42ft. 5in. | E. J. Bor, Great Britain | 1880 |
| 43ft. | Frank Lambrecht, U.S.A. | 1883 |
| 43ft. 9in. | J. OBrien, Great Britain | 1885 |
| 43ft. 11in. | George Gray, U.S.A. | 1887 |
| 44ft. 5in. | George Gray, U.S.A. | 1888 |
| 46ft. 2in. | George Gray, U.S.A. | 1890 |
| 46ft. 3$\frac{1}{2}$in. | George Gray, U.S.A. | 1891 |
| 46ft. 7$\frac{3}{4}$in. | George Gray, U.S.A. | 1891 |
| 47ft. | George Gray, U.S.A. | 1893 |
| 48ft. 2in. | Dennis Horgan, Ireland | 1898 |
| 48ft. 7in. | Ralph Rose, U.S.A. | 1904 |
| 49ft. 6in. | Wesley Coe, U.S.A. | 1905 |
| 49ft. 7$\frac{1}{2}$in. | Ralph Rose, U.S.A. | 1907 |
| 49ft. 10in. | Ralph Rose, U.S.A. | 1908 |
| 51ft. | Ralph Rose, U.S.A. | 1909 |
| 51ft. 9$\frac{5}{8}$in. | Emil Hirschfeld, Germany | 1928 |
| 52ft. $\frac{3}{4}$in. | John Kuck, U.S.A. | 1928 |
| 52ft. 7$\frac{1}{2}$in. | Emil Hirschfeld, Germany | 1928 |
| 52ft. 7$\frac{1}{2}$in. | Franz Danda, Czechoslovakia | 1931 |
| 52ft. 7$\frac{7}{8}$in. | Zygmunt Heljasz, Poland | 1932 |
| 53ft. $\frac{1}{2}$in. | Leo Sexton, U.S.A. | 1932 |
| 53ft. 1$\frac{3}{4}$in. | Franz Danda, Czechoslovakia | 1932 |
| 54ft. 1in. | John Lyman, U.S.A. | 1934 |
| 55ft. 1$\frac{1}{2}$in. | Jack Torrance, U.S.A. | 1934 |
| 55ft. 5in. | Jack Torrance, U.S.A. | 1934 |
| 57ft. 1in. | Jack Torrance, U.S.A. | 1934 |
| 58ft. $\frac{3}{8}$in. | Charles Fonville, U.S.A. | 1948 |
| 58ft. 4$\frac{3}{8}$in. | James Fuchs, U.S.A. | 1949 |
| 58ft. 5$\frac{1}{2}$in. | James Fuchs, U.S.A. | 1950 |
| 58ft. 8$\frac{1}{2}$in. | James Fuchs, U.S.A. | 1950 |
| 58ft. 10$\frac{1}{2}$in. | James Fuchs, U.S.A. | 1950 |
| 59ft. 2$\frac{1}{4}$in. | Parry O'Brien, U.S.A. | 1953 |
| 60ft. 10in. | Parry O'Brien, U.S.A. | 1954 |
| 63ft. 2in. | Parry O'Brien, U.S.A. | 1956 |
| 65ft. 7in. | William Nieder, U.S.A. | 1960 |
| 65ft. 10in. | William Nieder, U.S.A. | 1960 |
| 65ft. 10$\frac{1}{2}$in. | Dallas Long, U.S.A. | 1962 |
| 70ft. 7$\frac{1}{4}$in. | Randy Matson, U.S.A. | 1965 |
| 71ft. 5$\frac{1}{2}$in. | Randy Matson, U.S.A. | 1967 |
| 71ft. 7in. | Al Feuerbach, U.S.A. | 1973 |

## PROCEDURE

The modern technique of putting the shot is fairly well standardized, and the methods used by the different throwers vary only slightly from one another. The thrower grips the shot as illustrated in Figure 13–1. Starting near the backside of a seven-foot ring he moves across the ring in the direction of the put while hopping on one leg, then puts the shot while re-

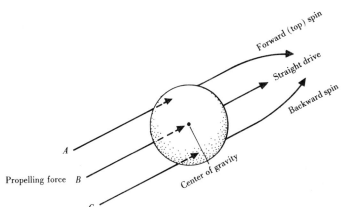

FIG. 13–1.   The motion of a projected object is influenced by the exact point of
application of the propelling force.   In putting the shot the force should be applied
directly through the center of the ball.

FIG. 13–2.   Two methods of holding
the shot.

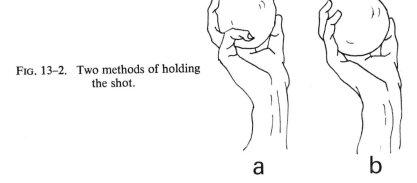

FIG. 13–3.   Position of the shot at the
beginning of movement across the ring.

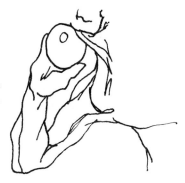

FIG. 13–4 (a–m). Sequence drawings of correct technique in putting the shot.

maining inside the ring. According to the rules the thrower may touch the inside surface of the stopboard and ring but may not touch the top surface of the board or ring and may not touch any place outside the ring until after the put has been marked. The shot must land within the designated area.

The distance of a throw is measured along a straight line from the nearest edge of the first mark made by the ball to the inside edge of the stopboard nearest such mark. A diagram of the throwing area appears in Chapter 19.

## SHOT PUT TECHNIQUE

The distance the shot travels depends upon its *velocity* at the moment of release and the *angle of projection*. The optimum angle of projection will vary depending on the height of the release and the distance of the put, but it will be approximately 38°. Provided the angle of release is optimum, then the velocity is the factor that determines the distance of the throw. Hence, the correct technique is the one that will result in the greatest velocity at release. It is important that the propelling force is applied through the center of the shot. Otherwise part of the force will be wasted in causing the shot to spin instead of projecting it forward and upward (Figure 13-1).

### Holding the Shot

For a right-handed putter the procedure for gripping the shot is to hold it in the left hand and lay the right hand loosely on top with the fingers spread slightly. Then turn the right hand over with the shot resting on the base of the fingers and push it under the jaw firmly against the neck. The saying "clean palm—dirty fingers—dirty neck" characterizes the proper position (Figures 13-2 and 13-3).

### The Stance at the Back of the Circle

The shot putter assumes a position at the rear of the circle with his weight on the right foot, which is placed close to the rim and pointing toward the rear. The left foot is placed approximately 18" closer to the middle of the circle with only the toe touching lightly for balance. During this preliminary stance, the left arm is held aloft to aid in balance. The head faces the rear with the eyes focused on a point six to ten feet behind the circle. The shoulders are square to the rear, and the right elbow is underneath the shot but held away from the chest (Figure 13-4a).

### The Glide

The purpose of the glide is to gain momentum while moving across the ring, and to lead into the correct position for the delivery (thrust). The initial movement is to lower the trunk and raise the left leg, causing the body to form a "T" with all the weight carried on the right leg. At this point, the shot should be outside the rear of the circle to increase the distance through which the force can be applied. The head, shoulders and hips remain square to the rear of the circle, and the right leg flexes in preparation for the drive across the ring (Figure 13-4b, c).

From the "T" position, the left thigh is swung downward and forward, and then driven back in a straight line toward the front of the circle. The back is kept low and straight. During the drive across the circle, the emphasis is upon attaining a tremendous split between the legs, which results in longer contact with the ground. The last contact with the rear of the circle will be the heel of the right foot. The glide must be long, low and fast, with the sole of the right foot barely clearing the surface. This results in maximum horizontal speed across the ring (Figure 13-4d, e, f, g and Figure 13-5).

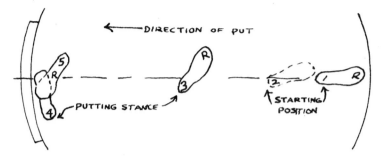

FIG. 13-5.   Foot pattern in movement across the ring (shot put).

FIG. 13-6.   Body actions during the early phase of delivery.

### The Throwing Position

The performer must arrive in a position of power at the front half of the circle.   The transition from the glide to the throwing position is completed as the right foot lands in the center of the circle with the toes pointed only slightly to the left.   This is followed immediately by the drive of the left leg hard and low against the stopboard at a point slightly to the left of center.   Any delay in the landing of the left foot results in a loss of momentum.   In this position, the shoulders are still square to the rear of the ring, the eyes are still focused on a point behind the circle and the right elbow is still underneath the shot (Figure 13-4g).

### The Delivery

At the completion of the glide, the putting action is initiated by rolling the head upward (eye focus leaves the ground) to guide the right shoulder and elbow into a high position. Simultaneously the right leg is straightened violently, driving against the resistance of the left leg which acts as a fulcrum. At the same time the vigorous trunk rotation and extension contributes to the forward-upward drive of the shot. This action is aided by a hard outward turning of the right heel, and a swift pull of the left arm high and away to the left. The left leg remains slightly flexed. As the trunk approaches an erect position, the right elbow is lifted to shoulder level, the eyes and chest are raised, and the back is arched. As the body weight passes over the left foot, the arm strikes. The arm strike is accompanied by a straightening of the left leg (Figures 13–4g through k and 13–6).

### The Release

The right foot leaves the ground ahead of the left foot. The instant before the left foot breaks contact, the putter gives the shot a final wrist and finger snap (Figures 13–4j, k; 13–7; 13–8).

### The Reverse

The reverse must be simple and natural. It is accomplished by reversing the feet, pointing the right shoulder and hip in the direction of the throw,

FIG. 13–7. The final phase of the delivery.

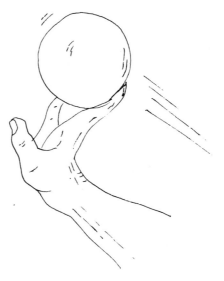

Fɪɢ. 13–8. Hand and finger action just prior to release.

bending the right knee and hip to lower the center of gravity and stretching the left leg toward the rear of the circle (Figure 13-4k, l, m).

## APPLICATION OF SCIENTIFIC PRINCIPLES

The correct application of the following scientific laws and principles is fundamental to effective shot put performances.

*The velocity of a body is changed only when acted upon by an additional force. The produced acceleration is proportional to and in the direction of the force.* The shot putter has only a short distance over which he can accelerate the shot. The more force applied the faster he can accelerate it and thus the greater will be the final velocity (velocity at moment of release). In other terms, maximum force must be applied over the contact distance in order to accelerate the shot as rapidly as possible.

*If a force is applied to a body (or object) the body develops greater velocity as the distance over which the force is applied increases.* In order to produce maximum final velocity, it is important for the thrower to apply force over as much distance as possible in order that he can accelerate the shot over a longer period of time. This is part of the justification for starting with the back in the direction of the throw, which allows additional distance for force application.

*In throwing or pushing activities, one or both feet should be kept in firm contact with the surface until the force-providing movements are completed.* If this principle is violated, the body loses part of its stability and, therefore, part of its ability to apply great force to the shot. Firm contact with the surface stabilizes the body and permits it to apply maximum force to the projectile (Figure 13–4j).

*The final velocity is the result of the sum of the velocities of the body seg-ments contributing to the act, if the forces are applied in a single direction and in the proper sequence and timing.* At the moment the shot is released it is traveling at a velocity approximately equal to the sum of the velocities of all of the contributing body movements. This includes movement across the ring, rotary movement of the total body and angular movements of the different body segments contributing to the throwing action. An in-crease in the speed of any of the contributing movements will result in a corresponding increase in the final velocity of the shot.

*The force of muscle contraction is increased by applying initial tension on the muscles (putting the muscles on stretch).* The dip at the beginning of the movement across the ring is very important because it places the leg and back extensor muscles on sudden stretch, and this results in more vigorous contractions. During the thrusting phase, the hip thrust and the whiplike actions of the trunk and arm places the throwing muscles on stretch and causes them to contract with greater force than usual (Figure 13–4e).

*In any explosive performance the next force in sequence should be applied at the peak of the prior force.* In putting the shot, if any force (movement) is out of sequence or out of timing, it tends to destroy the effectiveness of the forces which preceded it. Each force must be timed in such a way that it receives the full benefit of the previous forces and builds upon them.

*When performing activities in which two or more consecutive motions contribute to movement in the same direction, there should be no pause between the motions.* In putting the shot there should be no pause between the movement across the ring and the thrusting action. This is a total movement. Otherwise the effects of the first movement are diminished or lost prior to the beginning of the subsequent movement.

*A correct follow-through is essential to a maximum effort performance.* In putting the shot the reversal (follow-through) allows the performer to maintain balance and prevent fouling. If the reversal were eliminated or done incorrectly the performer would have to begin to diminish his force sooner, thereby reducing the total force and the final velocity (Figure 13-4m).

*An object remains in flight only as long as it takes to move through the vertical plane.* Horizontal distance has no influence on flight time. The higher the shot is projected, the longer it will remain in flight, and the more time it will have to travel horizontally. The correct combination of height and horizontal velocity results in maximum distance.

*When the beginning and ending points are on the same plane, the optimum angle of projection is 45° from the surface.* But when the beginning point is higher than the ending point (as in the case of putting the shot), the angle of projection is less than 45°. In putting the shot the optimum angle is influenced by the height of the point of release and the horizontal distance the shot covers. For a six-foot shot putter who throws 60', the optimum angle is about 35° from the surface.

*If a force is applied directly through the center of gravity of an object, only linear motion will result, whereas if the force is applied off center then part of the force will contribute to rotary motion and part to linear motion.* In the case of putting the shot the application of force should be directly through the center, thus causing all of the force to contribute toward linear (or curvilinear) motion with no force used to cause rotary motion (Figure 13–1).

## COMMON FAULTS AND HOW TO CORRECT THEM

Following are common faults among shot putters along with recommended correction techniques. They were identified through correspondence and consultation with shot put experts.

### Movement Across the Circle

Fault:  Failure to keep the shoulders and hips square to the rear of the ring for as long as possible, and the trunk and legs flexed as far as the putter's strength will justify.

Correction:  Keep the shot slightly to the right of the right knee during the movement across the ring, and be sure to keep the right knee and leg directly under the hips. Also, keep the eyes focused on a point six to ten feet directly behind the circle throughout the movement across the ring.

Fault:  Delay of the left leg coming to the ground immediately after the right leg lands (following the hop). This causes a loss of speed which has been built up during the glide.

Correction:  This error can result from crouching too low, thus making it easy to get the left leg too high. If this appears to be the problem, make it a point not to crouch so low. Also, try to increase the power of the right leg thus making it possible to straighten that leg more rapidly, which in turn will cause the left leg to come in contact with the ground earlier.

Fault:  Premature rotation of the hips prior to the left foot reaching the desired position. This causes the left foot to land in the "bucket."

Correction:  Draw a line across the circle in the direction of the put and practice following the line from start to finish. Keep the eyes focused on a point six to ten feet directly behind the circle, and keep the left arm across the front of the chest as long as possible.

### The Delivery and Release

Fault:  Attempting to "strike" before the left foot has landed. (The "strike" is the forward-upward thrust of the arm with which the shot is put.)

Correction:  The arm should not "strike" until the left foot has landed because little force can be generated without both feet on the ground. Thus, this error is a matter of timing and is best corrected by self-analysis on film, and concentration on correct timing.

Fault:          Rotation of the hips too early, which causes an early arm strike.
Correction:     Concentrate on moving the left hip around and then up.  Also, practice putting from the standing position, starting in a low crouch with the left arm across the chest and the back facing the direction of the put.  Emphasize correct timing of hip rotation in connection with extension of the legs and trunk.
Fault:          Failure to drive the hips first forward and then up.
Correction:     Utilize the standing put, concentrate on the correct hip movements.
Fault:          Failure to keep the left elbow at shoulder height during the early phase of the arm strike.
Correction:     Concentrate on keeping the upper arm at right angles with the trunk of the body (at shoulder height).
Fault:          Failure to keep the head and eyes in line with the flight of the shot, during and after the release.
Correction:     Concentrate on very fast foot actions keeping the right foot as low to the ground as possible (a fast shuffle).  This will allow the body to face the shot just at the time of release.

## THE TRAINING SCHEDULE

The following recommended training schedule can serve as an important guide for all shot putters but probably it will need to be adjusted to fit the needs of any particular athlete because athletes vary considerably in age, maturity and state of conditioning.

### Summer

During the summer the athlete should maintain a high level of general conditioning by participating regularly in vigorous activities which he enjoys.  Emphasis should be on running and overall muscular development.  This should be supplemented by an exercise program which emphasizes the development of strength and power in the muscle groups used the most in shot putting (see the recommended exercises at the end of this chapter).  Employment which involves heavy muscular work is beneficial.

### Fall

Lift weights Monday, Wednesday and Friday (see exercises at the end of this chapter) to increase power.  Run wind-sprints regularly and work a considerable amount on technique.

### Winter

During the winter months the shot putter should increase the intensity of the exercise program in an effort to build strength to near-maximum level by the beginning of the competitive season.  Also, he should run wind-sprints regularly and work to improve his technique.  The following program is based on the assumption that the athlete is preparing for the outdoor season.  If he is preparing for the indoor (winter) season, then this program should be followed during the late fall.

Monday:
1. Jog one-quarter mile.
2. Run wind-sprints for one-half mile, sprinting 50 yards and walking 50 yards.
3. Do stretching exercises involving the large muscles of the chest, the back and shoulders.
4. Do 10 push-ups (repeat three times) executed from the fingertip position.
5. Do 20 puts from a standing position, concentrating on leg extension and proper delivery.
6. Do 20–30 puts by gliding across the circle, concentrating on form. Remember, the shot should be carried low in the hand for the first two weeks in order to avoid injuring the fingers.
7. Take 6–10 starts from the blocks, sprinting 25 yards each time.
8. Lift weights (see exercises at the end of this chapter).

Tuesday:
1. Jog one-quarter mile.
2. Run wind-sprints for one-half mile.
3. Do stretching exercises.
4. Take 10–20 puts from a standing position.
5. Do 10–20 puts across the circle.
6. Lift weights (only selected muscle groups which need emphasis).

Wednesday:
1. Jog one-quarter mile.
2. Run wind-sprints for one-half mile.
3. Do stretching exercises.
4. Do 10 push-ups (repeated three times) from fingertip position.
5. Put 10 times from a standing position.
6. Take 20 puts moving across the circle. Put hard enough to get proper timing but not at an all-out effort for the first two weeks.
7. Take 6–10 starts from the blocks, sprinting 25 yards each time.
8. Lift weights.

Thursday:
1. Jog one-quarter mile.
2. Run wind-sprints for one-half mile.
3. Do stretching exercises.
4. Take 10–20 puts from a standing position.
5. Do 10–20 puts across the circle.
6. Lift weights (same as Tuesday).

Friday:
1. Jog one-quarter mile.
2. Run wind-sprints for one-half mile.
3. Do stretching exercises.

Saturday:
1. Do preparatory exercises.
2. Put five to seven times for distance (do not do this the first three or four weeks of training).
3. Lift weights.

## Spring (Early and Middle Portion)

Monday:
1. Jog one-quarter mile.
2. Run wind-sprints one-half mile, running 50 yards and walking 50 yards.
3. Do stretching exercises.
4. Do 10 push-ups (repeat three times) from the fingertip position.
5. Take 10 puts from a standing position.
6. Take 15–25 puts across the circle.
7. Take 6–10 starts from the blocks, sprinting 25 yards each time.

Tuesday:

    8. Review action movies of yourself.

    9. Lift weights.

    1. Jog one-quarter mile.

    2. Do stretching exercises.

    3. Do 10 push-ups (repeat three times) from the fingertip position

    4. Take 10 puts from a standing position.

    5. Take 10 puts at all-out effort in competition with teammates.

    6. Take six starts from the blocks, sprinting 25 yards each time.

Wednesday:

    1. Jog one-quarter mile.

    2. Run wind-sprints for one-half mile.

    3. Do stretching exercises.

    4. Do five push-ups (repeat three times) from fingertip position.

    5. Take 10–15 puts from a standing position.

    6. Do 15–25 puts using the whole circle.

    7. Lift weights.

Thursday:

    1. Jog one-quarter mile.

    2. Run wind-sprints for one-half mile.

    3. Do stretching exercises.

    4. Do five push-ups (repeat three times) from fingertip position.

    5. Take 10 puts from a standing position.

    6. Take seven puts under meet conditions.

    7. Take six starts from the blocks, running 25 yards each time.

Friday

    Study motion pictures of yourself and others in action. Get plenty of sleep and rest. Prepare yourself mentally and physiologically for your best effort on Saturday. Be confident and ready.

Saturday:

    1. The day of competition—arrive at the stadium in plenty of time to dress slowly and get properly warmed up for competition.

    2. Jog one lap.

    3. Do stretching exercises.

    4. Take three starts, and run 25 yards each time.

    5. Take four to five puts from a standing position.

    6. Take five puts across the circle. (Do not put with all-out effort.)

    7. Do your best on each throw after competition begins. It is unwise to save up for one all-out effort.

    8. Lift weights.

### Late Spring (May–June)

During the late season the shot putter will do the same kind of training as during the mid season. It is important that during this period he keep his level of strength as high as possible while working on speed and the fine points of correct technique.

## CONDITIONING EXERCISES

The conditioning program for shot putters should be designed to develop *strength* and *speed* in the following muscles, because these muscles are of prime importance in shot putting: ankle plantar flexors; knee extensors; hip extensors; trunk and hip rotators; trunk extensor; shoulder girdle elevators and protractors; shoulder flexors (horizontal position); elbow extensors; wrist flexors; and finger flexors.

In Chapter 2 are explanations of how to develop strength and speed effectively—the combination of which is power. It is recommended that the reader study the appropriate sections in that chapter. The particular exercises which should be done by putters follow. The exercises are illustrated in Appendix A.

Bench press—exercise #4
Arm raise (supine)—exercise #6
Arm press (standing)—exercise #5
Wrist flexion—exercise #11
Hand grip—exercise #12
Trunk extension—exercise #18
Body curl—exercise #16
Trunk rotation (standing)—exercise #19
Trunk rotation (supine)—exercise #15
Trunk lateral flexion—exercise #17
Half squat—exercise #22
Leg press—exercise #20
Heel raise—exercise #23
Quadriceps drill—exercise #24

# CHAPTER 14

# The Discus Throw

The most classic of all throwing events, the discus, is richly illustrated in the art and literature of ancient times. The early Greeks included it in their pentathlon contest, and it was one of the events in the ancient Olympics. From fragments of early stone models (about 500 B.C.) it can be concluded that the discus sometimes used for practice had a diameter of about 11″ and weighed nearly 15 pounds. For actual competition, however, the implement used most often by the Greeks was the metal discus which weighed between four and nine pounds. Little is known about the rules of the event in early times and even less about the distances achieved.

The Greeks themselves initiated the modern revival of this event in 1870 when it was listed on the program of a major athletic event held in Athens. At the inaugural of the modern Olympics in 1896 in Athens, the Greeks thought they had the inside track. But much to their surprise, the longest throw was 95′7½″ made by Robert Garrett of the U.S.A. Garrett also won the shot put and placed second in the long jump and third in the high jump—a remarkable combination for one athlete.

The world record at the end of the nineteenth century was held by Charles Henneman of the United States who achieved 118′9″. By 1912 the record had been improved to 156′1⅜″ held by James Duncan of the United States. The first thrower to surpass 170′ was Harold Andersson of Sweden in 1934. During the 1940s Adolfo Consolini of Italy was the world's outstanding discus thrower and his best performance was 181′6⅜″ in 1948. During the late 1940s and early 1950s Fortune Gordien and Sim Ines both of the United States contested each other regularly for world supremacy. They both exceeded the 180-foot mark several times and Gordien broke the world record three different times. His best throw was 194′6″ in 1953.

Since 1960 the world competition has been dominated by three men.

Alfred Oerter, the first man to exceed 200', and Jay Silvester, both of the United States, and Ludvik Danek of Czechoslovakia. All of these men have exceeded the 200-foot mark several times. Silvester became the world record holder with a mark of 224'5" which he accomplished in 1968. The following is a complete list of world records that have been recorded since 1896 when Robert Garrett threw 95'7½".

| Distance | Recorder-holder and country | Year |
|---|---|---|
| 95ft. 7½in. | Robert Garrett, U.S.A. | 1896 |
| 118ft. 9in. | Charles Henneman, U.S.A. | 1897 |
| 120ft. 7¾in. | Martin Sheridan, U.S.A. | 1901 |
| 127ft. 8¾in. | Martin Sheridan, U.S.A. | 1902 |
| 133ft. 6½in. | Martin Sheridan, U.S.A. | 1904 |
| 135ft. 5in. | Martin Sheridan, U.S.A. | 1906 |
| 136ft. 10in. | Martin Sheridan, U.S.A. | 1907 |
| 139ft. 10½in. | Martin Sheridan, U.S.A. | 1909 |
| 141ft. 4⅜in. | Martin Sheridan, U.S.A. | 1911 |
| 145ft. 9½in. | James Duncan, U.S.A. | 1912 |
| 156ft. 1⅜in. | James Duncan, U.S.A. | 1912 |
| 156ft. 2½in. | Thomas Lieb, U.S.A. | 1924 |
| 157ft. 1⅝in. | Glenn Hartranft, U.S.A. | 1925 |
| 158ft. 1¾in. | Clarence Houser, U.S.A. | 1926 |
| 163ft. 8¾in. | Eric Krenz, U.S.A. | 1929 |
| 167ft. 5⅜in. | Eric Krenz, U.S.A. | 1930 |
| 169ft. 8⅞in. | Paul Jessup, U.S.A. | 1930 |
| 171ft. 11¾in. | Harold Andersson, Sweden | 1934 |
| 174ft. 2½in. | Willi Schroeder, Germany | 1935 |
| 174ft. 8¾in. | Archie Harris, U.S.A. | 1941 |
| 175ft. | Adolfo Consolini, Italy | 1941 |
| 177ft. 11in. | Adolfo Consolini, Italy | 1946 |
| 180ft. 2¾in. | Robert Fitch, U.S.A. | 1946 |
| 181ft. 6⅜in. | Adolfo Consolini, Italy | 1948 |
| 185ft. 2¾in. | Fortune Gordien, U.S.A. | 1949 |
| 186ft. 11in. | Fortune Gordien, U.S.A. | 1949 |
| 194ft. 6in. | Fortune Gordien, U.S.A. | 1953 |
| 196ft. 6½in. | Edmund Piatowski, Poland | 1959 |
| 196ft. 6½in. | Richard Babka, U.S.A. | 1960 |
| 199ft. 2½in. | Jay Silvester, U.S.A. | 1961 |
| 200ft. 5½in. | Alfred Oerter, U.S.A. | 1962 |
| 202ft. 2¾in. | Vladimir Trusenev, U.S.S.R. | 1962 |
| 204ft. 10½in. | Alfred Oerter, U.S.A. | 1962 |
| 211ft. 9½in. | Ludvik Danek, Czechoslovakia | 1964 |
| 213ft. 11in. | Ludvik Danek, Czechoslovakia | 1965 |
| 218ft. 4in. | Jay Silvester, U.S.A. | 1968 |
| 224ft. 5in. | Jay Silvester, U.S.A. | 1968 |
| 224ft. 5in. | Ricky Bruch, Sweden | 1972 |

## PROCEDURE

The modern technique of throwing the discus is rather well standardized, and the methods used by the different throwers vary only slightly from each other. The thrower grips the discus as illustrated in Figure 14–1. Starting near the back side of a ring 8'2½" in diameter, with the back generally in the direction of the intended throw, the thrower moves across the ring while

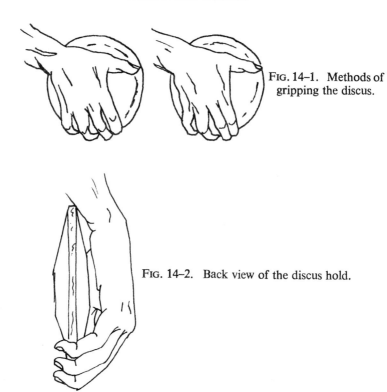

Fig. 14–1. Methods of gripping the discus.

Fig. 14–2. Back view of the discus hold.

doing one and one-half spins with the total body. Then he thrusts the discus in the intended direction while remaining inside the circle. According to the rules, the thrower may touch the inside surface of the ring but may not touch the top surface or any point outside the ring. The discus must land within the designated area. The distance of a throw is measured along a straight line from the nearest point of contact the discus makes with the surface to the inside edge of the circle nearest that point, along an extended radius of the circle. (See the illustration and description of the throwing area in Chapter 19.)

## DISCUS THROWING TECHNIQUE

The velocity of the discus at the moment it is released is the single most important factor in the distance of the throw. This velocity varies directly with the amount of force applied to the discus and the distance of force application. Other important factors include the angle at which the discus is projected, and the position of the implement during its flight.

### The Grip

The pads of the ends of the fingers should be turned over the rim, and the hand positioned slightly behind the implement's center of gravity with the fingers spread evenly. It is very important that the wrist remain straight (see Figures 14–1 and 14–2).

### The Starting Position and Preliminary Swing

The starting position depends upon the distance of the turn, which varies from one and one-half to one and three-quarter turns. The thrower assumes a stance at the back of the circle with his back generally facing the direction of the throw and his feet slightly wider than his hips. The preliminary swings, which should be restricted to two or three, involve swinging the discus at about shoulder level (palm down), in an easy and relaxed manner. During the preliminary swings, the shoulders remain level, the back straight and the head up. The free arm is wrapped loosely across the chest. On the final preliminary swing, the arm is swung back as far as possible so that the body weight is over a straight right leg. At this point the body is twisted far to the right to develop maximum torque, and the right arm is at about an 80° angle behind the shoulder. Relaxation should still be maintained (Figure 14–4b).

### Moving Into the Turn

The initial movement into the turn will strongly influence the success of the subsequent movements. With the discus trailing the plane of the shoulders at an 80° angle, the movement into the turn is initiated by bending the knees and transferring the weight to the left foot, while sitting back slightly. The correct movement is one of turning the hips and left leg in the direction of the throw while swinging the right leg up and out, in a circular motion, over the rim at the rear of the circle (Figure 14–4c,d).

### Run Across the Circle

The run across the circle is initiated by the driving action of the left leg, synchronized with the swing of the right leg. This produces a running stride. During this driving phase, the right leg, which is very slightly flexed, swings in a fairly close but natural arc around the left leg, then the

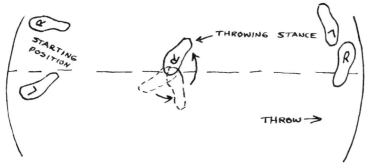

FIG. 14–3. Foot pattern during movement across the ring (discus).

a

b

c

d

e

f

g

h

Fig. 14-4 (a-l). Sequence drawings of correct technique in the discus throw.

right foot is planted as quickly as possible. This drive carries the thrower halfway across the circle. The fast leg action speeds up the hips so that they remain a fraction ahead of the plane of the shoulders. The shoulders, which are still well ahead of the trailing discus, remain level.

At this point, the right leg lands in the center of the circle with the knees partly flexed and the toes pointing 45° to the rear. The left leg, which has remained near the rear of the circle, now scissors rapidly past the right leg in a natural arc and lands heel first near the front of the ring. The objective now is to attain a coiled-spring position of the body so that the right side of the body can be driven against and around a relatively stable left side. As the left leg scissors past the right, the thrower strives to get his left foot planted at the front of the circle as soon as possible, slightly to the left of the direction of the throw. The thrower is now in the coiled position. His left hip is pointing toward the direction of the throw, his right shoulder is facing the rear, his throwing arm is well behind the shoulder, his left arm is curled and the discus is flat (Figures 14–3 and 14–4d through i).

### Thrust

The uncoiling action of the body is initiated by a vigorous extension of the right leg. The right heel is twisted outward to give the longest possible extension at the ankle. The right leg extension causes the right hip to move forward and upward, and transfers more of the body weight onto a slightly flexed left leg. Simultaneously, or slightly after, the right shoulder is driven forward to initiate a long and powerful slinglike action of the throwing arm (Figure 14–4i, j).

### Release

The left leg, which has remained in contact with the circle to allow for an effective forward hip drive against its resistance, is now extended vigorously, simultaneously with the last portion of the arm sling to give the discus a final lift. The release from the hand is a squeezing action in which the discus is spun clockwise into flight by squeezing it in such a manner that it leaves the pad of the index finger last. This clockwise rotation gives the discus stability in flight (Figures 14–4j, k and 14–5).

### Reversal

The objective of the reversal is to serve as a follow-through after the thrust and to retain balance in order to avoid fouling. As soon as the discus

Fig. 14–5. Follow-through is essential to maximum force in throwing, putting and striking performances. The discus throw is an example.

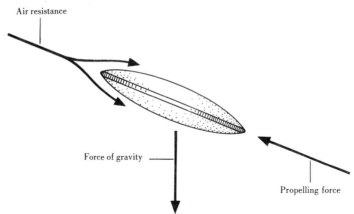

Air resistance

Force of gravity

Propelling force

FIG. 14–6. There are three forces acting on an object in flight (discus). The flight pattern is changed by altering any of the forces.

leaves the hand, the feet are reversed and the right leg is bent to lower the body mass, which aids in regaining balance. The body continues to turn as part of a natural follow-through (Figure 14–4k, l).

## APPLICATION OF SCIENTIFIC PRINCIPLES

The following are explanations of scientific principles which apply to the discus throw.

*In throwing or pushing activities one or both feet should be kept in contact with the surface until the force providing movements are completed.* If a discus thrower breaks contact between his feet and the surface before the main-force-providing movements are complete, the force applied to the discus will be reduced because the body loses part of its stability once it becomes suspended. Also, the driving force from the legs ends when contact is broken (Figure 14–4k).

*If a force is applied to an object the object develops greater velocity as the distance of force application is increased.* Thus the discus thrower should apply force through at least one and one-half complete turns and through a full slinging motion with the arm. If all else remains equal, the longer the distance of force application the greater will be the acceleration and, therefore, the greater will be the final velocity of the discus.

*When a constant force causes a body to rotate, lengthening the radius of the body slows the rotation while shortening the radius increases the rotation.* As a discus is held farther from the body during the spin (radius lengthened), it provides more resistance and the spin is slowed. For this reason, the discus is kept closer to the body during the early phase of the spin. However, at the time of release the discus should be away from the body as far as the arm can reach, because the longer the arc through which it moves the greater will be its velocity, assuming that rotational speed of the body is constant.

*The final velocity is the result of the sum of velocities of the body segments contributing to the act, if the forces are applied in a single direction and in the proper sequence and timing.* At the moment of release the discus is traveling at a velocity approximately equal to the sum of the velocities of all the contributing body movements. This includes linear movement across the ring, rotary movement of the body and angular movements of the different body segments contributing to the thrusting action. An increase in the speed of any of the contributing movements will result in a corresponding increase in the final velocity of the discus.

*The force of muscle contractions may be increased by increasing the initial tension on the muscles (putting the muscles on stretch).* The thrusting action following the spin is initiated with hip rotation, caused by the driving action of the right leg. With the right hip thrust forward and the shoulders and throwing arm trailing far behind, the body is in a wound-up position. This places the throwing muscles on stretch, and they immediately respond causing the unwinding and whipping action of the trunk and arm. The sudden stretch of the throwing muscles causes them to respond with stronger contractions (Figure 14–4b, h).

*When performing activities in which two or more consecutive movements contribute to motion in the same direction, there should usually be no pause between the movements.* In throwing the discus there should be no pause between the movements across the ring and the thrusting action. The throw is one continuous motion from beginning to end, where the discus continually increases in velocity until the moment of release, which is the climax of the velocity building actions.

*Successful performance often calls for effectively combining translatory and rotary motions.* The discus throw results from a combination of several movements. The thrower moves the total body linearly from the back to the front of the circle and in doing so overcomes the inertia of the discus to that motion. He rotates the total body with ever increasing velocity as he advances across the ring. He then thrusts the discus by use of body rotation and the action of the throwing arm. These combined motions, if performed correctly and with proper sequence and timing, will produce maximum final velocity of the discus.

*The less surface an object presents, the less will be the air resistance.* If a discus wobbles, it causes a larger surface to be presented to the air and this results in increased resistance, thus reducing the distance of the flight. Likewise, if a discus is projected in a position where its long axis is not in line with its direction of movement, the implement will present a larger area and will meet more air resistance (Figure 14–6).

*A correct follow-through is essential to a maximum effort performance.* In throwing the discus the reversal (follow-through) allows the performer to continue to accelerate until the moment of release. Without a correct follow-through the thrower tends to diminish his rate of acceleration prior to release, and the final velocity is lessened.

*The length of time an object remains in flight depends on the height it attains.* An object remains in flight only as long as it takes to move through the vertical plane of flight, and the time is not influenced by the horizontal component. Thus, the higher a discus is hurled, the longer it remains in flight, and the more time it has to travel horizontally. On the other hand, force used to propel the discus vertically cannot be used to propel it horizontally. Therefore, one of the keys to success is to get the right combination of vertical and horizontal force, thus resulting in the optimal angle of projection.

*When the beginning and ending points are on the same plane, the optimum angle of projection for maximum distance is 45° from the surface.* Because of the aerodynamics involved in the flight of the discus, this principle does not fully apply. However, it is still worth taking into consideration. Actually, the discus should typically be thrown at about 38° from the surface. However this angle of projection varies depending on the wind conditions.

## COMMON FAULTS AND HOW TO CORRECT THEM

The following common faults were identified through correspondence with experts in the discus throw. The suggestions on how to correct the faults were obtained from some of the best-qualified competitors and coaches.

### The Spin

Fault:       Failure to keep the shoulders level, the head up and the back straight during the spin.

Correction:  Drill with dummy footwork along a line across the ring. Try to hit the center of the ring with the right foot as it strikes the ground following the first step. Concentrate on leg bend, keeping the head and eyes level. Also, concentrate on sitting back, as if sitting on a chair. Some discus throwers have found it helpful to strap a discus to the hand in order to eliminate the necessity of concentrating on the carry and the release. This makes it possible to practice many turns in a short period, and more attention can be given to balance, correct footwork and timing.

Fault:       Failure to keep the throwing arm relaxed and well behind the body prior to the final thrust.

Correction:  Turn the head toward the arm which holds the discus in order to increase the arm extension and the body torque. Also, concentrate on forcing the arm back as far as possible and consciously maximize the torque.

Fault:       Failure to attain a constant buildup of momentum across the circle.

Correction:  Concentrate on starting the turn slowly and building up speed constantly to an explosive release. Some throwers have found that if the initial movement is too fast, it is difficult to maintain correct sequence and timing of movements later in the turn. During the constant acceleration of the discus it is important to keep the discus in the same arc, striving for the maximum effective radius. Some throwers have found it helpful to strap the discus to the hand while correcting this error, because it affords a chance to concentrate on acceleration without paying particular attention to the carriage of the discus or to the thrust.

### The Delivery (Thrust)

Fault:        Failure to have the discus far enough behind the body at the beginning of the delivery.

Correction:   Utilize the same correcting technique as described under the second fault. Also concentrate on a vigorous hip thrust, keeping the arm well behind. This contributes to increased body torque.

Fault:        Failure to accelerate throughout the delivery.

Correction:   Concentrate on continued acceleration to a point beyond release. Pay special attention to correct timing and rhythm which will aid in continued acceleration. Force the acceleration to the very end of the throw.

Fault:        Failure to initiate the final thrust at a time when the most force can be applied to the discus for the longest possible arc.

Correction:   This fault is a result of an error in timing. Special attention should be given to the sequence and timing of the different movements associated with the initiation of the thrust until the timing becomes as perfect as possible.

Fault:        Failure to impart the optimum rotation on the discus as it leaves the hand. This is necessary to create the gyroscopic effect which stabilizes the discus in flight.

Correction:   Place the middle finger against the index finger in order to stabilize the index finger. The discus should be squeezed with the index finger as it rolls off the middle portion of that finger. Some throwers find it helpful to use a bowling drill where the discus is gripped with the correct technique and the arm is swung in a relaxed position, forward and backward like a pendulum. The discus is then released and rolled along the ground.

Fault:        Faulty hand action at release which causes the discus to wobble in flight.

Correction:   Be sure to apply sufficient pressure on the discus with the thumb because this adds a stabilizing effect. Sometimes the faulty hand action at release is due to not keeping the discus in the same arc throughout the delivery phase. It is essential to concentrate on pulling the discus through a constant, steady, smooth arc, without any jerky motion. Also it is important to cover the discus as thoroughly as possible with the hand in order to be able to control it with ease.

## THE TRAINING SCHEDULE

The following recommended training schedule can serve as an important guide. But in all likelihood it will need to be adjusted to fit the requirements of any particular athlete because of differences in age, maturity and condition of athletes.

### Summer

During this season the discus thrower should maintain a high level of conditioning by participating regularly in vigorous activities which he enjoys. Emphasis should be upon activities which include running and overall muscular development. This program should be supplemented by specific exercises to maintain strength and power in the muscles involved the most in discus throwing (see the recommended exercises at the end of this chapter). Summer employment which involves heavy muscular work is beneficial.

### Fall

During the fall the discus thrower should do heavy weight lifting on Monday, Wednesday and Friday for the purpose of developing additional power. Also he should run wind-sprints regularly and do a considerable amount of work on throwing technique. The program can be similar to the daily schedule described for the winter season.

### Winter

During the winter months the thrower should continue weight lifting for the development of power; at the same time he should work extensively on discus throwing drills. Running should continue to be a part of the program.

Monday:
1. Jog one-quarter mile.
2. Run wind-sprints for one-half mile, sprinting 50 yards and walking 50 yards.
3. Do stretching exercises which involve the muscles of the back, shoulders and chest.
4. Throw 15–20 times from the standing position.
5. Practice the turn 10 minutes without the discus.
6. Make 15–20 throws with the turn, concentrating on form rather than speed.
7. Lift weights (see conditioning exercises at the end of this chapter).

Tuesday:
1. Jog one-quarter mile.
2. Run 50 yard wind-sprints, same as on Monday.
3. Do stretching exercises, same as on Monday.
4. Throw 15 times from the standing position.
5. Practice the turn for 10 minutes without throwing.
6. Practice 15–20 throws with the turn, concentrating on form. No all-out throws should be taken for the first two weeks.

Wednesday:
1. Jog one-quarter mile.
2. Run wind-sprints for one-half mile.
3. Do stretching exercises, same as on Monday.
4. Take 15–20 throws from the standing position.
5. Work for 10 minutes on the turn without throwing.
6. Throw 15–20 times out of the circle with the turn.
7. Do six starts out of the blocks running 25 yards.
8. Lift weights.

Thursday:
1. Jog one-quarter mile.
2. Run wind-sprints for a half mile.
3. Do stretching exercises.
4. Make 10 throws from the standing position.
5. Practice the turn for 10 minutes without throwing.
6. Do several throws (15–20) out of the circle with turn. Work on form emphasizing timing and follow-through.

Friday:
1. Jog one-quarter mile.
2. Run wind-sprints for one-half mile.
3. Do stretching exercises.
4. Study movies.

Saturday:
1. Do preparatory exercises.
2. Throw for distance.
3. Lift weights.

## Spring (Early and Middle Portion)

Monday:
1. Jog one-quarter mile.
2. Run wind-sprints for one-half mile, running 50 yards and walking 50 yards.
3. Do stretching exercises which involve the muscles of the back, shoulders and chest.
4. Throw 10–15 times from the standing position.
5. Practice the turn in the circle without throwing for 10 minutes.
6. Throw 15–20 times from the circle with the turn. Emphasize timing and speed.
7. Lift weights.

Tuesday:
1. Jog one-quarter mile.
2. Run wind-sprints for one-half mile.
3. Do stretching exercises.
4. Throw 10 times for maximum distance, competing with teammates.
5. Take 10 throws from the standing position.
6. Take six starts out of the blocks sprinting 25 yards each time.

Wednesday:
1. Jog one-quarter mile.
2. Run wind-sprints for one-half mile.
3. Do stretching exercises.
4. Take 10 throws from the standing position.
5. Practice the turn in the circle for 10 minutes, working on speed and timing.
6. Throw 10–15 times from the circle with the turn, emphasize speed and timing.
7. Lift weights. (Use relatively light weight and concentrate on speed. This weight training work out should be less exhausting than the one done on Monday.)

Thursday:
1. Jog one-quarter mile.
2. Run wind-sprints for one-half mile.
3. Do stretching exercises.
4. Take 10 throws from the standing position.
5. Throw seven times from the circle as if in competition.
6. Take six starts outs of the blocks, sprinting 25 yards.

Friday:
Study motion pictures of yourself and others in action. Get plenty of sleep and rest. Prepare yourself mentally and physiologically for your best effort on Saturday. Be confident. Be ready.

Saturday: 1. Arrive at the stadium in plenty of time to dress slowly and get properly warmed up for the competition.
2. Jog one lap.
3. Do stretching exercises.
4. Take three starts and run 25 yards each time.
5. Take five throws from the standing position.
6. Throw five times with turns from the circle; however do not throw with all-out effort.
7. Do your best on each throw after competition begins. It is unwise to save up for one all-out effort.
8. Lift weights after competition.

### Late Spring (May–June)

During this phase of the season the discus thrower will typically do the same kinds of training as during the mid season. While keeping his strength level at the highest point possible, he should concentrate on the fine points of technique and speed of movement.

## CONDITIONING EXERCISES

It is important for discus throwers to have a high level of strength combined with a great amount of speed. Therefore, a conditioning program which develops these characteristics is essential.

The best procedures for increasing *strength* and *speed* (*power*) are explained in Chapter 1. It is recommended that the reader study the appropriate sections of that chapter and base the conditioning program on that information. The specific exercises that should be included in the conditioning program are listed below. The exercises are illustrated in Appendix A.

Bench press—exercise #4
Arm curl—exercise #3
Arm raise (supine)—exercise #6
Rowing—exercise #13
Lateral arm raise (standing)—exercise #7
Hand grip—exercise #12
Trunk extension—exercise #18
Trunk flexion (incline board)—exercise #14
Body curl—exercise #16
Trunk rotation (standing)—exercise #19
Trunk rotation (supine)—exercise #15
Half squat—exercise #22
Leg press—exercise #20
Quadriceps drill—exercise #24
Heel raise—exercise #23

CHAPTER **15**

# Javelin Throw

The use of javelins and spears as implements in war and hunting can be traced to antiquity. As an athletic contest the javelin throw was in the program of both the Olympic Games of ancient Greece and the Tailteann Games of Ireland. In the second half of the nineteenth century javelin throwing was introduced by the Hungarians and Germans and subsequently became an athletic event among the Scandinavians. The first prominent name in the modern history of the event was Sweden's Eric Lemming who dominated the javelin throw for more than a decade. Lemming's best effort was in 1912 when he threw 204'5$\frac{3}{8}$".

Soon after Lemming's reign the Finnish people adopted the javelin throw as their national event and great emphasis was placed upon it. As a result, the Finns soon captured the javelin monopoly from the hands of their Swedish cousins. Between 1930 and 1936, Matti Jarvinen of Finland established the world record 10 different times. His best throw was 253'4$\frac{1}{2}$" in 1936. He was succeeded by another Finn, Yrjo Nikkanen, who threw 258'2$\frac{3}{8}$" in 1938 to establish a world record that stood until 1953.

Among the first great American javelin throwers were Frank "Bud" Held, Cy Young and Bill Miller, all of whom were slight, 165–170 pounders. Held, a slow comer, had his ups and downs for several years, and in the 1952 Olympics placed only ninth behind his American teammates Cy Young, the champion at 242'1$\frac{1}{2}$", and second place man Bill Miller, at 237'8$\frac{1}{2}$". After lengthy experimentation, Held devised a new javelin which possessed some of the characteristics of a glider. He was the first to take advantage of his own invention, and in August of 1953 he became the first javelin thrower to exceed 260'. On that day he established the world record at 263'10". Later he improved the record with a throw that exceeded 268'.

**236**

Taking advantage of Held's new invention along with improved training and performance techniques, several throwers exceeded the 260-foot mark, and the world record kept moving upward. The first person to exceed the 300-foot mark was Terje Pedersen of Norway who threw 300'11" in 1964. Subsequently, Klaus Wolferman of Germany set the current world record at 308'8" in 1973. The following list of world records shows the tremendous achievements of javelin throwers since Harold Anderson set the record at 120' in 1904.

| Distance | Recorder-holder and country | Year |
|---|---|---|
| 120ft. | Harold Andersson, Sweden | 1904 |
| 175ft. 6in. | Eric Lemming, Sweden | 1906 |
| 188ft. | Eric Lemming, Sweden | 1908 |
| 191ft. $2\frac{1}{8}$in. | Eric Lemming, Sweden | 1911 |
| 198ft. $11\frac{3}{8}$in. | Eric Lemming, Sweden | 1912 |
| 200ft. $1\frac{11}{20}$in. | Julius Saaristo, Finland | 1912 |
| 204ft. $5\frac{5}{8}$in. | Eric Lemming, Sweden | 1912 |
| 216ft. $10\frac{3}{8}$in. | Jonni Myyra, Finland | 1919 |
| 218ft. $6\frac{7}{8}$in. | Gunnar Lindstrom, Sweden | 1924 |
| 229ft. $3\frac{1}{8}$in. | Eino Penttila, Finland | 1927 |
| 232ft. $11\frac{5}{8}$in. | E. H. Lundquist, Sweden | 1928 |
| 234ft. $9\frac{3}{4}$in. | Matti Jarvinen, Finland | 1930 |
| 235ft. $2\frac{7}{8}$in. | Matti Jarvinen, Finland | 1930 |
| 235ft. $9\frac{7}{8}$in. | Matti Jarvinen, Finland | 1930 |
| 239ft. $3\frac{1}{4}$in. | Matti Jarvinen, Finland | 1930 |
| 242ft. $10\frac{1}{4}$in. | Matti Jarvinen, Finland | 1932 |
| 243ft. $8\frac{3}{8}$in. | Matti Jarvinen, Finland | 1933 |
| 244ft. $9\frac{3}{8}$in. | Matti Jarvinen, Finland | 1933 |
| 249ft. $8\frac{1}{8}$in. | Matti Jarvinen, Finland | 1933 |
| 251ft. $6\frac{1}{8}$in. | Matti Jarvinen, Finland | 1934 |
| 253ft. $4\frac{1}{2}$in. | Matti Jarvinen, Finland | 1936 |
| 255ft. $5\frac{3}{4}$in. | Yrjo Nikkanen, Finland | 1938 |
| 258ft. $2\frac{3}{8}$in. | Yrjo Nikkanen, Finland | 1938 |
| 263ft. 10in. | Franklin Held, U.S.A. | 1953 |
| 268ft. $2\frac{1}{2}$in. | Franklin Held, U.S.A. | 1955 |
| 281ft. 2in. | Egil Danielsen, Norway | 1956 |
| 282ft. $3\frac{1}{2}$in. | Albert Cantello, U.S.A. | 1959 |
| 284ft. 7in. | Carlo Lievore, Italy | 1961 |
| 300ft. 11in. | Terje Pedersen, Norway | 1964 |
| 304ft. 1in. | Jay Kinnunen, Finland | 1969 |
| 307ft. 9in. | Janis Lusis, U.S.S.R. | 1972 |
| 308ft. 8in. | Klaus Wolferman, W. Germany | 1973 |

## PROCEDURE

The javelin is gripped at the handle in the manner illustrated in Figure 15–2. During the approach run the thrower carries the javelin horizontally above the shoulder at a height slightly above the ear, and with the javelin pointed in the direction of the throw. At the completion of the approach the javelin is delivered from behind the scratch line. To be a legal throw the javelin must strike the ground point first within the boundaries of the throwing area. The throw is measured from the point where the javelin first strikes the ground to the inside edge of the scratch line nearest that point (see diagram of throwing area in Chapter 19).

The javelin must consist of three parts: a metal head, a shaft and a cord grip. The shaft, which may be made of metal or wood, tapers from the middle to both ends. The metal head must terminate in a sharp point. The specifications of the javelin include the following:

Weight:     No less than 1 pound, 12¼ ounces (800 grams)
Length:     Between 8'6⅜" (260 cm) and 8'10¼" (270 cm)
Diameter:   Between 1" (25 mm) and 1.181" (30 mm)

### JAVELIN THROW TECHNIQUE

The distance the javelin can be thrown is dependent upon: 1) velocity at the moment of release; 2) an optimum angle of projection; and 3) maximum stability in flight.

The speed of the javelin at release is determined by the forces acting upon it, thus the javelin thrower must apply as much force to the javelin as possible through a long range of motion, and the forces must be in line with the direction of the throw.

Although the optimum angle of release for a projectile, the point of release and landing of which are the same height above the ground, is 45° the optimum angle of release for the javelin varies between 30° and 40°.

Fig. 15–1. Body position going into the final stride before the throw.

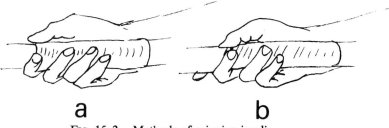

a　　　　　　　b

Fig. 15-2. Methods of gripping javelin.

This is due partly to the fact that the javelin is released at a height greater than the point of landing, but another factor that influences the angle even more is the aerodynamics associated with the unique construction of the implement. The angle of release for expert throwers is about 35°.

### The Grip

A correct javelin grip provides a firm hold with part of the hand behind the ledge of the binding, and allows the javelin to lie diagonally along the palm and not across it. This insures a straighter and more efficient pull. The two popular grips are the "horseshoe," preferred by the majority of the top-flight throwers, and the "thumb and second finger" grip (Figure 15-2).

### The Carry

The javelin should be carried with the hand above the shoulder in a manner that does not impede the running action. The point should be tipped slightly upward to aid in the withdrawal, and to lend to a more relaxed carry. The throwing arm should form a right angle at the elbow, and the hand should be allowed to move forward and backward with a springlike action during the run.

### The Approach Run

The objective of the approach is to attain maximum controllable velocity. Hence, the length of the approach must be sufficient to allow this. Top flight throwers use approach runs of 80'–90'. The run is separated into a preliminary phase of 10–12 strides, and a transition phase, usually five strides. During the preliminary phase the emphasis is upon a smooth buildup of velocity utilizing a high knee lift. The transition phase begins with the withdrawal of the javelin as the right foot hits the check-mark on the final stride of the preliminary run. The javelin is withdrawn in a straight line movement, close to the ear, and over the throwing shoulder. This is accompanied by trunk rotation, allowing the right shoulder to shift backward. During the withdrawal, the hips and feet remain facing the direction of the throw to maintain maximum forward velocity. The chin

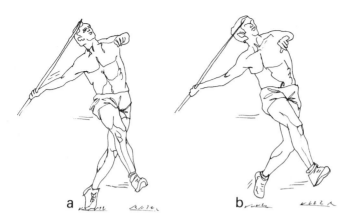

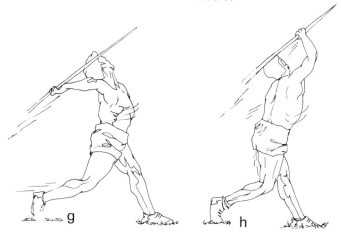

FIG. 15-3 (a-k). Sequence drawings of correct technique in the javelin throw.

moves forward and upward, and the free arm is wrapped loosely across the front of the body. The javelin must be completely withdrawn by the end of the second stride of the transition phase.

### The Cross-Over Stride

The objective of the cross-over stride is to get the legs ahead of the center of gravity to attain a more pronounced backward lean, which increases the range of motion during the delivery. The cross-over stride must be short and fast, as the right foot crosses in front of the left. It is executed by a fast pick-up of the right knee. The hips remain well forward and they rotate only a small amount away from the direction of the throw. The legs should be kept ahead of the body. The feet remain pointed directly in the line of approach, and the free arm is wrapped loosely across the body (Figure 15–3a, b).

### The Throwing Stride

The objective of the throwing stride is to place the left leg far forward of the body to increase the range of motion during the delivery. The stride is done quickly in order to continue the acceleration of the center of gravity. There are two acceptable styles for the throwing stride: the *straight leg style* and the more popular *bent leg style*. The bent leg style is used by a majority of the top-flight javelin throwers. The advantages of this style include: 1) a better application of force in a straighter line; 2) less decrease in body acceleration; and 3) a longer range of motion during the delivery. In selecting the style to be used, the coach and athlete must weigh the advantages mentioned above, against the disadvantage of throwing from a slightly lower release position. Ideally, the javelin should be launched at the highest possible point.

The throwing stride is performed by bringing the left leg, which was allowed to trail the right leg during the cross-over stride, through quickly into a long stride. The left foot lands heel-first with the knee held rigid. At this point, the left knee is either kept rigid or is allowed to bend, according to which style the thrower utilizes. Meanwhile, the right leg drives the hips forward and upward to a position over the left foot, at which time the arm and shoulder muscles contract vigorously to pull the javelin through a path high over the shoulder. The arm action is accompanied by a movement of the head to the left, without dropping the left shoulder. This enhances the actions of the right arm and shoulder. During the arm action the elbow leads the hand as the hand moves in a path straight over the shoulder, with emphasis upon a long, fast, straight pull, to a point of release high above and directly over the left leg (Figure 15–3c through h).

### The Recovery Stride

Once the javelin has been released, the right leg is brought forward into a running stride. The weight is quickly transferred to the right leg, which flexes quickly to lower the center of gravity and to absorb the forward momentum. Sometimes the recovery stride is followed by one or two hops to help maintain balance, and to complete the deceleration of the body (Figure 15–3i, j, k).

## APPLICATION OF SCIENTIFIC PRINCIPLES

Following are explanations of how certain principles apply to the javelin throw. These principles are fundamental to excellent performance in this event.

*The velocity of a body is changed only when acted upon by an additional force. The produced acceleration is proportional to and in the direction of the force.* One of the prime objectives of the javelin thrower is to accelerate the javelin as much as possible in order to achieve maximum velocity at the moment of release (final velocity). The thrower is limited to a certain range of motion during which he can accelerate the implement. Therefore, maximum force is necessary during the throwing action in order to achieve maximum velocity of the javelin within the restriction of the range through which force can be applied.

*If a force is applied to a body (or object) the body develops greater velocity as the distance of force application is increased.* This indicates that in throwing the javelin the throwing muscles should be fully extended at the beginning of the throw so they can apply force to the javelin through as much distance as possible. In other terms the range of the throwing motion should be extended maximally, within the limitations of good throwing technique (Figure 15–3).

*In throwing activities one or both feet should be kept in firm contact with the surface until the force-providing movements are completed.* If the javelin thrower breaks contact with the ground before the main force-providing movements are completed, the force applied to the javelin will be reduced because the body loses its stability and the ability to drive with the legs once contact is broken (Figure 15–3i).

*The force of muscular contraction may be increased by increasing the initial tension on the muscle (putting the muscles on stretch).* Sudden stretching of the muscles activates the stretch reflex, and this causes a stronger stimulus and a stronger initial contraction. Also, a fully extended muscle can contract through a full range of motion and thereby apply force over a longer distance. Thus, the thrower should purposely place the muscles on stretch as he initiates the throw, in order to get the strongest and longest muscle contractions possible (Figure 15–3f).

*All forces should be applied as directly as possible in the direction of the intended motion.* In the javelin throw, it is especially important that forces be applied to the javelin in a straight line direction. Any forces which deviate from that direction will tend to be either noncontributing or disruptive to the flight of the javelin.

*The final velocity is the result of the sum of the velocities of the body segments contributing to the act, if the forces are applied in a single direction and in the proper sequence and timing.* At the moment of release the javelin is traveling at a velocity approximately equal to the sum of the velocities of all of the contributing body movements. This includes linear movement resulting from the approach run, and the angular movements of the different body segments contributing to the throwing action. An increase in the speed of any of the contributing movements will result in a corresponding increase in the final velocity of the javelin.

*In any explosive performance the next force in sequence should be applied at the peak of the prior force.* If any force in the javelin throw is out of sequence or out of timing, the effectiveness of the forces which preceded it tend to be destroyed. Each force must be timed in such a way that it receives the full benefit of the preceding forces, and builds upon them.

*When performing activities in which two or more consecutive motions contribute to movement in the same direction, there should be no pause between the motions.* This means that the javelin thrower should have no pauses between the various phases of the throw. For example, there should be no pause between the approach run and the cross-over steps and no pause between the cross-over steps and the throwing stride, etc. Any pause will tend to destroy the velocity that has been developed up to that point.

*Objects that are dense and streamlined are influenced less by air resistance. The less surface an object presents, the less will be the retarding effects of air resistance.* This indicates that a javelin should be hurled *straight* in order that it will present its smallest surface, the tip, in the direction of movement. Quivering of the javelin while in flight will increase its air resistance considerably, and thus reduce its distance. Also excessive spin will increase air resistance.

*A correct follow-through is essential to a maximum-effort performance.* In the javelin throw the follow-through action permits the thrower to continue maximum application of force up to the moment of release, after which the velocity of the body is diminished as a result of the follow-through actions. Inadequate follow-through will tend to restrict the maximum application of force prior to the time of release (Figure 15–3k).

*The length of time an object remains in flight depends upon the height it attains. It remains in flight only as long as it takes to move through the vertical plane.* This means that the higher the javelin is projected the longer it will remain in flight, thus allowing more time for it to travel horizontally. However, if the angle of projection is too steep, then too much of the propelling force is directed vertically while horizontal force is sacrificed, and distance is lost.

*In throwing activities where maximum distance is the goal, final velocity in the intended direction is fundamental to success.* Since it is already established that the javelin will remain in flight as long as it takes to move through its vertical plane, then the factor that will determine how far it travels horizontally during that time is the velocity it has in the horizontal direction.

*When the beginning and ending points are on the same plane, the optimum angle of projection is 45° from the surface.* The javelin should deviate from the 45°-angle for two reasons: 1) it is projected from a point slightly higher than its point of landing, and 2) the aerodynamics of the javelin causes it to have a floating action. For these reasons the angle of projection for the javelin is approximately 35 °. This angle varies slightly with the distance of the throw, wind conditions and the differences in aerodynamics of javelins.

## COMMON FAULTS AND HOW TO CORRECT THEM

The following faults were identified by experts in the javelin throw, and the suggested corrections were provided by coaches of some of the best throwers.

### The Approach and Cross-Over

Fault:  Loss of momentum during the cross-over stride caused by poor execution of the cross-over.

Correction:  Use a five-step approach and concentrate on accelerating during the final cross-over step. Practice on repeat 25–50-yard cross-over step runs. Also, concentrate on keeping both feet pointed generally in the direction of the throw. This produces a much better running base and reduces the loss of velocity.

Fault:  Failure to plant the left foot in a proper position at the completion of the throwing stride to act effectively as a fulcrum.

Correction:  Concentrate on a "heel-first toe-forward" plant while utilizing a hard approach with easy throws. Also, practice in an area where foot prints can be easily checked, then erased. Emphasize releasing the javelin from a position directly over the left foot.

Fault:  Allowing the tail of the javelin to drop too low prior to release.

Correction:  Hold the arm higher during the cross-over strides and keep the eyes on the javelin point, which is close to the face. Concentrate on keeping the palm of the hand facing upward. Also, keep the throwing shoulder approximately level with the other shoulder, and do not lower the head when it turns to the left.

### The Delivery

Fault:  Failure to align the javelin and the driving force of the arm in the direction of the throw.

Correction:  Concentrate on keeping the palm of the hand facing upward. Also remember that since the delivery force must be directly along the shaft and in the plane from which the javelin is to be released, the elbow should remain pointed in the direction of the throw during the delivery.

Fault:  Loss of momentum between the run and the delivery.

Correction:  Practice cross-over runs, concentrating on driving the right knee across fast and low. Drill repeatedly on a three-stride approach and throw, concentrating on driving with the right cross-over leg and a "heel-first toe-forward" left foot plant. Emphasize conversion of forward momentum into the throw.

Fault:  Failure of the elbow to precede the forearm during the delivery.

Correction:  Concentrate on proper hand position. It is essential that the palm be up to allow the elbow to come through first. Also, point the elbow in the direction of the throw during the thrust.

Fault:  Throwing with the arm too far away from the head (sidearm).

Correction:  Avoid leaning away from the javelin and concentrate on releasing the javelin high over the left leg. Practice throwing with a weighted javelin or another object that is heavier than a javelin. **During the** withdrawal, bring the javelin directly back so that the shaft lies along the forearm and close to the ear. Keep the palm in an upward position throughout and do not lean away from the line of delivery.

Fault:              Failure to explode at the moment of release.

Correction:   Concentrate on stretching the throwing muscles by forcing the chest high, arching the back and reaching back with the throwing arm. Let the stretch initiate the explosive contractions of the muscles.

Fault:              The angle of projection is too low.

Correction:   Concentrate on keeping the palm of the hand facing upward. Also, concentrate on reaching high during the release, and looking high during the delivery phase.

### THE TRAINING SCHEDULE

The following is a recommended training schedule which will serve as a guide and which can be adjusted to fit the needs of any particular athlete.

#### Summer

During the summer the javelin thrower should maintain a high level of general conditioning by participating regularly in vigorous activities which he enjoys. Running and throwing type games are especially good. This should be supplemented by specific exercises to keep a high level of strength and endurance in the muscles involved in throwing the javelin. (See the recommended exercises at the end of this chapter.) Summer employment involving heavy muscular work is generally beneficial.

#### Fall

During the fall the thrower should weight train Monday, Wednesday and Friday, and he should run wind-sprints regularly. Also he should do a considerable amount of work on throwing technique.

#### Winter

During the winter months the thrower should continue his running drills with emphasis on short sprints, and he should increase the intensity of the exercise program. Also he should work on the cross-over steps used in his approach and do a considerable amount of throwing at less than maximum effort to improve his technique.

Monday:     1. Jog one-quarter mile.
2. Run one-half mile of wind-sprints, running 50 yards and walking 50 yards.
3. Do stretching exercises to loosen up shoulder, back, chest, side and groin muscles.
4. Throw the javelin at less than maximum for 10–15 minutes at a target 30′ away, to loosen up the shoulder and elbow.
5. Run through the approach to the foul line 10–15 times.

6. Take 15–20 throws, working on timing. Start with a slow run and gradually increase speed. Do not throw hard; let the momentum of the run take care of the distance attained.
7. Lift weights (see recommended exercises at the end of this chapter).

Tuesday:
1. Jog one-quarter mile.
2. Run one-half mile of wind-sprints.
3. Do stretching exercises, same as Monday.
4. Throw the javelin for 15 minutes at a target 50′ away.
5. Run through the steps to the foul line 15 times.
6. Take 15–20 throws, working on form. Always work from behind the foul line.
7. Work for 15 minutes on parallel bar and high bar exercises and the rope climb.

Wednesday:
1. Jog one-quarter mile.
2. Run one-half mile of wind-sprints.
3. Do stretching exercises.
4. Throw for 15 minutes at a target 50′ away.
5. Run through the steps to the foul line 10–15 times.
6. Take 15–20 throws, working on release and angle of flight of the javelin.
7. Take six starts out of the blocks, sprinting 25 yards each time.
8. Lift weights.

Thursday:
1. Jog one-quarter mile.
2. Run one-half mile of wind-sprints.
3. Do stretching exercises.
4. Do short throws for 10 minutes to loosen up the elbow and shoulder.
5. Run from five to eight times up and down the field, carrying the javelin as in the approach run. Stay relaxed. Practice the front cross-over step periodically during the run.
6. Take 10–15 throws using a complete approach; throw with three-quarter effort.

Friday:
1. Jog one-quarter mile.
2. Run one-half mile of wind-sprints.
3. Do stretching exercises.

Saturday:
1. Warm up.
2. Throw for long distance in competition with teammates. (Do not throw for maximum distance.)
3. Lift weights.

## Spring (Early and Middle Portion)

Monday:
1. Jog one-quarter mile.
2. Run one-half mile of wind-sprints, running 50 yards and walking 50 yards.
3. Do stretching exercises to loosen up the muscles of the shoulder, chest, back and groin.
4. Take short throws for 10 minutes to loosen up the elbow and shoulder.
5. Run through the approach steps to the foul line from five to eight times.
6. Take 15 throws; 10 throws for form and 5 for distance.
7. Lift weights (see exercises at the end of this chapter).

Tuesday:    1. Jog one-quarter mile.
            2. Run one-half mile of wind-sprints.
            3. Do stretching exercises.
            4. Take short throws for 10 minutes to loosen up the elbow and shoulder.
            5. Run through the approach to the foul line 8–10 times.
            6. Take 10 throws, working on both speed of run and form in throwing.
            7. Work for 15 minutes on parallel bar and high bar exercises, and the rope climb.

Wednesday:  1. Jog one-quarter mile.
            2. Run one-half mile of wind-sprints.
            3. Do stretching exercises.
            4. Take short throws for 10 minutes to loosen up the elbow and shoulder.
            5. Run through the approach to the foul line 8–10 times.
            6. Take seven throws for distance competing against teammates.
            7. Take six starts out of blocks, sprinting 25 yards each time.
            8. Lift weights.

Thursday:   1. Jog one-quarter mile.
            2. Run one-half mile of wind-sprints.
            3. Do stretching exercises.
            4. Take short throws for 10 minutes.
            5. Run through steps to the foul line 8–10 times.
            6. Throw easy 10 times, working on form.  During the last part of the season it is possible that no throwing will be done on Thursday.

Friday:     Rest and study movies of yourself and other throwers, and prepare yourself mentally and physiologically for competition.

Saturday:   1. Report to the stadium in plenty of time to dress slowly and warm up.  Make your best effort on each throw.
            2. Lift weights.

### Late Spring (May–June)

During this period the javelin thrower will ordinarily do the same kind of training as during the mid season.  He should keep his strength level as high as possible, work on the fine points of his throwing technique; concentrate on matters having to do with the flight of the javelin; and work to improve his speed of movement through the throwing motions.

## CONDITIONING EXERCISES

Javelin throwers must have a reasonably high level of strength, combined with a tremendous amount of speed in the movements involved in throwing. The following exercises will contribute to the desired muscular development of athletes competing in this event.  Even though the development of both strength and speed is important, speed is the more important of the two components.  This is because the javelin is a relatively light implement. In the throwing of heavier implements such as the shot, strength is proportionately more important.

In Chapter 1 are explanations of how to develop strength and speed. This information should be applied in designing the conditioning program. The specific exercises recommended for javelin throwers follow. The exercises are illustrated in Appendix A.

Arm press (standing)—exercise #5
Arm raise (supine)—exercise #6
Supine pull-over—exercise #2
Upper arm rotation—exercise #8
Hand grip—exercise #12
Trunk flexion—exercise #14
Trunk rotation (supine)—exercise #15
Trunk rotation (standing)—exercise #19
Half squats—exercise #22
Heel raise—exercise #23
Quadriceps drill—exercise #24

CHAPTER 16

# Hammer Throw

There exists an interesting drawing of Henry VIII in the act of throwing a conventional sledge hammer in a test of skill. Throwing an implement of this kind was for centuries a pastime of the nobility and populace alike in and around the British Isles.

The implement presently known as the hammer was introduced by Americans in 1887, and the early history of the event as it is performed today was made almost exclusively in the United States. However, the men who ruled in American circles in the early years were large-framed individuals of Irish extraction, and were nicknamed "The Irish Whales."

James Mitchell, the first great thrower of the modern era, reigned supreme on the American scene for about 10 years, and set a world record of 140′11″ in 1892. John Flanagan, another Irish immigrant, broke the record seven times in eight years. He was the first to break the barriers of 150′, 160′, 170′ and 180′. He was three times Olympic champion, and in 1909, at the age of 36, he climaxed his brilliant career with a mighty throw of 184′4″.

Next in line of great Irish-American throwers were Matt McGrath and Pat Ryan. For years these two battled at distances which were far ahead of their contemporaries. In 1911 McGrath set the world record at 187′4″. Ryan's reply came two years later when he raised the standard to 189′6½″.

The Europeans had practically neglected the hammer throw until after 1930 when they suddenly caught a burst of enthusiasm. During the 1930s and 1940s athletes from Germany and Hungary became especially prominent in this event. In 1938 Edwin Blask of Germany broke Pat Ryan's 25-year old record with a throw of 193′6⅞″. Imre Nemeth of Hungary dominated the world competition during the 1940s, holding the world record three different times and having a best throw of 196′5½″ accomplished in 1950.

During the 1950s the Russians came on strong, and since then the event has been dominated by athletes from Russia, Hungary, Norway, Germany and the United States. The world record has changed hands several times and is currently held by Walter Schmidt of Germany at 250'8". Following is a list of the official world's records that have been set since 1890.

| Distance | Recorder-holder and country | Year | Distance | Recorder-holder and country | Year |
|---|---|---|---|---|---|
| | | | 193ft. 6⅞in. | Erwin Blask, Germany | 1938 |
| 130ft. 8in. | James Mitchell, U.S.A. | 1890 | 193ft. 7½in. | Imre Nemeth, Hungary | 1948 |
| 140ft. 11in. | James Mitchell, U.S.A. | 1892 | 195ft. 5¼in. | Imre Nemeth, Hungary | 1949 |
| 147ft. | John Flanagan, U.S.A. | 1896 | 196ft. 5½in. | Imre Nemeth, Hungary | 1950 |
| 150ft. 8in. | John Flanagan, U.S.A. | 1897 | 197ft. 11½in. | Jozsef Csermak, Hungary | 1952 |
| 151ft. 10½in. | John Flanagan, U.S.A. | 1898 | 200ft. 11in. | Sverre Strandli, Norway | 1952 |
| 164ft. 6in. | John Flanagan, U.S.A. | 1899 | 204ft. 7in. | Sverre Strandli, Norway | 1953 |
| 167ft. 4½in. | John Flanagan, U.S.A. | 1900 | 207ft. 9¾in. | M. P. Krivonosov, U.S.S.R. | 1954 |
| 171ft. 9in. | John Flanagan, U.S.A. | 1901 | 211ft. ½in. | M. P. Krivonosov, U.S.S.R. | 1955 |
| 172ft. 11in. | John Flanagan, U.S.A. | 1904 | 220ft. 10in. | M. P. Krivonosov, U.S.S.R. | 1956 |
| 173ft. 7in. | Matt McGrath, U.S.A. | 1907 | 225ft. 4in. | Harold Connolly, U.S.A. | 1958 |
| 184ft. 8in. | John Flanagan, U.S.A. | 1909 | 230ft. 9in. | Harold Connolly, U.S.A. | 1960 |
| 187ft. 4in. | Matt McGrath, U.S.A. | 1911 | 231ft. 10in. | Harold Connolly, U.S.A. | 1962 |
| 189ft. 6½in. | Patrick Ryan, U.S.A. | 1913 | 241ft. 11in. | Gyula Zsivotzky, Hungary | 1965 |
| | | | 250ft. 8in. | Walter Schmidt, Germany | 1971 |

## PROCEDURE

Even though hammer throwing technique has changed considerably during the evolution of the event, the modern technique is rather standardized and the methods used by the different throwers vary only slightly.

The thrower grasps the handle of the hammer as illustrated in Figure 16–1. While inside the ring seven feet in diameter he does two preliminary swings of the hammer, followed by three body turns, and then the delivery (power burst). The objective is to develop as much velocity of the hammerhead as possible, then project it at the optimum angle.

According to the rules, the hammer may be thrown by any method desired. But the thrower may not touch the top surface of the ring or any point outside the ring until the throw has been marked. The hammer

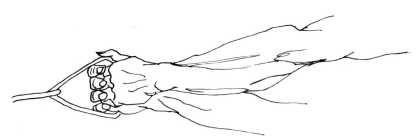

FIG. 16–1.   Correct method of gripping the hammer.

must land within the designated area (Figure 19–5). The distance of a throw is measured along a straight line from the nearest edge of the first mark made by the ball to the inside edge of the circle nearest such mark.

### HAMMER THROWING TECHNIQUE

When the angle of projection is constant, then velocity is the primary factor influencing throwing distance. The faster the hammer is moving when released, the farther it will travel. The velocity of the hammerhead at release is dependent upon: 1) the turning speed of the hammer thrower; 2) the radius of the arc through which the hammerhead sweeps; and 3) the force applied to the hammer during the final thrust (delivery).

The *turning speed of the thrower* results from the three major sources of power. All of these sources must be developed optimally if the thrower is to experience success. The *first* and primary source is the legs (especially the right leg) as they exert a strong driving action prior to each turn. The *second* source is torque, which is generated between each turn by completing the turn with the legs and hips well ahead of the plane of the shoulders. This sets the stage for unwinding of the body between turns. The *third* source is the body weight. As the hammerhead sweeps through each high point, the thrower hangs down from the hammer's pull by collapsing the left knee quickly to let the body sink ahead of the hammer. This sudden pull results in an increase in hammerhead velocity.

The importance of a *long radius* of the *hammerhead arc* is often overlooked. Many throwers concentrate too much on turning speed, which may result in pulling the shoulders back to counter against centrifugal force. By doing this, the hammer's radius is reduced, causing a decrease in the hammerhead velocity. It has been found that experienced throwers can improve their performance several feet by increasing the hammer's effective radius one inch, providing all other factors remain constant.

The *power burst (delivery)* is accomplished by the explosive straightening of the right leg and then the left leg, and vigorous unwinding and straightening of the trunk.

### The Initial Stance

The right-handed thrower assumes a stance at the rear of the circle with the back to the direction of the throw. The feet are slightly more than shoulder width apart, with the left foot planted just to the left of the center line pointing directly forward, and the right foot pointing outward about 40°. The hammerhead rests on the ground far to the right of the body. The left shoulder is dipped with the left arm fully extended and reaching across the front of the body. In this stance about ninety percent of the body weight rests on the right foot. The knees are partly flexed, the hips are cocked to the right and the eyes are focused toward the right.

### Preliminary Winds (Swings)

The purpose of the two winds is to accelerate the hammerhead, and to prepare for the first turn. The winds are acomplished mostly by the driving force of the legs and trunk. The first wind is initiated by quickly shifting the hips leftward, transferring the weight onto the left foot, then pulling the hammer with considerable force. As the hammerhead rises to knee level, the weight is shifted back to the right foot. The hands pass quickly over and behind the head with the upper arms kept close to the ears. The hands should reach as far to the rear as possible. This is when the hammerhead reaches its high point. As the hammerhead descends, the body weight shifts ahead of the hammer to the left foot, and the knees flex quickly and deeply to increase the velocity of the hammer. As the hammer starts to rise again, the left shoulder is dipped considerably and the weight is immediately shifted to the right foot for additional drive from that leg. This action is immediately followed by the hands passing over and behind the head again, but quicker than the first time. (Study Figure 16–2a through k.)

Throughout the winding phase it is extremely important to: 1) keep the arms semi-relaxed; 2) keep the head and eyes focused toward the right; 3) swing the hammer in a relatively flat plane, not allowing the hands to rise higher than shoulder level; 4) keep the low point of the hammerhead well to the right of the body during each wind; 5) keep the knees partially flexed; 6) keep the hips low in a sitting-back position when pulling on the hammer; and 7) reach outward with the arms and shoulders in order to cause the hammer to sweep through a large arc.

### Transition From the Winds Into the Turn

The transition is initiated by quickly rotating the shoulders to the right to catch the hammer early in its descent from the second wind (Figure 16–2j). At this point, the knees are flexed quickly and deeply. The body rotation is initiated by shifting the weight to the left foot, ahead of the hammer, and countering by lowering the hips back into a sitting position and bending forward at the waist. This increases the effective radius of the

Fig. 16–2 (a–y). Sequence drawings of correct technique in the hammer throw.

hammerhead and aids in controlling the centrifugal force (Figure 16–2k, l). At the moment the hammer reaches its low point, and before it passes the right knee, the thrower starts to pivot on the left heel and right toe. The first part of the leg to move into the turn is the left knee. This is followed closely by the left foot. The right foot pushes off with considerable force as it pivots, and then skims *very* close to the ground and close to the left heel and alights quickly. This action drives the legs and hips around with increased velocity and insures completion of the turn well ahead of the hammer. The hammer is swept to the left to insure an effective completion of the first turn (Figure 16–2j through o).

During the first turn, it is important to: 1) keep the left knee flexed; 2) sit back at the hips and bend forward at the waist; 3) turn the head and hips simultaneously; 4) lead into the turn with the left leg rather than the head; 5) sweep the right foot close to the ground and close to the left heel; 6) let the hammer rise naturally to its highest point; 7) hang the body down to prevent the force of the rising hammer from lifting the body off the ground; and 8) refrain from forcing the hammer with the arms at any time during the transition or the swing.

### The Power Stroke of the First Turn

If the first turn has been properly done according to the above criteria, the body should have completed the turn well ahead of the hammer and, thus, should have generated substantial torque. From the instant the hammer passes its highest point, the hammerhead will continually pick up speed until the right foot completes its push into the next turn. This phase is called the *power stroke* and is extremely crucial because more hammerhead velocity can be generated during this phase than during any other time. To insure the most effective transfer of leg power to the hammer during the power stroke, the legs must apply their maximum force before the hammer passes its low point at approximately 330° from a point at the back of the circle. This means the thrower must be firmly on his left foot before the hammer passes its low point (Figure 16–2n through p).

The success of the power stroke depends upon: 1) an early landing on the ball of the right foot before the hammer passes 270°; 2) the eyes facing the general direction of the hammer; 3) both legs being deeply flexed until the right foot is in place, which insures a strong lifting action; 4) sweeping a wide arc; 5) sitting back over the left foot to counter against centrifugal force; and 6) exerting enough leg force to sweep the hammer swiftly to the left.

### The Second and Third Turns

The second and third turns are done in the same manner as the first. However, the hammer is accelerated with each successive turn; therefore, excellent timing and concentration are necessary in order to maintain balance and do the movements correctly and precisely with ever increasing speed (Figure 16–2p through v).

### The Power Burst and Delivery

As the hammer rises during the early part of the third turn the arms and shoulders are extended to increase the hammer's radius and momentum. As the hammer sweeps to its highest point, the thrower continues to sit back with whatever force is required to maintain a well-flexed left leg, and to keep the weight on the left foot. He concentrates on placing the right foot in its correct position before the hammer reaches 270°. The right foot must land on the ball of the foot, slightly forward but not too far away from the left foot, angled slightly inward. At the instant the right foot lands both legs must be flexed. As the hammer descends the left leg collapses somewhat, and the left shoulder dips considerably to get the body into a strong lifting position with the weight settled primarily on the left foot. This must be accomplished before the hammer reaches its last low point. The thrower accelerates the hammer by pushing vigorously to the left with the right leg. This acceleration is aided by a violent straightening of the left leg and by throwing the head and shoulders backward while pointing the chin in the direction of the throw. This lifting action supplements the tremendous momentum of the hammer and is so explosive that the hammer rips from the fingers at the last instant when it is a little above shoulder height. A successful delivery is the climax of successive tight turns taken progressively faster, where control is maintained to the very end (Figures 16–2v through y, and 16–3).

Fig. 16–3. Follow-through action after releasing the hammer.

## APPLICATION OF SCIENTIFIC PRINCIPLES

Following are discussions of principles which are fundamental to correct technique in the hammer throw. Nonadherence to any of these principles will reduce performance.

*For greater stability, the base of support should be enlarged, the center of gravity lowered and the mass increased.* To maintain body stability while moving rapidly and swinging the hammer, the thrower spreads his feet (at certain times) to widen the base of support (but not too much or this will slow turning speed), and lowers the center of gravity by flexing at the knees and hips. By this means (combined with the stabilizing effects of strong muscle contractions) he is able to stay in the ring while completing the throw.

*One or both feet should be kept in firm contact with the surface until the object is released so the total effect of the muscle contractions may be directed to the throw.* If the athlete is off the ground the hammer will receive insufficient driving force. Also, because of the momentum of the swinging hammer, the athlete must stay in contact with the surface so he can control the hammer and release it in the correct direction. The best type of turn to use to remain in contact with the ground is the heel-toe turn on the left foot. This allows the right foot to stay in contact with the ground longer and thus permits the athlete to provide force with that leg over a large distance on each turn.

*The greater the friction between the supporting surface and the body parts in contact with that surface, the greater is the stability.* The surface of the throwing area is roughly finished to provide adequate friction between the surface and athlete. To get just the right amount of friction the athlete wears shoes which tend to grip the surface but still permit the necessary mobility. Free pivoting on the heel and ball of the foot must be permitted while unwanted slippage is prevented.

*Centrifugal force creates a tendency for an object to continue in motion in a straight line. The greater the centrifugal force, the greater must be the compensating centripetal force in order to keep the body moving in the intended direction.* A great amount of centrifugal force is produced by the hammer when it is swinging at top speed (400 to 500 pounds of force). This force will pull the thrower out of the ring if he does not keep his feet on the ground and sit back vigorously to counter the centrifugal force. The faster the hammer moves the greater must be the compensating forces in order to control the hammer and keep it in its circular path. But, in countering the centrifugal force the thrower must be careful to not reduce the effective radius of the hammer (Figure 16–2q).

*When the angular velocity of rotation remains constant, the lever's velocity and, therefore, its propelling force is directly proportional to its length.* To increase the velocity of the hammerhead, the thrower lengthens the effective radius of rotation as much as possible. He does this by extending the arms, rolling the shoulders forward, and sitting back only enough to resist the centrifugal force of the hammer. If all else remains equal the larger the arc, the greater will be the velocity of the hammerhead (Figure 16–2m).

*Acceleration is proportional to the force causing it, provided the mass is held constant. Therefore, when force is doubled the rate of acceleration doubles and when force is tripled the rate of acceleration also triples (except for the effects of the increased air resistance).* The acceleration of the hammer up to the time of release determines the final velocity, which is fundamental to the distance of the throw. Therefore, it is very important to accelerate the hammer to a maximum velocity by applying great force to the hammer while keeping the effective radius long.

*When a force is applied to a body, the body develops greater velocity as the distance of force application increases.* The hammer thrower applies force to the implement over an unusually long distance (two winds and three turns). If he applied the force over a shorter distance, then the final velocity of the hammer would be less. Theoretically, if the force is great enough additional velocity could be developed by doing an additional turn. But, practical experience has proven that two winds and three turns, with an effective delivery, are optimal, because other factors enter in, such as the problem of maintaining control and equilibrium (Figure 16–2).

*A total force (or velocity) is the sum of the forces (or velocities) of each body segment contributing to the act if the forces are applied in a single direction and in proper sequence and timing.* During the different phases of the throw there are numerous forces applied with different body segments. If the forces contribute their maximum in the intended direction with each force being added to the preceding forces at the point of greatest velocity, then the final velocity of the manner will be maximum. Its total force (or final velocity) will be equal to the sum of all the contributing forces (or velocities).

*In performances that require a sequence of movements and where each movement builds on the preceding movements, there should be no pause between the movements.* The different phases of the hammer throw are two swings, three turns and the delivery. These phases should be completed from the beginning to the end without pause in the application of force. Each subsequent movement should be perfectly timed so that it adds a maximum amount to the velocity developed by the prior movements.

*When the beginning and ending points are on the same level, the optimum angle of projection with which to gain maximum distance is 45° from the surface.* The hammer is released at shoulder height (about five feet) and travels approximately 200'. Under these conditions the hammer should be projected at near, but slightly less than 45° (about 42°) from the surface.

*An object remains in flight only as long as it takes to move through the vertical plane. The horizontal component of flight is not related to the flight time.* The force of gravity is ever present, and it is represented by the mass (weight) of the hammer (16 pounds). As soon as contact is broken with the hammer, the force of gravity begins to diminish its vertical velocity. Finally, gravity overcomes the vertical force, and the hammer begins to descend. The flight time is the time required for the hammer to move up to whatever height it attains and down again. The horizontal distance it travels has no influence on its time in flight. Because of this, it is important for the hammer to reach optimum height so it will be in flight long enough to reach its maximum horizontal distance. The correct combination of forces in the vertical and horizontal directions will result in about a 42° angle of projection.

*A performer must select, unconsciously in skillful actions, the muscles which are most effective for the task. In a maximum effort event, the stronger the muscles and the more muscles that are brought into action, the greater will be the force.* In the hammer throw the whole body becomes involved. The arm, shoulder and trunk muscles carry the hammer through the first two revolutions and then hold the hammer in a circular path as the athlete rotates with the hammer. The leg muscles carry the athlete through the turns and maintain balance as the body weight counteracts the force of the swinging hammer, and thus provides the main driving force to accelerate the hammer. In the final thrust the legs extend, the trunk rotates and the arms and shoulders pull and lift the hammer into flight. It is apparent that unless the correct muscles become involved at precisely the right times the accelerating forces will be less than maximum.

*A correct follow-through eliminates the tendency to decelerate an action prior to its completion. Two other purposes exist for follow-through: 1) to maintain balance; and 2) to protect the joints by gradually slowing the body parts.* The follow-through in the hammer is the continuation of the rotation. Without a correct follow-through the athlete will reduce acceleration prior to release, and the result will be less final velocity. The athlete lets the arms continue to swing; he swings the left foot around the right and extends it to the rear of the ring. At the same time he lowers his center of gravity by flexing the right leg. These actions decelerate him gradually and help him to maintain control and stay in the ring after the release (Figure 16–3).

## COMMON FAULTS AND HOW TO CORRECT THEM

The following common faults among hammer throwers were identified through correspondence and consultation with experts in the event. The suggestions on how to correct the faults were obtained from some of the best qualified competitors and coaches.

Fault:        Failure to maintain relaxation of the arms during the winds.
Correction:   Sway the body side-to-side, letting the body weight counter the pull of the hammer. Also concentrate on keeping the arms relaxed.
Fault:        Bending the arms during the turns.
Correction:   Concentrate on letting the arms out full length. Remember the

hammer is thrown with the body, and the arms are used primarily as a connection between the body and the hammer. Concentrate on letting the hammer revolve through the largest possible arc. Also, utilize a single wind, walking around rather than attempting heel-toe turns in a circle. This allows an easier way to maintain a feeling of arm and shoulder relaxation without having to think of the mechanics of the turn. Try to memorize that feeling.

Fault: Lifting the right foot too early at the start of each turn.

Correction: Concentrate on keeping the right toe on the ground until you are facing the direction of the throw. The toe should lift at about the time the front of the right knee touches the back of the left knee.

Fault: Pulling back with the shoulders rather than sitting back to compensate for centrifugal force.

Correction: Stand erect and then sit so that the shoulders, hips, and head are in a vertical plane directly over the heels. Retain this position during the turns, while keeping the arms relaxed and extended. Consciously attempt to reach (stretch) with the arms rather than pull. Also, while practicing with a weighted hammer (i.e., a hammerhead weighing 20 pounds) concentrate on keeping the arms relaxed and the shoulders relatively passive. The extra pull of the weighted hammer will force you to sit.

Fault: Failure to keep the body ahead of the hammer during the turns.

Correction: Keep your hips ahead of your shoulders and drag the hammer. Lead it; do not let it lead you. Also, emphasize relaxation of the upper body while aggressively working the legs to keep the hips in front of the hammer.

Fault: Failure to attain a maximum potential radius through which the hammer sweeps.

Correction: Place a towel at the low point of the arc and attempt to hit it during each preliminary wind. Continue to move the towel farther away so you have to stretch to hit it.
Also, use a short hammer during practice. The short hammer can be controlled more easily, and you can concentrate on the body position that will result in a maximum radius arc.

Fault: Allowing the left foot to leave the ground before or during the hammer release.

Correction: Lifting the left foot prematurely is a result of the low point of the ball having shifted to the center or to the left of center. Concentrate on delivering over the left leg, so you can "feel it in your toes." Also, pivot on the toes of both feet with a lifting, twisting motion, and deliver with a fully extended upright body, releasing the hammer on its way up and at shoulder height, or slightly higher.

## THE TRAINING SCHEDULE

The following schedule is for an experienced hammer thrower. It can serve as an important guide but might need to be adjusted to fit a particular athlete because athletes vary in age, maturity and state of conditioning.

### Summer

During the summer the hammer thrower should maintain a high level of physical conditioning by participating regularly in vigorous activities which he enjoys. Emphasis should be on activities that involve the whole body. These activities should be supplemented by specific exercises to keep a high level of strength in the muscle groups used the most in throwing the hammer (see the recommended exercises at the end of this chapter). Summer employment involving heavy muscular work is beneficial.

### Fall

During the fall the hammer thrower should lift weights Monday, Wednesday and Friday to increase power (see exercises at the end of this chapter). He should run wind-sprints regularly and do a considerable amount of work on technique.

### Winter

During the winter months the athlete should increase the intensity and the frequency of the exercise program, placing emphasis on the development of strength and speed. Also, during this period he should do a considerable amount of work on hammer-throwing drills.

Monday:
1. Jog one-quarter mile.
2. Run wind-sprints for one-half mile, sprinting 50 yards and walking 50 yards.
3. Do stretching exercises involving the muscles of the chest, shoulders, back and hip regions.
4. Do 10–15 easy throws without the spin, concentrating on correct hip and shoulder movements and causing the hammer to move through the maximum effective radius.
5. Do 8–10 easy throws including the spin, concentrating on form and timing.
6. Do 8–10 throws concentrating on buildup of speed during the spin. Concentrate on putting power into the spin but do not concentrate too much on the power of the thrust at this time.
7. Take 8–10 starts from the blocks, sprinting 25 yards each time.
8. Lift weights (see exercises at end of this chapter).

Tuesday:
1. Jog one-quarter mile.
2. Run wind-sprints for one-half mile.
3. Do stretching exercises.
4. Take 10–12 throws without spin.
5. Take 10–12 throws with the spin, concentrating on the drive during the spin.
6. Lift weights.

Wednesday:
1. Jog one-quarter mile.
2. Run wind-sprints for one-half mile, sprinting 50 yards and walking 50 yards.
3. Do stretching exercises involving the muscles of the chest, shoulders, back and hip regions.
4. Do 10–15 throws without the spin concentrating on correct hip and shoulder movements and causing the hammer to move through the maximum effective radius.

5. Take 10–15 throws, including the spin, and concentrate on correct footwork and timing during the movement in the spin. The throws should be considerably less than maximum.
6. Take 8–10 throws where the emphasis is upon the buildup of speed during the spin and increasing the maximum effective radius of the hammer. The main emphasis should be upon the driving power during the spin.
7. Take 6–10 starts from the blocks, sprinting 25 yards each time.
8. Lift weights.

Thursday:
1. Jog one-quarter mile.
2. Run wind-sprints for one-half mile.
3. Do stretching exercises.
4. Take 10–12 throws without spin.
5. Take 10–12 throws with the spin, concentrating on the drive during the spin.
6. Lift weights.

Friday:
1. Jog one-quarter mile.
2. Run wind-sprints for one-half mile.
3. Do stretching exercises.
4. Do a very limited amount of work with the hammer, concentrating on coordination and timing involved in spin and thrust.

Saturday:
1. Do preparatory exercises.
2. Throw from five to seven times for distance.
3. Lift weights.

## Spring (Early and Middle Portion)

Monday:
1. Jog one-quarter mile.
2. Run wind-sprints for one-half mile, running 50 yards and walking 50 yards.
3. Do stretching exercises.
4. Do 10 throws without the spin, concentrating on the movements of the hips and shoulders.
5. Take 12–15 throws, including the spin, concentrating on the buildup of speed to near maximum prior to the thrust.
6. Take 6–10 starts from the blocks, sprinting 25 yards each time.
7. Review action movies of yourself.
8. Lift weights.

Tuesday:
1. Jog one-quarter mile.
2. Do stretching exercises.
3. Take 10 throws without the spin.
4. Take 12–15 throws, including the spin, concentrating on the fine points of correct technique and the maximum effective radius of the hammer.
5. Take five throws, including the spin, concentrating on a fast build-up of speed during the spin and a smooth transition from the spin into a vigorous thrust.
6. Take six starts from the blocks, sprinting 25 yards each time.

Wednesday:
1. Jog one-quarter mile.
2. Run wind-sprints for one-half mile.
3. Do stretching exercises.
4. Do 5–10 throws, without the spin, concentrating on correct body movements.

                  5. Do 10–15 throws at less than maximum, but concentrating on a fast buildup of speed during the spin and a smooth transition into the thrust.

                  6. Lift weights.

Thursday:    1. Jog one-quarter mile.

                  2. Run wind-sprints for one-half mile.

                  3. Do stretching exercises.

                  4. Take five or six throws, without the spin.

                  5. Take seven near-maximum throws as if you were in competition.

                  6. Take six starts from the blocks, sprinting 25 yards each time.

Friday:      Study motion pictures of yourself and others in action. Get plenty of sleep and rest. Prepare yourself mentally and physiologically for the competition on Saturday. Be confident and ready.

Saturday:    1. Day of competition—arrive at the stadium in plenty of time to dress slowly and get properly warmed up before competition.

                  2. Jog one lap.

                  3. Do stretching exercises.

                  4. Take three starts and run 25 yards each time.

                  5. Throw four or five times, without the spin.

                  6. Take four or five throws, including the spin, but do not throw at maximum effort. Concentrate on coordination and timing.

                  7. Do your best on each throw after competition begins. It is unwise to save up for one all-out effort.

                  8. Lift weights.

### Late Spring (May–June)

During the late season the hammer thrower will ordinarily do the same kind of training as during the mid season, except he might want to increase the volume. It is very important that he maintain a high level of strength. During this period emphasis should be placed on the fine points of correct technique along with increasing speed of movement.

## CONDITIONING EXERCISES

The conditioning program for hammer throwers should develop both strength and speed in the muscle groups involved in hammer throwing. The program should emphasize the development of the legs and trunk, but development of the arms and shoulders is also important. The hammer is thrown with the whole body, but the speed that can be developed during the spins is influenced greatly by the strength and speed of contraction of the muscles in the legs and trunk. In Chapter 1, explanations are given of how to increase strength and speed. The conditioning program should be designed in accordance with that information. The particular exercises that should be emphasized by hammer throwers are the following. The exercises are illustrated in appendix A.

Bench press—exercise #4
Arm curl—exercise #3
Arm raise (supine)—exercise #6

Rowing—exercise #13
Lateral raise (standing)—exercise #7
Hand grip—exercise #12
Trunk rotation (standing)—exercise #19
Trunk rotation (supine)—exercise #15
Trunk extension—exercise #18
Trunk lateral flexion—exercise #17
Body curl—exercise #16
Half squat—exercise #22
Leg press—exercise #20
Quadriceps drill—exercise #24

# Part V

# Administration of Track and Field

# CHAPTER 17

# Promoting Track and Field

Most of the information in this chapter is aimed at promoting track and field in secondary schools. But some of the suggestions and ideas are also applicable at the college level.

The track and field coach is the one man most responsible for the promotion of his sport. Getting the school and community solidly behind the track team involves a give-and-take situation. The coach should encourage those around him to support his program and at the same time he should show interest in other school and community activities.

The following list includes specific suggestions for securing the good will and cooperation of the school administrators and faculty. In each situation the coach will have to decide which of these suggestions are workable.

1. Stress excellence in both athletics and academics.
2. Ask administrators and faculty members to act as officials at meets.
3. Invite school personnel to travel with the team when feasible.
4. Check periodically with the other teachers to find out whether the athletes are performing well in class.
5. Distribute track schedules to all teachers and extend personal invitations to attend the meets.
6. Insist that the track men act like gentlemen on and off the field.
7. Have a track dress-up day on the day of the meet. Identification tags add to the prestige of the athletes.

Included below are possible ways to promote track and field in the community.

1. Send personal letters to interested people.
2. Distribute wallet-sized schedules.

3. Circulate handouts advertising the meets.

4. Display photographs in public buildings of track stars, past and present.

5. Submit articles to the local and state newspapers.

6. Sponsor a summer recreational track program.

7. Have a track and field "Dad's" club.

8. Promote "PeeWee" track and field.

9. Organize a booster club to support the program.

Obviously the job of track and field coach is no position for a lazy man. One must have an abundance of energy to attend to the innumerable details associated with the program.

### GETTING THE ATHLETES OUT

It is a challenge for the coach to get athletes to come out for the team. His success in this undertaking depends on his personality, the example he sets and the kind of program he offers.

The coach must be sincerely enthusiastic and capable of instilling in team members a consuming desire to excel. He should be a person the team members respect and admire. Following is a list of leadership suggestions for the coach.

1. Remember that nothing is more essential to good coaching than a close personal relationship between the coach and each athlete. When an athlete feels the coach is sincerely interested in his progress he will make a stronger effort to conform to the coach's desires.

2. About one month before the beginning of regular practice prepare appropriate notices indicating the day practice begins and inviting all eligible students to try out.

3. Follow up by making personal contacts with prospective team members.

4. One week before practice begins, launch an all-out campaign for candidates. Notices (more extensive than the early notices) should be printed in the school newspaper. Articles should be submitted about the success of last year's team and about returning veterans and prospective point winners. At this time the season schedule ought to be released and posters displayed. The track should be worked into good condition and equipment placed on the field. Awards won by returning veterans might be put on display in a trophy case. Suddenly make track an important part of school life.

5. A school assembly emphasizing track will stimulate additional interest. A good track and field film which is interesting and educational to the whole student body might be shown along with a talk given by an outstanding athlete from outside the school who will stress the value of track and field.

The first meeting of candidates should be well-organized and reasonably short. The coach should talk briefly to the whole group giving them the essential information. Then it might be wise to station the best returning veteran in each event at a different location on the gymnasium floor; divide the remaining candidates into as many groups as there are stations; instruct each group to spend five minutes at each station, during which time the veteran occupying the station will lecture on his particular event. At the end of the meeting each prospective track athlete will have gained new knowledge about each event.

One thing that should be made clear at this time is that every team member will practice regularly, and that members will practice together as a team at a scheduled time.

At the second meeting the candidates should be on the field and dressed for practice. The practice session should be well-organized so that time will not be wasted. The initial practice sessions should be easy and enjoyable but everyone ought to be engaged constantly in worthwhile activity. As the athletes become better conditioned, the workouts can be more strenuous.

## MAINTAINING INTEREST

In order to have a successful track and field team there needs to be a reasonably large number of skillful athletes, and interest must be maintained at a high level for the duration of the season. The athletes should feel that the program helps to fulfill certain physical, social and emotional needs. Some methods which may be used to stimulate and maintain interest are listed below.

1. Invite well-known athletes to speak at track team meetings.

2. Provide attractive bulletin board displays, including school track records, district records, news clippings of current team members and action photographs of outstanding performers. The display should be neatly arranged and changed often.

3. Make workouts as much fun as possible and give abundant praise for a job well-done.

4. Create pride in individuals when they have completed a difficult workout by letting them and others know of their accomplishments.

5. Be democratic and fair in making decisions concerning team members. When a member does not make the traveling squad, encourage him to try harder to make the next trip.

6. Remember that some potential team members are not mature enough to make the team one year but might be point winners the next year.

7. Try to give each athlete some individual attention every day.

8. Let team members and others feel the pride you as a coach have in your team.

9. End every workout so that each person has a little energy left and is not totally exhausted.

10. Talk about the positive rather than the negative aspects of a hard workout and encourage others to do likewise.

11. Have the team captain and varsity members encourage new candidates who are trying to make the team. Often this will be more effective than encouragement from the coach.

12. Occasionally set up triathlon, pentathlon and decathlon contests for intrasquad competition.

13. Always speak of the team with pride and respect.

### KEEPING THE ATHLETES INVOLVED

Once the coach has assembled a team he faces the challenge of keeping them in training. Many potential point winners drop out because they become stale or feel that no one has interest in their progress. To keep this from happening it is important to work as closely with each individual as possible. Maintain in each member an attitude that is conducive to hard work and a winning spirit. Here are some ideas that may help to prevent members from leaving the team.

1. Place inspiring and challenging mottos or statements where team members will see them. Examples: "The difficult can be done right away, the impossible takes a little longer;" "When the going gets tough, the tough get going," etc.

2. Provide the athletes with good equipment and private lockers with the name of the sport and the athlete on the front.

3. Use a "Who's Who in Track." This display could consist of a list of the best 10 performers in each event in the district. Keen rivalries are stimulated by an open display of comparative marks.

4. Develop a tradition of winning. The athletes will feel it an honor to be on the team and will have an obligation to uphold the reputation.

5. Install an attractive trophy case where team trophies can be permanently displayed and where individual awards can be temporarily shown.

6. Provide T-shirts that have the school name and the word "track" stenciled on them. This gives identity and prestige.

7. Make interesting reading material on track and field available in the school library. *Track and Field News* is an important publication which should be in every school library. It is helpful if local businesses have a copy for their customers to read while sitting in waiting rooms.

8. Encourage each team member to keep a personal diary of his daily workout schedule and of his progress.

9. Maintain favorable relations with the press, radio and television. Strive to bring team members as much recognition as they earn so long as it is beneficial to the individual and the team.

10. Provide a challenging, yet reasonable schedule. Do not schedule

meets with teams excessively stronger or much weaker than your own. Keep your team in its class.

11. In the larger meets give individual awards to each place winner in each event. The awards need not be expensive or elaborate.

12. At the end of the season there should be a few highly valued awards given, such as a high point track and field award, most improved athlete and team captain award.

13. Take as many team members as possible to large meets and coaching clinics.

### OTHER VALUABLE SUGGESTIONS

1. Set up a track council consisting of one or two track team members from each class. This council should assist in formulating team rules and have an important part in enforcing the rules. Publicity, team parties and other activities can be organized through the council.

2. Do not drop athletes from the team who show a reasonable amount of interest and make some progress.

3. Sponsor a competitive cross country program in your school.

4. Encourage the conduct of track meets and cross country running in junior high schools in order to stimulate early interest in the sport.

5. Encourage jogger clubs in the community where whole families can participate together and where they can get advice about their physical conditioning.

6. Promote interclass and intramural meets. People learn to enjoy competing through experience in competition.

7. Hold an awards banquet at the end of the year where parents and friends are invited. Arrange for a dynamic speaker.

### NEWS MEDIA

The coach or meet director should be sure the public is aware of when and where each meet is to be held. It is also important that the news media have some interesting information to create public enthusiasm.

Every coach should take the initiative to meet with sports writers and seek their cooperation in developing his sport. The coach should not become overbearing by expecting everything he thinks important to appear in print. However, many times writers are not aware of accomplishments in track or of the personnel on the team. They will often welcome information that will gain public interest. The following are ways that can bring the coaching staff and members of the press together.

1. Drop by the reporters' offices for informal visits.

2. Invite writers to private luncheon meetings.

3. Invite school and local reporters to travel with the team to meets.

4. When league or conference meetings are being held, extend invitations to media personnel.

5. Hold special sports information days when reporters can get information and photographs of squad members.

## SPORTS BROCHURE

A colorful and well-organized sports brochure will add a great deal to the track program. High school brochures can be sent to college coaches to inform them of possible candidates for scholarships. College coaches can use them as an aid in recruiting potential team members. College brochures can serve an excellent purpose in bringing publicity and recognition to the team. The following ideas are essential in making brochures interesting and informative.

1. An attractive cover with the picture of one of the outstanding athletes on it, along with the name and address of the institution
2. A list of the athletic staff with their addresses and telephone numbers
3. A meet schedule for the coming year, including starting times
4. An alphabetical roster of team members

Other information that might be included:

1. Facts about the school
   A. Location
   B. Historical information
   C. Principal or president
   D. Enrollment
   E. Conference or league
   F. School colors
   G. School nickname and/or mascot
   H. History of the sport
2. Results of past meets
3. Prospects for the coming year in each event
4. Information about the coaches
5. Photographs of squad members in action
6. Records for the different events
   A. World records
   B. National high school or collegiate records
   C. League or conference records
   D. School records
   E. Stadium records

### Meet Program

At least a simple mimeographed program ought to be prepared for each dual meet and a more elaborate one for larger meets. The program should include:

1. For high school (each event):
   A. National record
   B. State record

    C. Regional record

    D. School record

  2. For college (each event):

    A. World record

    B. National record

    C. College record

    D. Meet record

    E. Stadium record

For large meets the following additional information might be included in the program to add luster to the meet.

  1. A colorful cover with the date, time and location of the meet

  2. Welcome statement from some prominent person

  3. A list of meet officials

  4. A list of events, giving starting times

  5. A table showing how the meet is to be scored for each event

  6. Previews about outstanding performers in the meet

  7. Action photographs

  8. Entry list for each event along with year in school and best performance for the year

  9. Past champions for each event, giving winning mark and year accomplished

CHAPTER **18**

# Organization and Conduct of Meets

Track meets range from relatively simple dual meets to large and complex championship meets. Regardless of the size and importance of the meet, careful planning is essential. Division of responsibilities must be made well in advance and each person must correlate his plans with others who have responsibilities.

The following information pertains to a large and highly organized event such as a major championship meet. Smaller and less complex meets would require proportionately less involvement. An important word of caution is that track meets are seldom over-organized, but they are frequently under-organized.

## GAMES COMMITTEE

The primary purpose of the games committee is to give the meet director assistance and guidance with organizing and promoting the meet. This committee should include representatives for housing, transportation, public relations, promotion, traffic control, etc. The committee should have a chairman, secretary and treasurer, all of whom would be different than the meet director. The committee should formulate a budget for the meet and then assign the meet director to proceed with organizing and conducting the meet within the framework of the budget, and with the assistance of the individuals on the committee.

## MAJOR RESPONSIBILITIES OF THE MEET DIRECTOR

The director is the key official behind the success of a meet. He must have a thorough working knowledge of a meet, possess the ability to work with people and be able to coordinate all of the various aspects of the meet. Working with the games committee, he must be certain that all of the following responsibilities are handled:

1. *Sanction of the Meet.* If the meet is not sanctioned by the appropriate state, regional and national organizations, the eligibility of certain athletes might be placed in jeopardy and those athletes who break records might not receive their due credit.

2. *Advanced Information to Coaches and Athletes.* The date of the meet, a list of events and entry information should be sent to the coaches of potential contestants well in advance of the meet.

3. *Promotion of the Meet.* An adequate promotional program should be conducted, involving members of the different news media along with those interested in promoting the meet on a local level.

4. *Entries.* Some time after the initial announcement of the meet, but well before the meet, entry forms should be distributed to the coaches of potential contestants. The forms should be accompanied by thorough and clear instructions, and the deadline date for entries should be indicated.

5. *Entry Fees.* If an entry fee is to be charged, the amount should be determined early enough to be stated in the initial information sent to coaches and athletes. Also the official entry form should state the amount of the fee, and the fee should be submitted with the entry.

6. *Transportation and Housing.* These responsibilities should probably be placed directly with a subcommittee where the chairman of the committee is responsible to be sure that adequate arrangements are made and that appropriate information is provided to the coaches of potential contestants. Included with this information should be directions relative to entry routes into the community, directions on how to get to the housing areas and information about the competition areas.

7. *Admission Charges.* Admission fees should be in line with the caliber of the meet and the potential interest in it. State and local taxes must be considered. Usually there are three different prices for seats—reserved, general admission-adult and student.

8. *Advanced Ticket Sales.* Advanced ticket sales is one good way to advertise a meet. Sometimes businesses will help sponsor the meet by purchasing a group of tickets which they in turn disperse to their customers. In return, the businesses receive certain kinds of publicity in connection with the meet.

9. *Complimentary Tickets.* In order to create the best relations with track and field enthusiasts, clear-cut policies regarding complimentary tickets should be enforced. These tickets should be handled with great discretion.

10. *Printed Programs.* A printed program can add much interest for spectators and participants alike. The program should include a listing of the appropriate records for each event, a list of the events along with

spaces for filling in the winners, and interesting information about selected athletes and coaches.

11. *Awards.* A special subcommittee should be appointed to determine the kinds of awards to be given, to obtain the awards and to arrange for their presentation.

12. *Concessions.* It must be decided whether concessions should be available and, if so, what they should include and who should manage them. The concessions should be well-organized and supervised.

13. *Police Security.* Adequate policemen from either the local police force or the school security force should be on hand and they should have specific instructions relative to their responsibilities.

14. *Parking.* If a large attendance is expected, then a parking plan should be worked out and an adequate number of well-qualified parking attendants should be on hand.

15. *Ceremony and Pageantry.* It must be decided early what ceremonies and pageantry will be held in connection with the meet and the necessary arrangements should be made well in advance.

16. *First Aid and Medical Arrangements.* A physician should be on duty and he should be in charge of a well-equipped first aid station; the station should be in a location known to meet officials, coaches and athletes.

17. *Competition Facilities.* The track and field area should be checked carefully for both legal and safety specifications well in advance of the meet in order that any necessary adjustments or repairs can be made prior to the meet. It would be unfortunate to have a record disallowed because the competition area did not fit official specifications.

18. *Weighing of Equipment.* The one who weighs equipment should be well-qualified and should have good quality measuring equipment. He should be stationed at a convenient location known to the coaches and competitors.

19. *Dressing Facilities.* The team members should be provided with accommodations as convenient as possible to the place of competition. They should be notified in advance whether towels will be furnished. An adequate number of dressing room attendants should be on duty to insure security and proper conduct in the dressing areas.

20. *Press Box Services.* The final results of the meet should reach the press and coaches as soon as possible. Sufficient secretarial help and secretarial machines should be provided and an adequate number of runners should be available to relay material from the officials to those who record.

21. *Ushers.* When reserved seats are sold, ushers must be available to help spectators find their seats. This assignment is often given to a service club within the school.

22. *Controlling Athletes and Coaches on the Field.* Much confusion can be avoided by having a clear-cut policy concerning who may be on the field. As much as possible, coaches and athletes should be kept in the

stands and they should be placed in prescribed areas. It is important that coaches and athletes be fully informed on what is expected of them in this regard and the policy should be enforced by security personnel. The announcer can help by stating the policy at regular intervals throughout the meet. In some cases, it might be necessary to disqualify habitual offenders.

23. *Briefing of Coaches and Athletes.* Coaches and athletes should be informed of the various policies and procedures of the meet. Also, each athlete should have a competitor's number attached to the back of his shirt. The coaches should be held responsible to disperse the necessary information and material to the team members.

24. *Establishment of New Records.* The appropriate measuring devices and the proper record forms should be available to the recorder and referee in case new records are established.

25. *Preparation of Competitive Areas.* All competitive areas must be properly prepared and marked prior to the beginning of competition.

26. *Identification of Officials.* All meet officials should be furnished with some kind of identification such as an official's ribbon, badge, vest or cap. This is necessary in order to keep only authorized personnel on the field.

27. *Press Passes.* Authorized photographers and sports writers should be provided with press passes which will enable them to go to the various competition areas.

28. *Drawing (Scratch) Meeting.* This meeting can be a frustrating experience for all concerned if it is not well-organized and properly conducted. The person in charge should be thoroughly familiar with the procedures to be followed and an adequate amount of good clerical help should be on hand.

29. *Expenses Paid to Athletes.* Under AAU and IAAF rules travel fares and per diem are allowed. Financial aid for those who must travel great distances might be included in the budget. This will help insure the presence of top performers at the meet.

30. *Anemometers.* An anemometer should be placed along the side of each straight-away and a person should be stationed there who is qualified to read and report wind velocity accurately.

31. *Briefing of Officials.* Prior to the day of the meet the meet director should call a meeting of all head officials to make certain that each one is well-informed of his duties. Each official should have access to the rules which govern his particular assignment. A few alternate officials should be on hand in case certain other officials are absent.

## ASSIGNMENT OF OFFICIALS

The rules governing meets and the exact duties of each official are described in the official rule book. The content of this section does not duplicate all of the information found there. It only gives an overview of the main responsibilities of the key officials.

The following chart shows the officials that are normally needed. However, the exact number of officials varies with the size of the meet and its duration. Therefore, the chart would need to be adjusted to fit the particular situation. Usually some excellent officials can be recruited from the school faculty and local businessmen. If there is a local track and field association, this organization can furnish a number of well-qualified officials.

| | | |
|---|---|---|
| Meet Director: _____ | | |
| Referee: _____ | | |
| Starter: _____ | Asst. Starter: _____ | |
| Announcer: _____ | | |
| Clerk of Course: _____ | Asst. Clerk: _____ | |
| Scorer: _____ | | |
| Marshal: _____ | | |
| Timers: | 1. _____(Head) | 2. _____ |
| | 3. _____ | 4. _____ |
| | 5. _____ | 6. _____ |
| Finish Judges: | 1. _____(Head) | 2. _____ |
| | 3. _____ | 4. _____ |
| | 5. _____ | 6. _____ |
| Inspectors: | 1. _____(Chief) | 2. _____ |
| | 3. _____ | 4. _____ |
| High Jump Judges: | 1. _____(Chief) | 2. _____ |
| | 3. _____ | |
| Long Jump Judges: | 1. _____(Chief) | 2. _____ |
| | 3. _____ | |
| Triple Jump Judges: | 1. _____(Chief) | 2. _____ |
| | 3. _____ | |
| Pole Vault Judges: | 1. _____(Chief) | 2. _____ |
| | 3. _____ | |
| Shot Put Judges: | 1. _____(Chief) | 2. _____ |
| | 3. _____ | |
| Discus Throw Judges: | 1. _____(Chief) | 2. _____ |
| | 3. _____ | |
| Javelin Throw Judges: | 1. _____(Chief) | 2. _____ |
| | 3. _____ | |
| Hammer Throw Judges: | 1. _____ | 2. _____ |
| | 3. _____ | |
| Starting Block Attendants: | 1. _____ | 2. _____ |
| | 3. _____ | |
| Hurdle Crew: | 1. _____ | 2. _____ |
| | 3. _____ | 4. _____ |
| | 5. _____ | 6. _____ |
| Anemometer Readers: | 1. _____ | 2. _____ |

### Meet Director

Sometimes the meet is managed by the meet director alone. However, in the case of large meets the director sometimes has three assistants in charge of equipment, field events and track events. It is the responsibility of the director to be sure that all the various events of the meet are run efficiently.

### Referee

The referee is the chief official of the meet. Some of his responsibilities are:

1. To make the final decision on matters involving disqualifications.

2. To interpret matters that are not clearly covered in the rules.

3. To verify the validity of a record that has been set by checking watches, height, distance, wind velocity and other necessary matters.

4. To decide place winners of running events when a film interpretation is necessary.

5. To instruct other officials on the interpretation of rules and other matters which may be in question.

### Starter

The starter should have control over all aspects of the start. His decisions are final and without appeal. He has the following specific responsibilities:

1. To start races promptly once the clerk of course has turned the participants over to him.

2. To give the appropriate instructions concerning the rules and conditions of the race.

3. To fire the signal for the last lap of races one mile and longer.

4. To make certain that the starting block crew places the blocks appropriately and at the right places and that the blocks are moved from locations where they will interfere with the continuance of a race.

5. With the aid of the assistant starter, to make sure the contestants get off to a fair start.

In performing his duties, the starter ought:

1. To make sure that every start is conducted strictly according to the rules.

2. To make sure that he does not upset the emotional control of the runners. This can be best accomplished by making sure the runners are fully informed of what is expected of them and by the starter himself using a calm and cool approach when conducting the start.

3. To stand on the outside edge of the track and slightly in front of the runners so they can see him.

4. To signal to the head timer and head finish judge and receive signals back from them indicating that they are ready. The standard commands given by the starter are the following:

A. "Remove your sweat clothes and stand behind your blocks."

B. A blast on a whistle which signifies to the timers and judges that the starter is ready. Usually the head judge will reply with two blasts of the whistle.

C. "Take your marks." Upon this command the competitors move into their starting blocks. At this time the starter raises the pistol above his shoulder.

D. "Set." The competitors move to the set position and simultaneously the starter raises the pistol higher or gives some other signal which signifies to the timers and judges that the runners are set.

E. Pistol shot. The competitors are to be held between 1.4 and 2.0 seconds in a motionless set position before the gun is fired.

The equipment needed by the starter includes a .32 caliber pistol and shells with black or colored powder which can be seen by the timers and judges, a .22 caliber pistol used for recall purposes, a whistle and a brightly colored starter's arm sleeve.

### Announcer

The announcer has a considerable amount of control over how fast the meet moves, how well the coaches and athletes are kept informed, and how interesting the meet is to the spectators. He should be a genuine track and field authority and enthusiast who has a pleasing voice and can give the spectators interesting information such as world, national, state and school records and points of interest about individual competitors. In the finals of each event the announcer ought to name each athlete before he performs and give his time or distance as soon as it is available. In order to do this the announcer needs a sufficient number of assistants who can provide up-to-date information. The announcer is the on-the-scene public information person.

### Clerk of Course

The clerk of course is responsible for the following duties:

1. To obtain a list of the competitors in each event.

2. To assign the competitors to heats and lanes in accordance with the rules and the other information furnished to him.

3. To get the competitors to their areas of competition prior to the prescribed time the competition should begin.

4. To turn the competitors over to the starter when it is time for the competition to begin.

### Head Timer and Timers

Efficient timing requires quick reflexes and concentration. Good quality stopwatches should be obtained in sufficient number and checked for accuracy by a qualified watchsmith. The timers should be positioned on an elevated step-stand at the finish line.

When the race is about ready to start the head timer should announce "gun-up" to get the timers' attention. As the gun is fired the timers should be looking at the gun so they can start their watches as they see the smoke. The timers should watch the runners until they get within 10–15 yards of the finish line, then they should sight down the finish line and be ready to stop the watch as soon as a runner's torso touches the finish line. The head timer is responsible for the following:

1. To check out the watches from the equipment manager and hand them to the timers.

2. To assign the other timers to their specific duties.

3. To collect and record the times following each race.

4. To determine the official time from the recorded times and submit the official time to the scorer and the announcer.

5. To have the referee check the readings on the watches when a record has been set.

6. To alert the timers when it is time to start the next race.

Each individual timer is responsible for the following:

1. To become familiar with the operation of the watch.

2. To record the time shown by the watch at the end of each race.

3. To keep the time posted on the watch until the head timer has given the signal to reset the watches.

4. To avoid discussing or comparing times with other timers until the official time has been recorded.

5. To return the watch to the head timer at the completion of the meet.

It is strongly recommended that electronic timers be used when possible, because this adds to timing accuracy, and reduces the number of judges needed.

### Head Finish Judge and Finish Judges

Top caliber finish judges are necessary if confusion and unfairness are to be avoided. A competent finish judge is alert, unbiased and calm. He must be able to make accurate and fair judgments under the pressures of exciting competition. They should be placed at the finish line and standing on graduated steps. It is recommended that a judge watch the runners as they come down the track until they get about 10 yards from the finish line, then shift his line of vision along the finish line and pick his runner. The runner on the inside lane and the one on the outside lane are the ones most often overlooked. The finish judges should be made aware of this. As the runner crosses the finish line, the judge should follow him down the track and obtain his number, name and school: this information should be recorded on the judge's card and handed to the head judge. The head finish judge is responsible:

1. To obtain pencils and place-picking cards and to distribute them to the finish judges.

2. To instruct finish judges on procedures to be followed.

3. To signal to the starter that officials are ready.

4. To gather and record the results immediately following each event.

5. To send the results immediately to the scorer and announcer.

6. To resolve any discrepancies on place winners that may occur.

The following are the responsibilities of the finish judges:

1. To position themselves where they can best do the job and be alert to their assignments.

2. To know the rules for picking place winners.

3. To record the place winner's number, name and school and immediately give the results to the head finish judge.

4. Not to discuss decisions with other judges.

### Chief Inspector and Inspectors

There should be at least four inspectors, one of whom is the chief inspector. The inspectors must be familiar with the various infractions of the rules that can result in disqualification. Some of the infractions which must be watched for by inspectors are: cutting in front of another runner too soon, elbowing, running out of an assigned lane, over-running the baton exchange zone or not running over a hurdle properly. The responsibilities of the chief inspector are:

1. To instruct the inspectors of the various infractions that they should watch for.

2. To place the inspectors where they can best perform their assigned duties.

3. To ask the starter to instruct runners to avoid committing fouls.

4. To report infractions to the referee and aid him in making the correct decision relative to disqualification.

The responsibilities of the inspectors are:

1. To become thoroughly familiar with the infractions which may result in disqualification and be alert in watching for infractions.

2. To report violations of the rules to the chief inspector.

3. To avoid discussing violations with anyone other than the chief inspector and the referee.

### Chief Field Judge

In large meets there is sometimes a chief field judge to oversee all the field events, one chief judge for each separate event and other judges as events may require. The chief field judge (if there is one) serves under and carries out the duties of the referee as they relate to the field events. Specifically, his responsibilities are:

1. To make every effort to insure a fair and equal opportunity for every contestant to do his best. For example, he may change the place or conditions of the competition if there is adequate justification for doing so.

2. To assume responsibility for inspecting, weighing and measuring of all implements and apparatus used in the field events, and ascertaining that no contestant uses an implement that is not approved.

3. To make certain that field events begin on schedule and are conducted properly.

4. To check and certify the official results for each event upon its completion and turn the results over to the announcer and recorder.

5. To inspect all measurements of record performances and recommend approval or disapproval.

The chief judge of each field event serves under the chief field judge and, with the help of his assistant judges, has the following responsibilities:

1. To conduct his event in accordance with the rules.

2. To judge competitors' efforts as being fair or foul.

3. To supervise his assistants in their duties.

4. To report the final results to the head field judge.

### The Marshal

The duty of the marshal and his assistants is to keep all areas of the track and field clear and unobstructed in accordance with the policies governing the meet. Unauthorized personnel, inactive officials, noncompeting athletes, photographers, public communication representatives, etc. should be assigned special areas where they do not interfere with the proper conduct of the competition. The marshal should make sure that the various people stay in their restricted areas.

## REMEMBERING THE DETAILS
## CHECKLIST

### Items to Do in Advance of the Meet

( ) Go through the normal reservation procedure to schedule all needed facilities, and be sure there are no conflicts.

( ) Write to judges reminding them of the time and place, and giving other information they need.

( ) Arrange for parking of buses and cars.

( ) Prepare written instructions describing the duties of each official.

( ) Check arrangements for lockers, towels and shower facilities.

( ) Check the publicity arrangements.

( ) Arrange to have the training room facilities available.

( ) Prepare a diagram showing the dressing room arrangements for each team.

( ) If visiting teams are planning to stay overnight, either arrange housing or send them information regarding the available facilities.

( ) Arrange for the printing and distribution of the program.

( ) Distribute passes to guests and officials, or prepare a pass gate list.

### Items to Check the Day of the Meet

( )  Check the facilities and have all of the equipment ready and available.
( )  Have the clipboards, pencils and event cards ready to be picked up by the head officials.
( )  Distribute packets to the coaches, including all the material and information they need for their team members.
( )  Present officials with a list of their duties.
( )  Meet with head officials and coaches a short time before the meet if needed.
( )  Start the meet on time.

( )  ### Equipment and Facilities to be Arranged

( )  Clipboards, pencils and either scratch pads or judging forms
( )  The public address system and a completed announcer's information form
( )  Chairs and tables as needed for judges, recorders, scorers and announcer
( )  Ticket booths and supplies needed for selling tickets
( )  Record player, a record of the national anthem and a national flag
( )  Finishing tapes
( )  Starting guns
    One .32 pistol plus shells
    One .22 pistol plus shells
( )  Two starter sleeves
( )  Eight stopwatches
( )  Pegs for marking distances in the throwing events
( )  Flags for marking conference, stadium and world records
( )  Forms for reporting the place winners in each event
( )  Master scorecard
( )  Equipment for weighing and measuring throwing implements
( )  Flash cards for the number of laps to run in the distance events
( )  Contestants' numbers for each school and pins to fasten on the numbers
( )  Marking of lanes
( )  Nine starting blocks—carrier to move starting blocks to different locations
( )  Six high jump and pole vault cross bars
( )  High jump standards and pit
( )  Pole vault standards and pit
( )  Long jump toe board
( )  Javelin toe board
( )  Six batons for relay races
( )  Cross bar lifter for pole vault
( )  Distance and height indicators (markers) for each throwing and jumping event
( )  Officials' caps, jackets or labels to identify the officials
( )  Marking of the several competitive areas in accordance with official rules
( )  Official rule books
( )  Duplicating machine and typewriters
( )  Measuring tapes to check the heights and distances in field events
( )  Towels for wiping off the discus, hammer and shot after each throw
( )  Water truck, if needed
( )  Officials' passes
( )  Parking passes
( )  Victory stand, if needed
( )  Decorative flags, if needed
( )  Medals and trophies

*Items to Do After the Meet*

( )  Duplicate the results and distribute them to interested persons
( )  Call local papers and radio and television stations, giving them a resume of the action and the final results
( )  Return any equipment loaned to you for the meet
( )  Prepare a written report for future reference, including suggestions on how the meet can be improved

# CHAPTER 19

# Track and Field Construction

A school administrator or track coach may be asked to direct or assist in the planning and construction of a new track and field facility or the remodeling of an old one. Of necessity most facilities must accommodate several sports. The concern here, however, is with the facilities needed for track and field. An overall track and field layout is shown in Figure 19–1. Details are given later in the chapter on the construction of the track, throwing areas and jumping areas.

In addition to the design and layout of the track and the throwing and jumping areas, there are certain other important considerations.

1. The seating capacity of the stadium should be sufficient to meet the needs of the near future with plans for expansion to satisfy predicted long range needs. The number of seats required will be influenced by: A) the sports served by the stadium; B) school enrollment; C) population of the geographic area; and D) the enthusiasm of the local people for athletics.

2. When possible, the topography where the field will be placed should be fairly level, free from stone formations near the surface and have good drainage.

3. The long dimension of the field should run north and south to minimize sun glare.

4. An area protected from excessive wind is best because of the adverse effects of wind on running and field events.

5. Adequate parking space and accessibility to traffic routes are important considerations.

6. Dressing and shower facilities should be provided in the stadium unless the school gymnasium is nearby to allow convenient access for the athletes.

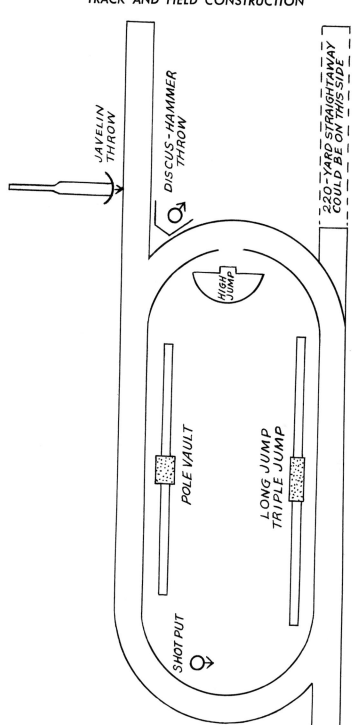

FIG. 19–1. Track and field layout.

7. The track should be placed no closer to the boundary of the seating and other obstacles than is provided for in the official rules.

8. The plan should provide for an emergency care room, ticket booths, concession stands, rest rooms and equipment storage areas.

9. The facilities should be located for maximum convenience of all of those who will use them.

10. Aesthetics should receive strong consideration.

11. Accessibility of public services such as sewer, electricity, gas and water supplies is important.

## DIMENSIONS AND MEASUREMENTS

More accuracy is required in track and field facilities than practically any other sports areas because the activity deals with precise measurements of times and distances. Many a record has been disallowed because when the facilities were checked, it was found that the track was a few inches too short, or the throwing or jumping area had too much slope. During the construction phase it is wise to employ the services of a well-qualified surveyor to check all measurements and grades. The areas that need to have exact measurements are:

1. Throwing areas: javelin, discus, shot and hammer throwing areas and sectors.

2. Jumping areas: long jump and triple jump, pole vault and high jump runways, takeoff areas and pits.

3. Track: levelness of the track; distance around.

4. Permanent track measurements: hurdle placements; steeplechase (water jump and placement of hurdles); baton-passing zones; track lanes; start and finish lines.

Special characteristics of the track are:

1. It should be an oval a minimum of 440 yards long, measured along a line 12″ from the curb.

2. It should be at least 24′ wide to permit a minimum of six 48″ lanes.

3. Finish lines should have white posts placed on each side of the track and at least one foot away from the track to aid the finish judges.

## TRACK COMPOSITION

When selecting material for construction consider such items as cost, availability, maintenance and durability. Different situations call for different kinds of base construction, depending on the money available, and the drainage problems at the particular location. Some of the better tracks where drainage is an important consideration and an all-weather surface is not used have been constructed as follows:

1. Top surface composed of three to six inches of cinders that have passed through a $\frac{1}{4}$ inch mesh screen. The cinders should contain a binder of one part clay.

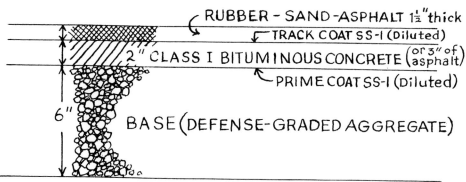

RUBBER – SAND –ASPHALT 1½"thick

TRACK COAT SS-I (Diluted)

2" CLASS I BITUMINOUS CONCRETE (or 3"of asphalt)

PRIME COAT SS-I (Diluted)

6" BASE (DEFENSE-GRADED AGGREGATE)

SUBGRADE (Compacted)

# CROSS SECTION OF A RUBBER-ASPHALT TRACK

Fig. 19–2. Track composition.

2. Middle layer composed of five to twelve inches of medium-sized cinders or gravel, leveled and rolled with a roller.

3. Bottom layer composed of four to ten inches of crushed stones, cinders, slag or crushed bricks. (This material should be rolled with a heavy roller to make it uniform.)

If an all-weather surface is to be used the base construction can be much simpler. Figure 19–2 shows the cross section of a typical rubber-asphalt track.

Six kinds of track surfaces are discussed here giving the advantages and disadvantages of each. The all-weather tracks have become very popular in the last few years and there is a strong trend toward all-weather facilities.

*Cinder Track*
  *Advantages:*

   1. Material is usually readily available.
   2. It does not stick to shoes when wet.
   3. The track packs easily.
   4. It does not get hard or bake.
   5. Weeds do not readily grow in it.

  *Disadvantages:*

   1. Footing may be loose after some use.
   2. Drainage can be a problem.
   3. It requires frequent care to be kept in good condition.
   4. Cinder tracks need to be marked prior to each meet.
   5. When runners fall, cinder surfaces cause considerable injury.

*Clay Track*
  *Advantages:*

    1. It provides solid and safe footing (when dry).
    2. A clay track is a fast track when properly prepared.

  *Disadvantages:*

    1. It does not drain well.
    2. It gets hard and bakes.
    3. A clay track has to be marked frequently for practice and meets.
    4. Weeds growing through the surface can be a problem.

*Rubber-Asphalt Track*
  *Advantages:*

    1. There is less chance that meets and practices will need to be cancelled because of rain.
    2. Markings are permanent.
    3. It provides good footing.
    4. The firmness can be altered by the application of water.
    5. Maintenance costs are minimal.
    6. A rubber-asphalt track is not as expensive to construct as other all-weather tracks.
    7. It is usually easy on athletes' legs and feet.

  *Disadvantages:*

    1. When the temperature gets too hot the track tends to get soft.
    2. If too much asphalt and too little rubber are used it will get too hard and be injurious to the athletes' legs and feet.
    3. Asphalt mixture may adhere to runner's spikes at certain temperatures.

*Tartan Track*
  *Advantages:*

    1. It withstands any kind of weather: rain, cold or heat.
    2. Any length spikes can be used.
    3. The surface is nonslip.
    4. Maintenance costs are minimal.
    5. Markings are permanent.
    6. It produces fast times.

  *Disadvantages:*

    1. The price may be prohibitive.
    2. The track is too hard for continuous sustained training.

*Astro-Turf Track*
  *Advantages:*

    1. There is resistance to moisture and mildew.
    2. The track requires little maintenance.

3. Excellent traction is provided.

4. It produces fast times.

5. Markings are permanent.

*Disadvantages:*

1. The price may be prohibitive

2. The track is too hard for continuous and sustained practice sessions.

### FIELD AREAS

The area for each field event is unique and requires precise construction. Following are important characteristics of each of the field areas.

#### Long Jump and Triple Jump Areas

Considerations when planning long and triple jump areas are:

1. Drainage and base construction of the runway should be the same as the running track.

2. To enhance drainage the runway should be four to six inches higher than the adjoining areas, and it should be at least 130' long.

3. The landing pit, takeoff board and runway must all be level with each other.

4. The takeoff board must be constructed of wood, eight inches wide and at least four feet long.

5. The takeoff board must be fixed firmly in the ground, preferably attached to a timber buried under the surface (Figure 19–3).

6. In the long jump the landing pit should be nine feet wide, and the distance between the scratch line and the nearer edge of the pit should be no less than three feet and three inches (12' is recommended). The distance between the scratch line and the far edge of the pit should be at least 33'.

7. In the triple jump the pit should be nine feet wide, and the nearer edge of the pit should be at least 36' from the scratch line (39' is recommended).

#### Pole Vault Area

The runway should be designed and constructed as explained for the long jump runway. The top surface of the box and the surface area where the standards rest should be on exactly the same level as the runway. The distance between the vertical uprights should be not less than 12' or more

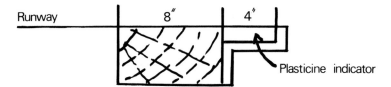

FIG. 19–3. Takeoff board for long jump and triple jump.

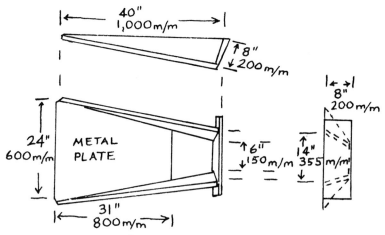

FIG. 19–4.    Pole vault box.

than 14'2". The pins on which the cross bar rests may protrude no more than three inches and must be round, smooth and perfectly horizontal. The vaulting box may be constructed of either wood or metal (Figure 19–4).

### High Jump Area

The high jump approach area should provide at least 50' of level surface where the jumper may approach the bar anywhere within a 180° arc. The takeoff area should be perfectly level and composed of the same material as the track and runways. The distance between the vertical uprights should be not less than 12' or more than 13'2". The surface on which the cross bar rests should be flat and measure $1\frac{1}{2}''$ by $2\frac{3}{8}''$. The cross bar should rest along the narrow dimension of the support. The high jump pit should have minimum dimensions of 16' wide by 12' deep. It should be high enough and of a composition which will provide a completely safe and comfortable landing.

### Shot Put Area

The shot is put from inside a metal ring seven feet in diameter (inside dimension). The surface within the ring should be of concrete or similar material. Although cinders or clay are legal these surfaces are not advised. The circle shall be divided in half by a two-inch line extending 30" outside each side of the circle and measured at right angles to the center of the throwing sector. The stop board shall be an arc of wood firmly fixed so that its inner edge coincides with the inner edge of the shot put circle. The stop board and circle are to be painted white. The maximum inclination of the sector shall be 1:1000 (see Figure 19–5).

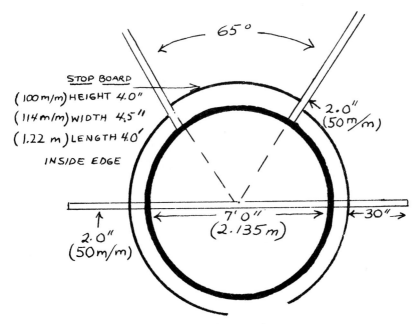

Fig. 19–5. Shot put ring.

### Discus Throw Area

The discus shall be thrown from inside a circle 8′2½″ in diameter (inside dimension). The circle is to be formed by a metal ring painted white, and the surface inside the circle should be of concrete or similar material, although cinder or clay surfaces are legal but not advised. The throwing sector shall be marked by two radial lines two inches wide which form a 60° angle extending from the center of the circle. The maximum inclination of the sector shall be 1:1000. Where spectators are close by it is recommended that the throwing area be partially enclosed by a wire mesh cage for the protection of the spectators (Figure 19–6).

### Hammer Throw Area

The hammer throw area is the same as the area for the discus throw except that for the hammer throw the circle is seven feet in diameter. It is strongly recommended that the throwing area be partially enclosed by a wire mesh cage for the protection of spectators.

### Javelin Throw Area

The run-up surface should be level and covered with turf, clay, or all-weather surfacing. The foul board shall be made in the shape of an arc with a radius of 26′3″. It shall be made of wood or metal two inches wide, painted white and sunk flush with the ground. The run-up boundaries

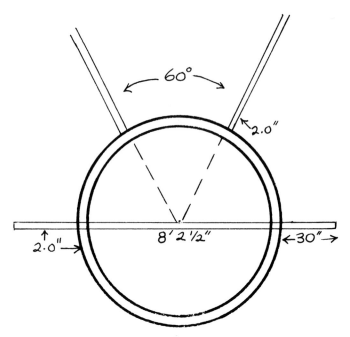

FIG. 19–6.   Discus throw ring.

shall be marked by two parallel lines two inches in width and 13'1½" apart, extending backward from the extremities of the throwing arc.    The maximum length of the run-up area should be 120' and its minimum length 110'.   The sector shall be marked by radial lines two inches wide extending from the center of the circle represented by the arc of the foul board.   The area within the sector shall be on the same level as the throwing area, with a maximum deviation of 1:1000 permitted (Figure 19–7).

### DRAINAGE REQUIREMENTS

Drainage problems vary with the immediate surroundings of the field and its subsoil.   Where artificial drainage is required, storm sewers and catch basins should be placed both inside and outside the track itself. Figure 19–8 shows a detailed drawing of one kind of drainage catch basin.

Surface drains and catch basins should be placed every 100', and about 12 to 15" away from both the inside and outside track curbs.   They should be connected to the lateral drains by a four to six inch tile or iron pipe that empties into a storm sewer.

Drains should be cut through the curb around the track every 10'.   A "V" cut in the curb with a one-percent grade to the infield area is sufficient (Figure 19–9).

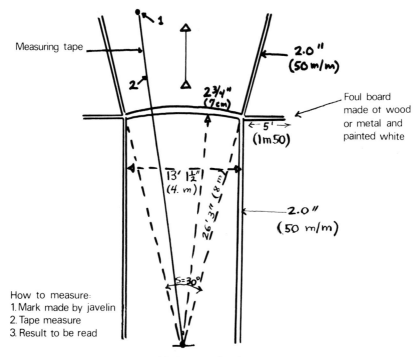

Measuring tape

2.0" (50 m/m)

2¾" (7 cm)

Foul board made of wood or metal and painted white

←5'→ (1m 50)

13' 1½" (4. m)

26' 3" (8 m)

2.0" (50 m/m)

6=30°

How to measure:
1. Mark made by javelin
2. Tape measure
3. Result to be read

FIG. 19–7. Javelin throw area.

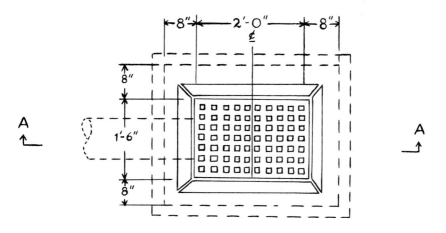

←8"→←—2'-0"—→←8"→
¢

8"

1'-6"

8"

A

A

TOP VIEW
FIG. 19–8. Drain catch basin.

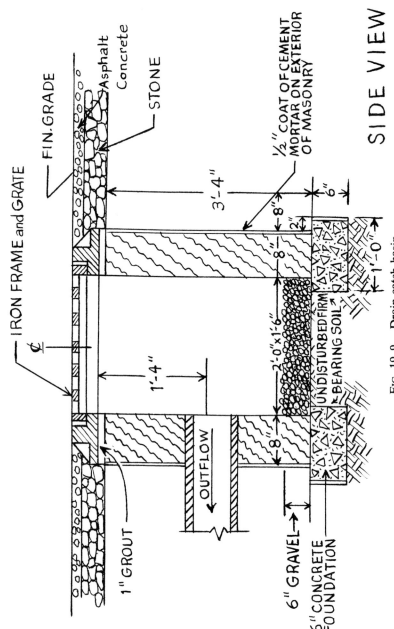

FIG. 19-9. Drain catch basin.

## OTHER IMPORTANT CHARACTERISTICS

In some cases it is desirable to fence the stadium area. When this is done, an eight-foot chain link fence is usually the most desirable.

Seating is an important consideration in order to enhance spectator interest. Careful consideration should be given to the design of the seating arrangement and the construction of the seats in order that the seats will contribute rather than detract from the enjoyment of the spectators.

Press box facilities are desirable and should be included if it is financially feasible to do so. The size of the press box and its exact specifications would vary with the local situation. In any event, it should have the following characteristics:

1. It should be located above the seats.

2. It should face the east in order to reduce the sun glare.

3. It should be large enough to accommodate the needs and serve the purposes for which it is designed.

4. It should have adequate electrical outlets, phones, private booths and furnishings.

A scoreboard, either manually or electrically operated, can add much interest for both spectators and contestants. It should show times, distances, heights and team scores.

The communications system should include a public address system and intercommunication system. The public address system should have adequate volume and a clear and understandable tone. An intercommunication system should be provided from both sides of the field to the press box. Microphone hookups should be placed both in the press box and in the lower part of the stadium near the field.

Weather-tight storage space is necessary for taking care of hurdles, pits, standards, etc. Usually such space is provided underneath the seats.

# Part VI

# Appendices

# Conditioning Exercises

Exercises can be used effectively to develop strength, muscular endurance or flexibility. It is important for the correct approach to be taken in order that the exercise program will be efficient in developing the desired characteristic.

In order to develop *strength*, of which a certain amount of muscular endurance is a by-product, the muscles must be contracted regularly against heavy resistance.

Conversely, *muscular endurance* can be developed with very little effect on strength by contracting the muscles regularly against lighter resistance for many repetitions. Refer to Chapter 2 for detailed explanations of strength and endurance development programs.

*Flexibility* can best be developed by the slow stretching method as opposed to bobbing or rapid stretching. Slow stretching means that an exercise is performed which puts the muscles on stretch and the position is held for several seconds while the stretched muscles are consciously relaxed and permitted to extend fully. The exercise is repeated several times in succession. Additional information about flexibility appears in Chapter 2.

## EXERCISES

1. *Straight Arm Forward Raise.* While in a standing position hold a barbell with the forward grip in front of the hips in a straight arm position. Keeping the arms straight, raise the barbell to a position in front of the shoulders, then lower it to the beginning position.

**303**

2. *Supine Pullover.* Assume a supine position (on the back) on a mat with the arms fully extended behind the shoulders. Grasp a barbell and while keeping arms straight, raise the barbell to a position directly above the face, then return it to the beginning position.

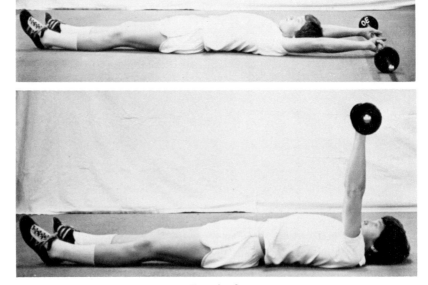

Exercise 2

3. *Arm Curl.* Using the reverse grip, grasp a barbell and lift it to a position in front of the hips. Keeping the elbows stabilized at the sides, flex the elbows raising the barbell to a position in front of the chest, then lower it to the beginning position in front of the hips.

Exercise 3

4. *Bench Press.* Assume a supine position on a bench with the feet flat on the floor to stabilize the body. Grasp the barbell with both hands and lower it slowly toward the chest, then press it upward to the straight arm position.

Exercise 4

5. *Arm Press* (*standing*). Using a barbell, lift the weight to shoulder height, then press it upward until the arms are fully extended. Lower the weight to shoulder height again and repeat the pressing exercise as many times as desired.

Exercise 5

6. *Arm Raise* (*supine*).    Lie on a bench with the arms stretched outward and hyperextended at the shoulders.    Place a dumbbell in each hand, then while keeping the arms straight, raise the dumbbells to a position above the shoulders.    Return the weights to the starting position.

Exercise 6

7. *Lateral Arm Raise* (*standing*).    While in a standing position, hold a dumbbell in each hand and raise the arms laterally to shoulder height, then return the weights to the beginning position.

Exercise 7

8. *Upper Arm Rotation.*  Assume a supine position on a mat and place the arms flat on the mat at shoulder height and with the elbows forming 90° angles.  Grasp a barbell with both hands and raise it to a position above the face, keeping the two elbows in contact with the mat.  This exercise can be done using dumbbells and one arm at a time if preferred.

Exercise 8

9. *Pull-ups.*  Hang on a chinning bar using the forward grip.  Pull the body upward until the chin reaches the bar, then lower the body to the beginning position.  Additional resistance can be added by use of a weighted belt or by another person pulling downward on the body.

10. *Handstand Push-ups.*  Assume a handstand position.  While another person holds the feet to stabilize the body, lower the chin to the floor, then push up to the beginning position.

11. *Wrist Flexion.* With the hand and forearm extended beyond the edge of a table and with the wrist extended, place a dumbbell in the hand. Flex the wrist as far as possible, then return the wrist to the extended position.

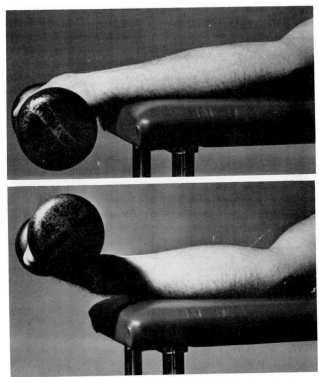

Exercise 11

12. *Hand Grip.* Place a ball in the hand, such as a handball or a firm tennis ball. Squeeze the ball repeatedly with great force. This exercise can be done at any time of the day in any location.

13. *Rowing.* Using a rowing machine, practice the rowing exercise. If a rowing machine is not available a substitute exercise is to place a dumbbell in each hand, bend over at the hips and practice the rowing action in an up and down direction.

14. *Trunk Flexion* (*incline board*).    Set the board at the desired angle and assume the supine position with the feet hooked in the loop.    Place a weight either behind the head or on the chest and do the sit-up exercise.

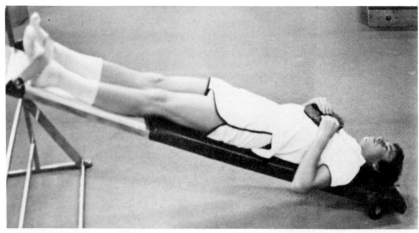

Exercise 14

15. *Trunk Rotation* (*supine*).    Assume a supine position on the incline board with weight held behind the head.    Do a sit-up rotating the trunk so that the right elbow reaches a position outside the left knee.    Repeat to the opposite side.

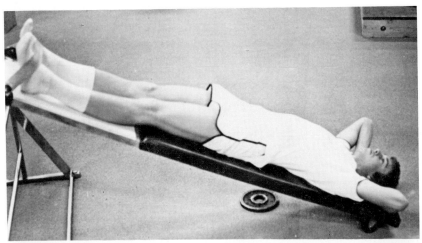

Exercise 15

16. *Body Curl* (*incline board*). With the board placed at the desired angle, assume a supine position with the feet in the loop and the knees elevated. Clasp the hands behind the head then flex the trunk and reach the elbows beyond the knees. Return to the supine position.

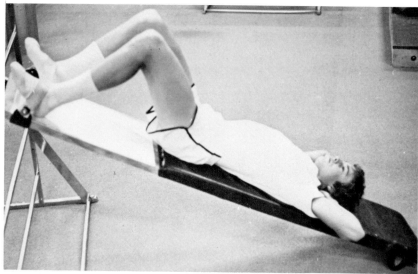

Exercise 16

17. *Trunk Lateral Flexion.* While in a standing position, hold a dumbbell in one hand. Bend the trunk from side to side as far as possible, working against the weight of the dumbbell. Repeat with the dumbbell in the opposite hand.

18. *Trunk Extension.* Assume a standing position with feet spread apart to aid in stability and with a barbell in front of the body. Bend at the hips and waist, grasp the barbell and lift the barbell by extending the trunk and hips to a standing position. Extreme caution should be taken with this exercise to be sure to not injure the back.

Exercise 18

19. *Trunk Rotation* (*standing*).    With a barbell resting on the shoulders and with the body in a stable position, rotate the trunk to the right and then to the left.

Exercise 19

20. *Leg Press.* Using a leg press machine, of which there are several varieties, extend the legs against heavy resistance.

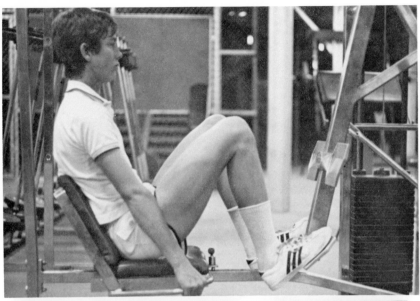

Exercise 20

21. *Jumping Jack.* With a barbell placed on the shoulders and with one foot slightly in front of the other, spring into the air and change the position of the two feet. Repeat several times in succession.

22. *Half-squat.* With a barbell on the shoulders, lower the body to the half-squat position then raise it back to the beginning position.

Exercise 22

23. *Heel Raise.* Using an appropriate machine, place the balls of the feet on the edge of the surface with the ankles fully flexed. Raise the heels from the floor, extending the ankles to the fully extended position, then return to the beginning position.

24. *Quadriceps Drill.*   Using a quadriceps apparatus, extend the knees to a straight-leg position, then return to the beginning position.

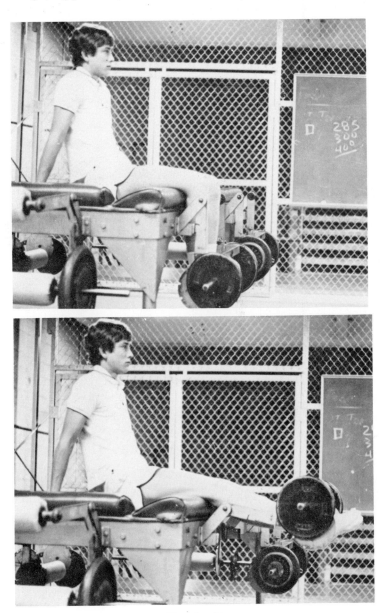

Exercise 24

25. *Leg Raise* (*supine*).   While lying on the back, take hold of a bench or barbell to stabilize the shoulder region.   Keep the legs straight and raise them to the vertical position, then return to beginning position.   Resistance can be added by wearing weighted shoes or by having another person provide resistance.

26. *Leg Raise* (*high bar*).   While hanging on a high bar keep the knees straight and raise the legs forward until they reach the horizontal position, then return to the starting position.

Exercise 26

27. *Hip Flexion* (*lead leg*).   This exercise is for hurdlers and jumpers. Attach a weight to the foot of the lead leg.   Stabilize the body, then while keeping the knee straight, raise the lead leg to a position in front of the hip, then lower it to the beginning position.

28. *Vertical Jump Drill.*   This exercise is especially for jumpers.   Jump vertically and reach as high as possible.   Rest for three or four seconds, then repeat the jump.   Do a large number of repetitions.

APPENDIX **B**

# Track and Field Records

| Event | World | American | NCAA | Jr. College | High School |
|---|---|---|---|---|---|
| 100-yard | 9.1 | 9.1 | 9.1 | 9.2 | 9.3 |
| 220-yard (straightaway) | 19.5 | 19.5 | 19.5 | 20.5 | 20.2 |
| 220-yard (turn) | 20.0 | 20.0 | 20.0 | | |
| 440-yard | 44.5 | 44.5 | 44.5 | 46.1 | 45.8 |
| 880-yard | 1:44.9 | 1:44.9 | 1:45.9 | 1:48.6 | 1:48.8 |
| One-mile | 3:51.1 | 3:51.1 | 3:51.1 | 3:56.1 | 3:58.3 |
| Two-mile | 8:17.8 | 8:22.0 | 8:33.1 | 8:52.4 | 8:41.5 |
| Three-mile | 12:50.4 | 12:53.0 | 12:53.0 | 13:47.5 | |
| Six-mile | 26:47.0 | 27:11.6 | 27:21.8 | | |
| Ten-mile | 47:12.8 | | | | |
| Fifteen-mile | 1:12:48.2 | | | | |
| One-hour | 12 miles, 1478 yds. | | | | |
| 100-meter | 9.9 | 9.9 | 9.9 | | |
| 200-meter (straightaway) | 19.5 | 19.5 | 19.5 | | |
| 200-meter (turn) | 19.8 | 20.0 | 20.0 | | |
| 400-meter | 43.8 | 43.8 | 43.8 | | |
| 800-meter | 1:44.3 | 1:44.3 | 1:44.3 | | |
| 1000-meter | 2:16.2 | | | | |
| 1500-meter | 3:33.1 | 3:33.1 | 3:33.1 | | |
| 2000-meter | 4:56.2 | | | | |
| 3000-meter | 7:39.6 | | | | |
| 5000-meter | 13:13.6 | 13:22.8 | 13:22.8 | | |
| 10,000-meter | 27:38.4 | 27:51.4 | 28:08.0 | | |
| 20,000-meter | 58:06.2 | | | | |
| 25,000-meter | 1:15:22.6 | | | | |
| 30,000-meter | 1:31:30.4 | | | | |
| 3000-meter steeplechase | 8:22.0 | 8:26.4 | 8:26.4 | | |

| Event | World | American | NCAA | Jr. College | High School |
|---|---|---|---|---|---|
| **Hurdles** | | | | | |
| 120-yard and 110-meter high | 13.0 | 13.0 | 13.0 | 13.5 | 13.5 |
| 220-yard and 200-meter low (straightaway) | 21.9 | 21.9 | | | |
| 200-meter (full turn) | 22.5 | 22.5 | | | |
| 400-meter intermediate | 47.8 | 48.4 | 48.8 | | |
| 440-yard intermediate | 48.8 | 48.8 | 48.8 | 51.2 | |
| **Field Events** | | | | | |
| High jump | 7–6¼ | 7–6¼ | 7–6¼ | 7–1½ | 7–1½ |
| Pole vault | 18–5¾ | 18–5¾ | 18–½ | 16–11 | 16–7 |
| Long Jump | 29–2¼ | 29–2¼ | 27–4¼ | 26–2¾ | 25–9½ |
| Triple jump | 57–1 | 56–0 | 55–9¼ | 51–10¾ | 52–6¼ |
| Shot put | 71–7 | 71–5½ | 71–5½ | 62–1 | 72–3¼ |
| Discus throw | 224–5 | 224–5 | 213–9¼ | 187–5 | 201–3 |
| Hammer throw | 250–8 | 235–11 | 231–3 | 167–9 | |
| Javelin throw | 304–1 | 300 | 300 | 273 | 254–11 |
| **Relays** | | | | | |
| 440-yard | 38.6 | 39.0 | 38.6 | 40.4 | 40.2 |
| 880-yard | 1:21.7 | 1:21.7 | 1:21.7 | 1:24.1 | 1:25.4 |
| One-mile | 3:02.8 | 3:03.5 | 3:03.5 | 3:08.2 | 3:11.8 |
| Two-mile | 7:11.6 | 7:16.3 | 7:16.3 | 7:29.3 | 7:41.9 |
| Four-mile | 16:02.8 | 16:09.0 | 16:09.0 | 17:00.4 | |
| 400-meter | 38.2 | 38.2 | | | |
| 800-meter | 1:22.1 | | | | |
| 1600-meter | 2:56.1 | 2:56.1 | | | |
| 3200-meter | 7:08.6 | | | | |
| 6000-meter | 14:49.0 | | | | |
| Distance medley | | 9:31.8 | 9:31.8 | 9:51.0 | |
| Sprint medley | | | 3:14.8 | 3:22.8 | 3:23.3 |
| 480 yard shuttle | | | 56.7 | 53.7 | |

# APPENDIX C

# Distance Conversion Tables

## CONVERSION OF METERS TO FEET AND INCHES

| M. | Ft. | In. | M. | Ft. | In. | M. | Ft. | In. | M. | Ft. | In. |
|----|-----|-----|----|-----|-----|----|-----|-----|----|-----|-----|
| 1 | 3 | 3⅜ | 26 | 85 | 3⅝ | 51 | 167 | 3⅞ | 76 | 249 | 4⅛ |
| 2 | 6 | 6¾ | 27 | 88 | 7 | 52 | 170 | 7¼ | 77 | 252 | 7½ |
| 3 | 9 | 10⅛ | 28 | 91 | 10⅜ | 53 | 173 | 10⅝ | 78 | 255 | 10⅞ |
| 4 | 13 | 1½ | 29 | 95 | 1¾ | 54 | 177 | 2 | 79 | 259 | 2¼ |
| 5 | 16 | 4⅞ | 30 | 98 | 5⅛ | 55 | 180 | 5⅜ | 80 | 262 | 5⅝ |
| 6 | 19 | 8¼ | | | | 56 | 183 | 8¾ | | | |
| 7 | 22 | 11⅝ | 31 | 101 | 8½ | 57 | 187 | 0⅛ | 81 | 265 | 9 |
| 8 | 26 | 3 | 32 | 104 | 11⅞ | 58 | 190 | 3½ | 82 | 269 | 0⅜ |
| 9 | 29 | 6⅜ | 33 | 108 | 3¼ | 59 | 193 | 6⅞ | 83 | 272 | 3¾ |
| 10 | 32 | 9¾ | 34 | 111 | 6⅝ | 60 | 196 | 10¼ | 84 | 275 | 7⅛ |
| | | | 35 | 114 | 10 | | | | 85 | 278 | 10¼ |
| 11 | 36 | 1⅛ | 36 | 118 | 1⅜ | 61 | 200 | 1⅝ | 86 | 282 | 1⅝ |
| 12 | 39 | 4½ | 37 | 121 | 4¾ | 62 | 203 | 5 | 87 | 285 | 5 |
| 13 | 42 | 7¾ | 38 | 124 | 8⅛ | 63 | 206 | 8⅜ | 88 | 288 | 8⅜ |
| 14 | 45 | 11⅛ | 39 | 127 | 11⅜ | 64 | 209 | 11¾ | 89 | 291 | 11¾ |
| 15 | 49 | 2½ | 40 | 131 | 2¾ | 65 | 213 | 3 | 90 | 295 | 3⅛ |
| 16 | 52 | 5⅞ | | | | 66 | 216 | 6⅜ | | | |
| 17 | 55 | 9¼ | 41 | 134 | 6⅛ | 67 | 219 | 9¾ | 91 | 298 | 6½ |
| 18 | 59 | 0⅝ | 42 | 137 | 9½ | 68 | 223 | 1⅛ | 92 | 301 | 9⅞ |
| 19 | 62 | 4 | 43 | 141 | 0⅞ | 69 | 226 | 4½ | 93 | 305 | 1¼ |
| 20 | 65 | 7⅜ | 44 | 144 | 4¼ | 70 | 229 | 7⅞ | 94 | 308 | 4⅝ |
| | | | 45 | 147 | 7⅝ | | | | 95 | 311 | 8 |
| 21 | 68 | 10¾ | 46 | 150 | 11 | 71 | 232 | 11¼ | 96 | 314 | 11⅜ |
| 22 | 72 | 2⅛ | 47 | 154 | 2⅜ | 72 | 236 | 2⅝ | 97 | 318 | 2¾ |
| 23 | 75 | 5½ | 48 | 157 | 5¾ | 73 | 239 | 6 | 98 | 321 | 6⅛ |
| 24 | 78 | 8⅞ | 49 | 160 | 9⅛ | 74 | 242 | 9⅜ | 99 | 324 | 9½ |
| 25 | 82 | 0¼ | 50 | 164 | 0½ | 75 | 246 | 0¾ | 100 | 328 | 0⅞ |

## CONVERSION OF STANDARD RACE DISTANCES
(Yards to Meters, Meters to Yards)

| Yards | Meters | Meters | Yards |
|--------|---------|---------|-----------|
| 100 | 91.44 | 100 | 109.36 |
| 220 | 201.17 | 200 | 218.72 |
| 440 | 402.34 | 400 | 437.44 |
| 880 | 804.67 | 800 | 874.88 |
| 1 mile | 1609.35 | 1500 | 1640.40 |
| 2 mile | 3218.70 | 3000 | 3280.80 |
| 3 mile | 4828.05 | 5000 | 5468.00 |
| 6 mile | 9656.10 | 10,000 | 10,936.00 |

# Decathlon Scoring Values of Commonly Made Marks

| 100 Meter Dash | | | | | | | |
|---|---|---|---|---|---|---|---|
| 12.0 — 580 | 20–6 — 660 | 39–0 — 591 | 6–1 — 725 |
| 11.9 — 601 | 20–9 — 675 | 39–6 — 602 | 6–2 — 751 |
| 11.8 — 622 | 21–0 — 693 | 40–0 — 612 | 6–3 — 769 |
| 11.7 — 643 | 21–3 — 708 | 40–6 — 622 | 6–4 — 796 |
| 11.6 — 665 | 21–6 — 725 | 41–0 — 632 | 6–5 — 813 |
| 11.5 — 687 | 21–9 — 742 | 41–6 — 642 | 6–6 — 840 |
| 11.4 — 710 | 22–0 — 757 | 42–0 — 652 | 6–7 — 857 |
| 11.3 — 733 | 22–3 — 774 | 42–6 — 661 | 6–8 — 882 |
| 11.2 — 756 | 22–6 — 791 | 43–0 — 671 | 6–9 — 900 |
| 11.1 — 780 | 22–9 — 806 | 43–6 — 682 | 6–10 — 925 |
| 11.0 — 804 | 23–0 — 822 | 44–0 — 691 | |
| 10.9 — 828 | 23–3 — 836 | 44–6 — 700 | 400 Meters |
| 10.8 — 853 | 23–6 — 853 | 45–0 — 710 | 55.0 — 603 |
| 10.7 — 879 | 23–9 — 869 | 45–6 — 720 | 54.5 — 621 |
| 10.6 — 905 | 24–0 — 883 | 46–0 — 729 | 54.0 — 640 |
| 10.5 — 932 | 24–3 — 899 | 47–0 — 747 | 53.5 — 659 |
| 10.4 — 959 | 24–6 — 915 | 48–0 — 766 | 53.0 — 679 |
| 10.3 — 986 | 24–9 — 929 | 49–0 — 784 | 52.8 — 687 |
| 10.2 — 1014 | 25–0 — 945 | 50–0 — 803 | 52.6 — 695 |
| | | 51–0 — 820 | 52.4 — 703 |
| | Shot Put | 52–0 — 839 | 52.2 — 712 |
| Long Jump | 35–0 — 509 | 53–0 — 859 | 52.0 — 720 |
| 19–0 — 557 | 36–0 — 530 | | 51.8 — 728 |
| 19–3 — 573 | 36–6 — 547 | High Jump | 51.6 — 736 |
| 19–6 — 591 | 37–0 — 551 | 5–9 — 634 | 51.4 — 744 |
| 19–9 — 607 | 37–6 — 561 | 5–10 — 652 | 51.2 — 753 |
| 20–0 — 624 | 38–0 — 571 | 5–11 — 680 | 51.0 — 762 |
| 20–3 — 642 | 38–6 — 581 | 6–0 — 707 | 50.8 — 770 |

| | | | |
|---|---|---|---|
| 50.6 — 779 | *Discus* | 12–0 — 717 | 175–0 — 677 |
| 50.4 — 788 | 100–0 — 485 | 12–3 — 736 | 180–0 — 697 |
| 50.2 — 797 | 105–0 — 519 | 12–6 — 757 | 185–0 — 715 |
| 50.0 — 805 | 110–0 — 552 | 12–9 — 775 | 190–0 — 735 |
| 49.8 — 814 | 115–0 — 585 | 13–0 — 796 | 195–0 — 754 |
| 49.6 — 824 | 120–0 — 616 | 13–3 — 817 | 200–0 — 773 |
| 49.4 — 833 | 125–0 — 648 | 13–6 — 835 | 205–0 — 791 |
| 49.2 — 842 | 130–0 — 678 | 13–9 — 856 | 210–0 — 810 |
| 49.0 — 852 | 135–0 — 708 | 14–0 — 874 | 215–0 — 828 |
| 48.5 — 875 | 140–0 — 737 | 14–3 — 894 | 220–0 — 845 |
| 48.0 — 898 | 145–0 — 766 | 14–6 — 913 | |
| | 150–0 — 795 | 14–9 — 930 | *1500 Meters* |
| *High Hurdles* | 155–0 — 823 | 15–0 — 950 | 5:30 — 259 |
| | 160–0 — 850 | 15–3 — 969 | 5:25 — 282 |
| 17.0 — 660 | 165–0 — 877 | 15–6 — 986 | 5:20 — 306 |
| 16.8 — 676 | 170–0 — 904 | 15–9 —1005 | 5:15 — 330 |
| 16.6 — 694 | 175–0 — 930 | 16–0 —1021 | 5:10 — 355 |
| 16.4 — 712 | 180–0 — 956 | | 5:00 — 408 |
| 16.2 — 730 | | *Javelin* | 4:50 — 464 |
| 16.0 — 748 | *Pole Vault* | 130–0 — 485 | 4:45 — 494 |
| 15.8 — 767 | 10–0 — 543 | 135–0 — 508 | 4:40 — 525 |
| 15.6 — 787 | 10–3 — 564 | 140–0 — 530 | 4:35 — 556 |
| 15.4 — 807 | 10–6 — 587 | 145–0 — 552 | 4:30 — 590 |
| 15.2 — 827 | 10–9 — 607 | 150–0 — 574 | 4:25 — 624 |
| 15.0 — 848 | 11–0 — 630 | 155–0 — 595 | 4:20 — 660 |
| 14.8 — 870 | 11–3 — 652 | 160–0 — 616 | 4:15 — 696 |
| 14.6 — 892 | 11–6 — 672 | 165–0 — 637 | 4:10 — 735 |
| 14.4 — 914 | 11–9 — 694 | 170–0 — 657 | 4:05 — 775 |
| | | | 4:00 — 816 |

# Books, Journals and Articles

Included in this appendix are lists of rule books, textbooks, journals and articles which are interesting and useful to both coaches and athletes.

## RULE AND RECORD BOOKS

*National Collegiate Athletic Association Track and Field Guide*, Box 757, Grand Central Station, New York, New York, 10027.

*Official Track and Field Handbook of the Amateur Athletic Union of the United States*, 233 Broadway, New York, New York, 10007.

*National Federation of State High School Athletic Associations Track and Field Rules and Record Book*, 7 South Dearborn Street, Chicago, Illinois, 60603.

*Handbook of the Internal Amateur Athletic Federation*, Halton House, 23 Halborn, London E.C. 1, England.

*Handbook of the Amateur Athletic Association of Britain*, 54 Torrington Place, London W.C.1, England.

*International Athletic Annual.* Published by World Sports, 2 Salisbury Square, London E.C.4, England.

## JOURNALS

*Athletic Journal.* 1719 Howard St., Evanston, Illinois, 60202 (monthly).

*Clinic Notes.* National Collegiate Track Coaches Association, 1643 South State St., Ann Arbor, Michigan, 48104 (annual).

*Coach and Athlete.* 1421 Mason Street, N.W., Atlanta, Georgia, 30324 (monthly).

*Journal of Applied Physiology.* 9650 Wisconsin Ave., N.W. Washington, D.C., 20014 (monthly).

*Scholastic Coach.* 33 West 42nd Street, New York, New York 10036 (monthly).

*The Amateur Athlete.* 233 Broadway, New York, New York, 10007 (monthly).

*Track and Field.* U.S. Track & Field Coaches Association, 745 State Circle, Ann Arbor, Michigan, 48104 (quarterly).

*Track and Field News.* P. O. Box 296, Los Altos, California, 94022 (monthly).

*Track Technique.* P. O. Box 296, Los Altos, California, 94022 (quarterly).

*World Sports.* 2 Salisbury Square, Fleet St., London E.C.4, England (monthly).

## BOOKS

Cretzmeyer, F. X., Alley, L. E. and Tipton, C. M.: *Bresnahan and Tuttle's Track and Field Athletics*. 7th ed., St. Louis: The C. V. Mosby Co., 1969.

Dyson, G.: *The Mechanics of Athletics*. London: University of London Press, 1962.

Jordon, P.: *Track and Field for Boys*. Chicago: Follett Publishing Company, 1968.

Doherty, J. K.: *Modern Track and Field*. 2nd ed., Englewood Cliffs, New Jersey: Prentice-Hall, Inc., 1963.

Jensen, C. and Schultz, G. W.: *Applied Kinesiology*. New York: McGraw-Hill Book Co., 1970.

Jensen, C. R. and Fisher, G.: *Scientific Basis of Athletic Conditioning*. Philadelphia: Lea & Febiger, 1972.

Gordon, J. A.: *Track and Field, Changing Concepts and Modern Techniques*. 2nd ed., Boston: Allyn and Bacon Company, 1972.

Gardner, J. and Purdy, G.: *Computerized Running Training Programs*. P.O. Box 296, Los Altos, California: Tafnews Press, 1970.

## TRACK TECHNIQUE INDEX

This index emphasizes issues 20–46 of *Track Technique* (1965–1973), however a few carefully selected articles from earlier issues are listed. The number indicates the issue in which the article appears. *Track Technique* is a quarterly journal devoted totally to track and field with emphasis on training and performance techniques. It is published by *Track and Field News*, P.O. Box 296, Los Altos, California.

### Altitude

1. Adjusting to Altitude by Buddy Edelen, #22.
2. Effects of Mexico City Training, #29.
3. From the Desk of Fred Wilt, #22, #30.
4. Physiology of Altitude Acclimatization by LeMesurier, #27.
5. Possible Effects of Altitude Upon Performance by Paish, #20.
6. Project Mexico City by LeMesurier, #28.
7. Project Olympics by E. Dickinson and M. Piddington, #32.
8. Training for Altitude by E. W. Banister, #26.

### Cross Country

1. Cross Country Training by Alex Francis, #25.
2. Cross Country Training for National-Class Races by Tony Farrell, #41.
3. Fartlek Variations for Cross Country Training by Red Estes, #43.

### Decathlon

1. Balance—The Decathlon Keyword by Robin C. Sykes, #45.
2. Decathlete by Les Mitchell, #23.
3. Decathlon Training, West German Style by Friedel Schirmer, #42.
4. How They Train—Phil Mulkey by Jim Hay, #10.

### Diet and Nutrition

1. Blood Test as a Guide to Training by K. Rompotti, #1.
2. Food and Nutrition—I Graphic Health Chart, #17; II Graphic Health Chart, #18.
3. From the Desk of Fred Wilt, #15.
4. Nutrition of the Athlete by N. N. Yakovlev Part I, #20; Part II, #21; Part III, #22; Part IV, #23; Part V, #24; Part VI, #25; Part VII, #26.
5. Training and Diet for Track and Field by A. M. Traill, #31.
6. Use of Salt in Training by John Sterner, #20.

### Discus Throw

1. A Hurry-Up Program of Developing Weightmen by Gordon Scoles, #35.
2. Analysis of the Discus Throw by Paul Ward, #37.
3. Bill Neville's Training Profile by Fred Wilt, #25.
4. Bob Humphrey's Training Profile by Fred Wilt, #23.
5. Cinematographic Analysis of the Discus Throw by D. Stolberg and Wayne D. Van Huss, #20.
6. Discus and the Wind by Jan Vrabel, #21.
7. Discus Technique Discussion by E. Wachowsky and Pat Tan Eng Yoon, #22.
8. Discus Throwing by Jacques Van de Aberle, #24.
9. Discus Throwing—chart by Canadian Department of National Health and Welfare, #30.
10. Photo Sequence of Ludvik Danck, #21.
11. Teaching the Discus Throw by Wilf Paish, #42.
12. Year-Round Discus Training by Olga Connolly, #46.

### Drugs

1. Examination of Doping in Sport by W. T. Pink, #31.
2. From the Desk of Fred Wilt, #25.
3. Use of Hormones as Anabolic Agents by R. Pickering, #29.

### Equipment and Facilities

1. Cost-Free All Weather Track, #5.
2. From the Desk of Fred Wilt, #14, #15, #20.
3. Instant Heart Rate Table, #21.
4. New Equipment—Long Jump Sight Bar, #3.
5. Sand and Oil, A New "All Weather" Track by Traill, #11.

### Exercise

1. Abdominal Strengthening by Jack Hutchinson, #32.
2. Book Review: Physiology of Exercise, #1.
3. Early Season Warm-up by John T. Powell, #18.
4. General Warmup Exercise Program by G. Laurel, #12.
5. Review of Warming Up by B. P. Garfoot, #30.

### Hammer Throw

1. Development of Young Hammer-Throwers by J. Lutkowski, #39.
2. Dynamics of Hammer Throwing by Vladimir Kuznyetsov, #34.
3. Fundamental Skills of Throwing the Hammer by Johnson, #28.
4. Gyula Zsivotzky—Training Profile by Sandor Harmati, #26.

5. Hammer and Shot Flight Angles and Velocities by K. O. Bosen, #24.
6. Hammer Throwing by Gabor Simonyi, Part III, #23.
7. Hammer Throwing (Chart), #42.
8. Some Mechanical Features of the Hammer Release by B. Hopper, #31.
9. Speed and Path of the Hammer by V. Kuznyetsov, #25.
10. Teaching Beginning Hammer Throwers by Irving S. Black, #46.
11. The Hammer and Javelin for High School by Dick Held, #41.

### High Jump

1. Analyzing the Fosbury Flop by Klement Kerssenbrock, #41.
2. Crossing the Bar From a Left Foot Take-off by Housden, #19.
3. Do Athletes Defy the Law of Gravity? by R. V. Ganslen, #3.
4. Experimental Isometric Program for Track by Wesley K. Ruff and Payton Jordan, #7.
5. High Jump, The, by Vladimir M. Dyatchkov, #34.
6. High Jump Exercises by W. Djatschkov, #25.
7. High Jumping by V. M. Dyatchkov, #36.
8. High Jumping—chart by Canadian Department of National Health and Welfare, #31.
9. High Jumping Style of Robert Shavlakadze by B. Diachkov, #2.
10. High Jumping—with Photos by John Dobroth, #27.
11. Improving Spring in the High Jump by Adam Bezeg, #28.
12. Introduction to High Jumping by Geoffrey Elliott, #26.
13. Length of Flight in the High Jump by K. Kerssenbrock, #21.
14. Mechanical Analysis of the High Jump by P. Page, #32.
15. New Ideas for the High Jump, Long Jump and Steeplechase by Napoleon Bercaru, #45.
16. Specialized Exercises for High Jumpers, by V. M. Dyatchkov, #34.
17. The High Jump Approach by T. Chityakov, #40.
18. Twisting High Jumper by G. M. Elliott, #21.
19. Two Rules in Movement by Fred Housden, #28.
20. Valeriy Brumel's Approach, Speed and Rhythm by Karel Spilar, #44.

### Hurdles

1. Action Analysis of Anatoliy Mikhailov, High Hurdler by John T. Powell, #13.
2. Analysis of High Hurdles Clearance by L. J. Mitchell and B. J. Hopper, #44.
3. Art of Hurdling by Brother Justin, #39.
4. Bend Running in the Quarter Hurdles by L. Mitchell, #33.
5. Blaine Lindgren—Photo Sequence by Karel Novak, #24.
6. Experimental Isometric Program for Track by Wesley K. Ruff and Payton Jordan, #7.
7. First Hurdle Attack by Jagmohan Singh, #41.
8. 400-Meter Hurdles Training and Technique by Borivoj Bartusek, #38.
9. Future of the One-Lap Hurdles by Les Mitchell, #28.
10. Glenn Davis—How He Trains by Fred Wilt, #10.
11. How I Train 400m Hurdlers by Ulrich Jonath, #14.
12. How They Train—Lee Calhoun by Don Kavadas, #8.
13. How They Train—Gert Potgieter by Fred Wilt, #2.
14. Hurdle Training Integral Part of Total Training by Gerhardt Schmolinski, #45.
15. Hurdling—chart by the Canadian Department of National Health and Welfare, #24.
16. Hurdle Points to Ponder by K. O. Bosen, #15.

17. Hurdle Reference Chart by Fred Wilt, #17.
18. Pace Judgment and Stride Plan in 400 Meter Hurdles by J. Singh, #20.
19. Planning Hurdles Training by Les Mitchell, #31.
20. Points Sometimes Overemphasized in High Hurdles by J. Singh, #21.
21. Preliminary Conditioning of H.S. Sprints and Hurdles by Fred Wilt, #21.
22. Rex Cawley—How He Trains by Jerry Smith, #29.
23. Sprint Hurdling by Fred Housden, #27.
24. Starting in the High Hurdles by Les Mitchell, #26.
25. Suggestions for Development of Hurdle Endurance by Jagmohan Singh, #23.
26. Some Observations on the High Hurdles by Les Mitchell, #37.

### Interval Training

1. An Appraisal of Interval Training by Michael Down, Part III, #20; Part IV, #21; Part V, #22; Part VI, #23; Part VII, #24; Part VIII, #25; Part IX, #26; Part X, #27; Part XI, #28; Part XII, #29.
2. A Physiological Basis for Interval Training by Leonard Almond, #37.
3. From the Desk of Fred Wilt, #29.
4. Influence of Interval Training on Blood Sugar Level by D. N. Mathur and K. Vankeleshwaralu, #35.
5. Interval Sprint Training by Dieter Berben, #24.
6. The Specificity of Interval Training by John Bloomfield, #44.

### Javelin

1. Analysis of European Javelin Throwers by W. Paish, #27.
2. An Experimental Isometric Program for Track by Wesley K. Ruff and Payton Jordan, #7.
3. Finnish Javelin Throwing—A Comparative Viewpoint by M. G. Wade, #28.
4. Javelin Aero-Dynamics by Richard B. Ganslen, #30.
5. Javelin Lessons from Budapest by John FitzSimons, #32.
6. Javelin Refutation by Michael G. Wade, #23.
7. Javelin Techniques of World Class Performers by Paish, #24.
8. Javelin Throwing (chart), #40.
9. Javelin Throwing, Russian Style by V. Massalitis, #33.
10. The Hammer and Javelin for High School by Dick Held, #41.
11. Throwing the Javelin by Fred Housden, #38.
12. Vladimir Kuznyetsov—Photo Sequence by Karel Novak, #22.

### Long Distance

1. Bob Schul—How He Trains by Mihaly Igloi, #30.
2. Derek Clayton—How He Trains by Fred Wilt, #32.
3. Distance Running Training Weekend by Tony Ward, #25.
4. From the Desk of Fred Wilt, #29.
5. Kip Keino's Training Profile by Fred Wilt, #23.
6. Michel Jazy—How He Trains by Jo Mallejac, #22.
7. Observing Mihaly Igloi by Arnd Kruger, #30.
8. Telescoping—The Acid Test of Distance Training by Lucas, #25.

### Long Jump

1. A New View of Distance Training by Richard Amery, #46.
2. Basic Long Jump Teaching by Harvey Greer, #44.
3. Clarke-Clayton on Distance Training, #42.

4. Discovering Potential Distance Runners by James W. Bradshaw, #40.
5. Distance Training, Development Blamed for Stress Fractures by Frederick L. Behling, #45.
6. Fun and Games in Distance and Cross-Country Running by M. Thomas Woodall, #39.
7. Igor Ter-Ovanesyan—Photo Sequence by Karel Novak, #24.
8. Long and Triple Jumping Questions and Answers by Fred Housden, #40.
9. Long Jumping (chart), #38.
10. Long Jump Technique Analysis by Achmed El Khadem Cairo and Bill Huyck, #24.
11. L.S.D.—Long Slow Distance by Joe Henderson, #38.
12. New Ideas for the High Jump, Long Jump and Steeplechase by Napoleon Bercaru, #45.
13. Rhythm Runups for Long and Triple Jumps by B. McWatt, #34.
14. Ter-Ovanesyan on the Long Jump by I. Ter-Ovanesyan, #27.
15. Training of the Long Jump by Antanas Vaupsas, #30.

## Marathon

1. Coach Arthur Lydiard's Training Methods by Fred Wilt, #7.
2. From the Desk of Fred Wilt, #13.

## Mechanics

1. Basic Mechanical Principles of Running by John Powell, #1.
2. Basic Running Form by S.A. Embling, #24.
3. Book Review: Efficiency of Human Movement, #6.
4. Book Review: The Mechanics of Athletics, #9.
5. Development of Maximum Explosive Efforts by Hopper, #27.
6. Do Athletes Defy the Law of Gravity? by Ganslen, #3.
7. Foot Plant in Running by Toni Nett, #15.
8. Fundamental Mechanics by B. R. P. McWatt, #8.
9. Mechanical Quantities in Track by B. J. Hopper, #25.
10. Mechanics Without Tears by Fred Wilt, #28.
11. Nutation and Precession in Athletics by Hopper, #22.
12. Striding Movements During the Push-off by Korenberg, #23.
13. Units and Measurements in Mechanics of Track by Bernard Hopper, #26 and #29.

## Middle Distance

1. Bill Crothers' Training Profile by Fred Wilt, #23.
2. Calculating Potential of 440 and 880 Runners by Farrell, #20.
3. Distance Running Training Weekend by Tony Ward, #25.
4. Jim Ryun—How He Trains by Bob Timmons, #31.
5. Jurgen May's Training Profile by Dr. Reiss, #23.
6. Kip Keino's Training Profile, #23.
7. Michel Jazy—How He Trains by Jo Mallejac, #22.
8. Middle Distance Running by Wilf Paisch, #41.
9. Middle Distance Training, #32.
10. Modern Concepts of Middle Distance Training by Tony Ward, #30.
11. Observing Mihaly Igloi by Arnd Kruger, #30.
12. Principles of Training Middle-Distance Runners by John Bork, #39.
13. Specific Fitness for Middle Distance Running by Brown, #25.

14. Telescoping—The Acid Test of Distance Training by Lucas, #25.
15. Varying Work Loads in Middle Distance Training by Yevgeniy Kashlakov, #43.

### Pole Vault

1. A-B-C's of Fiberglass Vaulting, #17.
2. Advantages of Fiberglass Poles by James G. Hay, #24.
3. Answers to Fiberglass Vaulting Questions by Morcom, #18.
4. Approach to Analysis of Fiberglass Pole Vaulting by Housden, #13.
5. Aubrey Dooley—How He Trains by Jim Hay, #9.
6. Brian Sternberg—Vaulting Profile by Bill Perrin, #16.
7. C. K. Yang—Vaulting Profile by Bill Perrin, #15.
8. Coaching Fiberglass Vaulters in High School by Englund, #20.
9. Coaches in Session by G. H. G. Dyson, #16.
10. Considerations in the Use of Fiberglass Poles by Jarver, #10.
11. Development of Fiberglass Vaulting Technique by R. J. Hoke, #42.
12. Experimental Isometric Program for Track by Ruff and Jordan, #7.
13. Mechanical Energy in Pole Vaulting by James Hay, #33.
14. Pentti Nikula—Photo Sequence by Karel Novak, #25.
15. Pole Vaulting (chart), #35.
16. Pole Vault Technique by Gerhard Jeitner, #28.
17. Review of Modern Pole Vaulting by Richard W. Bowers, #39.
18. Teaching Beginners to Vault in Ten Easy Steps by Olsen, #21.
19. Teaching Fiberglass Vaulting by Tom Olsen, #21.
20. Vaulting with Flexible Poles by Geoffrey M. Elliott, #26.
21. Vaulting with the Fiberglass Pole by Erich Lindner, #23.

### Psychology and Motivation

1. Some Psychological Traits of the Successful Coach by Ogilvie and Tutko, #33.
2. Why Do We Run? by Brian Mitchell, #21.

### Relays

1. Art of Baton Passing by Jal D. Pardivala, #24.
2. 440 Yard Relay Checkmark Chart by Tom Echer, #22.
3. From the Desk of Fred Wilt, #20.
4. Relay Racing in Schools by B. J. Lancastle, #42.
5. Relay Racing—chart by Canadian Department of National Health and Welfare, #32.
6. Relays with Speed by J. Huitorel, #27.
7. Some Aspects of the Non-Visual Relay Pass by Derek Priestman, #37.
8. Teaching the Sprint Relay in Schools by Kelvin B. Giles, #45.

### Shot Put

1. Analysis of Dallas Long's Shot Putting by Bob Ward, #39.
2. Analysis of the Trajectory of the Shot by Brian Garfoot, #32.
3. Approach to the Shot Put by Bill Huyck, #30.
4. Arthur Rowe—Action Analysis by John T. Powell, #8.
5. Bob Humphrey's Training Profile by Fred Wilt, #23.
6. Experimental Isometric Program for Track by Ruff and Jordan, #7.
7. Explosive Power for the Shot Put by John P. Jesse, #14.
8. Foot Contact at the Instant of Release in Throwing, #9.
9. Hammer and Shot Flight Angles and Velocities by Bosen, #24.

10. Perfection of Shot Put Technique by Peter Tschiene, #37.
11. Shot Put Questions and Answers, #24.
12. Shot Put Questions and Answers, #29.
13. Shotputting—chart by Canadian Department of National Health and Welfare, #23.
14. Specialized Exercises for Shot Putters by O. Grigalka, #31.
15. Suppleness for the Shot Put by Peter Schiene, #27.
16. Thoughts on Shot Put Technique by Hannes Booysen, #43.

### Sprints

1. Armin Hary's Training by Toni Nett, #27.
2. Characteristics of the Running Stride by B. J. Hopper, #38.
3. Experimental Isometric Program for Track by Ruff and Jordan, #7.
4. Foot Plant in Running by Toni Nett, #15.
5. Forward Lean in Sprinting by H. A. L. Chappan, #5.
6. Glenn Davis—How He Trains by Fred Wilt, #10.
7. How They Train—Bobby Morrow by Fred Wilt, #4.
8. How They Train—Frank Budd by Fred Wilt, #7.
9. How They Train—George Kerr by Fred Wilt, #4.
10. How They Train—Otis Davis by Fred Wilt, #3.
11. How to Improve Speed by Nikolay Ozolin, #44.
12. Mike Larrabee—How He Trains, #20.
13. One Style of Sprinting by Rajko Miler, #22.
14. Preliminary Conditioning of H.S. Sprints and Hurdlers by Fred Wilt, #21.
15. Rex Cawley—How He Trains by Jerry Smith, #29.
16. Running the Curve by Richard P. Dodge, #25.
17. Sprinting—chart by Canadian Department of National Health and Welfare, #29.
18. Stature, Leg Length, and Stride Frequency by Karel Hoffmann, #46.
19. Strength Training for Sprinters by Eugeniusz Kruczalak, #35.
20. Theoretical Examples of Sprint Training by Fred Wilt, #34.
21. The Sprint Start by Brother Justin, #41.

### Steeplechase

1. Experimental Isometric Program for Track by Ruff and Jordan, #7.
2. Gaston Roelants—How He Trains by Fred Wilt, #9.
3. Hints on Steeplechasing by Denis Watts, #41.
4. New Ideas for the High Jump, Long Jump and Steeplechase by Napoleon Bercaru; #45.
5. Steeplechase Technique and Training by Tony Saunders, #35.
6. Water Jump Clearance Analysis, #29.
7. Zdzislaw Krzyskowiak—How He Trains, #9.

### Strength Training

1. Book Review: Better Athletics Through Weight Training, #6.
2. Discus Throwing—chart by Canadian Department of National Health and Welfare, #30.
3. Experimental Isometric Program for Track by Ruff and Jordan, #7.
4. Explosive Power for the Shot Put by John P. Jesse, #14.
5. High Jumping—chart by Canadian Department of National Health and Welfare, #31.
6. How I Train the Yugoslavian High Jumpers by Zivkovic, #14.

7. Isometric Exercises and Their Value to the Athlete by Willee, #6.
8. New Lift for the Sprinter by Les Mitchell, #5.
9. Problems Involved in the Training of Soviet High Jumpers by Vladimir Dyachkov, #5.
10. Re-Evaluation of Isometric Training by Pickering, #27.
11. Shot Put Questions and Answers by G. F. D. Pearson, #24.
12. Shotputting—chart by Canadian Department of National Health and Welfare, #23.
13. Specialized Exercises for Shot Putters by Otto Grigalka, #31.
14. Strength and Flexibility Exercise for Track and Field, #30.
15. Winter Conditioning and Training for Triple Jumpers by H. Kleinen, #20.

### Tactics and Strategy

1. Code of Tactical Commands by Pyotr Bolotnikov, #28.
2. How to Look Back While Running by D. B. Kelly, #20.

### Training (Distance Training)

1. Distance Running Training Weekend by Tony Ward, #25.
2. First Principles of Running Training by Brian Mitchell, #26.
3. Telescoping—The Acid Test of Distance Running by Lucas, #25.

### Triple Jump

1. Double Arm Action in Triple Jumping by Gabor Simonyi, #43.
2. Long and Triple Jump Questions and Answers by Fred Housden, #40.
3. Polish Triple Jumping by Tom McNab, #29.
4. Rhythm Runups for Long and Triple Jumps by Bishop McWatt, #34.
5. Triple Jumping (chart), #39.
6. Triple Jump Technique by Jack Lowe, #37.
7. Triple Jump Training by Tadeusz Starzynski, #45.
8. Vitold Kreyer—Photo Sequence by Karel Novak, #22.
9. Winter Conditioning and Training for Triple Jumpers by Kleinen, #20.

APPENDIX **F**

# Glossary

1. *A.A.U.*  Amateur Athletic Union.
2. *Acceleration*  Rate of increase in velocity.
3. *Aerobic*  Physiological processes occurring in the presence of and by the use of oxygen.
4. *Agility*  The ability to change directions of the body or its parts rapidly—demonstrated in such movements as dodging, zigzagging, stopping, starting and reversing direction quickly.
5. *Agonistic muscle*  A muscle which contributes to the desired movement by its concentric contraction.
6. *Alveoli*  The tiny air sacs in the lungs where gases are exchanged between the lungs and the blood.
7. *Anaerobic*  Physiological processes occurring with no oxygen present and without the use of oxygen.
8. *Anchor*  The fourth and last position on a relay team.
9. *Angle of delivery (or angle of projection)*  The angle at which a missile travels in relation to the ground as it leaves the hand of the thrower (same as angle of trajectory).
10. *Angle of trajectory*  See Angle of delivery.
11. *Angular velocity*  Speed of movement in a rotary (an angular) path.
12. *Antagonistic muscle*  A muscle which acts in opposition to the desired movement. One which must relax to allow the movement to occur.
13. *Axis*  A fixed point around which a moving object revolves.
14. *Ball-heel*  Refers to contact with the ground where the ball of the foot strikes before the heel.
15. *Barbell*  A piece of weight training apparatus used for lifting with both hands.
16. *Body whip*  A vigorous movement of the body resulting in a whiplike action of body parts.
17. *Breaking (start)*  The act of leaving the starting mark before the official has fired the starting pistol.
18. *Breasting the yarn (tape)*  The act of contacting the yarn with the chest at the finish of the race.
19. *Cadence*  Rhythm and rate of motion.

20. *Cardiac output*  Volume of blood pumped through the left ventricle of the heart in one minute.
21. *Center of gravity*  The point of intersection of the three primary planes of the body.  The exact center of the body.  The point around which the body would rotate freely in all directions if it were free to rotate.
22. *Centrifugal force*  The force that tends to keep a moving object in motion along a straight line.  The force that resists a change in direction of movement.
23. *Centripetal force*  The force that causes a moving object to turn.  The force which opposes centrifugal force.
24. *Check-mark*  An aid to ensure accuracy of stride; usually a mark at the side of the runway.
25. *Concentric contraction*  The shortening of a muscle due to a stimulus.  Opposite of eccentric contraction.
26. *Conditioned reflex*  A reflex pattern which is learned as opposed to being inborn.
27. *Contractile force (muscle)*  The amount of tension applied by a muscle or group of muscles during contraction.
28. *Coordination*  The act of various muscles working together in a smooth concerted way.  Correct and precise timing of muscle contractions.
29. *Deceleration*  Rate of decrease in velocity.
30. *Density*  The relationship of mass to volume.  The weight of an object compared to its size.
31. *Diathermy*  Local increase of temperature of the tissues by electric current.
32. *Dynamic contraction*  See Isotonic contraction.
33. *Eccentric contraction*  Controlled lengthening of a muscle.  The muscle becomes longer as it contracts because the resistance is greater than the contractile force.  Opposite of concentric contraction.
34. *Echelon*  Placement of athletes in staggered positions at the start of a race around a curve so that all competitors run an equal distance.
35. *Endurance*  Ability to resist fatigue and recover quickly after fatigue.
36. *Expiration*  Expelling air from the lungs.
37. *Extension*  Movement of a body segment that increases the angle at the joint; straightening the joint.
38. *Fartlek system (speed play)*  A plan of athletic exercises, semistructured in nature, whereby the athlete determines the type, intensity and duration of his activity.
39. *Flexibility*  That property of muscles and connective tissue which allows full range of motion.
40. *Flexion*  Movement of a body segment that decreases the angle at the joint; bending the joint.
41. *Free leg*  The leg which is not driving but the one that is free to swing into a specific position.
42. *Gather*  Preparation or positioning of the body for an explosive movement.
43. *Hyperventilation*  The condition caused by forced deep breathing in which too much air pressure causes dizziness and/or unconsciousness.
44. *Impetus*  The property possessed by a moving body by virtue of its weight and its motion; the equivalent of momentum.
45. *Inertia*  A property of matter by which it remains at rest or in uniform motion in a straight line unless acted upon by some external force.
46. *Interval running*  Practice exercises in which the athlete runs specified distances interspersed with intervals of jogging or rest.
47. *Isometric contraction*  A contraction in which muscle tension is applied but the muscle does not shorten because it does not overcome the resistance.

48. *Isotonic contraction* A contraction in which muscle fibers shorten as a result of stimulus.
49. *Jumping leg* The leg that is in contact with the ground and that imparts force to the body.
50. *Kilogram* Equivalent to 2.2 pounds; 1000 grams.
51. *Kinesthetic sense* A sense of awareness, without the use of the other senses, of muscle and joint positions and actions.
52. *Lever (body)* A rigid bar comprised of one or more bones which revolves about a fulcrum (joint).
53. *Ligament* Tough connective tissue which binds bones together, forming joints.
54. *Medley* A relay race in which the various sectors are of unequal lengths.
55. *Meter* The metric unit of measure equal to 39.37 inches or 100 centimeters.
56. *Momentum* The property of a moving body that is equal to force required to bring the body to rest. Momentum = mass X velocity.
57. *Muscle boundness* A pathological condition brought on by improper training in which the joints lose some of their range of motion due to muscle enlargement and tightness.
58. *N.C.A.A.* National Collegiate Athletic Association. The organization which governs college athletics in the United States.
59. *Neuromuscular* Pertaining to nerves and muscles.
60. *N.F.S.H.S.A.A.* National Federation of State High School Athletic Associations.
61. *Overload* The process of demanding more performance from a system than is ordinarily required.
62. *Oxygen debt* A condition which results when the demand for oxygen is greater than the supply.
63. *Passing zone* The distance prescribed by relay racing rules within which the baton must be exchanged.
64. *Phasic contraction* See Isotonic contraction.
65. *Pinched off* Having both the forward and sideward paths blocked (applies to a runner).
66. *Power* The product of force and velocity. The ability to apply force at a rapid rate.
67. *Pulled muscle* An injury in which a portion of the fibers of a mucle are pulled apart or torn.
68. *Range of motion* The amount of movement that occurs in a joint, expressed in degrees.
69. *Reaction time* That time between a signal to respond and the beginning of the response.
70. *Recovery leg* The swinging leg during the running stride.
71. *Recovery phase* That part of the running stride when the leg is swinging forward into position for the oncoming drive.
72. *Reflex* An immediate response to a situation in which the thought process is bypassed.
73. *R.M. (repetition maximum)* The maximum number of repetitions that can be accomplished against a given amount of resistance in weight training.
74. *Rock-up* The action involved in shifting the body weight from the whole foot to the ball of the foot.
75. *Rotation* Movement of a body segment around its own longitudinal axis.
76. *Scratch line* The front edge of the takeoff board in a jumping event.
77. *Shuttle hurdle race* A relay race in which a team of hurdlers (usually four) races back and forth on the hurdle course.

78. *Skeletal muscles*   Also called striated, motor and voluntary muscles.   Muscles which attach to and cause movements of the skeleton.
79. *Skill*   Demonstrated neuromuscular coordination—the act of performing the correct movements in correct sequence and timing.
80. *Stability*   Firmness in position.   Ability to withstand external force.
81. *Stabilizer muscle*   Any muscle that acts to stabilize or fix a body segment in order for another segment to move on it.
82. *Staggered*   See Echelon.
83. *Stamina*   Endurance or staying power.
84. *Static contraction*   See Isometric contraction.
85. *Steady state*   A condition where the supply of oxygen to the tissues is equal to the demand for oxygen.
86. *Steeplechase*   A race where hazards such as hurdles and water jumps are erected in the course of the runners.
87. *Stop board*   A curved block of wood placed along the front edge of the shot put circle as a restraining device.
88. *Stretch reflex*   An automatic reflex causing skeletal muscles to contract, brought on by sudden stretching of the muscles.
89. *Stroke volume (heart)*   The volume of blood pumped out of the left ventricle with each contraction.
90. *Supine position*   Face up or front up.
91. *Takeoff foot*   The foot from which the athlete drives off the ground in jumping or leaping.
92. *Technique*   The form used for the performance of an event.
93. *Tendon*   A tough fibrous tissue that connects muscles to bones.
94. *Thrust*   To exert force upon or against an object so as to move in a desired direction.
95. *Timing*   The proper time relationship between two or more movements.
96. *Tonic contraction*   See Isometric contraction.
97. *Translatory motion*   Motion in which an object moves from one point to another point, as opposed to rotary motion.   It can occur in either a linear or a curvilinear path.
98. *Tying up*   A condition brought on by fatigue in which the athlete overtenses certain muscles and thereby detracts from a relaxed performance.
99. *Vital capacity*   The total amount of air that can be forced out of the lungs after a forced inhalation.

# Index

(Numbers in *italics* refer to illustrations)

Aerobic-anaerobic relationship, 15–16
Aerobic training, 13–15
Age, strength and, 11
Akii-Bua, John, 120, 130
Alcohol, 30
Amphetamines, 30
American Medical Association, 31
Anaerobic training, 15
Andersson, Arne, 72
Andersson, Harold, 222, 237
Arm curl, 305
Arm press, 307
Arm raise, 308
Articles, track and field, 328–335
Astrand, P. O., 14
Athletes, 272–275
    traits of, 5
ATP, 13–15

Bannister, Roger, 72
Baton passing, variations of, 140–143
Beamon, Bob, 163
Bench press, 306
Berger, R. A., 6, 7
Best, C. H., 26
Blask, Edwin, 250
Body curl, 314
Body maintenance, hints for, 35
Books, reference, 328
Boston, Ralph, 163

Breathing, while running, 82–83
Brochures, 276
Brooks, Marshall, 147
Brumel, Valeriy, 148

Caffeine, 30
Carbohydrates, nutrition and, 26
Carr, Sabin, 188
Cator, Silvio, 163
Chase, Stephen, 106
Clark, Ellery, 147
Clark, R. S. J., 19
Coaching, hints for, 35–39
Cocaine, 29
Colbeck, Edward H., 63
Collett, Wayne, 120, 127, 133
Competitive hints, 35–39
Computerized training programs, 95
Conditioning exercises, 303–320
    arm curl, 305
    arm press, 307
    arm raise, 308
    bench press, 306
    body curl, 314
    for discus throw, 235
    for distance races, 105
    half squat, 318
    for hammer throw, 266–267
    hand grip, 311
    handstand push-ups, 310

Conditioning exercises—(*continued*)
  heel raise, 318
  for high hurdles, 118
  for high jump, 162
  hip flexion, 320
  for intermediate hurdles, 135
  for javelin throw, 249
  jumping jack, 318
  lateral arm raise, 309
  leg press, 317
  leg raise, 320
  for long jump, 176
  for pole vault, 203
  pull-ups, 310
  quadriceps drill, 319
  for quarter mile, 71
  rowing, 311
  for shot put, 221
  for sprints, 62
  straight arm forward raise, 303
  supine pull-over, 304
  for triple jump, 187
  trunk extension, 315
  trunk flexion, 312
  trunk lateral flexion, 315
  trunk rotation, 313, 316
  upper arm rotation, 310
  vertical jump drill, 320
  wrist flexion, 311
Consolini, Adolfo, 222
Continuous fast running, training
  technique, 93–94
Conversion, of distances, 323–324
Cooper, K. H., 15
Correction, of faults. *See* Faults
  and corrections
Cunningham, Glen, 72
Cureton, T. K., 27
Cushman, Clifford, 131

da Silva, Adhemar, 178
Danek, Ludvik, 223
Davis, Glenn, 119
Davis, Otis, 67
Davis, Walter, 147
Definitions. *See* Glossary
Decathlon scoring tables, 325–326
DeLorme, T., 6
DeVries, H. A., 20, 33
Discus throw, 222–235
  conditioning exercises for, 235
  faults and corrections for, 231–232

Discus throw—(*continued*)
  foot touch pattern for, 225
  grip for, 224
  history of, 222–223
  procedure for, 223
  records for, 222–223
  scientific principles applied to,
    229–231
  training schedule for, 232–235
  technique of, 224–229, *226–227*
    movement across the ring, 225
    moving into turn, 225
    preliminary swing, 225
    release, 228
    reversal, 228
    starting position, 225
    thrusting action, 228
Distance conversion tables, 323–324
Distance races, 72–105
  conditioning exercises for, 105
  faults and corrections for, 83–86
  history of, 72–73
  overtraining for, 96–97
  records for, 73–76
  scientific principles applied to, 83
  speed work, importance of, 95–96
  steeplechase and, 88
  technique for, 77–83
    arm action, 81–82
    back kick, 80–81
    breathing, 82–83
    foot action, 78–79
    knee lift, 80–81
    leg action, 80–81
    posture, 81–82
    relaxation, 77
    stride, 79–81
  training for, 76–77
  training systems for, 89–96
    continuous fast running, 93–94
    fartlek training, 90–91
    interval training, 89–90
    long slow distance, 93
    Lydiard system, 91–93
    speed play, 90–91
  training techniques for, 94–95
    acceleration sprinting, 95
    fast interval, 94
    hollow sprinting, 95
    interval sprinting, 94
    repetition running, 94
    repetition sprints, 94
    slow interval, 94

Drainage. *See* Track and field construction
Dray, Walter, 188
Drugs, 29–31. *See also specific drugs*
Dumas, Charles, 148
Duncan, James, 222

Eastman, Ben, 63
800-meter run. *See* Distance running
880-yard run. *See* Distance running
Endurance, 12–19
  aerobic, 13–15
  anaerobic, 15
  cardiovascular, 12, 13–16
  factors influencing, 18–19
    age and, 18
    body temperature and, 19
    circulatory efficiency and, 18
    fatty tissue and, 18
    pace and, 19
    respiratory efficiency and, 18
    sex and, 18
    skill and, 18
    strength and, 18
  interval training for, 14–16
  methods of increasing, 12–16
  muscular, 12, 13
  overload and, 14
  physiological changes and, 16–19
  programs for developing, 17
  training, 76–77
Energy cost, speed and, 22
Evans, Lee, 63, 66–68
Exercises, conditioning, 303–320. *See also* Conditioning exercises

Falls, H. B., 16
Fartlek training, 90–91
Fats, nutrition and, 26
Faults and corrections,
  for discus throw, 231–232
  for distance races, 83
  for hammer throw, 262–263
  for high hurdles, 114–116
  for high jump, 157–158
  for intermediate hurdles, 125–127
  for javelin throw, 245–246
  for long jump, 172–174
  for pole vault, 198–200
  for quarter mile, 68–69
  for shot put, 217–218
  for sprints, 58–60

Field events, hints about, 36–37
Filiput, Armando, 129
Flanagan, John, 250
Flexibility, 22
Fonville, Charles, 207
Food(s). *See also* Nutrition
  fad, 28
  supplements, 27–28
Foot action in running, 78–79
Foot touch pattern in running, 46–47
Fosbury, Dick, 158–160
Fosbury technique, of high jumping, 158–160
400-meter sprint. *See* Quarter mile
440-yard sprint. *See* Quarter mile
Frinolli, Roberto, 120–121
Frische, Eric, 138
Fuchs, James, 207

Gardner, J. B., 95
Gardner, Robert, 188
Garrett, Robert, 222–223
George, Walter, 72
Gooch, Franklin H., 163
Gordien, Fortune, 222
Glossary, 336–339
Gray, George, 207
Greene, Charlie, 46, 138
Grose, J. E., 19
Groudin, Edward, 163

Hagg, Gunder, 72
Haines, Jim, 138
Half squat, 318
Hammer throw, 250–267
  conditioning exercises for, 266–267
  faults and corrections for, 262–263
  grip for, 252
  history of, 250–267
  procedure for, 251–252
  records for, 251
  scientific principles applied to, 260–262
  technique for, 252–259, *254–257*
    delivery, 259
    first turn, 258
    follow-through, 259
    initial stance, 253
    power burst, 259
    power stroke, 258
    preliminary winds, 253
    second turn, 258–259

Hammer throw, technique for—(*cont.*)
  third turn, 259
  transition into the turn, 253
  training schedule for, 263–267
Hand grip, 311
Handstand push-ups, 310
Hansen, Fred, 188
Heel raise, 318
Hemery, Dave, 120
Henneman, Charles, 222
Henninge, Gerhardt, 120
Hettinger, Theodor, 8
High hurdling, 106–118
  conditioning exercises for, 118
  exercises for, 113
  faults and corrections for, 114–116
  history of, 106–107
  procedure for, 107
  records for, 107
  technique for, 107–114
    after the last hurdle, 112–113
    between hurdles, 112
    to first hurdle, 108
    over hurdle, 110–112
    starting, 107
  training schedule for, 116–118
High jumping, 147–162
  conditioning exercises for, 162
  faults and corrections for, 157–158
  history of, 147–148
  procedure for, 148–149
  records for, 148
  rules for, 148–149
  scientific principles applied to, 155–156
  technique for, 149–155, 158–160
    action in the air, 154
    approach, 149–152, 159–160
    arm and shoulder action, 154
    clearance of the bar, 154–155, 160
    foot plant, 152–153
    Fosbury flop, 158–160
    horizontal momentum, 153
    landing, 155, 160
    lead leg action, 153–154
    straddle roll, 149–155
    takeoff, 152–154, 160
  training schedule for, 160–162
Hines, Jim, 54
Hints, coaching and competitive, 35–39
Hip flexion, 320
History, 3. *See also specific events*
Holmer, Gosta, 90

Horine, George, 147
Hurdling. *See* High hurdling *and* Intermediate hurdling

Ines, Sim, 222
Intermediate hurdling, 119–135
  change of stride patterns for, 125
  conditioning exercises for, 135
  faults and corrections for, 125–127
  form for, 124
  history of, 119–120
  procedure for, 121
  race plan for, 128–129
  records for, 120
  scientific principles applied to, 125
  step patterns for, 127–128, 129–131
  technique for, 121–125, 127–128
    after last hurdle, 125
    between hurdles, 123–125
    to first hurdle, 121–123
    importance of, 127
    over first hurdle, 123
    starting, 121
  training schedule for, 133–135
  220-yard splits, 131–133
Interval training, 14–16, 89–90

James, Larry, 68
Jarvinen, Matti, 236
Javelin throw, 236–249
  conditioning exercises for, 248–249
  faults and corrections for, 245–246
  grip for, 239
  history of, 236–237
  procedure for, 237–238
  records for, 237
  scientific principles applied to, 242–244
  technique for, 238–242, *240–241*
    approach run, 239
    cross over stride, 241–242
    recovery stride, 242
    throwing stride, 242
  training schedule for, 246–249
Journals, 327
Jumping events, 145–203. *See also specific events*
Jumping jack, 318

Karnoven, M. J., 15
Kashkarov, Igor, 148
Kraenzlein, Alvin, 106

Larrabee, Mike, 66–68
Lateral arm raise, 309
Leg press, 317
Leg raise, 320
Lemming, Eric, 236
Lituyea, Yuri, 130
Long jump, 163–176
    conditioning exercises for, 176
    faults and corrections for, 172–174
    history of, 163
    procedure for, 165
    records for, 163–164
    scientific principles applied to, 170–172
    technique for, 165–170
        action in the air, 167–169
        approach run, 165–166
        landing, 169–170
        takeoff, 166–167
    training schedule for, 174–176
Long, Max W., 63
Long slow distance training technique, 93
Lydiard, Arthur, 91–93
Lydiard system, of training, 91–93

MacDonald, Bobby, 44
MacIntyre, Bob, 138
Mann, Ralph, 120–122, 126–127, 130–131, 133
Marijuana, 29
Matson, Randy, 207
Matzdorf, Pat, 148
Meriwether, Delano, 46
Meters, converted to feet, 323–324
Milburn, Rodney, 106
Miller, A. T., 26
Miller, Bill, 236
Minerals, 27
Mitchell, James, 250
Moore, Charles, 129–130
Morehouse, L. E., 26
Muller, E. A., 8
Muscle, contraction of, 20–22
    size of, strength and, 11
Muscular power, 19–20
Myers, Lawrence, 63

Nallett, Jean Claude, 133
Nambu, Chuhei, 178
Narcotics, 29
Nemeth, Imre, 250
News media, use of, 275

Nieder, William, 207
Nikkanen, Finn Yrjo, 236
Nurmi, Paavo, 72
Nutrition, 25–28
    carbohydrate sources and, 26
    distribution of food intake and, 28
    fad foods and, 28
    fat sources and, 26
    food supplements and, 27
    minerals and, 27
    proportions of different foods and, 26
    protein sources and, 27
    vegetarians and, 28
    vitamins and, 27
    wheat germ and, 27

O'Brien, Parry, 207–208
Oda, Mikio, 178
Oerter, Alfred, 223
Official(s), list of, 282
    responsibilities of, 278–287
        announcer, 284
        clerk of course, 284
        field judge, 286–287
        finish judge, 285–286
        games committee, 278
        inspector, 286
        marshal, 287
        meet director, 278–281, 283
        referee, 283
        starter, 283–284
        timer, 284–285
Olympics, 3
Omni-directional resistance, 10
Opium, 29
Overloading, for endurance, 14
    for strength, 7, 9
Overtraining, of distance runners, 96–97
Owen, John Jr., 44

Pace, importance of, 19
Paddock, Charles, 54
Page, William, 147
Pedersen, Terje, 237
Pender, Mel, 138
Perez, Pedro, 178
Performance, preparation for, 1–39
Physiological changes, endurance and, 16–19
    strength and, 10
Plummer, Adolph, 63
Pole vault, 188–203
    conditioning exercises for, 203

Pole vault—*(continued)*
  faults and corrections for, 198–200
  history of, 188–189
  pole bend and, 196–197
  pole selection and, 190
  procedure for, 189
  records for, 189
  rules of, 189
  scientific principles applied to, 197–198
  technique for, 189–197
    approach run, 190
    clearing the bar, 196
    landing, 196
    pole grip and carry, 191
    pole plant, 191
    pole release, 196
    pull-up and push-up, 195
    rock back, 195
    takeoff, 194
  training schedule for, 200–203
Posture, running, 81–82
Potgieter, Gert, 119, 130
Power, 19
  how to increase, 19
  importance of, 19, 56
Pre-competition, procedures for, 32–34
  pre-meet meal, 32
  warm-up, 33–34
Programs, for track and field meets, 276–277
Promoting track and field, 271–277
Proteins, nutrition and, 27
Pull-ups, 310
Purcell, John, 178
Purty, G. J., 95

Quadriceps drill, 319
Quarter mile sprint, 63–71
  faults and corrections for, 68–69
  history of, 63–64
  race plan for, 66–67
  records for, 64
  running technique for, 64–68
  scientific principles applied to, 68–69
  starting technique for, 64
  training schedule for, 69–71
  200 meter splits, 66
Questad, Larry, 138

Race(s), distance, 72–105
  relay, 136–143
  strategy, 37–39

Ratios of the hop, step and jump, 182
Reaction time, 22–23
Records, track and field, 321–322. *See also specific events*
References, books and journals, 327–335
Relaxation, while running, 77
Relay racing, 136–143
  baton passing, 140–143
  history of, 136
  records for, 136–137
  running order for, 143
  technique for, 138–143
Resistance, omni-directional, 10
Rhoden, George, 67
Ridley, John H., 63
Rodahl, K., 14
Rohmert, W., 8
Rose, Ralph, 207
Rowing, 311
Rubin, Dale, 138
Rule and record books, 327
Running events, 41–143. *See also specific events*
  hints for, 37
Running technique. *See specific events*
Ryan, Pat, 250
Ryun, Jim, 73

Schmidt, Walter, 250
Scientific principles, application of,
  to discus throwing, 229–231
  to distance running, 83
  to hammer throwing, 260–262
  to high hurdling, 114
  to high jumping, 155–156
  to intermediate hurdling, 125
  to javelin throwing, 242–244
  to long jumping, 170–172
  to pole vaulting, 197–198
  to quarter mile running, 68–69
  to shot putting, 215–217
  to sprinting, 57–58
  to triple jumping, 182–183
Seagren, Bob, 188
Sedatives, 29
Shelton, Ernie, 147
Shot put, 207–221
  conditioning exercises for, 221
  faults and corrections for, 217–218
  foot pattern across ring in, 213
  history of, 207
  holding methods for, 209
  procedure for, 208

Shot put—(*continued*)
  propelling forces in, 209
  records for, 207–208
  scientific principles applied to, 215–217
  technique for, 211–215
    beginning stance, 212
    delivery, 213–214
    glide across ring, 212
    reversal, 214
  training schedule for, 218–221
Silvester, Jay, 223
Sitkin, Vladimir, 148
Skill, importance of, 23
Smith, John, 63, 66
Smith, Ronnie Ray, 138
Smoking, 31
Southern, Eddie, 119
Speed, 20–21
  how to improve, 21
  importance of, 20
  influence of on energy cost, 22
  leg, in sprinting, 56
  of muscle contraction, 20
  relationship to body temperature, 21
Speed play training, 90–91
Speed training for distance runners, 95–96
Sprinting, 43–62. *See also* Sprints
  action, characteristics of, 52–54
  arm action for, 52
  faults and corrections, 58–60
  finish and, 54–55
  foot touch pattern for, 46–47
  keys to success and, 55
  leg action for, 53
  leg speed for, 56
  length of stride for, 56
  poise and, 52
  relaxation and, 52
  scientific principles applied to, 57–58
  start in, 47–52
  technique for, 46–54
Sprints, 43–62
  conditioning exercises for, 62
  flexibility, importance of, 55–56
  history of, 43–44
  power, importance of, 56
  quarter-mile, 63–71
  records for, 44–45
  self-confidence and, 55
  short, 43–62
  starting technique for, 47–52

Sprints, starting technique for—(*cont.*)
    drive out of the blocks, 50–51
    position in the blocks, 47–49
    set position, 49–50
    training schedule for, 60–62
Staleness. *See* Overtraining
Steeplechase, 87–88. *See also* Distance running
Stepanov, Yuri, 148
Straight arm forward raise, 303
Strategy, race, 37–39
Strength, 5–12
  comparison of methods and, 9
  components of, 5
  curve, 10
  dynamic, 6–8
  factors which influence, 11–12
  functional overload and, 9
  guidelines for, 7
  isometric, 6, 8–9
  isotonic, 6–8
  isometric-isotonic method, 9
  methods of increasing, 6
  overloading, 7
  physiological changes which accompany, 10
  principles underlying, 9–10
  static 6, 8–9
Stride, in distance running, 79–80
  in sprinting, 56
Supine pull-over, 304
Sweeney, Michael, 147

Tajima, Naoto, 178
Taylor, N. B., 26
Tewskbury, Walter, 119
Thomson, Earl, 106
Throwing events, 205–267. *See also specific events*
Tobacco, 31
Toribio, Simeon, 147
Torrance, Jack, 207
Towns, Forrest, 106
Track and field, history of, 4. *See also specific events*
  performance trends in, 4
  popularity of, 4
Track and field articles, 328–335
Track and field, construction of, 290–301
    drainage of, 298, *299, 300*
    field areas, construction of, 295–300
      discus throw, 297
      hammer throw, 297

Track and field, construction of, field areas—(*continued*)
  high jump, 296
  javelin throw, 297–298
  long jump, 295
  pole vault, 295–296
  shot put, 296
  triple jump, 295
  track, astro-turf, 294–295
    cinder, 293
    clay, 294
    composition of, 292–295
    rubberized asphalt, 294
    tartan, 294
  facilities of, 301
  layout of, *300*
Track and field meets, 278–289
  administration of, 269–301
  checklist for, 287–289
  equipment and facilities for, 288
  organization and conduct of, 278–289
Training, 13–15. *See also* Training schedule(s) *and specific events*
  aerobic, 13–15
  anaerobic, 15
  interval, 14–16
  strength and, 11
Training schedule(s), for discus throw, 232–235
  for hammer throw, 263–267
  for half-mile, 97–99
  for high-hurdles, 118
  for high jump, 160–162
  for intermediate hurdles, 133–135
  for javelin throw, 246–249
  for long jump, 174–176
  for marathon, 100–104
  for one mile, 100–104
  for pole vault, 200–203
  for quarter mile, 71
  for shot put, 218–221
  for six mile, 100–104
  for sprints, 60–62
  for three mile, 100–104
  for triple jump, 185–187
Training systems, for distance runners, 89–96. *See also* Distance running
Triple jump, 177–187
  conditioning exercises for, 187
  faults and corrections for, 183–184
  history of, 177
  procedure for, 178
  ratios for, 182

Triple jump—(*continued*)
  records for, 177–178
  scientific principles applied to, 182–183
  technique for, 178–182
    approach run, 178–179
    hop, 179
    jump, 182
    step, 181
  training schedule for, 185–187
Trunk extension, 315
Trunk flexion, 312
Trunk lateral flexion, 315
Trunk rotation, 313, 316
220 yard sprint style, 57

Uelses, John, 188
Upper arm rotation, 310

Vaughn, Ben, 46
Vaulting pole, selection of, 190
Vegetarians, 28
Vertical jump drill, 320
Vitamins, 27

Warm-up, 33–34
  effects of, 33
  guidelines for, 34
  reasons for, 33
Warmerdam, Cornelius, 188
Weight, control of, 34–35
Weight training methods, 6. *See also* Strength
Wheat germ, 27
Whitney, Ron, 120, 131
Wilkins, A. L., 6
Williams, Wes, 130, 133
Wolferman, Klaus, 237
Work, 13
  aerobic, 13
  anaerobic, 13
World records, 44–45. *See also specific events*
  for 100 yards, 44
  for 100 meters, 45
  for 220 yards, 45
  for 200 meters, 45–46
  for 440 yards, 64
  for 400 meters, 64
  for 880 yards, 73
  for 800 meters, 73
  for one mile, 74
  for 1500 meters, 74–75

World records—(*continued*)
    for three miles, 75
    for 5000 meters, 75
    for six miles, 75–76
    for 10,000 meters, 76
    for 440 yard hurdles, 120
    for 400 meter hurdles, 120
    for relays, 136–137

World records, for relays—(*continued*)
    440 yard, 137
    400 meter, 137
    one mile, 137
    1600 meter, 137
Wrist flexion, 311

Young, Cy, 236